# Readings in American Foreign Policy

## PROBLEMS AND RESPONSES

Edited by
# GLENN P. HASTEDT
James Madison University

ROWMAN & LITTLEFIELD
*Lanham • Boulder • New York • London*

Executive Editor: Traci Crowell
Associate Editor: Molly White
Senior Marketing Manager: Karin Cholak
Marketing Manager: Deborah Hudson
Production Editor: Janice Braunstein
Compositor: Coghill Composition Co.
Cover Designer: Meredith Nelson
Cover Image: Greg Baker/AFP/Getty Images

Credits and acknowledgments for material borrowed from other sources, and reproduced with permission, appear on the appropriate page within the text.

Published by Rowman & Littlefield
A wholly owned subsidary of The Rowman & Littlefield Publishing Group, Inc.
4501 Forbes Boulevard, Suite 200, Lanham, Maryland 20706
www.rowman.com

Unit A, Whitacre Mews, 26-34 Stannary Street, London SE11 4AB, United Kingdom

British Library Cataloguing in Publication Information Available

**Library of Congress Cataloging-in-Publication Data**

Readings in American foreign policy : problems and responses / edited by Glenn P. Hastedt, James Madison University.
       pages cm
    Includes bibliographical references.
    ISBN 978-1-4422-4964-6 (cloth : alk. paper) — ISBN 978-1-4422-4965-3 (pbk. : alk. paper) — ISBN 978-1-4422-4966-0 (electronic)
    1. United States—Foreign relations—21st century.   I. Hastedt, Glenn P., 1950–
JZ1480.R23   2016
327.73—dc23

                                                                                           2015014727

∞ ™ The paper used in this publication meets the minimum requirements of American National Standard for Information Sciences—Permanence of Paper for Printed Library Materials, ANSI/NISO Z39.48-1992.

Printed in the United States of America

# CONTENTS

Denotes think tank analysis.

# INSTRUCTOR GUIDE

The following table provides summaries for each reading, including key ideas and concepts. To facilitate in structuring your course, readings are also linked to relevant chapters in my text: *American Foreign Policy: Past, Present, Future*, Tenth Edition (Rowman & Littlefield, 2015), 978-1-4422-4161-9 (paperback), 978-1-4422-4162-6 (ebook).

| Key Ideas, Concepts, and Perspectives | American Foreign Policy: Past, Present, Future, Tenth Edition |
|---|---|
| **PART I: DEFINING FOREIGN POLICY** | |
| 1. **Excerpts from President Obama's Address to West Point Graduates** <br><br> Obama makes the case for U.S. global leadership. He reviews the major foreign policy problems facing the United States and argues that the United States continues to be powerful militarily and strong economically. | **Chapter 1:** Defining Foreign Policy Problems <br> **Chapter 2:** The Global Context |
| 2. **Robert Kagan, "Allure of Normalcy: What America Still Owes the World"** <br><br> Kagan argues that the world is heading into a new period of disorder reminiscent of the 1930s that cannot be avoided unless the United States once again embraces Its global responsibilities and abandons its search for "normalcy" and withdrawal. | |
| 3. **David C. Unger, "A Better Internationalism"** <br><br> Unger points out elitism of crisis management internationalism; calls for a new constructive internationalism; and looks at climate change, development, and nuclear issues. | |
| 4. **Barry R. Posen, "Pull Back: The Case for a Less Activist Foreign Policy"** <br><br> Posen argues Republicans and Democrats both want a domineering foreign policy and calls for abandoning hegemonic policies for one of restraint. He looks at the Middle East, NATO, Asia. | |

| Key Ideas, Concepts, and Perspectives | *American Foreign Policy: Past, Present, Future,* Tenth Edition |
|---|---|

## PART II: GLOBAL PROBLEMS

5. **Excerpt from the U.S. Intelligence Community's "Worldwide Threat Assessment"**
   This excerpt presents the 10 major global threats facing the United States covering such diverse issues as terrorism, cyber threats, counterspace, organized crime, economic issues, health risks, and mass atrocities.

   **Chapter 2:** The Global Context
   **Chapter 4:** Learning from the Past

■ 6. **Yun Sun, "China's New Calculations in the South China Sea"**
   Sun argues that from China's perspective it must abandon a policy of restraint and change the status quo through all necessary means. From its perspective the South China Sea is seen as indispensable.

7. **Samuel Charap and Jeremy Shapiro, "How to Avoid a New Cold War"**
   Focusing on the Ukrainian crisis, it is asserted that the United States needs a broad strategy for addressing U.S.-Russian problems and avoiding a "great man" theory of history. The authors discuss economic sanctions, NATO, and EU.

8. **Elizabeth Dickinson, "Fighting the Last War"**
   Colombia's success in defeating its narco-terrorism insurgency has been cited as a model that can be used in Mexico and elsewhere in Latin America. The author argues these countries will have to find their own solutions.

9. **Excerpts from the Congressional Research Service's "U.S. and International Health Responses to the Ebola Outbreak in West Africa"**
   The Ebola crisis caught the United States and the world community unprepared. This reading presents an overview and evaluation of the U.S. response. Looking to the future, it presents issues for Congress and U.S. assistance programs.

10. **Fawaz A. Gerges, "ISIS and the Third Wave of Jihadism"**
    Gerges describes ISIS as adhering to a doctrine of total war and as having taken operational leadership of the global jihadist movement by default. The author also argues there is no easy solution for the West.

## PART III: SOCIETAL INFLUENCES ON U.S. FOREIGN POLICY

11. **Excerpts from the Congressional Research Service's "Keystone XL Pipeline Project: Overview and Recent Developments"**
    This CRS report provides an overview of the tension between societal interests and national interest in the

    **Chapter 3:** The American National Style
    **Chapter 5:** Society

---

■ Denotes think tank analysis.

Keystone XL Pipeline project. The history of the project is reviewed as well as the controversies over whether the president or Congress has the power to authorize it and the competing evaluations of its merits.

12. **Fredrik Logevall and Kenneth Osgood, "The Ghost of Munich: America's Appeasement Complex"**
Americans find it hard to accept the idea of failure in foreign policy. Accordingly, they view Munich and the policy of appeasement as synonymous with naiveté and weakness. Logevall and Osgood examine the origins of these terms and trace their impact on American foreign policy.

■ 13. **"Debate: Should the United States Increase or Decrease Its Spending for Defense?"**
Focusing on such issues as sequestration, the size of the defense budget, and sharing the defense burden with other countries, representatives from three think tanks look at defense spending.

14. **David J. Danelo, "The Courage Crisis"**
Focusing on the problem of children refugees coming into the United States, this essay argues a major part of the problem is the lack of courage of both parties to address the underlying issues, which are examined in the context of a debate between Samuel Huntington and Robert Kaplan.

## PART IV: INSTITUTIONS AND U.S. FOREIGN POLICY

15. **Excerpts from the State Department's "Quadrennial Diplomacy and Development Review"**
This first State Department effort at a general review of its operations was intended to be a blueprint for building civilian power and better positioning the State Department and USAID to partner with the military and other U.S. agencies in responding to conflicts and crises.

**Chapter 6:** Congress
**Chapter 7:** Presidency
**Chapter 8:** Bureaucracy
**Chapter 9:** Policy-Making Models

■ 16. **Ken Gude, "Understanding Authorizations for the Use of Military Force"**
Gude reviews the War Powers Act and argues it is time for Congress and Obama to work together on a new authorization of force against ISIS that contains geographic and time limitations.

17. **David Rothkopf, "National Insecurity: Can Obama's Foreign Policy Be Saved?"**
Rothkopf argues that many of Obama's foreign policy problems are of his own making and from an unwillingness to learn from past errors or manage his foreign policy team. Rothkopf further contrasts

Obama on these points with improvement in Bush's
White House foreign policy process.

18. **Daniel L. Byman and Benjamin Wittes,
"Reforming the NSA: How to Spy after Snowden"**
Byman and Wittes suggest a new consensus is
emerging that the NSA must retain many of its
capabilities but become more open about its
operations. In addition, they review post-9/11 history
of the NSA and suggest reforms.

## PART V: RESPONSES

19. **Excerpts from President Obama's Remarks on
American Foreign Policy toward Syria, 2012–2014**
This set of three commentaries by President Obama
provides a time line and overview of his
administration's efforts to establish a policy to deal
with the crisis in Syria.

20. **Gareth Evans, "R2P: Looking Back, Looking
Forward"**
This reading looks at Responsibility to Protect (R2P)
from four perspectives: as a normative force, an
institutional catalyst, a preventive framework, and a
reactive framework.

■ 21. **Franklin D. Kramer and Melanie J. Teplinsky,
"Cybersecurity and Tailored Deterrence"**
Kramer and Teplinsky call for moving from a defense-
oriented cybersecurity strategy to one built around
deterrence. While the authors assert there is no silver
bullet, they identify a series of targeted actions against
cyber aggressors to reduce cyber risk.

22. **Clyde Prestowitz, "A Tale of Two Trade Deals"**
Prestowitz reviews the geostrategic benefits of
proposed regional free trade agreements with Asia and
Europe. He sees the Trans-Pacific Partnership as a
''lose-lose'' deal and favors moving ahead with the one
with Europe.

23. **Bijan Khajehpour, Reza Marashi, and Trita Parsi,
"The Trouble with Sanctions"**
Three Iranian experts challenge the logic of U.S. trade
sanctions against Iran. They examine the forces
driving economic sanctions along with their impact on
the complexion of Iranian domestic politics.

**Chapter 10:** Diplomacy
**Chapter 11:** Economic
Instruments
**Chapter 12:** Military
Instruments: Big Wars
**Chapter 13:** Military
Instruments: Small Wars

| Key Ideas, Concepts, and Perspectives | *American Foreign Policy: Past, Present, Future*, Tenth Edition |
| --- | --- |

## PART VI: EMERGING ISSUES

24. **Excerpt from the National Intelligence Council's "Global Trends 2030: Alternative Worlds"**
This global forecasting effort creates scenarios for the future based on long-term trends and potential game-changers. This reading also examines the U.S. foreign policy impact on future global conditions.

**Chapter 4:** Learning from the Past
**Chapter 9:** Policy-Making Models
**Chapter 14:** Alternative Futures

25. **Max Boot, "More Small Wars: Counterinsurgency Is Here to Stay"**
Using Afghanistan and Iraq as his reference point, Boot examines ten key lessons that must be learned by policy makers if they are to succeed in the inevitable next round of small wars that the United States will face.

■ 26. **Molly Elgin-Cossart, "Delivering Development after 2015"**
Elgin-Cossart looks at such problems as improving domestic resource mobilization, development assistance, and the level of private financing as a means to achieve the post-2015 Millennium Development Goals.

■ 27. **Excerpts from Taryn Fransen and Casey Cronin's "A Critical Decade for Climate Policy: Tools and Initiatives to Track Our Progress"**
Fransen and Cronin introduce different forms of climate policy and use the concept of the lifecycle of climate policy tracking to highlight the efforts of public and private groups to accomplish the goal of measuring climate change.

28. **Michael J. Boyle, "Is the U.S. Drone War Effective?"**
Boyle examines the issue of the strategic and tactical value of drones in the fight against terrorism and gives special attention to the short- and long-term dangers to U.S. foreign policy of using drones on too large a scale.

# PREFACE

President John F. Kennedy often remarked that "domestic politics can defeat us; foreign policy can kill us." During the Cold War there was no shortage of foreign policy problems supporting Kennedy's cautionary observation about the inherent dangers in responding to foreign policy problems. The Korean War (1950–1953), a series of Berlin crises (1958–1962), the Cuban missile crisis (1962), a series of Arab-Israeli wars (1948, 1957, 1967, 1973, 1982), the Vietnam War (1950s–1975), the fall of the Shah of Iran (1979), the Russian invasion of Afghanistan (1979), and the proliferation of nuclear weapons immediately come to mind as foreign policy problems that fit the spirit of Kennedy's warning.

The end of the Cold War brought about a notable change in outlook on foreign policy problems for many. No longer were foreign policy problems seen as an endless series of threatening conditions. Instead, the end of the Cold War brought with it a "peace dividend." Freed from external national security threats, the United States could now turn its attention to domestic policy problems as well as engage in more positive and cooperative foreign policy undertakings such as building democracy, promoting human rights, and addressing global environmental problems.

The terrorist attacks of September 11, 2001, shattered this optimism, and for many Kennedy's words once again seemed to ring true. The death of Osama bin Laden in 2011, the end of fighting in Afghanistan and Iraq, and the onset of the Arab Spring in 2010 combined to inject a renewed sense of optimism into how the overall state of global affairs and the challenges facing American foreign policy were viewed. This optimism proved to be short-lived with the start of civil war in Syria in 2011, charges the Syrian government was using chemical weapons against its opponents, and the rise to prominence of ISIS along with the continued diplomatic conflict with Iran over its pursuit of nuclear weapons capability. Once again, the dangers inherent in foreign policy seemed all too real, leaving little room for cooperative foreign policy ventures.

It is against this complex backdrop of potentially high stakes and conflicting optimistic and pessimistic assessments of the state of world politics that President Barack Obama has had to construct a foreign policy. His administration has had to confront a variety of problems, ranging from the ongoing (terrorism, global warming, nuclear proliferation, and human rights) to the periodically recurring (immigration, the rise of challenging powers, and global epidemics) to the new (cyber threats, civil war in Syria, and the collapse

Ukraine). Not surprisingly, the responses adopted have brought forward a wide range of debates. In some cases commentators question whether a problem really exists or if the problem is misinterpreted. Others debate whether too little or too much is being done or if American resources are being properly used. Still others debate whether the response chosen has been successful or made the situation worse.

In order to help students gain an understanding of the scope of the debate over the conduct of American foreign policy today and the proper direction it should take in the future, the selections in *Readings in American Foreign Policy: Problems and Responses* are organized thematically into six parts. Each part begins with a recent government document that either provides students with a general overview of the topics covered or a discussion of a key issue raised in the section. We have also included readings either written by authors living and working outside the United States or that appeared in journals published abroad. The goal here is to expand the range of commentary on American foreign policy to which students are exposed.

- **Part I: Defining Foreign Policy** consists of readings designed to present students with an overview of how the overall direction of American foreign policy today is viewed by leading commentators and the types of concerns they will see expressed in later readings. It begins with a statement of American foreign policy by President Obama in order to provide a common starting point for class discussions and student analysis.
- **Part II: Global Problems** introduces students to the range of foreign policy problems facing the United States. The readings provide a concrete foundation on which later discussions of policy responses can be built as well as fleshing out the overarching evaluative commentaries on American foreign policy presented in part I. The first reading in this part is the 2015 Threat Assessment presented to Congress by the intelligence community.
- **Part III: Societal Influences on U.S. Foreign Policy** contains readings designed to help students recognize that constructing responses to foreign policy problems is not just a matter of responding to events abroad but also involves calculations about how foreign policy responses fit in with traditional ways of viewing global problems, the intersection of foreign and domestic policies, and the ever-present need for domestic political support for foreign policy initiatives. The first reading in this section is a study by the Congressional Research Service on the Keystone XL Pipeline, a policy response that cuts across the lines of domestic and foreign policy.
- **Part IV: Institutions and U.S. Foreign Policy** provides students with insight into the operation and foreign policy impact of key institutions involved in the making and implementing of American foreign policy. Included here are commentaries both on Congress and the presidency as well as on key bureaucratic actors. The first reading introduces students to one of those bureaucracies. It presents excerpts from the first State Department Quadrennial Diplomacy and Development Review.

- **Part V: Responses** is designed to move student thinking beyond the point of identifying foreign policy problems to evaluating the strengths and weaknesses of responses to foreign policy problems. The readings present critiques of existing responses and advocate new foreign policy initiatives for current foreign policy problems. The lead essay here consists of a set of excerpts from President Obama's public comments on how his administration was responding to the crisis in Syria.
- **Part VI: Emerging Issues** directs student attention to possible future foreign policy problems. The readings selected introduce students to problems whose general outlines are already visible and hold the potential for becoming increasingly prominent. The first reading in this part is by the National Intelligence Council and presents students with a broad conceptualization of future trends into which the more concrete problems addressed in the readings can be placed.

The overarching goals of *Readings in American Foreign Policy: Problems and Responses* are twofold. The first is to present a set of readings that will help students (a) gain a deeper understanding of the nature of the problems facing American foreign policy, (b) develop informed opinions about what strategies to follow in responding to them, and (c) understand the domestic and international constraints policy makers face in constructing American foreign policy. The second goal is to help students develop their critical thinking skills so that they will be able to move beyond the present to being better able to analyze and evaluate future American foreign policy problems and responses.

We have included a number of special features in *Readings in American Foreign Policy: Problems and Responses* to help students realize these goals. First, the readings in each part are preceded by a short introductory essay that provides students with historical and conceptual reference points to help them place the readings in the broader literature on American foreign policy. Each introductory essay ends with a set of **Big Picture Questions**, which are designed to help students identify the overarching issues addressed by the readings and to better see them as a whole. Second, each reading is followed by a set of **Critical Thinking Questions**, which are designed to help students identify and reflect on key questions and issues raised by the reading both for present and future American foreign policies. Third, selections from think tanks are included throughout the book. Identified as **think tank analyses**, these readings provide students with perspectives on American foreign policy not traditionally found in textbooks. Think tanks play an increasingly prominent role in helping policy makers identify problems and responses in American foreign policy. By including examples of think tank analyses from across the political spectrum, we hope to help students better see the commonalities, differences, and linkages among traditional academic analyses of American foreign policy, that of think tanks, and the actual decisions made by policy makers.

To aid instructors in using *Readings in American Foreign Policy: Problems and Responses* in their classes, we have included an **Instructor Guide.** It presents a capsule summary of the key features of each reading with a special emphasis on the key concepts used, the central theme of the reading, the perspective taken by the author, and whether it is a think tank analysis. Linkages are also provided for how *Readings in American Foreign Policy: Problems and Responses* can be used with the tenth edition of my textbook, *American Foreign Policy: Past, Present, and Future*, which is also published by Rowman & Littlefield.

Special thanks are owed to those who helped move *Readings in American Foreign Policy: Problems and Responses* from an idea to a book. Clement E. Adibe, DePaul University; Eric Blanchard, Columbia University; Philip Brenner, American University; Nader Entessar, University of South Alabama; and Brian Urlacher, University of North Dakota, provided important feedback on the selection of readings. Traci Crowell strongly supported the project from the very beginning and provided invaluable advice in strengthening the structure and organization of *Readings in American Foreign Policy: Problems and Responses*. Molly White guided the project through production and offered excellent feedback and insight into the organization of the sections and the introductory essays. I also wish to thank Lindsey Schauer for copyediting and Rima Weinberg for proofreading.

# Defining
# Foreign Policy

Debates over the proper direction of American foreign policy are a recurring phenomenon in American politics. The twentieth century began with a debate over the outcome of the Spanish-American War of 1898 that left the United States as the colonial power in the Philippines. The merits of joining the League of Nations and pursuing a policy of isolationism followed the conclusion of World War I. The period immediately after World War II brought forward debates over whether the proper goals of American foreign policy in containing Soviet expansionism were global in scope or limited to key strategic areas. The adoption of expansive goals ultimately led to the U.S. involvement in Vietnam, which began in the 1950s and did not end until 1975. That experience left in its wake continuing debates over the goals and objectives of American foreign policy as well as the United States' proper place in the world.

Without a clear starting point, debates on questions such as these about the correct path for the United States to follow, what alternatives are open to the United States, or how to think about success and failure are unlikely to produce agreement. Instead of clarifying matters, confusion will continue and agreement on how to proceed becomes more difficult.

In studying the evolution and practice of American foreign policy, commentators have put forward a number of suggestions on how we might go about creating a more precise understanding of what foreign policy means. One is to make a distinction between foreign policy as a specific action or set of actions (i.e., giving foreign aid or sending troops into a country) and foreign policy as a strategic pathway or objective (i.e., neutrality, deterrence, freedom of the seas). This distinction is intended to remind us that what is important is not just winning the war but what was accomplished by winning the war. A second is to make a distinction between foreign policy as a set of statements (declaratory foreign policy) and foreign policy as implemented (action foreign policy). The point here is that a country might support human rights in official documents and speeches yet do little to address human rights violations.

Other commentators have sought to sharpen our thinking about what it is that foreign policies are intended to accomplish and what they need to succeed. With regard to the first point it has been suggested that we need to define the boundaries and relationship of the "national interest" and the "global interest." It is often presented as if they are competing concepts, but is this necessarily so? Might they not support each other under some circumstances? In terms of the requirements for success, one of the most influential arguments was put forward by newspaper columnist Walter Lippmann in the 1940s. He argued that the primary problem standing in the way of a successful foreign policy was an imbalance between the goals being sought and the means available to realize them. In his view this imbalance, or gap, held harmful long- and short-term consequences for American foreign policy.

The contemporary debate on defining American foreign policy revolves around three overlapping questions. The first deals most narrowly with President Barack Obama's foreign policy. Critics argue it lacks a central purpose (a guiding strategy or pathway) and that it consists of little more than a series of improvised undertakings (foreign policy as specific actions). A second debate exists over the proper strategic direction that American foreign policy should take. Opinions here vary greatly, running from a Tea Party position that is generally skeptical of any notion that the United States has a special responsibility to bring order to the world or that events beyond U.S. borders are particularly threatening to a neo-conservative position that holds that the United States has a special responsibility and capability to lead in world affairs. In between are found liberal and conservative commentators holding a variety of positions that on the whole embrace some degree of global involvement, with terrorism being identified as the primary threat. An outlier position in this debate argues that the world has become too complex for any single strategic foreign policy position to succeed and that improvisation may, in fact, be the best solution among bad choices.

The third debate is over the United States' standing in the world and speaks to the continued relevance of the need to link foreign policy goals and power resources. The Cold War ended with the United States as the unchallenged hegemonic global power. To many, the situation today looks far different. The overwhelming U.S. military power resources did not stop the 9/11 attacks, and its economic power resources did not protect the United States from the effects of the 2008 global economic crisis. More recently it has faced challenges from both a declining power (Russia) and a rising power (China). Participants in this third debate ask, in light of these developments, should (or must) the United States change its foreign policy goals or the means by which it seeks to realize them?

The readings in the section begin with President Obama's May 28, 2014, speech to West Point graduates in which he outlined his administration's foreign policy agenda. Not surprisingly, it received the same mixed reaction that accompanied his foreign policy from the start of his presidency. For us, it provides the reference point for thinking about defining foreign policy. We follow with three different perspectives authored by scholars on how to think about strategic options in making U.S. foreign policy. Each provides a different vantage point from which to evaluate President Obama's vision of American foreign policy.

The first, "Allure of Normalcy," is by Robert Kagan and was published virtually at the same time Obama gave his speech at West Point. Where Obama spoke of pragmatism, Kagan spoke of America's continued responsibility for global peace and order, ending his essay with, "Perhaps Americans can be inspired in this way again. . . . There is no superpower waiting in the wings to save the world if this democratic superpower falters." According to the second vision, "A Better Internationalism," David C. Unger argues that American internationalism often amounts to little more than micro-meddling in the affairs of other states and the pursuit of the national interest as defined by a tight-knit foreign policy elite. He calls for adopting a "constructive internationalism" that emphasizes global involvement and peaceful cooperation. Next, Barry R. Posen, in "Pull Back: The Case for a Less Activist Foreign Policy," makes the case for replacing what he characterizes as a foreign policy based on an "undisciplined, expensive, and bloody strategy" with one based on the principle of restraint. No longer would the United States pursue global reforms; instead it would focus on narrow national security interests, thus preserving U.S. prosperity and security in the long run.

## BIG PICTURE QUESTIONS

1. What are the major philosophical differences between Kagan, Unger, and Posen's positions? Which position do you agree with most?
2. How compatible are U.S. national interests and the global interest? Under what conditions might tensions between them arise?
3. What are the most important concerns other countries have about the conduct and content of U.S. foreign policy today?

## SUGGESTED READINGS

Richard Betts, "Pick Your Battles," *Foreign Affairs* 93 (November 2014), 15–24.
Daniel Drezner, ed., *Avoiding Trivia: The Role of Strategic Planning in American Foreign Policy* (Washington, DC: Brookings, 2009).

David Fitzgerald, *Learning to Forget* (Stanford, CA: Stanford University Press, 2013).

Bruce Jentleson, "Strategic Recalibration," *Washington Quarterly* 37 (January 2014), 115–36.

Christopher Layne, "This Time It's Real: The End of Unipolarity and the Pax Americana," *International Studies Quarterly* 6 (2012), 205–13.

# 1

# President Obama's Address to West Point Graduates

This is a particularly useful time for America to reflect on those who have sacrificed so much for our freedom, a few days after Memorial Day. You are the first class to graduate since 9/11 who may not be sent into combat in Iraq or Afghanistan. When I first spoke at West Point in 2009, we still had more than 100,000 troops in Iraq. We were preparing to surge in Afghanistan. Our counterterrorism efforts were focused on al Qaeda's core leadership—those who had carried out the 9/11 attacks. And our nation was just beginning a long climb out of the worst economic crisis since the Great Depression.

Four and a half years later, as you graduate, the landscape has changed. We have removed our troops from Iraq. We are winding down our war in Afghanistan. Al Qaeda's leadership on the border region between Pakistan and Afghanistan has been decimated, and Osama bin Laden is no more. And through it all, we've refocused our investments in what has always been a key source of American strength: a growing economy that can provide opportunity for everybody who's willing to work hard and take responsibility here at home.

In fact, by most measures, America has rarely been stronger relative to the rest of the world. Those who argue otherwise—who suggest that America is in decline, or has seen its global leadership slip away—are either misreading history or engaged in partisan politics. Think about it. Our military has no peer. The odds of a direct threat against us by any nation are low and do not come close to the dangers we faced during the Cold War.

Meanwhile, our economy remains the most dynamic on Earth; our businesses the most innovative. Each year, we grow more energy independent. From Europe to Asia, we are the hub of alliances unrivaled in the history of nations. America continues to attract striving immigrants. The values of our founding inspire leaders in parliaments and new movements in public squares around the globe. And when a typhoon hits the Philippines, or schoolgirls are kidnapped in Nigeria, or masked men occupy a building in Ukraine, it is America that the world looks to for help. So the United States is and remains

Excerpted from "Remarks by the President at the United States Military Academy Commencement Ceremony," The White House Office of the Press Secretary, May 28, 2014.

the one indispensable nation. That has been true for the century passed and it will be true for the century to come.

But the world is changing with accelerating speed. This presents opportunity, but also new dangers. We know all too well, after 9/11, just how technology and globalization has put power once reserved for states in the hands of individuals, raising the capacity of terrorists to do harm. Russia's aggression toward former Soviet states unnerves capitals in Europe, while China's economic rise and military reach worries its neighbors. From Brazil to India, rising middle classes compete with us, and governments seek a greater say in global forums. And even as developing nations embrace democracy and market economies, 24-hour news and social media makes it impossible to ignore the continuation of sectarian conflicts and failing states and popular uprisings that might have received only passing notice a generation ago.

It will be your generation's task to respond to this new world. The question we face, the question each of you will face, is not whether America will lead, but how we will lead—not just to secure our peace and prosperity, but also extend peace and prosperity around the globe.

Now, this question isn't new. At least since George Washington served as Commander-in-Chief, there have been those who warned against foreign entanglements that do not touch directly on our security or economic wellbeing. Today, according to self-described realists, conflicts in Syria or Ukraine or the Central African Republic are not ours to solve. And not surprisingly, after costly wars and continuing challenges here at home, that view is shared by many Americans.

A different view from interventionists from the left and right says that we ignore these conflicts at our own peril; that America's willingness to apply force around the world is the ultimate safeguard against chaos, and America's failure to act in the face of Syrian brutality or Russian provocations not only violates our conscience, but invites escalating aggression in the future.

And each side can point to history to support its claims. But I believe neither view fully speaks to the demands of this moment. It is absolutely true that in the 21st century American isolationism is not an option. We don't have a choice to ignore what happens beyond our borders. If nuclear materials are not secure, that poses a danger to American cities. As the Syrian civil war spills across borders, the capacity of battle-hardened extremist groups to come after us only increases. Regional aggression that goes unchecked—whether in southern Ukraine or the South China Sea, or anywhere else in the world—will ultimately impact our allies and could draw in our military. We can't ignore what happens beyond our boundaries.

. . .

Here's my bottom line: America must always lead on the world stage. If we don't, no one else will. The military that you have joined is and always will be the backbone of that leadership. But U.S. military action cannot be the only—or even primary—component of our leadership in every instance. Just because we have the best hammer does not mean that every problem is a nail. And because the costs associated with military action are so high, you should expect every civilian leader—and especially your Commander-in-Chief—to be clear about how that awesome power should be used.

So let me spend the rest of my time describing my vision for how the United States of America and our military should lead in the years to come, for you will be part of that leadership.

First, let me repeat a principle I put forward at the outset of my presidency: The United States will use military force, unilaterally if necessary, when our core interests demand it—when our people are threatened, when our livelihoods are at stake, when the security of our allies is in danger. In these circumstances, we still need to ask tough questions about whether our actions are proportional and effective and just. International opinion matters, but America should never ask permission to protect our people, our homeland, or our way of life.

On the other hand, when issues of global concern do not pose a direct threat to the United States, when such issues are at stake—when crises arise that stir our conscience or push the world in a more dangerous direction but do not directly threaten us—then the threshold for military action must be higher. In such circumstances, we should not go it alone. Instead, we must mobilize allies and partners to take collective action. We have to broaden our tools to include diplomacy and development; sanctions and isolation; appeals to international law; and, if just, necessary and effective, multilateral military action. In such circumstances, we have to work with others because collective action in these circumstances is more likely to succeed, more likely to be sustained, less likely to lead to costly mistakes.

This leads to my second point: For the foreseeable future, the most direct threat to America at home and abroad remains terrorism. But a strategy that involves invading every country that harbors terrorist networks is naïve and unsustainable. I believe we must shift our counterterrorism strategy—drawing on the successes and shortcomings of our experience in Iraq and Afghanistan—to more effectively partner with countries where terrorist networks seek a foothold.

And the need for a new strategy reflects the fact that today's principal threat no longer comes from a centralized al Qaeda leadership. Instead, it comes from decentralized al Qaeda affiliates and extremists, many with agendas focused in countries where they operate. And this lessens the possibility of large-scale 9/11-style attacks against the homeland, but it heightens the danger of U.S. personnel overseas being attacked, as we saw in Benghazi. It heightens the danger to less defensible targets, as we saw in a shopping mall in Nairobi.

So we have to develop a strategy that matches this diffuse threat—one that expands our reach without sending forces that stretch our military too thin, or stir up local resentments. We need partners to fight terrorists alongside us. And empowering partners is a large part of what we have done and what we are currently doing in Afghanistan.

. . .

I also believe we must be more transparent about both the basis of our counterterrorism actions and the manner in which they are carried out. We have to be able to explain them publicly, whether it is drone strikes or training partners. I will increasingly turn to our military to take the lead and provide information to the public about our efforts. Our intelligence community has done outstanding work, and we have to continue to protect sources and methods. But when we cannot explain our efforts clearly and publicly, we face terrorist propaganda and international suspicion, we erode legitimacy with our partners and our people, and we reduce accountability in our own government.

And this issue of transparency is directly relevant to a third aspect of American leadership, and that is our effort to strengthen and enforce international order.

After World War II, America had the wisdom to shape institutions to keep the peace and support human progress—from NATO and the United Nations, to the World Bank and IMF. These institutions are not perfect, but they have been a force multiplier. They reduce the need for unilateral American action and increase restraint among other nations.

Now, just as the world has changed, this architecture must change as well. At the height of the Cold War, President Kennedy spoke about the need for a peace based upon, "a gradual evolution in human institutions." And evolving these international institutions to meet the demands of today must be a critical part of American leadership.

Now, there are a lot of folks, a lot of skeptics, who often downplay the effectiveness of multilateral action. For them, working through international institutions like the U.N. or respecting international law is a sign of weakness. I think they're wrong. Let me offer just two examples why.

In Ukraine, Russia's recent actions recall the days when Soviet tanks rolled into Eastern Europe. But this isn't the Cold War. Our ability to shape world opinion helped isolate Russia right away. Because of American leadership, the world immediately condemned Russian actions; Europe and the G7 joined us to impose sanctions; NATO reinforced our commitment to Eastern European allies; the IMF is helping to stabilize Ukraine's economy; OSCE monitors brought the eyes of the world to unstable parts of Ukraine. And this mobilization of world opinion and international institutions served as a counterweight to Russian propaganda and Russian troops on the border and armed militias in ski masks.

This weekend, Ukrainians voted by the millions. Yesterday, I spoke to their next President. We don't know how the situation will play out and there will remain grave challenges ahead, but standing with our allies on behalf of international order working with international institutions, has given a chance for the Ukrainian people to choose their future without us firing a shot.

Similarly, despite frequent warnings from the United States and Israel and others, the Iranian nuclear program steadily advanced for years. But at the beginning of my presidency, we built a coalition that imposed sanctions on the Iranian economy, while extending the hand of diplomacy to the Iranian government. And now we have an opportunity to resolve our differences peacefully.

The odds of success are still long, and we reserve all options to prevent Iran from obtaining a nuclear weapon. But for the first time in a decade, we have a very real chance of achieving a breakthrough agreement—one that is more effective and durable than what we could have achieved through the use of force. And throughout these negotiations, it has been our willingness to work through multilateral channels that kept the world on our side.

The point is this is American leadership. This is American strength. In each case, we built coalitions to respond to a specific challenge. Now we need to do more to strengthen the institutions that can anticipate and prevent problems from spreading. For example, NATO is the strongest alliance the world has ever known. But we're now working with NATO allies to meet new missions, both within Europe where our Eastern allies must be reassured, but also beyond Europe's borders where our NATO allies must pull their weight to counterterrorism and respond to failed states and train a network of partners.

Likewise, the U.N. provides a platform to keep the peace in states torn apart by conflict. Now we need to make sure that those nations who provide peacekeepers have the training and equipment to actually keep the peace, so that we can prevent the type of killing we've seen in Congo and Sudan. We are going to deepen our investment in countries that support these peacekeeping missions, because having other nations maintain order in their own neighborhoods lessens the need for us to put our own troops in harm's way. It's a smart investment. It's the right way to lead.

. . .

You see, American influence is always stronger when we lead by example. We can't exempt ourselves from the rules that apply to everybody else. We can't call on others to make commitments to combat climate change if a whole lot of our political leaders deny that it's taking place. We can't try to resolve problems in the South China Sea when we have refused to make sure that the Law of the Sea Convention is ratified by our United States Senate, despite the fact that our top military leaders say the treaty advances our national security. That's not leadership; that's retreat. That's not strength; that's weakness. It would be utterly foreign to leaders like Roosevelt and Truman, Eisenhower and Kennedy.

I believe in American exceptionalism with every fiber of my being. But what makes us exceptional is not our ability to flout international norms and the rule of law; it is our willingness to affirm them through our actions. And that's why I will continue to push to close Gitmo—because American values and legal traditions do not permit the indefinite detention of people beyond our borders. That's why we're putting in place new restrictions on how America collects and uses intelligence—because we will have fewer partners and be less effective if a perception takes hold that we're conducting surveillance against ordinary citizens. America does not simply stand for stability or the absence of conflict, no matter what the cost. We stand for the more lasting peace that can only come through opportunity and freedom for people everywhere.

Which brings me to the fourth and final element of American leadership: Our willingness to act on behalf of human dignity. America's support for democracy and human rights goes beyond idealism—it is a matter of national security. Democracies are our closest friends and are far less likely to go to war. Economies based on free and open markets perform better and become markets for our goods. Respect for human rights is an antidote to instability and the grievances that fuel violence and terror.

A new century has brought no end to tyranny. In capitals around the globe—including, unfortunately, some of America's partners—there has been a crackdown on civil society. The cancer of corruption has enriched too many governments and their cronies, and enraged citizens from remote villages to iconic squares. And watching these trends, or the violent upheavals in parts of the Arab World, it's easy to be cynical.

But remember that because of America's efforts, because of American diplomacy and foreign assistance as well as the sacrifices of our military, more people live under elected governments today than at any time in human history. Technology is empowering civil society in ways that no iron fist can control. New breakthroughs are lifting hundreds of millions of people out of poverty. And even the upheaval of the Arab World reflects the rejection of an authoritarian order that was anything but stable, and now offers the long-term prospect of more responsive and effective governance.

. . .

Ultimately, global leadership requires us to see the world as it is, with all its danger and uncertainty. We have to be prepared for the worst, prepared for every contingency. But American leadership also requires us to see the world as it should be—a place where the aspirations of individual human beings really matters; where hopes and not just fears govern; where the truths written into our founding documents can steer the currents of history in a direction of justice. And we cannot do that without you.

---

## CRITICAL THINKING QUESTIONS

1. Is the United States as strong and powerful as Obama states in his speech?
2. What are core U.S. foreign policy interests? What are the second- and third-tier interests?
3. What foreign policy problems would you remove from the speech if it was given today? What would you add?

# 2

# Allure of Normalcy

## WHAT AMERICA STILL OWES THE WORLD

Robert Kagan

## I.

Almost 70 years ago, a new world order was born from the rubble of World War II, built by and around the power of the United States. Today that world order shows signs of cracking, and perhaps even collapsing. The Russia-Ukraine and Syria crises, and the world's tepid response, the general upheaval in the greater Middle East and North Africa, the growing nationalist and great-power tensions in East Asia, the worldwide advance of autocracy and retreat of democracy—taken individually, these problems are neither unprecedented nor unmanageable. But collectively they are a sign that something is changing, and perhaps more quickly than we may imagine. They may signal a transition into a different world order or into a world disorder of a kind not seen since the 1930s.

If a breakdown in the world order that America made is occurring, it is not because America's power is declining—America's wealth, power, and potential influence remain adequate to meet the present challenges. It is not because the world has become more complex and intractable—the world has always been complex and intractable. And it is not simply war-weariness. Strangely enough, it is an intellectual problem, a question of identity and purpose.

Many Americans and their political leaders in both parties, including President Obama, have either forgotten or rejected the assumptions that undergirded American foreign policy for the past seven decades. In particular, American foreign policy may be moving away from the sense of global responsibility that equated American interests with the interests of many others around the world and back toward the defense of narrower, more parochial national interests. This is sometimes called "isolationism," but that is not the right word. It may be more correctly described as a search for normalcy. At

Robert Kagan is a senior fellow at the Brookings Institution and a contributing editor at *The New Republic*. He is the author, most recently, of *The World America Made*. This article was originally published by *The New Republic* in May 2014 and is reprinted with permission from the author.

the core of American unease is a desire to shed the unusual burdens of responsibility that previous generations of Americans took on in World War II and throughout the cold war and to return to being a more normal kind of nation, more attuned to its own needs and less to those of the wider world.

If this is indeed what a majority of Americans seek today, then the current period of retrenchment will not be a temporary pause before an inevitable return to global activism. It will mark a new phase in the evolution of America's foreign policy. And because America's role in shaping the world order has been so unusually powerful and pervasive, it will also begin a new phase in the international system, one that promises not to be marginally different but radically different from what we have known these past 70 years. Unless Americans can be led back to an understanding of their enlightened self-interest, to see again how their fate is entangled with that of the world, then the prospects for a peaceful twenty-first century in which Americans and American principles can thrive will be bleak.

To understand where America, and the world, may be heading, it is useful to remind ourselves where we have been—of the choices that Americans made decades ago and of the profound, world-changing consequences of those choices.

For Americans, the choice was never been between isolationism and internationalism. With their acquisitive drive for wealth and happiness, their love of commerce, their economic and (in earlier times) territorial expansiveness, and their universalistic ideology, they never had it in them to wall themselves off from the rest of the world. Tokugawa Japan and Ming China were isolationist. Americans have always been more like republican Rome or ancient Athens, a people and a nation on the move.

When, roughly 70 years ago, American foreign policy underwent a revolutionary transformation, it was not a transformation from isolationism to internationalism. What Americans had rejected before World War II was a steady global involvement, with commitments to other nations and responsibilities for the general well-being of the world. That was what the so-called internationalists of the time wanted for the United States. Theodore Roosevelt, John Hay, Henry Cabot Lodge, Elihu Root, Henry Stimson, Woodrow Wilson, and many others believed that Americans ought to take on a much bigger role in world affairs, as befitted their growing power. The United States had become "more and more the balance of power of the whole globe," Roosevelt observed, and it ought to behave accordingly. And indeed, following the Spanish-American War and for the first two decades of the twentieth century, the United States did pursue a wider and deeper global involvement than it had ever done before, culminating in the dispatch of two million troops to France. When World War I ended, Wilson, like Roosevelt before him, ambitiously set out to make the United States a central player in world affairs. Beseeched by all the European powers after the war—for American financing aid to steady their economies and for American security guarantees against each other—Wilson wanted the United States to commit itself to an enduring global role. The world, he warned Americans, would be "absolutely in despair if America deserts it." Wilson's League of Nations (actually it had been Roosevelt's idea first), although couched in the idealistic language of universal principles and collective security, was meant above all to serve as the vehicle for American power and influence in support of a new liberal world order.

But Americans rejected this role. Disillusioned by the compromises and imperfections of the Versailles Treaty, mourning the loss of more than 100,000 dead soldiers, skeptical about American participation in the league, and spurred on by Republicans eager to defeat Wilson and recapture the White House, a majority of Americans came to oppose not only the league but also the internationalists' broad vision of America's global role. This was no absentminded lapse back into nonexistent isolationist traditions. It was a deliberate decision to turn away from the increasingly active global involvement of the previous two decades, to adopt a foreign policy of far greater restraint, and above all to avoid future military interventions beyond the Western Hemisphere. Wilson's Republican successors promised, and the American public welcomed, what Warren Harding called a "return to normalcy."

Normalcy in the 1920s did not mean isolation. Americans continued to trade, to invest, and to travel overseas; their navy was equaled in size only by Britain's, and had fleets in the Atlantic and the Pacific; and their diplomats pursued treaties to control the arms race and to "outlaw" war. Normalcy simply meant defining America's national interests the way most other nations defined theirs. It meant defending the homeland, avoiding overseas commitments, preserving the country's independence and freedom of action, and creating prosperity at home. The problems of Europe and Asia were not America's problems, and they could be solved, or not solved, without American help. This applied to global economic issues as well. Harding wanted to "prosper America first," and he did. The 1920s were boom years for the American economy, while Europe's postwar economies stagnated.

To the vast majority of Americans, normalcy seemed a reasonable response to the world of the 1920s, after the enormous exertions of the Wilson years. There were no obvious threats on the horizon. Postwar Weimar Germany was a faltering republic more likely to collapse than to take another stab at continental dominance. Bolshevik Russia was racked by civil war and economic crisis. Japan, though growing in power and ambition, was a fragile democracy with a seat on the League of Nations permanent council. To most Americans in the 1920s, the greatest risk to America came not from foreign powers but from those misguided "internationalists" and the greedy bankers and war profiteers who would involve the nation in foreign conflicts that were none of America's business.

This consensus was broad, deep, and bipartisan, and Americans stayed on the course of normalcy for two full decades. They did so even as the world order—no longer upheld by the old combination of British naval might and a relatively stable balance of power in Europe and Asia—began to fray and then collapse. The Japanese invasion of Manchuria in 1931; Hitler's rise to power in 1933; Mussolini's invasion of Ethiopia in 1935; Germany's remilitarization of the Rhineland, and the German and Italian intervention in the Spanish Civil War, in 1936; Japan's invasion of central China in 1937; Hitler's absorption of Austria, followed by his annexation and eventual conquest of Czechoslovakia in 1938 and 1939—all these events troubled and at times appalled Americans. They were not ignorant of what was going on. Even back then information traveled widely and rapidly, and the newspapers and newsreels were filled with stories about each unfolding crisis. Reports of Mussolini's dive-bombers dropping their ordnance on spear-carrying Ethiopians; Germany's aerial bombing of the civilian population of Guernica; Japan's rampage of rape, pillage, and murder in Nanking—they were horrific and regrettable. But they were not reasons for the United States to get involved. On the contrary, they were reasons for not getting involved. The worse things looked around the world, the more hopeless it all seemed, the less Americans wanted to have anything to do with it. The United States, it was widely believed, had no vital interests at stake in Manchuria, Ethiopia, Spain, or Czechoslovakia.

In fact, it was not clear that the United States had vital interests anywhere outside the Western Hemisphere. Even after the German invasion of Poland in 1939, and the outbreak of a general European war that followed, respected American strategic thinkers, priding themselves on "realistic thinking," the "banishment of altruism and sentiment" from their analysis, and "single-minded attention to the national interests," advised that, with two oceans and a strong navy standing between America and every great power in the world, the United States was invulnerable. A Japanese attack on, say, Hawaii, they ruled out as literally impossible. Republican Senator Robert A. Taft felt confident in saying that no power "would be stupid enough" to attack the United States "from across thousands of miles of ocean." Nor would the United States suffer appreciably if Nazi Germany did manage to conquer all of Europe, including Great Britain, which by 1940 the realists regarded as a foregone conclusion. Taft saw no reason why the United States could not trade and conduct normal diplomacy with a Europe dominated by Nazi Germany just as it had with Great Britain and France. As the historian Howard K. Beale put it, nations "do not trade with one another because they like each other's governments but because both sides find the exchange of goods desirable."

Holders of such views were tagged with the disparaging label of "isolationist," but as Hans Morgenthau later pointed out, they believed at the time that they were upholding the "realist tradition of American foreign policy." The United States should not range "over the world like a knight-errant," Taft admonished, "[protecting] democracy and ideals of good faith and [tilting] like Don Quixote against the windmills of fascism." Taft insisted on seeing the world as it was, not as idealists wished it to be. The European war was the product of "national and racial animosities" that had existed "for centuries" and would continue to exist "for centuries to come," he argued. To make a difference in the war, the United States would have to send millions of troops across the ocean, make an impossible amphibious landing on shores heavily defended by German forces, and then march across Europe against the world's strongest army. The very thought was inconceivable. Much as they might wish to help Europe, therefore, Americans had "no power, even if we have the will, to be its savior."

This view was so dominant and so politically popular that Franklin Roosevelt spent his first years in office muzzling his internationalist instincts and vowing to keep America out of another war—"I hate war!" he roared in a famous address in 1936. After Munich, however, he grew panicked, sensing that the Western powers, Britain and France, had lost the will to stand up to Hitler. And so he began trying to warn Americans of what he regarded as the coming threat. Yet it was difficult to counter the realists' hardheaded analysis. Roosevelt could not prove that American security was directly endangered by what was happening in Europe. He was left making a case that really did appeal more to sentiment and idealism than to demonstrable threats to the American homeland.

Even if the United States faced no immediate danger of military attack, Roosevelt argued, if Hitler, Mussolini, and Imperial Japan were allowed to have their way, the world would be a "shabby and dangerous place to live in—yes, even for Americans to live in." America would become a "lone island" in a world dominated by the "philosophy of force." The "institutions of democracy" would be placed at risk even if America's security was not, because America would have to become an armed camp to defend itself. Roosevelt urged Americans to look beyond their immediate physical security. "There comes a time in the affairs of men," he said, "when they must prepare to defend, not their homes alone, but the tenets of faith and humanity on which their churches, their governments, and their very civilization are founded. The defense of religion, of democracy, and of good faith among nations is all the same fight. To save one we must now make up our minds to save all."

Such arguments, along with the fall of France and the Battle of Britain, did help convince Americans that they had a stake in the outcome of the European struggle, but it did not convince them to go to war. That decision followed only after Pearl Harbor. The Japanese attack, Hitler's subsequent declaration of war, and America's full-scale entry into the conflicts in both Europe and Asia were a traumatic shock to Americans, especially for those in positions of power. That which had been deemed impossible had proved possible, and long-held assumptions about American security in a troubled world collapsed in a single day.

The events of 1941 forced a fundamental reassessment not only of America's global strategy but also of how to define America's interests. Even as they waged the struggle against Germany and Japan, Roosevelt and his advisers during the war began thinking of how the postwar world ought to be shaped, and they took as their guide what they considered the lessons of the previous two decades.

The first had to do with security. The Japanese attack had proved that vast oceans and even a strong navy no longer provided adequate defense against attack. More broadly, there was the realization—or rather the rediscovery—of an old understanding: that the rise of a hostile hegemonic power on the Eurasian landmass could eventually threaten America's core security interests as well as its economic well-being. As a corollary, there was the "lesson of Munich": would-be aggressors in Eurasia had to be deterred before they became too strong to be stopped short of all-out war.

Another lesson was that the United States had an interest in political developments in Eurasia. Walter Lippmann argued that, for Americans to enjoy both "physical security" and the preservation of their "free way of life," they had to ensure that "the other shore of the Atlantic" remained always in the hands of "friendly," "trustworthy" democracies. For two decades, people had sneered at "Woodrow Wilson's demand that the world must be made safe for democracy," Lippmann commented, but Wilson had been right. Under the control of "free governments the shores and waters of the Atlantic" had become the "geographical center of human liberty." The Atlantic Charter and Roosevelt's Four Freedoms reflected this revived conviction that the well-being of democracy in the world was not only desirable but important to America's security.

Then there was the global economy. In the late 1920s and throughout the 1930s, the United States had sought mostly domestic remedies for the Great Depression, raising its own tariffs, choking off lending abroad, refusing to join other nations in a common monetary policy, and generally protecting the American economy while ignoring the world economy. By 1941, however, Roosevelt and his advisers had concluded that both America's prosperity and its security depended on a healthy world economy. Poverty and economic dislocation had played a major role in the rise of both Hitler and Bolshevism. The United States bore much of the blame, for although it had been the world's leading economic power in the 1920s and 1930s, it had failed to play a constructive and responsible role in stabilizing the global economy.

Finally, there was the issue of American public support for global involvement. In the 1920s and 1930s, Americans had been allowed and even encouraged by their political leaders to believe that the United States was immune to the world's troubles. They could not be allowed to fall back into such complacency. They could no longer regard events thousands of miles away as of no concern to them. To Roosevelt, assuring public support for a larger and more consistent American role in the world was going to be among the greatest challenges after the war. Americans had to understand, as Reinhold Niebuhr wrote in April 1943, that "the world problem cannot be solved if America does not accept its full share of responsibility in solving it."

That share was to be sizeable. Convinced that World War II had been the result not of any single incident but rather of the overall breakdown of world order, politically, economically, and strategically, American leaders set out to erect and sustain a new order that could endure. This time it was to be a world order built around American economic, political, and military power. Europeans had proved incapable of keeping the peace. Asia was entirely unstable on its own. Any new order would depend on the United States. It would become the center of a new economic system that would encourage open trade and provide financial assistance and loans to nations struggling to stay afloat. It would take a substantial and active part in the occupation and transformation of the defeated powers, ensuring that some form of democracy took root in place of the dictatorships that had led those nations to war. America would also have to possess preponderant military strength and when necessary deploy sufficient power to preserve stability and security in Europe, Asia, and the Middle East.

Military force played a central part in the calculations of Roosevelt and his advisers as they set out to establish and defend the new liberal world order. "Peace must be kept by force," Roosevelt insisted. There was "no other way." He anticipated that an American occupation force of one million troops would be necessary to keep the peace in Europe, for at least a year and perhaps longer. During the war, the Joint Chiefs envisioned establishing military bases around the world in "areas well removed from the United States" so that any fighting would take place "nearer the enemy" rather than near American territory.

Roosevelt naturally hoped to avoid the repeated and extended deployment of American ground forces overseas, since he feared the public would not tolerate it. But he did expect that the United States would have to send at least planes and ships whenever called upon by the U.N. Security Council. As Cordell Hull insisted at the Dumbarton Oaks conference in 1944, American military forces had to be "available promptly, in adequate measure, and with certainty." In fact, Roosevelt anticipated that requests from the Security Council would be so frequent that he did not want the president to have to go to Congress each time for approval of the use of force. The Security Council had to have "the power to act quickly and decisively to keep the peace by force, if necessary," Roosevelt explained, and so the American representative had to be given advance authority to act.

Roosevelt supported the United Nations but was not a great believer in collective security. American power, he believed, would be the key. He saw the United Nations much as Wilson had seen the League of Nations, as a vehicle for U.S. global involvement. Indeed, as the historian Robert Dallek has noted, for Roosevelt the United Nations was partly meant to "obscure" the central role American power was to play in the new world order—obscure it, that is, from Americans.

# II.

This new American grand strategy for the postwar world could not have been a more radical departure from "normalcy." Its goals were not simply defense of the territory, prosperity, and sovereign independence of the American people, but also the promotion of a liberal world order that would defend not only America's interests but those of many other nations as well. The rise of a Eurasian hegemon would threaten other nations long before it would threaten the United States, for instance, yet Americans now accepted primary responsibility for preventing it. The new strategy was not selfless or altruistic. American officials believed that it was in the best interest of the United States. But neither did it fit the normal definition of the "national interest." As Dean Acheson explained, Americans had to learn to "operate in a pattern of responsibility which is greater than our own interests." This was the real revolution in American foreign policy.

The new strategy was not directed at any particular nation or any specific threat—at least not at first. The Soviet Union had not yet emerged as the next great challenge to the new global order. During World War II, Roosevelt and most other top officials expected mutual cooperation with the Soviets after the war, and even as late as 1945, Acheson still believed in the possibility of partnership with Moscow. Rather than responding to a specific threat, the new grand strategy aimed at preventing a general collapse of global order, which meant supporting an open international economic system, enforcing principles of international behavior, supporting, where possible, democratic governments, encouraging a minimum of respect for human rights, as defined in the U.N. Charter, and generally promoting the kind of world that suited Americans and those who shared their beliefs.

This new and wide-ranging set of goals and responsibilities completely reoriented the posture of American foreign policy. Instead of essentially leaning back, waiting for threats to emerge, responding, and then pulling back again, the new strategy required a constant and pervasive forward involvement in the affairs of the world. The new economic strategy aimed to prevent economic crises before they resulted in revolution or despotism. The new military strategy aimed to discourage would-be aggressors before they became aggressors, or as Roosevelt put it, to "end future wars by stepping on their necks before they grow up."

The new forward-leaning posture became especially pronounced as the postwar era transitioned into the cold war. The Marshall Plan aimed to shore up Western European economies and democracies before they collapsed and succumbed to communism. The Truman Doctrine aimed to bolster Greece and Turkey before they fell to communist subversion. When the communist revolution triumphed in China in 1949, American critics blamed the Truman administration for not doing enough to prevent it—a charge, fair or not, that no one would have thought to make before World War II. The unanticipated North Korean invasion of the South produced panic in Washington and, in the minds of Truman and his advisers, powerfully reinforced the "lesson of Munich." Henceforth the United States would have to be vigilant and ready to act, with force, anywhere in the world.

All of this was precisely what the anti-interventionist critics had warned about in the 1930s. Taft, a thoughtful and intelligent man, had indeed predicted that, once sent off to the war, American forces would never come home again. Victory would prove as much a curse as a blessing. American troops, Taft had warned, "would have to police Europe or maintain the balance of power there by force of arms" indefinitely. Beale had cautioned that, if freedom and democracy were the goals, as Roosevelt claimed, then the United States was going to have to "maintain democracy by armed force on the Continent of Europe" and keep a "navy large enough to establish 'freedom of the seas' . . . on all the oceans of the world." It was a prescription at once for bankruptcy and militarism at home and "unadulterated imperialism" abroad.

Roosevelt and other American statesmen originally hoped that the United States would not have to do everything by itself. Roosevelt planned to share global management among the "Four Policemen"—the United States, Great Britain, the Soviet Union, and China. And Truman in 1945 was bound and determined to slash the defense budget and bring as many troops home as possible. Yet within two years after the war ended, the new world order was already teetering on the edge of collapse along with hopes for global partnership with the other great powers. Britain quickly signaled its inability to play its historic role, even in the Mediterranean. China descended into civil war and revolution. And the Soviet Union emerged not as a supporter of the new order but, to American eyes, as its greatest opponent. The result was the disheartening realization that the United States was going to carry the lion's share of the burden, just as Taft had warned. As Acheson later put it, the United States was going to have to be "the locomotive at the head of mankind," while the rest of the world was going to be "the caboose."

Roosevelt had always worried that the American people would never accept such an expansive and seemingly open-ended global role. Three months before he died, in his last State of the Union address, in January 1945, he attempted to rally them for the task ahead. "In our disillusionment after the last war," he reminded the American public, "we gave up the hope of gradually achieving a better peace because we had not the courage to fulfill our responsibilities in an admittedly imperfect world. We must not let that happen again, or we shall follow the same tragic road again—the road to a third world war."

That was the last time, before 1989, that an American statesman would think of American global responsibilities without reference to the Soviet Union or to international communism. The onset of the cold war, the panicked American response to Soviet policies in Eastern Europe and in the Middle East, and the recurrent American paranoia about the danger of communist subversion at home answered FDR's fears about public support. To many Americans, Soviet communism seemed an even more direct threat to their way of life than Hitler and the Nazis. Fighting it, therefore, proved an easier strategy to comprehend and support than shouldering "responsibilities in an admittedly imperfect world." Although there was intense and often divisive debate over foreign policy during the cold war, and much dissent voiced by critics of anti-communist containment, especially during and just after the Vietnam war, a majority of Americans proved consistently willing to go to great lengths in the name of containing communism. In the late 1940s and 1950s, they provided billions of dollars for European reconstruction and made military alliances with former adversaries such as Japan and Germany and other European powers they had once disdained and mistrusted. They even extended nuclear guarantees to deter a Soviet conventional invasion of Europe, voluntarily making themselves targets of Soviet nuclear weapons in the event of a European war. In the 1950s and 1960s, they often spent 10 percent or more of their GDP on defense. They deployed hundreds of thousands of troops overseas, indefinitely, in Europe and Asia—almost a million during the Eisenhower years. They fought in costly wars in Korea and Vietnam, with uncertain and unsatisfying results.

Justifying everything in terms of the anti-communist struggle may have been, to borrow Acheson's phrase, "clearer than truth," but it worked. Fear of communism, combined with fear of the Soviet Union as a geopolitical threat, allowed a majority of Americans and American policymakers to view practically any policy directed against communist forces, or even against suspected communist forces, anywhere in the world as directly serving the nation's vital interests. In 1965, even David Halberstam believed that preventing a communist victory in Vietnam was "vital to our national interest." A decade and a half later, Jimmy Carter, who had come to office warning, not entirely unreasonably, against an "inordinate fear of communism," was forced to announce a dramatic shift of policy in response to a Soviet invasion of Afghanistan, a country that not two Americans in a million could have found on a map and where no direct American interest could be identified, other than the fact that the Soviets were there. Yes, the general feeling went, the United States had taken on unprecedented global responsibilities, but it had done so because American interests were directly threatened by an unprecedented global challenge.

So Americans for more than four decades proved willing to support the expansive and active foreign policy that Roosevelt and his advisers had envisioned—indeed, probably much more than they envisioned—and the results were extraordinary. In the half-century following World War II, the United States successfully established, protected, and advanced a liberal world order, carving out a vast "free world" within which an unprecedented era of peace and prosperity could flower in Western Europe, East Asia, and the Western Hemisphere. Although tensions between the United States and the Soviet Union sometimes rose to dangerous levels, the period was characterized above all by peace among the great powers. The United States and the Soviet Union did not come to blows, and just as importantly, the American presence in Europe and East Asia put an end to the cycles of war that had torn both regions since the late nineteenth century. The number of democracies in the world grew dramatically. The international trading system expanded and deepened. Most of the world enjoyed an unprecedented prosperity. There was no shortage of disasters and near-disasters, as well as the two costly wars in Asia—but the strategy was largely successful, so much so that the Soviet empire finally collapsed or voluntarily withdrew, peacefully, under the pressure of the West's economic and political success, and the liberal order then expanded to include the rest of Europe and most of Asia. All of this was the result of many forces—the political and economic integration of Europe, the success of Japan and Germany, and the rise of other successful Asian economies—but none of it would have been possible without a United States willing and able to play the abnormal and unusual role of preserver and defender of a liberal world order.

America's ability to play this role at all was due less to the special virtues of the American people than to some remarkable advantages that put the United States in a historically unique position. The most important advantage was geography. For centuries the world's cockpits of conflict had been in Europe, Asia, and the Middle East, where multiple powers shared common neighborhoods, jostled for primacy, and engaged in endless cycles of military competition and warfare. When the United States emerged as a great power at the end of the nineteenth century, it alone enjoyed fundamental security in a neighborhood in which it was already the unquestioned hegemon. This, along with its wealth and large population, gave the United States the ability to dispatch the bulk of its armed forces thousands of miles away to engage in protracted military operations. It also allowed the United States to station large numbers of troops permanently overseas if it so desired. And it could do all of this without leaving itself vulnerable to a neighboring power.

No other nation in the world was ever so situated. Even that other great island superpower, Great Britain, sat too close to the European continent to be invulnerable to attack, especially when the airplane and the long-range missile became major tools of warfare. Nor had Britain succeeded in securing its core strategic requirement: preventing the emergence of a hegemon on the continent. Although successful for two centuries in maintaining and managing its overseas empire, Britain failed to prevent the rise of German hegemony twice in the twentieth century, leading to two devastating wars that ultimately undid British global power. Britain failed because it had tried to play the role of balancer in Europe from "offshore." Britons' main concern was always defense of their far-flung empire, and they preferred to stay out of Europe if possible. Their inability or unwillingness to station troops on the continent in sufficient number, or at least reliably to guarantee that sufficient force would arrive quickly in an emergency, led would-be aggressors to calculate that decisive British military force would either not arrive on time or not arrive at all.

After World War II, Americans' unique geographical advantage made possible an unprecedented global strategy. The United States was able to move beyond traditional national defense and beyond offshore balancing. It was able to become effectively both a European power and an Asian power, with troops permanently stationed "onshore" in both theaters simultaneously. The presence of American troops acted to remove doubt by potential aggressors that the United States would fight if its allies were attacked. For the next seven decades, this American presence enforced a general peace and stability in two regions that for at least a century had known almost constant great-power conflict.

Just as remarkable was the degree to which the rest of the nations in the liberal world generally accepted and even welcomed America's overwhelming power. Again, the reason had as much to do with power and geography as with ideological affinity. It was true that for most nations in the world the

United States appeared to be a relatively benign hegemon. But the core geopolitical reality was that other nations faced greater and more immediate threats from their neighbors than from the distant Americans. When those neighbors grew menacing, they looked to the United States as a natural partner—comforting for its ability to project power and defend them but comforting also for its distance.

The United States thus violated some of the cardinal rules of international relations. For decades, realists had believed that the only peaceful and stable world order was one based on a multipolar balance of power, a "concert" of nations poised in rough equilibrium in a system that all the players regarded as necessary and legitimate—like Europe in the years following the Congress of Vienna. This was the world with which Henry Kissinger felt comfortable and which he constantly predicted, even in the 1960s, was just right around the corner. Unipolarity was supposed to be inherently unstable and short-lived, because other great powers would always band together to balance against a power grown too strong—as had happened in Europe in response to the rise of France and Germany in the nineteenth and twentieth centuries. Richard Nixon expressed this alleged realist truism in a speech, no doubt penned under Kissinger's influence, in 1972. "We must remember," Nixon declared, that "the only time in the history of the world that we have had any extended period of peace is when there has been balance of power. It is when one nation becomes infinitely more powerful in relation to its potential competitor that the danger of war arises. So I believe in a world in which the United States is powerful. I think it will be a safer world and a better world if we have a strong, healthy United States, Europe, Soviet Union, China, Japan, each balancing." But the United States was already disproving this thesis.

The broad acceptance of American power, best demonstrated by the large number of its allies and the absence of powerful nations joining the Soviet Union against it, created a unique situation in the world. No other nation in history had ever played such a role on a global scale, and arguably no other nation possibly could. The situation could not conform to a theory because it could not be replicated. It was sui generis.

Geography made it possible for the United States to play this unique role in the world, but as the 1920s and 1930s showed, the question of whether the United States would take it on was up to the American people. Nothing required them to play such an abnormal part in world affairs. During the cold war, they did it primarily out of fear of communism. But what would happen when the Soviet Union disappeared and the threat of communism vanished? The question seemed moot for four excruciatingly long decades when no one ever really expected the Soviet Union to give up the geopolitical competition. But the unanticipated fall of the Soviet empire and the collapse of international communism after 1989 inevitably raised anew the question of how to define America's purpose and its interests in the absence of an obvious threat. Suddenly, Americans were back to where Roosevelt had left off in the early 1940s, when the challenge had been to avoid the mistakes of the 1920s and 1930s. But would anyone remember the original grand strategy, devised in the brief moment before the Soviet Union arose to dominate American strategic thinking? Would the original grand strategy still seem relevant at the end of the twentieth century? Or had Americans, as the political scientist Robert Osgood worried in the 1950s, "become so transfixed by their fears of communism" that they had forgotten "what they are for in their obsession with what they are against"?

# III.

When the cold war ended, many did believe that the United States could finally unburden itself of the vast global responsibilities that it had shouldered for more than four decades. As in the 1920s, the world of the early 1990s seemed safe enough. The former Soviet Union was in a state of economic and political collapse; China, following the Tiananmen Square massacre, was diplomatically and economically isolated. Americans' biggest concern at the time was the booming economy of Japan, which, as it turned out, was just about to fall into 20 years of stagnation. So what grave threat required America to continue its abnormal, outsized role in the world? Could not the United States return to being more of a normal nation with a more normal definition of its national interests?

In September 1990, in an article titled "A Normal Country in a Normal Time," Jeane Kirkpatrick argued precisely that. With the Soviet Union collapsing, there was no longer a "pressing need for heroism and sacrifice." The cold war had given foreign policy "an unnatural importance" in American life. The "foreign policy elite" had grown accustomed to thinking of the United States as having "expansive, expensive, global purposes" that "transcended . . . apparent American interests." It was time for the United States "to focus again on its own national interests," by which she meant national interests as "conventionally conceived"—"to protect its territory, wealth, and access to necessary goods; to defend its nationals." This was the "normal condition for nations."

Kirkpatrick expressed what many felt after the fall of the Berlin Wall in 1989, and not just the followers of Patrick Buchanan, who found much to praise in her essay. Francis Fukuyama also argued that with communism vanquished and democracy triumphant, there were no other great geopolitical or ideological challenges on the horizon. The chief threat of the future—as he suggested in his famous essay "The End of History?"—would be boredom, the empty tediousness of life lived under a vapid, soul-killing Western liberalism. Others noted Paul Kennedy's warnings about "imperial overstretch" and worried that America's extensive global military commitments, no longer justified by a Soviet enemy, would put it at a disadvantage in a world where geoeconomics trumped geopolitics. Realists called for a sharp retraction of American military commitments overseas, the withdrawal of troops from Europe and Asia, and even a return to what they called the "offshore balancing" of the 1920s and 1930s.

Still, and remarkably, for the first two decades of the post-cold-war era the United States pursued the original pre-cold-war grand strategy. The event that set the tone for the next dozen years was comparatively minor. In August 1990, Saddam Hussein's Iraqi army invaded Kuwait, and in a matter of days conquered and annexed it. Brutal though the action was, by comparison with the seismic events of the bloody twentieth century, it was small beer. The border between the two nations, like most boundaries in the Arab world, had been arbitrarily drawn by the British Empire. Kuwait had been under Iraqi suzerainty under the Ottomans, and leaders in Baghdad had long regarded it as an Iraqi province. Saddam further justified the invasion as support for an allegedly popular (though largely manufactured) rebellion against the Kuwaiti royal family.

Inside and outside the Bush administration, self-described realists argued that the United States draw the line not at Kuwait but at Saudi Arabia. Kuwait's oil was not that important, Colin Powell argued, and the risks of "a major confrontation" with Saddam and his army were high, so the "most prudent" option would be to defend the Saudis. "We can't make a case for losing lives for Kuwait," Powell argued, "but Saudi Arabia is different." Dick Cheney worried that driving Saddam out of Kuwait was going to cost "one hell of a lot of money," that Americans had a "short tolerance for war," and that, after all, "the oil goes mostly to Japan." James Baker took a similar view, as did a majority of Democrats in Congress, as did a majority of Americans. A poll taken in November 1990 showed that 51 percent of Americans were opposed to trying to drive the Iraqis out of Kuwait by force and that only 37 percent were in favor of it. Most favored economic sanctions to punish Saddam.

Other Bush advisers, however, led by Brent Scowcroft, saw things differently. Saddam's invasion, they believed, was "the first test of the postwar system." For half a century the United States had taken the lead role in deterring and punishing would-be aggressors. Although driving Iraqi forces out of Kuwait would be "costly and risky," Scowcroft feared that failure to do so would set "a terrible precedent—one that would only accelerate violent centrifugal tendencies—in this emerging 'post-Cold War' era." Appeasement of aggression in one region would breed aggression elsewhere. To President Bush, it was all reminiscent of the 1930s. This time, he recalled in his memoirs, "I wanted no appeasement." Speaking to the American people on the eve of war, Bush described American objectives not in terms of national interests but in terms of a "new world order," in which "the rule of law, not the law of the jungle, governs the conduct of nations." Much like Roosevelt in 1939, he argued that "a world in which brutality and lawlessness are allowed to go unchecked isn't the kind of world we're going to want to live in."

Thus did Roosevelt's original grand strategy—the defense of a liberal world order against collapse, responding not to any single, specific threat but to whatever political, economic, or strategic challenges might arise—seem to reemerge after the long cold war. After 1990, the United States, despite occasional protectionist pressures at home, generally sought to expand free trade and worked in cooperation with other governments, even at moments of economic crisis, to prevent a collapse of the global economic system. The United States also undertook to expand its alliance system, especially in Central and Eastern Europe.

In the decade following the fall of the Berlin Wall, moreover, the United States also conducted a number of sizeable military operations—seven to be precise, roughly one every 17 months: in Panama (1989), Iraq (1991), Somalia (1992), Haiti (1994), Bosnia (1995), Iraq again (1998), and Kosovo (1999). None were a response to perceived threats to vital national interests. All aimed at defending and extending the liberal world order—by toppling dictators, reversing coups, and attempting to restore democracies in Panama and Haiti; preventing mass killing or starvation in Somalia, Bosnia, and Kosovo; deterring or reversing aggression in the Persian Gulf in 1991; and attempting to prevent the proliferation of nuclear or other weapons of mass destruction in Iraq in 1998. When Bush sent 30,000 troops to remove the corrupt dictator Manuel Noriega, it was not, as George Will wrote approvingly at the time, in order to pursue national interests "narrowly construed," but to fulfill "the rights and responsibilities that come with the possession of great power." When Bush then carried out in Somalia what was arguably the most purely humanitarian, and therefore most purely selfless, intervention in American history, he told the public, "I understand that the United States alone cannot right the world's wrongs." But the "people of Somalia need . . . our help" and "some crises in the world cannot be resolved without American involvement."

The United States, in short, was the "indispensable nation," as Bill Clinton would proclaim—indispensable, that is, to the preservation of a liberal world order. Such was the thinking behind most of Clinton's foreign policy initiatives: the enlargement of NATO, which included the extension of unprecedented military guarantees to such nations as Poland, the Czech Republic, and the Baltic states; the billions sent to try to save Boris Yeltsin's faltering democratic experiment in Russia; and the intense focus on containing North Korea, Iraq, and Iran, designated as "rogue states" because they defied the principles of a liberal world order. Conflicts in remote and troubled parts of the world were not considered irrelevant to American interests but were viewed within this broader context. After the massacre at Srebrenica in 1995, Clinton officials argued, according to David Halberstam, that "Serb aggression" was intolerable—not because it threatened American interests directly, which obviously it did not, but because it tore at "the very fabric of the West."

Even the American confrontation with Iraq, beginning in the late 1990s and culminating in the U.S. invasion in 2003, had begun as a world order issue, before it became subsumed by George W. Bush's "War on Terror." When President Clinton ordered four days of bombing and missile attacks against suspected Iraqi weapons production facilities at the end of 1998, he warned that, if Saddam were not stopped, "The community of nations may see more and more of the very kind of threat Iraq poses now: a rogue state with weapons of mass destruction, ready to use them or provide them to terrorists. . . . If we fail to respond today, Saddam and all those who would follow in his footsteps will be emboldened tomorrow." In the twentieth century, Americans had "often made the difference between chaos and community, fear and hope. Now, in the new century, we'll have a remarkable opportunity to shape a future more peaceful than the past." At the end of the day, George W. Bush's decision to remove Saddam Hussein, whether that decision was wise or foolish, was driven more by concerns for world order than by narrow self-interest. Of all the American interventions of the post-cold-war era, only the invasion of Afghanistan could be understood as directly related to America's own national security.

The long interventions in Iraq and Afghanistan certainly played a part in undermining American support, not just for wars but for the grand strategy that led to those wars. However, that support had been shaky from the beginning. Polls throughout the 1990s showed Americans wary of overseas interventions, even though the public generally supported their presidents when they used force. Opposition parties generally opposed the interventions undertaken by both Democratic and Republican presidents. Democrats voted against George H. W. Bush's Persian Gulf war; Republicans opposed the Clinton administration's interventions in Haiti and the Balkans as superfluous "international social work" and "nation-building" that were divorced from American national interests. Realists in the academy and the think tanks pecked away at successive administrations, warning of overreach and "imperialism." Perhaps like the cartoon character that runs beyond the edge of the cliff and hangs with legs churning in the air before falling, support for the globally active policies of the 1990s was a kind of forward inertia, fueled by the energy of the late cold war, and gravity was eventually going to bring it to Earth.

The conventional wisdom these days is that Americans are war-weary. But it may be more accurate to say they are world-weary. During the cold war, after all, Americans had much greater reason for war-weariness—Korea and Vietnam were 14 times more costly in terms of American deaths than Afghanistan and Iraq—but they never fully rejected the global anti-communist containment strategy that had gotten them into the wars. Today's mood seems more analogous to the 1920s. More than 50 percent of Americans today believe that the United States "should mind its own business internationally and let other countries get along the best they can on their own"—the highest number ever recorded since Pew started asking the question 50 years ago.

At the core of this public attitude is no doubt the desire to avoid more wars. But as the 1920s and 1930s showed, a determination to stay out of war can affect broader foreign and economic policies. In the 1930s, the desire to avoid war led Congress to pass the Neutrality Acts, to prevent Americans from even trading with belligerents in a foreign war lest the United States be dragged in on one side or the other. Such an action may be inconceivable today, but the reasoning behind it is visible. Polls these days show that Americans are not only averse to using military force but also to actions short of war. More than 50 percent agreed that it was "more important" that the United States "not get too involved in the situation in Ukraine" than that it "take a firm stand" against Russia, which 29 percent found more important. Many of those not wanting to get "too involved" may fear that any involvement could eventually lead to a possible military confrontation—and they're not entirely wrong. As in the 1920s and 1930s, Americans can see the slippery slope.

# IV.

Historians often refer to the "maturing" of American foreign policy since the nineteenth century. But if nations can learn, they can also unlearn. These days it is hard to watch both the conduct and the discussion of American foreign policy and not sense a certain unlearning, a forgetting of the old lessons on which the grand strategy was premised. Perhaps this was inevitable. World War II is as distant from today's "millennials" as the Civil War was from the generation of the 1930s. A generation that does not remember the cold war, but grew up knowing only Iraq and Afghanistan, is going to view America's role in the world differently. Combine that with the older generations that have tired of playing the old role, and it is hardly surprising that enthusiasm is flagging. Americans today are not isolationists, any more than they were in the 1920s. They favor the liberal world order insofar as they can see how it touches them. But they are no longer prepared to sacrifice very much to uphold it.

This is understandable. Americans have been Atlas carrying the world on their shoulders. They can be forgiven for feeling the temptation to put it down. Under the best of circumstances, playing the role of upholder of the liberal world order was always a monumental task. At the dawn of the American era, Truman called it "the most terrible responsibility that any nation ever faced." George Kennan was convinced that the American people were "not fitted, either institutionally or temperamentally, to be an imperial power in the grand manner." Actually, he underestimated them, for Americans maintained their global commitments for decades, better than most nations.

Yet the burden has been immense, and not just the obvious costs in lives and treasure. Americans have spent vast amounts on defense budgets, more than all other major powers combined. Can't U.S. allies carry more of the burden? The question has been asked since the dawn of the cold war, but the answer has always been: probably not. The same factors that have made the United States uniquely capable of supporting a world order—great wealth and power and the relative security afforded by geography—help explain why American allies have always been less capable and less willing. They have lacked the power and the security to see and act beyond their narrow interests. So where they failed before they will fail again. Even twenty-first-century Europeans, for all the wonders of their union, seem incapable of uniting against a predator in their midst, and are willing, as in the past, to have the weak devoured if necessary to save their own (financial) skins. There are moral costs, too. Like most people, Americans generally like to believe that they are behaving justly in the world, that they are on the side of the right. If possible, they like to have legal or institutional sanctions for their action, or at least the general approval of like-minded nations. On the two occasions in the past 100 years when the United States contemplated taking on a central role in global affairs, in 1918 and 1945, American leaders insisted on simultaneously creating world organizations that could, at least in theory, provide this legitimacy for American actions.

The problem is, the world lacks any genuine overarching legal or institutional authority, much less a democratic authority, to which all nations subordinate themselves. Questions of right and wrong are settled not according to impartial justice but usually according to the distribution of power in the system. Americans have usually had to use their power to enforce their idea of justice without any assurance beyond their own faith that they are right. This is a heavy moral burden for a democratic people to bear. In their domestic lives, Americans are accustomed to having that burden spread evenly across society. The people make the laws, the police enforce the laws, judges and juries mete out justice, and the prison officials carry out the punishment. But in the international sphere, Americans have had to act as judge, jury, police, and, in the case of military action, executioner. What gives the United States the right to act on behalf of a liberal world order? In truth, nothing does, nothing beyond the conviction that the liberal world order is the most just.

This moral conundrum was easier to ignore during the cold war, when every action taken, even in the most obscure corners of the world, was justified as being in defense of vital national interests. But actions taken in defense of world order are fraught with moral complexity. Americans and Europeans argue that Ukraine's sovereignty should be inviolate and that the people of Ukraine should be allowed to pursue their aspirations to be part of Europe. Vladimir Putin justifies his invasion of Crimea on the grounds of ancient historical ties and in response to American and European meddling in Russia's historical sphere of influence. Who is there to adjudicate between these competing claims of justice? Who can determine which side is right and which side is wrong? It does no good to invoke some allegedly superior twenty-first-century morality against an inferior nineteenth-century morality. No more in this century than in previous centuries is there either perfect morality or perfect justice to be found in the international system. Nor do great powers come to disputes with clean hands, in this or any other century. All are selfish; all are morally compromised. And indeed, the more power a nation has, the more it is likely to act in ways that cannot be squared with a Christian or Enlightenment morality.

Who is to say that even defense of the liberal world order is necessarily good? The liberal world order was never put to a popular vote. It was not bequeathed by God. It is not the endpoint of human progress, despite what our Enlightenment education tells us. It is a temporary and transient world order that suits the needs, interests, and above all the ideals of a large and powerful collection of people, but it does not necessarily fit the needs and desires of everyone. For decades many abroad and some Americans at home saw it as a form of Western imperialism, and many still do. Communism may have failed, but authoritarianism and autocracy live on. And it is that form of government, not democracy, that has been the norm throughout history. In recent decades the democracies, led by the United States and Europe, have had the power to shape the world. But who is to say that Putinism in Russia or the particular brand of authoritarianism practiced in China will not survive as far into the future as European democracy, which, outside of Great Britain, is itself only a little over a century old?

A liberal world order, like any world order, is something that is imposed, and as much as we in the West might wish it to be imposed by superior virtue, it is generally imposed by superior power. Putin seeks to impose his view of a world order, at least in Russia's neighborhood, just as Europe and the United States do. Whether he succeeds or fails will probably not be determined merely by who is right and who is wrong. It will be determined by the exercise of power.

This is a disturbing thought for a nation that has grown weary of exercising power. Hans Morgenthau once observed that Americans are attracted to the "illusion that a nation can escape . . . from power politics," that at some point "the final curtain would fall and the game of power politics would no longer be played." Many escapes have been offered over the past two decades. In 1989, Fukuyama told Americans that with the end of history there would be no more "serious ideological competitors left to liberal democracy." Liberal progress was inevitable, and therefore nothing need be done to promote or defend it. Such thoughts were echoed throughout the 1990s. The age of geopolitics had supposedly given way to the age of geoeconomics. What America needed in the new era was less "hard power" and more "soft power."

Such was the reigning conventional wisdom, at least from the end of the cold war until 2008 and the beginning of the financial crisis. Then the paradigm shifted. Suddenly, instead of the end of history, it was the end of America, the end of the West. Triumphalism turned to declinism. From the post–cold war utopia it became the post-American world. Yet this, too, turned out to be a form of escapism, for remarkably, whether the liberal world order was triumphing or America and the West were declining, the prescription remained the same: There was nothing to be done. Whereas before it had been unnecessary, and even wrong, for the United States to use its power to shape the world, now, suddenly, it was impossible, because the United States no longer had sufficient power.

Today more than 50 percent of Americans believe the United States plays "a less important and powerful role as a world leader than it did a decade ago." One senses that, for many Americans, this decline is not a reason for panic but comes as something of a relief. Less power means fewer responsibilities. A sense of futility, today as much as in the 1920s and 1930s, is both an invitation and a justification for a return to normalcy.

The sense of futility has affected policymakers, too. Senior White House officials, especially the younger ones, look at problems like the struggle in Syria and believe that there is little if anything the United States can do. This is the lesson of their generation, the lesson of Iraq and Afghanistan: that America has neither the power nor the understanding nor the skill to fix problems in the world.

This is also escapism, however, for there is a myth embedded in this plea of futility. It is that wielding power effectively was ever any easier than it is today. With rose-colored glasses we look back at the cold war and imagine that the United States used to get others to do what it wanted, used to know what it was doing, and used to wield such overwhelming power that the world simply bent to its will or succumbed to its charms. But American policy during the cold war, despite its ultimate success, was filled with errors, folly, many near-disasters, and some disasters. From the beginning, allies proved rebellious, resentful, and unmanageable. American domestic politics made sensible policies difficult and sometimes impossible to sustain. The world economy, and the American economy, lurched from crisis to crisis. American military power was at its best a most uncertain instrument. In Vietnam, whether inevitably or because of bad policymaking in Washington, it failed miserably. In Korea, it almost suffered a complete catastrophe. The most successful presidents of the era, from Truman to Reagan, did not always seem successful to their contemporaries and suffered significant setbacks in their foreign policies. Can the architects of today's foreign policies really believe that Acheson and his colleagues, or the policymakers in the Johnson or Nixon or Carter administrations, had an easier time of it?

Any nation's foreign policy is bound to fail more often than it succeeds. The attempt to influence the behavior of people even in the domestic setting is difficult enough. To influence other peoples and other nations without simply annihilating them is the most difficult of all human tasks. It is also in the very nature of foreign policy, as in human affairs generally, that all solutions to problems only breed more problems. This is certainly true of all wars. There is no perfect ending to any war, even those fought with the clearest and most straightforward of objectives. The Civil War did not put an end to the terrible plight of blacks in America, though it cost over half a million lives. World War II ended with the Soviet Union in control of half of Europe and opened the way to another four decades of superpower confrontation.

When a nation uses its power to shape a world order, rather than merely for self-defense or conquest, the tenuousness of solutions is even more pronounced. Military actions for world order preservation are almost by definition limited both in scope and objectives. World order maintenance requires operating in the gray areas between victory and defeat. The measure of success is often not how wonderful the end result is, but whether the unsatisfying end result is better or worse than the outcome if there had been no action. To insist on outcomes that always achieve maximum ends at minimal cost is yet another form of escapism.

Today, however, Americans seem overwhelmed by the difficulty and complexity of it all. They yearn to return to what Niebuhr called "the innocency of irresponsibility," or at least to a normalcy in which the United States can limit the scope of its commitments. In this way America has perhaps returned to the mood of the 1920s. There is a difference, however. In the 1920s, it was not America's world order that needed shoring up. Americans felt, mistakenly as it turned out, that it was Britain's and Europe's job to preserve the world order they had created. Today, it is America's world order that needs propping up. Will Americans decide that it matters this time, when only they have the capacity to sustain it?

You never miss the water 'til the well runs dry, or so the saying goes. One wonders whether Americans, including their representatives and their president, quite understand what is at stake. When President Obama first took office five years ago, Peter Baker of the *New York Times* reported that he intended to deal "with the world as it is rather than as it might be." It is a standard realist refrain and has been repeated time and again by senior Obama officials as a way of explaining why he decided against pursuing some desirable but unreachable "ideal" in this place or that. What fewer and fewer seem to realize, however, is that the last 70 years have offered Americans and many others something of a reprieve from the world "as it is."

Periods of peace and prosperity can make people forget what the world "as it is" really looks like, and to conclude that the human race has simply ascended to some higher plateau of being. This was the common view in Europe in the first decade of the twentieth century. At a time when there had not been a war between great powers in 40 years, or a major Europe-wide war in a century, the air was filled with talk of a new millennium in which wars among civilized nations had become impossible. Three quarters of a century and two world wars and a cold war later, millennial thoughts return. Studies cited by Fareed Zakaria purport to show that some "transformation of international relations" has occurred. "Changes of borders by force" have dropped dramatically "since 1946." The nations of Western Europe, having been responsible for two new wars a year for 600 years, had not even started one "since 1945." Steven Pinker observes that the number of deaths from war, ethnic conflict, and military coups has declined—since 1945—and concludes that the human race has become "socialized" to prefer peace and nonviolence.

The dates when these changes supposedly began ought to be a tip-off. Is it a coincidence that these happy trends began when the American world order was established after World War II, or that they accelerated in the last two decades of the twentieth century, when America's only serious competitor collapsed? Imagine strolling through Central Park and, after noting how much safer it had become, deciding that humanity must simply have become less violent—without thinking that perhaps the New York Police Department had something to do with it.

In fact, the world "as it is" is a dangerous and often brutal place. There has been no transformation in human behavior or in international relations. In the twenty-first century, no less than in the nineteenth and twentieth centuries, force remains the ultima ratio. The question, today as in the past, is not whether nations are willing to resort to force but whether they believe they can get away with it when they do. If there has been less aggression, less ethnic cleansing, less territorial conquest over the past 70 years, it is because the

United States and its allies have both punished and deterred aggression, have intervened, sometimes, to prevent ethnic cleansing, and have gone to war to reverse territorial conquest. The restraint showed by other nations has not been a sign of human progress, the strengthening of international institutions, or the triumph of the rule of law. It has been a response to a global configuration of power that, until recently, has made restraint seem the safer course.

When Vladimir Putin failed to achieve his goals in Ukraine through political and economic means, he turned to force, because he believed that he could. He will continue to use force so long as he believes that the payoff exceeds the cost. Nor is he unique in this respect. What might China do were it not hemmed in by a ring of powerful nations backed by the United States? For that matter, what would Japan do if it were much more powerful and much less dependent on the United States for its security? We have not had to find out the answers to these questions, not yet, because American predominance, the American alliance system, and the economic, political, and institutional aspects of the present order, all ultimately dependent on power, have mostly kept the lid closed on this Pandora's box.

Nor have we had to find out yet what the world "as it is" would do to the remarkable spread of democracy. Skeptics of "democracy promotion" argue that the United States has often tried to plant democracy in infertile soil. They may be right. The widespread flowering of democracy around the world in recent decades may prove to have been artificial and therefore tenuous. As Michael Ignatieff once observed, it may be that "liberal civilization" itself "runs deeply against the human grain and is achieved and sustained only by the most unremitting struggle against human nature." Perhaps this fragile democratic garden requires the protection of a liberal world order, with constant feeding, watering, weeding, and the fencing off of an ever-encroaching jungle. In the absence of such efforts, the weeds and the jungle may sooner or later come back to reclaim the land.

One wonders if even the current economic order reflects the world "as it is." A world in which autocracies make ever more ambitious attempts to control the flow of information, and in which autocratic kleptocracies use national wealth and resources to further their private interests, may prove less hospitable to the kind of free flow of commerce the world has come to appreciate in recent decades.

In fact, from the time that Roosevelt and Truman first launched it, the whole project of promoting and defending a liberal world order has been a concerted effort not to accept the world "as it is." The American project has aimed at shaping a world different from what had always been, taking advantage of America's unique situation to do what no nation had ever been able to do. Today, however, because many Americans no longer recall what the world "as it is" really looks like, they cannot imagine it. They bemoan the burdens and failures inherent in the grand strategy but take for granted all the remarkable benefits.

Nor do they realize, perhaps, how quickly it can all unravel. The international system is an elaborate web of power relationships, in which every nation, from the biggest to the smallest, is constantly feeling for shifts or disturbances. Since 1945, and especially since 1989, the web has been geared to respond primarily to the United States. Allies observe American behavior and calculate America's reliability. Nations hemmed in or threatened by American power watch for signs of growing or diminishing power and will. When the United States appears to retrench, allies necessarily become anxious, while others look for opportunities.

In recent years, the world has picked up unmistakable signals that Americans may no longer want to carry the burden of global responsibility. Others read the polls, read the president's speeches calling for "nation-building at home," see the declining defense budgets and defense capabilities, and note the extreme reticence, on the part of both American political parties, about using force. The world judges that, were it not for American war-weariness, the United States probably would by now have used force in Syria—just as it did in Kosovo, in Bosnia, and in Panama. President Obama himself recently acknowledged as much when he said, "It's not that it's not worth it. It's that after a decade of war, you know, the United States has limits." Such statements set the web vibrating. In East Asia, nations living in close proximity to an increasingly powerful China want to know whether Americans will make a similar kind of calculation when it comes to defending them; in the Middle East, nations worried about Iran wonder if they will be left to confront it alone; in Eastern Europe and the Baltic states, American security guarantees are meaningless unless Americans are able and willing to meet them.

Are they? No one has taken a poll lately on whether the United States should come to the defense of its treaty allies in the event of a war between, say, China and Japan; or whether it should come to the defense of Estonia in a Ukraine-like conflict with Russia. The answers might prove interesting.

Meanwhile, the signs of the global order breaking down are all around us. Russia's invasion of Ukraine and seizure of Crimea was the first time since World War II that a nation in Europe had engaged in territorial conquest. If Iran manages to acquire a nuclear weapon, it will likely lead other powers in the region to do the same, effectively undoing the nonproliferation regime, which, along with American power, has managed to keep the number of nuclear-armed powers limited over the past half century. Iran, Saudi Arabia, and Russia are engaged in a proxy war in Syria that, in addition to the 150,000 dead and the millions displaced, has further destabilized a region that had already been in upheaval. In East Asia, nervousness about China's rise, combined with uncertainty about America's commitment, is exacerbating tensions. In recent years the number of democracies around the world has been steadily declining, while the number of autocracies grows. If these trends continue, in the near future we are likely to see increasing conflict, increasing wars over territory, greater ethnic and sectarian violence, and a shrinking world of democracies.

How will Americans respond? If the test is once again to be "national interests" narrowly construed, then Americans may find all of this tolerable, or at least preferable to doing something to stop it. Could the United States survive if Syria remains under the control of Assad or, more likely, disintegrates into a chaos of territories, some of which will be controlled by jihadi terrorists? Could it survive if Iran acquires a nuclear weapon, and if in turn Saudi Arabia, Turkey, and Egypt acquire nuclear weapons? Or if North Korea launches a war on the South? Could it survive in a world where China dominates much of East Asia, or where China and Japan resume their old conflict? Could it survive in a world where Russia dominates Eastern Europe, including not only Ukraine but the Baltic states and perhaps even Poland? Of course it could. From the point of view of strict "necessity" and narrow national interest, the United States could survive all of this. It could trade with a dominant China and work out a modus vivendi with a restored Russian empire. Those alarmed by such developments will be hard-pressed, as Roosevelt was, to explain how each marginal setback would affect the parochial interests of the average American. As in the past, Americans will be among the last to suffer grievously from a breakdown of world order. And by the time they do feel the effects, it may be very late in the day.

Looking back on the period before World War II, Robert Osgood, the most thoughtful of realist thinkers of the past century, discerned a critical element missing from the strategic analyses of the day. Mere rational calculations of the "national interest," he argued, proved inadequate. Paradoxically, it was the "idealists," those who were "most sensitive to the Fascist menace to Western culture and civilization," who were "among the first to understand the necessity of undertaking revolutionary measures to sustain America's first line of defense in Europe." Idealism, he concluded, was "an indispensable spur to reason in leading men to perceive and act upon the real imperatives of power politics." This was Roosevelt's message, too, when he asked Americans to defend "not their homes alone, but the tenets of faith and humanity on which their churches, their governments, and their very civilization are founded."

Perhaps Americans can be inspired in this way again, without the threat of a Hitler or an attack on their homeland. But this time they will not have 20 years to decide. The world will change much more quickly than they imagine. And there is no democratic superpower waiting in the wings to save the world if this democratic superpower falters.

## CRITICAL THINKING QUESTIONS

1. Does the world need a leader? Must it be the United States? Will a return to accepting global responsibility occur?
2. Is the world headed for a renewed period of world disorder? What are the primary causes of this transformation?
3. What is a normal foreign policy? Has the United States ever had a foreign policy that fit your definition?

# 3

# A Better Internationalism

David C. Unger

GENOA—Internationalism has many different meanings, but constructive global citizenship should always be at its core. An internationalist
foreign policy for the developed countries would use their wealth, economic might, and military power to promote a better, more peaceful, more
prosperous world for everyone.

Unfortunately, the kind of policies American commentators typically label
internationalist today do not fit that definition. They feature micro-meddling
in the internal politics of sovereign nations large and small to support "pro-
American" politicians. They include the practice of waging militarily unwinna-
ble and internationally unpopular counter-insurgency wars in unreceptive
countries. And they require the stationing of U.S. troops in self-contained foreign bases that bind Washington to the whims of local despots. Subordinated
at best, are a host of truly internationalist goals like supporting locally rooted
democracy, sustainable development, human rights, environmental protection,
and arms control. These worthy aims frequently become lost in a welter of
complex local chess games played out against the designated enemy du jour—
international Communism, rogue states, global terrorism, a rising China.

For Americans, internationalism has become little more than a label for
the narrow pursuit of national interests as defined by a tight-knit political and
foreign policy elite. Accustomed to viewing the world through the concerns
of trade and investment interests, too many self-proclaimed internationalists
dismiss other concerns as dangerously unenlightened and self-centered.

Washington's so-called internationalists are especially ready to stigmatize
domestic critics of their ill-chosen wars as isolationists and foreigners as
narrow-minded nationalists with suspect motives. They subject to moral con-
descension and intellectual scorn anyone who questions whether American
military intervention is the most beneficial and long-lasting solution to the
problems of Afghanistan, Iraq, Somalia, Haiti, Bosnia, or Kosovo. They dis-
parage and try to thwart any United Nations initiative not promoted by the
United States. They question the internationalist credentials of other developed

David C. Unger is the Europe-based foreign affairs editorial writer for the *New York
Times* and adjunct professor at Johns Hopkins University, Bologna. David C. Unger,
*World Policy Journal* 29, no. 1: 101–10. Copyright © 2012 by Sage Publications.
Reprinted by permission of Sage Publications.

countries not prepared to march lockstep behind Washington's chosen military interventions or sanctions campaigns.

## A VERY WRONG PICTURE

Internationally unpopular policies of unilateral American self-assertion are being marketed by the United States as liberal internationalism, while those who question these policies and suggest non-military alternatives risk being denounced as neo-isolationist, naïve, parochial, or simply selfish.

Liberal internationalism has become code language in the United States for pressuring other governments, large and small, friendly and hostile, to do as Washington sees fit. It has become synonymous with maintaining overwhelming American military predominance on every ocean and every continent; for weaving a web of preferential trade agreements that carefully protect the privileges of American corporations abroad while exposing American workers at home to the leveling downdrafts of free market competition. Increasingly, the size and reach of America's military, rather than the strength and competitiveness of its economy and society, has become the measure of its international leadership and prestige.

This semantic sleight of hand has pushed more constructive and progressive forms of international engagement to the political and financial margins of American life.

Branding assertive American nationalism as internationalism is dishonest. It diverts attention from such truly international causes as reducing global arms spending and the risks of nuclear and conventional war, slowing destructive climate change, controlling and preventing infectious diseases, and improving the lives of the billions of people around the world still excluded from such basic benefits of modern life as clean water, adequate nutrition, and universal education. And it all too often leaves the world's wealthiest and most militarily powerful nation, the United States, playing a much smaller role in meeting the internationalist challenges of our times.

Three billion of the world's seven billion people now live on less than $2.50 a day. Some 10 million people die every year from preventable diseases that spring from poverty. That is 2,000 times the peak annual death toll from international terrorism. And millions of those lives lost to international neglect can be saved at a far lower economic cost, doing far less collateral damage to innocent civilians and far less reputational damage to the international standing of the United States than the unsuccessful wars waged over the past decade in the name of denying specific territorial havens to geographically mobile and ideologically shape-shifting international terrorists. Terrorism is an international security threat that must be fought. But not as it has been, through prolonged and costly counter-insurgency style wars in Muslim lands that evoke bitter memories of Western colonialism and play into the hands of propagandists for violent resistance.

Washington-style internationalism has been reduced to an internationalism of crisis management, which is scarcely internationalism at all. It is a great way to cut off important debates about United States foreign policy and make a show of good intentions toward complicated and intractable problems. But it is unsustainable, and its inevitable frustrations and disappointments risk pushing the broader American public into real isolationism at some cost to America's competitiveness and security. Yet that's where the United States seems headed no matter who wins the presidential election this November.

If Americans really want to use their nation's enormous power and prestige to bring about positive international change—my definition of constructive internationalism—they will need to make some hard choices about priorities and methods. In short, we must move quickly and adroitly to reclaim the good name of internationalism and suggest what a more constructive and progressive internationalism could look like in the world of 2012.

## ONE PLANET

Constructive internationalism sees us all living on one planet, with our primary international interest making that planet safer—from global warming, nuclear weapons, infectious diseases, and the widening inequalities that weaken democracy and help feed support for ideologies of hatred, xenophobia, and racism. It challenges the need for wars like Iraq and Afghanistan, while questioning laissez-faire models of globalization that have largely helped the 1 percent and left most of the 99 percent worse off. In 2008, constructive internationalists turned hopefully to Barack Obama. This year they seem to have no champion. Crisis-management internationalism, as peddled by Democrats like Obama and Republicans like Mitt Romney, seems to have lost most of its capacity to inspire.

Constructive internationalism would place far greater emphasis on peaceful international cooperation, sustainable and equitable development, and conventional as well as nuclear arms control. But it will sometimes require the use of international military force. So long as there are international aggressors and genocidal dictators, collective military action will have an important place in the internationalist tool kit.

Last year's NATO intervention in Libya provides an imperfect template. Broader international participation, better military coordination with anti-Gaddafi Libyans and a more robust United Nations resolution all would have helped. But Libya 2011 was everything Iraq 2003 was not. The revolt against Muammar Gaddafi was initiated by Libyans themselves and was broadly based. The Gaddafi regime had, and forfeited, the chance to come to terms with the Libyan people. Outside forces only became involved after the regime violated international norms by embarking on a war of annihilation against its own people. The United Nations Security Council acted at the behest of the Arab League. And while the Security Council's resolution authorized military action only to save civilian lives, NATO rightly stretched that mandate to provide air cover to rebel armies and civilians. A more literal reading of the resolution would have repeated the mistakes of Bosnia when UN peacekeepers took a formally neutral stance between aggressors and victims, rendering themselves helpless to stop massacres of unarmed civilians in Srebrenica and elsewhere.

The Obama administration, grasping at meaningless abstractions like "leading from behind," played a curiously stilted role in NATO's Libya operations. In the George W. Bush–Donald Rumsfeld era, Washington had unilaterally proclaimed an international division of military labor—the United States itself assuming the hard power tasks of destruction leaving the soft power work of stabilization, peacekeeping, and nation-building to European and other allies.

In Libya, Washington took on the front-end task of knocking out Libyan air defenses, then largely left it to the rest of NATO to keep Gaddafi loyalists from slaughtering civilians. The twofold aim was to force NATO into more equitable military burden sharing and to minimize the administration's domestic political exposure in a war-weary United States. The result was to withdraw highly accurate low flying American tank buster planes that might have held down friendly fire casualties among Libyan rebels and possibly shortened the war.

The United States, which has over-invested in the world's most powerful and specialized military assets, should develop more effective mechanisms for making these available for appropriately authorized international interventions. Ideally authorization should come from the United Nations Security Council. But that won't always be possible. The Security Council could certainly be paralyzed by a veto-wielding great power patron of a rampaging dictator so as happened in the case of Syria's Bashar al-Assad, fed by the chronic fear of China and Russia that a precedent for international action could be set by action ordered against internal dissent. In such instances, authorization may come from a relevant and inclusive regional body, like the Arab League in the case of Libya or the European Union in the Balkans. NATO, because of its cold war heritage and Washington's preponderant role, is an imperfect substitute. And American participation in internationalist military interventions must not slight the constitutional mechanisms of American democracy. Constructive internationalism is, by its nature, a form of democratic internationalism under the rule of law.

But future military interventions like the Libyan case will and should be rare. The real test of American constructive internationalism won't be dramatic hard power showdowns. Most of the world's first order challenges, like the basic needs of the bottom billions, destructive climate change, nuclear proliferation, and unsustainably unbalanced globalization cannot be solved by military force. They are not amenable to crisis-management internationalism—by Washington or any other global or regional power. And they are far too dangerous to keep ignoring or under-resourcing.

Dealing with these challenges will not require budget-busting aid programs or massive global transfers of wealth. What they need is sustained steady funding and commitment, which is harder than it sounds. Trillion-dollar wars are politically easier to fund than much more modest and constructive assistance programs. Consider the history of the United Nations Millennium Development Goals.

## GOALS, MILLENNIUM STYLE

These were set out in 2000 (hence the name) and have been endorsed by 193 nations. They set ambitious, but arguably achievable targets for 2015 including making primary schooling available to all and halving the proportion of the world's population living on less than $1 a day—those not eating enough to maintain health and strength and without regular access to clean water or basic sanitation. Looking beyond survival needs, the goals also call for a global partnership for development. At the same time, a partnership with the private sector would make essential drugs and information and communications technology available and affordable to the people of developing countries. Global progress has been achieved on all fronts, but unevenly, with China and Southeast Asia already exceeding some of the 15-year targets but much of sub-Saharan Africa and South Asia badly lagging.

In adopting the Millennium Development Goals, donor countries implicitly committed themselves to provide enough resources to achieve them. For nearly half a century, development aid equivalent to 0.7 percent of national income has been considered an appropriate benchmark for developed country donors. A few, mostly Scandinavian, countries meet or exceed this benchmark. The current worldwide average is 0.45 percent. The United States, though the biggest aid giver in dollar terms, is one of the lowest in percentage terms, providing less than 0.2 percent. Aid isn't the only factor in development, or even the main one, as successes in China and Southeast Asia demonstrate. But for countries trapped in deep poverty and outside the channels of globalized development—like much of sub-Saharan Africa—aid matters mightily.

Of course, not all aid is good aid. Some is stolen by kleptocrats, wasted by bureaucrats, or diverted to purchases of expensive weapons that contribute nothing to development. Aid should never be given without appropriate conditions and monitoring. That is a democratic political duty for donor nations, who are giving taxpayer dollars that might otherwise be spent at home. It is even more important for recipient nations. Many leaders insist that conditions and monitoring are an intolerable infringement of sovereignty. But if major donors agree on a standard set of conditions requiring accountability, transparency, and coherent development planning and apply them without exceptions, most recipient governments will go along, and those that don't will have to explain why to their own people.

Unfortunately, China has made accountability harder by offering unconditional aid to pariah leaders it courts for geopolitical reasons. A big challenge for constructive internationalism will be to coordinate aid programs and conditions more effectively. That would require negotiating terms of transparency and accountability that all significant donors will agree to abide by and enforce. China cannot be ignored. It will need to be courted. Beijing sometimes invests in pariahs as a kind of insurance that its access to vital resources and raw materials won't be cut off by Western-inspired embargoes and sanctions. A West less prone to going it alone on sanctions might find it easier to enlist Chinese cooperation on aid and development practices.

## REVERSING CLIMATE CHANGE

Destructive climate change has already become irreversible. But that only makes slowing the pace of global warming more urgent. Average global temperatures are now projected to rise by as much as 9 degrees Fahrenheit by the end of this century. The effects of these higher temperatures and changed rainfall patterns on current agricultural regions would be incalculable. The effects of the resulting rise in sea levels on coastal cities and low-lying land areas are all too calculable.

The failed 2009 UN climate conference at Copenhagen aimed to cut that rise to less than 4 degrees Fahrenheit. That would require reducing worldwide per capita emissions of carbon dioxide by more than 70 percent over the next 40 years—from seven metric tons per person to two metric tons. The United States, which spews out close to 20 metric tons per person, the second highest per capita emissions rate of any developed country (tiny Luxembourg is first) cannot continue to exempt itself from agreed mandatory limits, nor can China, the world's largest single source of atmospheric carbon dioxide. Its per capita rate—still below the global average rate at five to six metric tons—is one of the most rapidly rising. Nor can any other significant current or future emitter receive a free pass.

It may not be possible to move forward through conferences that require all 193 UN member states to arrive at full consensus on implementing environmental goals. A few retrograde governments, particularly if their countries are not big emitters, cannot be left to condemn the rest of the planet to ecological catastrophe. Constructive internationalism needs international legitimacy. But there is no legitimacy in structural paralysis. Countries ready to move ahead with binding emissions limits should do so, and encourage others to join them by establishing something like a free trade area of the environmentally virtuous, offering advantageous trade and investment deals to those who do. One such area could be built around some of Europe's more environmentally conscious high-income nations, which could then use their market power to woo other neighbors and trading partners. If such an area eventually encompassed the United States as well, no trading nation, China included, could afford to ignore its emissions standards.

Few countries would reap as many advantages as the United States from reducing greenhouse gases by reducing fossil fuel consumption. It is a developed country with a largely post-industrial economy. It has some of the world's most expensive low-lying real estate. Its foreign policy and military budgets have long been distorted by the need to assure Persian Gulf oil supplies. With less than 5 percent of the world's population, it currently consumes a grossly disproportionate 25 percent of the world's oil (and a similar disproportion of all fossil fuels). Yet through a quarter century of international debate about global warming and how to slow it, Washington has been a consistent outlier. No one country, or continent, for that matter, can slow global climate change on its own. But the United States has been doing far less than its good internationalist share.

Eventually, the visible signs of climate change will create political pressure on countries around the world to adopt much stricter emissions limits. It's essential that constructively internationalist political leaders heed the scientific consensus on what the planet can stand and then work to sell strict emissions limits to voters around the world.

## NUCLEAR RESTRAINT

Restraining nuclear weapons proliferation and reducing existing stockpiles of nuclear warheads should also be a priority area for constructive internationalism. Current American counter-proliferation policies are more geopolitical than universal. They aim at keeping nuclear weapons out of the hands of Iran's Islamic Republic and North Korea's Kim dynasty while ignoring, or even abetting, the rogue nuclear weapons programs of strategic allies like Israel and India, neither of which has signed the Nuclear Non-Proliferation Treaty.

Constructive internationalism is not just concerned with denying counter-deterrence capabilities to potential military adversaries. It must be equally concerned with making it less likely that nuclear weapons will be used in warfare, anywhere, with the appalling ecological, public health, and long-term economic consequences that would bring. It also needs to be universal. Absurdly large American and Russian nuclear arsenals and stockpiles, though much reduced since 1991, are still mired in the Cold War calculus of strategic parity and deliberate overkill. This makes it harder to convince would-be nuclear powers like Iran—or even Saudi Arabia if its Shiite neighbor explodes such a device—that having nukes is a token neither of national manhood nor sovereignty. Strategic missile defense systems capable of knocking down some, but not all, incoming missiles create perverse incentives for others to compensate by adding more offensive weapons.

If countries choose not to sign the Nuclear Non-Proliferation Treaty, they should not be eligible for civilian nuclear assistance from the United States or any other member of the international nuclear suppliers group. The special cut-out from this rule Washington pushed through for India sent all the wrong signals—to Pakistan today, perhaps to Egypt, Saudi Arabia, and Iraq tomorrow.

Constructive internationalism would work to break the perverse link between discouraging nuclear weapons and encouraging nuclear power. That contradictory impulse dates all the way back to Dwight Eisenhower's Atoms for Peace proposal of the 1950s. And it is incorporated in the ground rules of the International Atomic Energy Agency today. If a country signs and ratifies the Non-Proliferation Treaty, it has an absolute legal right to enrich uranium for nuclear power, as Iran, an NPT signatory, never ceases to point out.

The problem is that uranium can be enriched to bomb grade by the same processes that enrich it to reactor grade. IAEA safeguards and inspectors don't really help. Any treaty signatory can legally get itself to within a year of being able to build a bomb, and then just stay at that point until it decides to break out of the treaty and go further. That makes the NPT and IAEA safeguards weaker anti-proliferation tools than they need to be. Wider adoption of an optional additional protocol allowing surprise inspections would help, but not decisively. Countries could still move legally to the brink of a nuclear weapons break-out.

More useful would be to internationalize the fuel enrichment cycle, meaning all legal uranium enrichment would have to take place at international enrichment centers under full IAEA auspices. That way, non-nuclear weapons states could not master the enrichment technologies they need for bomb making. Countries would not accept this arrangement unless they were guaranteed their supplies of enriched fuel for reactor use would never be cut off as long as they remained treaty compliant. (There are no such guarantees today.) Some still would not accept it and would try to master the fuel cycle themselves. The penalty for doing so must be as high as the rest of the world can make it, including a full cutoff of uranium imports and civilian nuclear assistance. Companies that export civilian nuclear reactors and technologies won't like this. But the world will be safer if they are over-ruled.

## CONVENTIONAL FORBEARANCE, TOO

Conventional weapons kill too, though on a smaller scale. They feed wars, enable repression, and divert resources from development. They also create jobs and profits for weapons producers in the United States, the world's biggest arms exporter, with Russia second, Germany third. Constructive internationalism would pay more attention to the costs and less to the profits. In 2010, the Obama administration agreed to sell $60 billion worth of American weapons systems to Saudi Arabia over the next five to 10 years, the largest arms sale in American history. It includes advanced fighter jets, theater missile defense systems, and a full range of surveillance, troop transport, and attack helicopters. Yes, Iran is a potentially threatening neighbor. But selling still more advanced aircraft to Saudi Arabia's spendthrift royals will not provide much help against Iranian-sponsored terrorism or subversion.

There is a bigger issue, illustrated by the Saudi monarchy's leading role in helping neighboring Bahrain crush pro-democracy demonstrations last March. Out-of-touch autocratic regimes are being challenged across the Middle East, and no one would mistake the Saudis as allies of progressive change. If the role of the West in helping Libyans rid themselves of Gaddafi is a hopeful portent of constructive internationalism, selling arms to Saudi Arabia is a throwback to crisis management internationalism and a bet against the future of democracy movements in the Middle East and beyond.

## CONTROL CHALLENGES

The hardest, though among the most important, challenges facing constructive internationalism concern trade, investment, and globalization. A globalization more actively shaped and regulated by democratic civil society would be more financially balanced, more broadly beneficial, and more politically sustainable than the current regime.

Many of today's bilateral free trade agreements aren't worthy of the name. It does not take hundreds of pages of fine print to open markets to competition. Much of that legal verbiage, drafted out of public view and shielded from full public scrutiny, has been crafted at the behest of well-paid lobbyists to protect the interests of the firms they represent, while less well represented farmers abroad and factory workers at home are fed pieties about the creative logic of unregulated markets. Moreover, such lobbyists are hard at work wherever free trade agreements are in play—from Washington to Brussels, London to Geneva and beyond.

Meanwhile, the underlying ground rules of the World Trade Organization oblige governments to treat all goods alike, ignoring the working and environmental conditions where they are produced. That tends to make progressive national environmental and labor laws international competitive liabilities. So a contemporary version of the 1944 international economic compact that fashioned the post-war Bretton Woods economic system is essential. That brought three decades of exemplary prosperity, social mobility, and economic security to the then developed world of North America, Western Europe, and Japan. Helping design a similarly progressive successor system would mark a return to the creative American internationalism of the mid-1940s. It would also prevent freer trade from becoming a race to the bottom for poor and rich countries alike.

Bretton Woods succeeded because it allowed market economics and democratic civil society to work in tandem. It permitted limited capital and currency controls that let governments use Keynesian tools to fight recessions. Allowing democracy to reshape globalization would be good internationalist economics and good internationalist politics as well, helping to strengthen democracy in the developing and the developed world. Today's feeling that political parties are powerless in the face of blind market forces fuels cynicism and the rise of xenophobic populist parties promising solutions based on scapegoating immigrants and religious and ethnic minorities.

A new Bretton Woods should let countries take account of the labor and environmental conditions where the goods are produced, encouraging voluntary "coalitions of the virtuous." Built around countries that agree to abide by stricter standards on labor rights, product safety, and environmental emissions, each would grant others privileged trading access for conformity. Governments that have built their growth models on cheap labor and loose environmental rules will object. But such new trade arrangements, by linking these countries' future growth to higher standards, will provide strong market incentives to change practices in ways most consistent with their own societies.

Crisis management internationalism is an elitist, often violent, and always expensive process with a waning base of popular support in the United States and much of Europe as well. Alternatives suggested here would be more democratic and progressive—and worthy of the name internationalism.

## CRITICAL THINKING QUESTIONS

1. Is crisis management internationalism bad?
2. Pick a problem not discussed in this article and devise a constructive internationalism policy for it.
3. Is there a third form of internationalism other than crisis management and constructive internationalism?

# 4

# Pull Back

## THE CASE FOR A LESS ACTIVIST FOREIGN POLICY

Barry R. Posen

**D**espite a decade of costly and indecisive warfare and mounting fiscal pressures, the long-standing consensus among American policymakers about U.S. grand strategy has remained remarkably intact. As the presidential campaign made clear, Republicans and Democrats may quibble over foreign policy at the margins, but they agree on the big picture: that the United States should dominate the world militarily, economically, and politically, as it has since the final years of the Cold War, a strategy of liberal hegemony. The country, they hold, needs to preserve its massive lead in the global balance of power, consolidate its economic preeminence, enlarge the community of market democracies, and maintain its outsized influence in the international institutions it helped create.

To this end, the U.S. government has expanded its sprawling Cold War–era network of security commitments and military bases. It has reinforced its existing alliances, adding new members to NATO and enhancing its security agreement with Japan. In the Persian Gulf, it has sought to protect the flow of oil with a full panoply of air, sea, and land forces, a goal that consumes at least 15 percent of the U.S. defense budget. Washington has put China on a watch list, ringing it in with a network of alliances, less formal relationships, and military bases.

The United States' activism has entailed a long list of ambitious foreign policy projects. Washington has tried to rescue failing states, intervening militarily in Somalia, Haiti, Bosnia, Kosovo, and Libya, variously attempting to defend human rights, suppress undesirable nationalist movements, and install democratic regimes. It has also tried to contain so-called rogue states that oppose the United States, such as Iran, Iraq under Saddam Hussein, North Korea, and, to a lesser degree, Syria. After 9/11, the struggle against al Qaeda

Barry R. Posen is Ford International Professor of Political Science and Director of the Security Studies Program at the Massachusetts Institute of Technology. Reprinted by permission of *Foreign Affairs* 92, no. 1 (January/February 2013). Copyright © 2013 by the Council on Foreign Relations, Inc., www.ForeignAffairs.com.

and its allies dominated the agenda, but the George W. Bush administration defined this enterprise broadly and led the country into the painful wars in Afghanistan and Iraq. Although the United States has long sought to discourage the spread of nuclear weapons, the prospect of nuclear-armed terrorists has added urgency to this objective, leading to constant tension with Iran and North Korea.

In pursuit of this ambitious agenda, the United States has consistently spent hundreds of billions of dollars per year on its military—far more than the sum of the defense budgets of its friends and far more than the sum of those of its potential adversaries. It has kept that military busy: U.S. troops have spent roughly twice as many months in combat after the Cold War as they did during it. Today, roughly 180,000 U.S. soldiers remain stationed on foreign soil, not counting the tens of thousands more who have rotated through the war zones in Afghanistan and Iraq. Thousands of American and allied soldiers have lost their lives, not to mention the countless civilians caught in the crossfire.

This undisciplined, expensive, and bloody strategy has done untold harm to U.S. national security. It makes enemies almost as fast as it slays them, discourages allies from paying for their own defense, and convinces powerful states to band together and oppose Washington's plans, further raising the costs of carrying out its foreign policy. During the 1990s, these consequences were manageable because the United States enjoyed such a favorable power position and chose its wars carefully. Over the last decade, however, the country's relative power has deteriorated, and policymakers have made dreadful choices concerning which wars to fight and how to fight them. What's more, the Pentagon has come to depend on continuous infusions of cash simply to retain its current force structure—levels of spending that the Great Recession and the United States' ballooning debt have rendered unsustainable.

It is time to abandon the United States' hegemonic strategy and replace it with one of restraint. This approach would mean giving up on global reform and sticking to protecting narrow national security interests. It would mean transforming the military into a smaller force that goes to war only when it truly must. It would mean removing large numbers of U.S. troops from forward bases, creating incentives for allies to provide for their own security. And because such a shift would allow the United States to spend its resources on only the most pressing international threats, it would help preserve the country's prosperity and security over the long run.

## ACTION AND REACTION

The United States emerged from the Cold War as the single most powerful state in modern times, a position that its diversified and immensely productive economy supports. Although its share of world economic output will inevitably shrink as other countries catch up, the United States will continue for many years to rank as one of the top two or three economies in the world. The

United States' per capita GDP stands at $48,000, more than five times as large as China's, which means that the U.S. economy can produce cutting-edge products for a steady domestic market. North America is blessed with enviable quantities of raw materials, and about 29 percent of U.S. trade flows to and from its immediate neighbors, Canada and Mexico. The fortuitous geostrategic position of the United States compounds these economic advantages. Its neighbors to the north and south possess only minuscule militaries. Vast oceans to the west and east separate it from potential rivals. And its thousands of nuclear weapons deter other countries from ever entertaining an invasion.

Ironically, however, instead of relying on these inherent advantages for its security, the United States has acted with a profound sense of insecurity, adopting an unnecessarily militarized and forward-leaning foreign policy. That strategy has generated predictable pushback. Since the 1990s, rivals have resorted to what scholars call "soft balancing"—low-grade diplomatic opposition. China and Russia regularly use the rules of liberal international institutions to delegitimize the United States' actions. In the UN Security Council, they wielded their veto power to deny the West resolutions supporting the bombing campaign in Kosovo in 1999 and the invasion of Iraq in 2003, and more recently, they have slowed the effort to isolate Syria. They occasionally work together in other venues, too, such as the Shanghai Cooperation Organization. Although the Beijing-Moscow relationship is unimpressive compared with military alliances such as NATO, it's remarkable that it exists at all given the long history of border friction and hostility between the two countries. As has happened so often in history, the common threat posed by a greater power has driven unnatural partners to cooperate.

American activism has also generated harder forms of balancing. China has worked assiduously to improve its military, and Russia has sold it modern weapons, such as fighter aircraft, surface-to-air missiles, and diesel-electric submarines. Iran and North Korea, meanwhile, have pursued nuclear programs in part to neutralize the United States' overwhelming advantages in conventional fighting power. Some of this pushback would have occurred no matter what; in an anarchic global system, states acquire the allies and military power that help them look after themselves. But a country as large and as active as the United States intensifies these responses.

Such reactions will only grow stronger as emerging economies convert their wealth into military power. Even though the economic and technological capacities of China and India may never equal those of the United States, the gap is destined to narrow. China already has the potential to be a serious competitor. At the peak of the Cold War, in the mid-1970s, Soviet GDP, in terms of purchasing power parity, amounted to 57 percent of U.S. GDP. China reached 75 percent of the U.S. level in 2011, and according to the International Monetary Fund, it is projected to match it by 2017. Of course, Chinese output must support four times as many people, which limits what the country can extract for military purposes, but it still provides enough resources to hinder U.S. foreign policy. Meanwhile, Russia, although a shadow of its former Soviet self, is no longer the hapless weakling it was in the 1990s. Its economy is roughly the size of the United Kingdom's or France's, it has plenty of energy resources to export, and it still produces some impressive weapons systems.

# FIGHTING IDENTITY

Just as emerging powers have gotten stronger, so, too, have the small states and violent substate entities that the United States has attempted to discipline, democratize, or eliminate. Whether in Somalia, Serbia, Afghanistan, Iraq, or Libya, the U.S. military seems to find itself fighting enemies that prove tougher than expected. (Consider the fact that Washington spent as much in real terms on the war in Iraq as it did on the war in Vietnam, even though the Iraqi insurgents enjoyed little external support, whereas China and the Soviet Union lent major support to the Vietcong and the North Vietnamese.) Yet Washington seems unable to stay out of conflicts involving substate entities, in part because their elemental nature assaults the internationalist values that U.S. grand strategy is committed to preserving. Having trumpeted the United States' military superiority, U.S. policymakers have a hard time saying no to those who argue that the country's prestige will suffer gravely if the world's leader lets wars great and small run their course.

The enduring strength of these substate groups should give American policymakers pause, since the United States' current grand strategy entails open-ended confrontation with nationalism and other forms of identity politics that insurgents and terrorists feed off of. These forces provide the organizing energy for groups competing for power within countries (as in Bosnia, Afghanistan, and Iraq), for secessionist movements (as in Kosovo), and for terrorists who oppose the liberal world order (mainly al Qaeda). Officials in Washington, however, have acted as if they can easily undercut the power of identity through democratic processes, freedom of information, and economic development, helped along by the judicious application of military power. In fact, identity is resilient, and foreign peoples react with hostility to outsiders trying to control their lives.

The Iraq war has been a costly case in point. Officials in the Bush administration convinced themselves that a quick application of overwhelming military power would bring democracy to Iraq, produce a subsequent wave of democratization across the Arab world, marginalize al Qaeda, and secure U.S. influence in the region. Instead, Shiites, Sunnis, and Kurds stoked the violence that the United States labored to suppress, and Shiite and Sunni factions fought not only each other but also the U.S. military. Today's Shiite-dominated government in Baghdad has proved neither democratic nor effective. Sunni terrorists have continued to carry out attacks. The Kurdish parts of Iraq barely acknowledge their membership in the larger state.

By now, it is clear that the United States has worn out its welcome in Afghanistan, too. The Taliban continue to resist the U.S. presence, drawing their strength largely from Pashtun nationalism, and members of the Afghan security forces have, in growing numbers, murdered U.S. and other NATO soldiers who were there to assist them. Instead of simply punishing the Taliban for their indirect role in 9/11 and hitting al Qaeda as hard as possible, true to its global agenda, the Bush administration pursued a costly and futile effort to transform Afghanistan, and the Obama administration continued it.

## FRIENDS WITHOUT BENEFITS

Another problematic response to the United States' grand strategy comes from its friends: free-riding. The Cold War alliances that the country has worked so hard to maintain—namely, NATO and the U.S.-Japanese security agreement—have provided U.S. partners in Europe and Asia with such a high level of insurance that they have been able to steadily shrink their militaries and outsource their defense to Washington. European nations have cut their military spending by roughly 15 percent in real terms since the end of the Cold War, with the exception of the United Kingdom, which will soon join the rest as it carries out its austerity policy. Depending on how one counts, Japanese defense spending has been cut, or at best has remained stable, over the past decade. The government has unwisely devoted too much spending to ground forces, even as its leaders have expressed alarm at the rise of Chinese military power—an air, missile, and naval threat.

Although these regions have avoided major wars, the United States has had to bear more and more of the burden of keeping the peace. It now spends 4.6 percent of its GDP on defense, whereas its European NATO allies collectively spend 1.6 percent and Japan spends 1.0 percent. With their high per capita GDPs, these allies can afford to devote more money to their militaries, yet they have no incentive to do so. And so while the U.S. government considers draconian cuts in social spending to restore the United States' fiscal health, it continues to subsidize the security of Germany and Japan. This is welfare for the rich.

U.S. security guarantees also encourage plucky allies to challenge more powerful states, confident that Washington will save them in the end—a classic case of moral hazard. This phenomenon has caused the United States to incur political costs, antagonizing powers great and small for no gain and encouraging them to seek opportunities to provoke the United States in return. So far, the United States has escaped getting sucked into unnecessary wars, although Washington dodged a bullet in Taiwan when the Democratic Progressive Party of Chen Shui-bian governed the island, from 2000 to 2008. His frequent allusions to independence, which ran counter to U.S. policy but which some Bush administration officials reportedly encouraged, unnecessarily provoked the Chinese government; had he proceeded, he would have surely triggered a dangerous crisis. Chen would never have entertained such reckless rhetoric absent the long-standing backing of the U.S. government.

The Philippines and Vietnam (the latter of which has no formal defense treaty with Washington) also seem to have figured out that they can needle China over maritime boundary disputes and then seek shelter under the U.S.

umbrella when China inevitably reacts. Not only do these disputes make it harder for Washington to cooperate with Beijing on issues of global importance; they also risk roping the United States into conflicts over strategically marginal territory.

Georgia is another state that has played this game to the United States' detriment. Overly confident of Washington's affection for it, the tiny republic deliberately challenged Russia over control of the disputed region of South Ossetia in August 2008. Regardless of how exactly the fighting began, Georgia acted far too adventurously given its size, proximity to Russia, and distance from any plausible source of military help. This needless war ironically made Russia look tough and the United States unreliable.

This dynamic is at play in the Middle East, too. Although U.S. officials have communicated time and again to leaders in Jerusalem their discomfort with Israeli settlements on the territory occupied during the 1967 war, Israel regularly increases the population and dimensions of those settlements. The United States' military largess and regular affirmations of support for Israel have convinced Israeli hawks that they will suffer no consequences for ignoring U.S. advice. It takes two to make peace in the Israeli-Palestinian conflict, but the creation of humiliating facts on the ground will not bring a negotiated settlement any closer. And Israel's policies toward the Palestinians are a serious impediment to improved U.S. relations with the Arab world.

## A NIMBLER STRATEGY

The United States should replace its unnecessary, ineffective, and expensive hegemonic quest with a more restrained grand strategy. Washington should not retreat into isolationism but refocus its efforts on its three biggest security challenges: preventing a powerful rival from upending the global balance of power, fighting terrorists, and limiting nuclear proliferation. These challenges are not new, but the United States must develop more carefully calculated and discriminating policies to address them.

For roughly a century, American strategists have striven to ensure that no single state dominated the giant landmass of Eurasia, since such a power could then muster the resources to threaten the United States directly. To prevent this outcome, the United States rightly went to war against Germany and Japan and contained the Soviet Union. Although China may ultimately try to assume the mantle of Eurasian hegemon, this outcome is neither imminent nor inevitable. China's economy still faces many pitfalls, and the country is surrounded by powerful states that could and would check its expansion, including India and Russia, both of which have nuclear weapons. Japan, although it underspends on defense today, is rich and technologically advanced enough to contribute to a coalition of states that could balance against China. Other maritime Asian countries, even without the United States as a backstop, could also make common cause against China. The United States should maintain the capability to assist them if need be. But it should proceed cautiously in order to ensure that its efforts do not unnecessarily threaten China and thus encourage the very ambitions Washington hopes to deter or prompt a new round of free-riding or reckless driving by others in Asia.

The United States must also defend itself against al Qaeda and any similar successor groups. Since such terrorists can threaten Americans' lives, the U.S. government should keep in place the prudent defensive measures that have helped lower the risk of attacks, such as more energetic intelligence efforts and better airport security. (A less interventionist foreign policy will help, too: it was partly the U.S. military's presence in Saudi Arabia that radicalized Osama bin Laden and his followers in the first place.) When it comes to offense, the United States must still pursue terrorists operating abroad, so that they spend their scarce resources trying to stay alive rather than plotting new attacks. It will need to continue cooperating with other vulnerable governments and help them develop their own police and military forces. Occasionally, the U.S. military will have to supplement these efforts with air strikes, drone attacks, and special operations raids.

But Washington should keep the threat in perspective. Terrorists are too weak to threaten the country's sovereignty, territorial integrity, or power position. Because the threat is modest, and because trying to reform other societies by force is too costly, the United States must fight terrorism with carefully applied force, rather than through wholesale nation-building efforts such as that in Afghanistan.

Finally, a restrained grand strategy would also pay close attention to the spread of nuclear weapons, while relying less on the threat of military force to stop it. Thanks to the deterrence provided by its own massive nuclear forces, the United States faces little risk of a direct nuclear attack by another state. But Washington does need to keep nonstate actors from obtaining nuclear weapons or material. To prevent them from taking advantage of lax safeguards at nuclear facilities, the U.S. government should share best practices regarding nuclear security with other countries, even ones that it would prefer did not possess nuclear weapons in the first place. The United States does already cooperate somewhat with Pakistan on this issue, but it must stand ready to do more and ultimately to undertake such efforts with others.

The loss of a government's control over its nuclear weapons during a coup, revolution, or civil war is a far harder problem to forestall. It may be possible for U.S. forces to secure weapons in a period of instability, with the help of local actors who see the dangers for their own country if the weapons get loose. Conditions may lend themselves to a preventive military attack, to seize or disable the weapons. In some cases, however, the United States might have to make do with less sure-fire responses. It could warn those who seized the nuclear weapons in a period of upheaval that they would make themselves targets for retaliation if the weapons were ever used by terrorists. And it could better surveil international sea and air routes and more intensively monitor both its own borders for nuclear smuggling and those of the potential source countries.

These measures may seem incommensurate with the terrible toll of a nuclear blast. But the alternative strategy—fighting preventive conventional wars against nascent nuclear powers—is an expensive and uncertain solution to proliferation. The Obama administration's oft-repeated warning that deterrence and containment of a nuclear Iran is unacceptable makes little sense given the many ways a preventive war could go wrong and in light of the redundant deterrent capability the United States already possesses. Indeed, the more Washington relies on military force to halt proliferation, the more likely it is that countries will decide to acquire the ultimate deterrent.

A more restrained America would also have to head off nuclear arms races. In retrospect, the size, composition, doctrine, and highly alert posture of U.S. and Soviet nuclear forces during the Cold War seem unduly risky relative to the strategic problem those weapons were supposed to solve. Nuclear weapons act as potent deterrents to aggression, but significantly smaller forces than those the United States now possesses, carefully managed, should do the job. To avoid a replay of Cold War–style nuclear competition, the United States should pursue a new multilateral arms control regime that places ceilings on nuclear inventories and avoids hair-trigger force postures.

## RESTRAINT IN PRACTICE

A grand strategy of restraint would narrow U.S. foreign policy to focus on those three larger objectives. What would it look like in practice? First, the United States would recast its alliances so that other countries shared actual responsibility for their own defense. NATO is the easiest case; the United States should withdraw from the military command structure and return the alliance to the primarily political organization it once was. The Europeans can decide for themselves whether they want to retain the military command structure under the auspices of the European Union or dismantle it altogether. Most U.S. troops should come home from Europe, although by mutual agreement, the United States could keep a small number of naval and air bases on the continent.

The security treaty with Japan is a more difficult problem; it needs to be renegotiated but not abandoned. As the treaty stands now, the United States shoulders most of the burden of defending Japan, and the Japanese government agrees to help. The roles should be reversed, so that Japan assumes responsibility for its own defense, with Washington offering backup. Given concerns about China's rising power, not all U.S. forces should leave the region. But the Pentagon should pare down its presence in Japan to those relevant to the most immediate military problems. All U.S. marines could be withdrawn from the country, bringing to an end the thorny negotiations about their future on the island of Okinawa. The U.S. Navy and the U.S. Air Force should keep the bulk of their forces stationed in and around Japan in place, but with appropriate reductions. Elsewhere in Asia, the U.S. military can cooperate with other states to ensure access to the region should future crises arise, but it should not seek new permanent bases.

The military should also reassess its commitments in the Persian Gulf: the United States should help protect states in the region against external attacks, but it cannot take responsibility for defending them against internal dissent. Washington still needs to reassure those governments that fear that a regional power such as Iran will attack them and hijack their oil wealth, since a single oil-rich hegemon in the region would no doubt be a source of mischief. The U.S. military has proved adept at preventing such an outcome in the past, as it did when it defended Saudi Arabia and repelled Saddam's forces from Kuwait in 1991. Ground forces bent on invasion make easy targets for air attacks. The aircraft and cruise missiles aboard U.S. naval forces stationed in the region could provide immediate assistance. With a little advance notice, U.S. Air Force aircraft could quickly reinforce land bases maintained by the Arab states of the Gulf, as they did during the Gulf War when the regional powers opposed to Saddam's aggression prepared the way for reinforcement from the U.S. military by maintaining extra base capacity and fuel.

But U.S. soldiers no longer need to live onshore in Gulf countries, where they incite anti-Americanism and tie the U.S. government to autocratic regimes of dubious legitimacy. For example, Bahrain is suffering considerable internal unrest, which raises questions about the future viability of the United States' growing military presence there. The Iraq war proved that trying to install new regimes in Arab countries is a fool's errand; defending existing regimes facing internal rebellion will be no easier.

Under a restrained grand strategy, U.S. military forces could shrink significantly, both to save money and to send allies the message that it's time they did more for themselves. Because the Pentagon would, under this new strategy, swear off counterinsurgency, it could cut the number of ground forces in half. The navy and the air force, meanwhile, should be cut by only a quarter to a third, since their assets take a long time to produce and would still be needed for any effort to maintain the global balance of power. Naval and air forces are also well suited to solving the security problems of Asia and the Persian Gulf. Because these forces are highly mobile, only some need be present in key regions. The rest can be kept at home, as a powerful strategic reserve.

The overall size and quality of U.S. military forces should be determined by the critical contingency that they must address: the defense of key resources and allies against direct attack. Too often in the past, Washington has overused its expensive military to send messages that ought to be left to diplomats. That must change. Although the Pentagon should continue leading joint exercises with the militaries of other countries in key regions, it should stop overloading the calendar with pointless exercises the world over. Making that change would save wear and tear on troops and equipment and avoid creating the impression that the United States will solve all the world's security problems.

## LETTING GO

Shifting to a more restrained global stance would yield meaningful benefits for the United States, saving lives and resources and preventing pushback, provided Washington makes deliberate and prudent moves now to prepare its allies to take on the responsibility for their own defense. Scaling down the U.S. military's presence over a decade would give partners plenty of time to fortify their own militaries and develop the political and diplomatic machinery to look after their own affairs. Gradual disengagement would also reduce the chances of creating security vacuums, which opportunistic regional powers might try to fill.

U.S. allies, of course, will do everything they can to persuade Washington to keep its current policies in place. Some will promise improvements to their military forces that they will then abandon when it is convenient. Some will claim there is nothing more they can contribute, that their domestic political and economic constraints matter more than America's. Others will try to divert the discussion to shared values and principles. Still others will hint that they will bandwagon with strong neighbors rather than balance against them. A few may even threaten to turn belligerent.

U.S. policymakers will need to remain cool in the face of such tactics and keep in mind that these wealthy allies are unlikely to surrender their sovereignty to regional powers. Indeed, history has shown that states more often balance against the powerful than bandwagon with them. As for potential adversaries, the United States can continue to deter actions that threaten its vital interests by defining those interests narrowly, stating them clearly, and maintaining enough military power to protect them.

Of course, the United States could do none of these things and instead continue on its present track, wasting resources and earning the enmity of some states and peoples while infantilizing others. Perhaps current economic and geopolitical trends will reverse themselves, and the existing strategy will leave Washington comfortably in the driver's seat, with others eager to live according to its rules. But if the U.S. debt keeps growing and power continues to shift to other countries, some future economic or political crisis could force Washington to switch course abruptly, compelling friendly and not-so-friendly countries to adapt suddenly. That seems like the more dangerous path.

---

## CRITICAL THINKING QUESTIONS

1. What is the point beyond which a passive foreign policy fails?
2. Has past American foreign policy been "mindless and expansive," or was there a logic to it?
3. What is the bigger danger for an active U.S. foreign policy: push back and resistance or manipulation by other states?

# Global Problems

By definition, American foreign policy is outward looking. Its focus is on events and conditions beyond U.S. borders that either now or in the future could harm American interests and values—or offer the opportunity to advance them. Historically, American foreign policy has been organized around a number of competing views on the key foreign policy problems facing the United States. The earliest clear statement about identifying and ranking foreign policy problems came with the Monroe Doctrine (1823), which identified the Western Hemisphere as central to American security. In the mid-1800s the concept of Manifest Destiny was used to justify war with Mexico (1846) and continental expansion, which in turn led to the growing American interest in Asia as symbolized by Admiral Perry's "opening of Japan" in 1854. And in the early part of the twentieth century, the sense that events in Europe were not central to American security interests first voiced by the Monroe Doctrine regained political importance in the debate over isolationism following World War I.

A number of different starting points have been put forward for identifying and defining what constitutes an important foreign policy problem. One of the earliest was advanced by Alfred Mahan, who in 1890 emphasized the importance of controlling the seas for promoting commerce and national security as the proper foundation for a country's foreign policy. His writings were particularly influential on the thinking of Teddy Roosevelt and led Roosevelt's support of a strong navy. However, Mahan's writings did not go unchallenged. In 1904 Harold Mackinder put forward his heartland theory stressing the geopolitical importance of the world island (the land mass consisting of Europe, Asia, and Africa) to global domination and thus national security.

During the Cold War (generally defined as the period from 1947 to 1991) several additional starting points for thinking about how to identify important foreign policy problems began to emerge. One directed our attention to the global commons, those portions of "planet earth" that were not—and should not—be considered the possession of any one state or alliance system. The most frequently discussed commons were the atmosphere, polar regions, outer space, and the oceans. The health of the global commons was seen as vital to all countries and demanded international cooperation and protection. A second challenge to traditional ways of defining foreign policy problems was the call to give greater emphasis to the well-being of people. In this view foreign policy should not simply further the interests of countries, but it should advance the safety, prosperity, and rights of individuals.

Over the past decade still another perspective on defining foreign policy problems has come to the forefront: globalization. From this viewpoint advances in scientific discoveries and communication and transportation technologies have both brought people closer together but also highlighted differences among people. Similarly, scientific technological advances have both helped solve and manage some global problems but also contributed to their global spread, with health and environmental problems being cited most frequently. Critical to these challenges are (1) the speed by which people and events cross borders and (2) the inability of states to address these problems without the cooperation of others.

The correct ranking of foreign policy problems continues to be a point of controversy in the conduct of American foreign policy today. Disagreement exists over the merits of President Obama's "pivot" to Asia, by which he intended to heighten the attention given to Asia in U.S. foreign policy. The logical consequence is a decreased emphasis on Europe and Russia. This disagreement reflects the continued uncertainty over how to evaluate the relative importance of the world's geography in assessing U.S. strategic interests. Complicating matters further in making judgments about the relative importance of controlling oceans versus land to American foreign policy is the emergence of local and regional conflicts in the Middle East and Africa. Ongoing disagreement over how to deal with global health, environmental, and climatic problems along with the emerging question of to what extent international versus national laws should govern military and economic activity in the Arctic Ocean are testimony to the degree to which conflict over the global interest and national interest in commons regions continues to be a major source of contention in foreign policy making. Competing for attention with these geographically focused global challenges of today's world are challenges stemming from increased globalization. In recent years these challenges have ranged from stopping the spread of terrorism to stabilizing the value of the U.S. dollar to protecting Americans from global disease epidemics.

The first reading in this section presents the U.S. intelligence community's evaluation of the major global foreign policy problems facing the United States in 2015. The readings that follow provide overviews of specific foreign policy problems. Yun Sun looks at the rise of China as a competitor to the United States. In "China's New Calculations in the South China Sea," he argues that China's rising assertiveness is explained by its conclusion that past unilateral restraint in this region has done nothing to improve its overall position. Samuel Charap and Jeremy Shapiro, in "How to Avoid a New Cold War," use the crisis over control of Ukraine as the starting point to discuss U.S.-Russia relations. They argue the United States does not need to accept Russian domination over its neighbors and call for finding a balance between economic sanctions against Russia and forging a new working relationship with the nation. Elizabeth Dickinson examines the ongoing problem of narco-insurgencies facing the United States in Latin America. In "Fighting the Last War," she reviews U.S. policy toward Colombia and argues that Mexico and other countries in the region need to find their own unique solutions. Simply repeating the U.S. policy followed in Colombia will fail. One of the most recent global problems faced by the United States and other countries was the Ebola outbreak in West Africa. The excerpt from Congressional Research Service's October 2014 report on this health crisis reviews the U.S. response, the issues the crisis raises for Congress, and its long-term effects. Fawaz A. Gerges, in "ISIS and the Third Wave of Jihadism," argues there is no quick solution to the challenge presented by ISIS since its historical roots are deep and its current strength is rooted in the breakdown of state institutions and sectarian conflict spreading through the Middle East.

## BIG PICTURE QUESTIONS

1. Construct a chart of foreign policy problems facing the United States today and rate each on a scale of 1–10 in terms of their importance.
2. Which category of foreign policy problems represents the greatest challenge to American foreign policy: those rooted in geography and military power, those growing out of the global commons, or those linked to globalization?
3. Select six major foreign policy problems the United States has faced since the end of World War I. Rank them from high to low according to the degree to which the United States succeeded in its goals. What lessons can we learn from where it succeeded and where it failed?

## SUGGESTED READINGS

Intergovernmental Panel on Climate Change, *Climate Change 2014: Synthesis Report* (Geneva, 2014).

Michael Klare, "The Growing Threat of Maritime Conflict," *Current History* 112 (January 2013), 26–32.

Adam Liff and G. John Ikenberry, "Racing Toward Tragedy? China's Rise, Military Competition in the Asia Pacific and the Security Dilemma, "*International Security* 39 (Fall 2014), 52–91.

Anthony Richards, "Conceptualizing Terrorism," *Studies in Conflict and Terrorism* 37 (March 2014), 213–36.

David Shambaugh, "The Illusion of Chinese Power," *National Interest* 132 (July 2014), 39–48.

# 5

# Worldwide Threat Assessment

## CYBER

### Strategic Assessment

Cyber threats to U.S. national and economic security are increasing in frequency, scale, sophistication, and severity of impact. The ranges of cyber threat actors, methods of attack, targeted systems, and victims are also expanding. Overall, the unclassified information and communication technology (ICT) networks that support U.S. Government, military, commercial, and social activities remain vulnerable to espionage and/or disruption. However, the likelihood of a catastrophic attack from any particular actor is remote at this time. Rather than a "Cyber Armageddon" scenario that debilitates the entire U.S. infrastructure, we envision something different. We foresee an ongoing series of low-to-moderate level cyber attacks from a variety of sources over time, which will impose cumulative costs on U.S. economic competitiveness and national security.

- A growing number of computer forensic studies by industry experts strongly suggest that several nations—including Iran and North Korea—have undertaken offensive cyber operations against private sector targets to support their economic and foreign policy objectives, at times concurrent with political crises.

### Risk

Despite ever-improving network defenses, the diverse possibilities for remote hacking intrusions, supply chain operations to insert compromised hardware or software, and malevolent activities by human insiders will hold nearly all ICT systems at risk for years to come. In short, the cyber threat cannot be eliminated; rather, cyber risk must be managed. Moreover, the risk calculus employed by some private sector entities does not adequately account for foreign cyber threats or the systemic interdependencies between different critical infrastructure sectors.

### Costs

During 2014, we saw an increase in the scale and scope of reporting on malevolent cyber activity that can be measured by the amount of corporate data

Excerpted from "Statement for the Record, Worldwide Threat Assessment of the U.S. Intelligence Community," February 26, 2015.

stolen or deleted, personally identifiable information (PII) compromised, or remediation costs incurred by U.S. victims. For example:

- After the 2012–2013 distributed denial of service (DDOS) attacks on the U.S. financial sector, JPMorgan Chase (JPMorgan) announced plans for annual cyber security expenditures of $250 million by the end of 2014. After the company suffered a hacking intrusion in 2014, JPMorgan's CEO said he would probably double JPMorgan's annual computer security budget within the next five years.
- The 2014 data breach at Home Depot exposed information from 56 million credit/debit cards and 53 million customer email addresses. Home Depot estimated the cost of the breach to be $62 million.
- In 2014, unauthorized computer intrusions were detected on the networks of the Office of Personnel Management (OPM) as well as its contractors, U.S. Investigations Services (USIS) and KeyPoint Government Solutions. The two contractors were involved in processing sensitive PII related to national security clearances for Federal Government employees.
- In August 2014, the U.S. company, Community Health Systems, informed the Securities and Exchange Commission that it believed hackers "originating from China" had stolen PII on 4.5 million individuals.

## Attribution

Although cyber operators can infiltrate or disrupt targeted ICT networks, most can no longer assume that their activities will remain undetected. Nor can they assume that if detected, they will be able to conceal their identities. Governmental and private sector security professionals have made significant advances in detecting and attributing cyber intrusions.

- In May 2014, the U.S. Department of Justice indicted five officers from China's People's Liberation Army on charges of hacking U.S. companies.
- In December 2014, computer security experts reported that members of an Iranian organization were responsible for computer operations targeting U.S. military, transportation, public utility, and other critical infrastructure networks.

## Deterrence

Numerous actors remain undeterred from conducting economic cyber espionage or perpetrating cyber attacks. The absence of universally accepted and enforceable norms of behavior in cyberspace has contributed to this situation. The motivation to conduct cyber attacks and cyber espionage will probably remain strong because of the relative ease of these operations and the gains they bring to the perpetrators. The result is a cyber environment in which multiple actors continue to test their adversaries' technical capabilities, political resolve, and thresholds. The muted response by most victims to cyber attacks has created a permissive environment in which low-level attacks can be used as a coercive tool short of war, with relatively low risk of retaliation. Additionally, even when a cyber attack can be attributed to a specific actor, the forensic attribution often requires a significant amount of time to complete. Long delays between the cyber attack and determination of attribution likewise reinforce a permissive environment.

## Threat Actors

Politically motivated cyber attacks are now a growing reality, and foreign actors are reconnoitering and developing access to U.S. critical infrastructure systems, which might be quickly exploited for disruption if an adversary's intent became hostile. In addition, those conducting cyber espionage are targeting U.S. Government, military, and commercial networks on a daily basis. These threats come from a range of actors, including: (1) nation states with highly sophisticated cyber programs (such as Russia or China), (2) nations with lesser technical capabilities but possibly more disruptive intent (such as Iran or North Korea), (3) profit-motivated criminals, and (4) ideologically motivated hackers or extremists. Distinguishing between state and non-state actors within the same country is often difficult—especially when those varied actors actively collaborate, tacitly cooperate, condone criminal activity that only harms foreign victims, or utilize similar cyber tools.

### Russia

Russia's Ministry of Defense is establishing its own cyber command, which—according to senior Russian military officials—will be responsible for conducting offensive cyber activities, including propaganda operations and inserting malware into enemy command and control systems. Russia's armed forces are also establishing a specialized branch for computer network operations.

- Computer security studies assert that unspecified Russian cyber actors are developing means to access industrial control systems (ICS) remotely. These systems manage critical infrastructures such as electric power grids, urban mass-transit systems, air-traffic control, and oil and gas distribution networks. These unspecified Russian actors have successfully compromised the product supply chains of three ICS vendors so that customers download exploitative malware directly from the vendors' websites along with routine software updates, according to private sector cyber security experts.

### China

Chinese economic espionage against U.S. companies remains a significant issue. The "advanced persistent threat" activities continue despite detailed private sector reports, public indictments, and U.S. demarches, according to a computer security study. China is an advanced cyber actor; however, Chinese hackers often use less sophisticated cyber tools to access targets. Improved cyber defenses would require hackers to use more sophisticated skills and make China's economic espionage more costly and difficult to conduct.

## Iran

Iran very likely values its cyber program as one of many tools for carrying out asymmetric but proportional retaliation against political foes, as well as a sophisticated means of collecting intelligence. Iranian actors have been implicated in the 2012–2013 DDOS attacks against U.S. financial institutions and in the February 2014 cyber attack on the Las Vegas Sands casino company.

## North Korea

North Korea is another state actor that uses its cyber capabilities for political objectives. The North Korean Government was responsible for the November 2014 cyber attack on Sony Pictures Entertainment (SPE), which stole corporate information and introduced hard drive erasing malware into the company's network infrastructure, according to the FBI. The attack coincided with the planned release of a SPE feature film satire that depicted the planned assassination of the North Korean president.

## Terrorists

Terrorist groups will continue to experiment with hacking, which could serve as the foundation for developing more advanced capabilities. Terrorist sympathizers will probably conduct low-level cyber attacks on behalf of terrorist groups and attract attention of the media, which might exaggerate the capabilities and threat posed by these actors.

## Integrity of Information

Most of the public discussion regarding cyber threats has focused on the confidentiality and availability of information; cyber espionage undermines confidentiality, whereas denial-of-service operations and data-deletion attacks undermine availability. In the future, however, we might also see more cyber operations that will change or manipulate electronic information in order to compromise its integrity (i.e., accuracy and reliability) instead of deleting it or disrupting access to it. Decision making by senior government officials (civilian and military), corporate executives, investors, or others will be impaired if they cannot trust the information they are receiving.

■ Successful cyber operations targeting the integrity of information would need to overcome any institutionalized checks and balances designed to prevent the manipulation of data, for example, market monitoring and clearing functions in the financial sector.

# COUNTERINTELLIGENCE

We assess that the leading state intelligence threats to U.S. interests in 2015 will continue to be Russia and China, based on their capabilities, intent, and broad operational scopes. Other states in South Asia, the Near East, and East Asia will pose increasingly sophisticated local and regional intelligence threats to U.S. interests. For example, Iran's intelligence and security services continue to view the United States as a primary threat and have stated publicly that they monitor and counter U.S. activities in the region.

Penetrating the U.S. national decision-making apparatus and Intelligence Community will remain primary objectives for foreign intelligence entities. Additionally, the targeting of national security information and proprietary information from U.S. companies and research institutions dealing with defense, energy, finance, dual-use technology, and other areas will be a persistent threat to U.S. interests.

Non-state entities, including transnational organized criminals and terrorists, will continue to employ human, technical, and cyber intelligence capabilities that present a significant counterintelligence challenge. Like state intelligence services, these non-state entities recruit sources and perform physical and technical surveillance to facilitate their illegal activities and avoid detection and capture.

The internationalization of critical U.S. supply chains and service infrastructure, including for the ICT, civil infrastructure, and national security sectors, increases the potential for subversion. This threat includes individuals, small groups of "hacktivists," commercial firms, and state intelligence services.

Trusted insiders who disclose sensitive U.S. Government information without authorization will remain a significant threat in 2015. The technical sophistication and availability of information technology that can be used for nefarious purposes exacerbates this threat.

# TERRORISM

Sunni violent extremists are gaining momentum and the number of Sunni violent extremist groups, members, and safe havens is greater than at any other point in history. These groups challenge local and regional governance and threaten U.S. allies, partners, and interests. The threat to key U.S. allies and partners will probably increase, but the extent of the increase will depend on the level of success that Sunni violent extremists achieve in seizing and holding territory, whether or not attacks on local regimes and calls for retaliation against the West are accepted by their key audiences, and the durability of the U.S.-led coalition in Iraq and Syria.

Sunni violent extremists have taken advantage of fragile or unstable Muslim-majority countries to make territorial advances, seen in Syria and Iraq, and will probably continue to do so. They also contribute to regime instability and internal conflict by engaging in high levels of violence. Most will be unable to seize and hold territory on a large scale, however, as long as local, regional, and international support and resources are available and dedicated to halting their progress. The increase in the number of Sunni violent extremist groups also will probably be balanced by a lack of cohesion and authoritative leadership. Although the January 2015 attacks against Charlie Hebdo in Paris is a reminder of the threat to the West, most groups place a higher priority on local concerns than on attacking the so-called far enemy—the United States and the West—as advocated by core al Qa'ida.

Differences in ideology and tactics will foster competition among some of these groups, particularly if a unifying figure or group does not emerge. In some cases, groups—even if hostile to each other—will ally against common enemies. For example, some Sunni violent extremists will probably gain support from like-minded insurgent or anti-regime groups or within disaffected or disenfranchised communities because they share the goal of radical regime change.

Although most homegrown violent extremists (HVEs) will probably continue to aspire to travel overseas, particularly to Syria and Iraq, they will probably remain the most likely Sunni violent extremist threat to the U.S. homeland because of their immediate and direct access. Some might have been inspired by calls by the Islamic State of Iraq and the Levant (ISIL) in late September for individual jihadists in the West to retaliate for U.S.-led airstrikes on ISIL. Attacks by lone actors are among the most difficult to warn about because they offer few or no signatures.

If ISIL were to substantially increase the priority it places on attacking the West rather than fighting to maintain and expand territorial control, then the group's access to radicalized Westerners who have fought in Syria and Iraq would provide a pool of operatives who potentially have access to the United States and other Western countries. Since the conflict began in 2011, more than 20,000 foreign fighters—at least 3,400 of whom are Westerners—have gone to Syria from more than 90 countries.

# WEAPONS OF MASS DESTRUCTION AND PROLIFERATION

Nation-states' efforts to develop or acquire weapons of mass destruction (WMD), their delivery systems, or their underlying technologies constitute a major threat to the security of the United States, its deployed troops, and allies. Syrian regime use of chemical weapons against the opposition further demonstrates that the threat of WMD is real. The time when only a few states had access to the most dangerous technologies is past. Biological and chemical materials and technologies, almost always dual-use, move easily in the globalized economy, as do personnel with the scientific expertise to design and use them. The latest discoveries in the life sciences also diffuse rapidly around the globe.

## Iran Preserving Nuclear Weapons Option

We continue to assess that Iran's overarching strategic goals of enhancing its security, prestige, and regional influence have led it to pursue capabilities to meet its civilian goals and give it the ability to build missile-deliverable nuclear weapons, if it chooses to do so. We do not know whether Iran will eventually decide to build nuclear weapons.

We also continue to assess that Iran does not face any insurmountable technical barriers to producing a nuclear weapon, making Iran's political will the central issue. However, Iranian implementation of the Joint Plan of Action (JPOA) has at least temporarily inhibited further progress in its uranium enrichment and plutonium production capabilities and effectively eliminated Iran's stockpile of 20 percent enriched uranium. The agreement has also enhanced the transparency of Iran's nuclear activities, mainly through improved International Atomic Energy Agency (IAEA) access and earlier warning of any effort to make material for nuclear weapons using its safeguarded facilities.

We judge that Tehran would choose ballistic missiles as its preferred method of delivering nuclear weapons, if it builds them. Iran's ballistic missiles are inherently capable of delivering WMD, and Tehran already has the largest inventory of ballistic missiles in the Middle East. Iran's progress on space launch vehicles—along with its desire to deter the United States and its allies—provides Tehran with the means and motivation to develop longer-range missiles, including intercontinental ballistic missiles (ICBMs).

## North Korea Developing WMD-Applicable Capabilities

North Korea's nuclear weapons and missile programs pose a serious threat to the United States and to the security environment in East Asia. North Korea's export of ballistic missiles and associated materials to several countries, including Iran and Syria, and its assistance to Syria's construction of a nuclear reactor, destroyed in 2007, illustrate its willingness to proliferate dangerous technologies.

In 2013, following North Korea's third nuclear test, Pyongyang announced its intention to "refurbish and restart" its nuclear facilities, to include the uranium enrichment facility at Yongbyon, and to restart its graphite-moderated plutonium production reactor that was shut down in 2007. We assess that North Korea has followed through on its announcement by expanding its Yongbyon enrichment facility and restarting the reactor.

North Korea has also expanded the size and sophistication of its ballistic missile forces, ranging from close-range ballistic missiles to ICBMs, while continuing to conduct test launches. In 2014, North Korea launched an unprecedented number of ballistic missiles.

Pyongyang is committed to developing a long-range, nuclear-armed missile that is capable of posing a direct threat to the United States and has publicly displayed its KN08 road-mobile ICBM twice. We assess that North Korea has already taken initial steps toward fielding this system, although the system has not been flight-tested.

Because of deficiencies in their conventional military forces, North Korean leaders are focused on developing missile and WMD capabilities, particularly building nuclear weapons. Although North Korean state media regularly carries official statements on North Korea's justification for building nuclear weapons and threatening to use them as a defensive or retaliatory measure, we do not know the details of Pyongyang's nuclear doctrine or employment concepts. We have long assessed that, in Pyongyang's view, its nuclear capabilities are intended for deterrence, international prestige, and coercive diplomacy.

## China's Expanding Nuclear Forces

The People's Liberation Army's (PLA's) Second Artillery Force continues to modernize its nuclear missile force by adding more survivable road-mobile systems and enhancing its silo-based systems. This new generation of missiles is intended to ensure the viability of China's strategic deterrent by providing a second strike capability. In addition, the PLA Navy continues to develop the JL-2 submarine-launched ballistic missile (SLBM) and might produce additional JIN-class nuclear-powered ballistic missile submarines. The JIN-class submarines, armed with JL-2 SLBMs, will give the PLA Navy its first long-range, sea-based nuclear capability. We assess that the Navy will soon conduct its first nuclear deterrence patrols.

## Russia's New Intermediate-Range Cruise Missile

Russia has developed a new cruise missile that the United States has declared to be in violation of the Intermediate-Range Nuclear Forces (INF) Treaty. In 2013, Sergei Ivanov, a senior Russian administration official, commented in an interview how the world had changed since the time the INF Treaty was signed in 1987 and noted that Russia was "developing appropriate weapons systems" in light of the proliferation of intermediate- and shorter-range ballistic missile technologies around the world. Similarly, as far back as 2007, Ivanov publicly announced that Russia had tested a ground-launched cruise missile for its Iskander weapon system, whose range complied with the INF Treaty "for now." The development of a cruise missile that is inconsistent with INF, combined with these statements about INF, calls into question Russia's commitment to this treaty.

## WMD Security in Syria

In June 2014, Syria's declared CW stockpile was removed for destruction by the international community. The most hazardous chemical agents were destroyed aboard the MV CAPE RAY as of August 2014. The United States and its allies continue to work closely with the Organization for the Prohibition of Chemical Weapons (OPCW) to verify the completeness and accuracy of Syria's Chemical Weapons Convention (CWC) declaration. We judge that Syria, despite signing the treaty, has used chemicals as a means of warfare since accession to the CWC in 2013. Furthermore, the OPCW continues to investigate allegations of chlorine use in Syria.

# SPACE AND COUNTERSPACE

Threats to U.S. space systems and services will increase during 2015 and beyond as potential adversaries pursue disruptive and destructive counterspace capabilities. Chinese and Russian military leaders understand the unique information advantages afforded by space systems and services and are developing capabilities to deny access in a conflict. Chinese military writings highlight the need to interfere with, damage, and destroy reconnaissance, navigation, and communication satellites. China has satellite jamming capabilities and is pursuing antisatellite systems. In July 2014, China conducted a non-destructive antisatellite missile test. China conducted a previous destructive test of the system in 2007, which created long-lived space debris. Russia's 2010 Military Doctrine emphasizes space defense as a vital component of its national defense. Russian leaders openly assert that the Russian armed forces have antisatellite weapons and conduct antisatellite research. Russia has satellite jammers and is pursuing antisatellite systems.

# TRANSNATIONAL ORGANIZED CRIME

Transnational Organized Crime (TOC) is a global, persistent threat to our communities at home and our interests abroad. Savvy, profit-driven criminal networks traffic in drugs, persons, wildlife, and weapons; corrode security and governance; undermine legitimate economic activity and the rule of law; cost economies important revenue; and undercut U.S. development efforts.

## Drug Trafficking

Drug trafficking will remain a major TOC threat to the United States. Mexico is the largest foreign producer of U.S.-bound marijuana, methamphetamines, and heroin, and the conduit for the overwhelming majority of U.S.-bound cocaine from South America. The drug trade also undermines U.S. interests abroad, eroding stability in parts of Africa and Latin America; Afghanistan accounts for 80 percent of the world's opium production. Weak Central American states will continue to be the primary transit area for the majority of U.S.-bound cocaine. The Caribbean is becoming an increasingly important secondary transit area for U.S.- and European-bound cocaine. In 2013, the world's capacity to produce heroin reached the second highest level in nearly 20 years, increasing the likelihood that the drug will remain accessible and inexpensive in consumer markets in the United States, where heroin-related deaths have surged since 2007. New psychoactive substances (NPS), including synthetic cannabinoids and synthetic cathinones, pose an emerging and rapidly growing global public health threat. Since 2009, U.S. law enforcement officials have encountered more than 240 synthetic compounds. Worldwide, 348 new psychoactive substances had been identified, exceeding the number of 234 illicit substances under international controls.

## Criminals Profiting from Global Instability

Transnational criminal organizations will continue to exploit opportunities in ongoing conflicts to destabilize societies, economies, and governance. Regional unrest, population displacements, endemic corruption, and political turmoil will provide openings that criminals will exploit for profit and to improve their standing relative to other power brokers.

## Corruption

Corruption facilitates transnational organized crime and vice versa. Both phenomena exacerbate other threats to local, regional, and international security. Corruption exists at some level in all countries; however, the symbiotic relationship between government officials and TOC networks is particularly pernicious in some countries. One example is Russia, where the nexus among organized crime, state actors, and business blurs the distinction between state policy and private gain.

## Human Trafficking

Human trafficking remains both a human rights concern and a challenge to international security. Trafficking in persons has become a lucrative source of revenue—estimated to produce tens of billions of dollars annually. Human traffickers leverage corrupt officials, porous borders, and lax enforcement to ply their illicit trade. This exploitation of human lives for profit continues to occur in every country in the world—undermining the rule of law and corroding legitimate institutions of government and commerce.

## Wildlife Trafficking

Illicit trade in wildlife, timber, and marine resources endangers the environment, threatens rule of law and border security in fragile regions, and destabilizes communities that depend on wildlife for biodiversity and ecotourism. Increased demand for ivory and rhino horn in Asia has triggered unprecedented increases in poaching in Africa. Criminal elements, often in collusion with corrupt government officials or security forces, are involved in poaching and movement of ivory and rhino horn across Africa. Poaching presents significant security challenges for militaries and police forces in African nations, which often are outgunned by poachers and their allies. Illegal, unreported, and unregulated fishing threatens food security and the preservation of marine resources. It often occurs concurrently with forced labor in the fishing industry.

## Theft of Cultural Properties, Artifacts, and Antiquities

Although the theft and trafficking of cultural heritage and art are traditions as old as the cultures they represent, transnational organized criminals are acquiring, transporting, and selling valuable cultural property and art more swiftly, easily, and stealthily. These criminals operate on a global scale without regard for laws, borders, nationalities or the significance of the treasures they smuggle.

# ECONOMICS AND NATURAL RESOURCES

The global economy continues to adjust to and recover from the global financial crisis that began in 2008; economic growth since that period is lagging behind that of the previous decade. Resumption of sustained growth has been elusive for many of the world's largest economies, particularly in European countries and Japan. The prospect of diminished or forestalled recoveries in these developed economies as well as disappointing growth in key developing countries has contributed to a readjustment of energy and commodity markets.

## Energy and Commodities

Energy prices experienced sharp declines during the second half of 2014. Diminishing global growth prospects, OPEC's decision to maintain its output levels, rapid increases in unconventional oil production in Canada and the United States, and the partial resumption of some previously sidelined output in Libya and elsewhere helped drive down prices by more than half since July, the first substantial decline since 2008–2009. Lower-priced oil and gas will give a boost to the global economy, with benefits enjoyed by importers more than outweighing the costs to exporters.

## Macroeconomic Stability

Extraordinary monetary policy or "quantitative easing" has helped revive growth in the United States since the global financial crisis. However, this recovery and the prospect of higher returns in the United States will probably continue to draw investment capital from the rest of the world, where weak growth has left interest rates depressed.

Global output improved slightly in 2014 but continued to lag the growth rates seen before 2008. Since 2008, the worldwide GDP growth rate has averaged about 3.2 percent, well below its 20-year, pre-GFC average of 3.9 percent. Looking ahead, prospects for slowing economic growth in Europe and China do not bode well for the global economic environment.

Economic growth has been inconsistent among developed and developing economies alike. Outside of the largest economies—the United States, the EU, and China—economic growth largely stagnated worldwide in 2014, slowing to 2.1 percent. As a result, the difference in growth rates of developing countries and developed countries continued to narrow—to 2.6 percentage points. This gap, smallest in more than a decade, underscores the continued weakness in emerging markets, whose previously much-higher average growth rates helped drive global growth.

# HUMAN SECURITY

## Critical Trends Converging

Several trends are converging that will probably increase the frequency of shocks to human security in 2015. Emerging infectious diseases and deficiencies in international state preparedness to address them remain a threat, exemplified by the epidemic spread of the Ebola virus in West Africa. Extremes in weather combined with public policies that affect food and water supplies will probably exacerbate humanitarian crises. Many states and international institutions will look to the United States in 2015 for leadership to address human security issues, particularly environment and global health, as well as those caused by poor or abusive governance.

Global trends in governance are negative and portend growing instability. Poor and abusive governance threatens the security and rights of individuals and civil society in many countries throughout the world. The overall risk for mass atrocities—driven in part by increasing social mobilization, violent conflict, and a diminishing quality of governance—is growing. Incidents of religious persecution also are on the rise. Legal restrictions on NGOs and the press, particularly those that expose government shortcomings or lobby for reforms, will probably continue.

## Infectious Disease Continues to Threaten Human Security Worldwide

Infectious diseases are among the foremost health security threats. A more crowded and interconnected world is increasing the opportunities for human and animal diseases to emerge and spread globally. This has been demonstrated by the emergence of Ebola in West Africa on an unprecedented scale. In addition, military conflicts and displacement of populations with loss of basic infrastructure can lead to spread of disease. Climate change can also lead to changes in the distribution of vectors for diseases.

■ The Ebola outbreak, which began in late 2013 in a remote area of Guinea, quickly spread into neighboring Liberia and Sierra Leone and then into dense urban transportation hubs, where it began spreading out of control.

Gaps in disease surveillance and reporting, limited health care resources, and other factors contributed to the outpacing of the international community's response in West Africa. Isolated Ebola cases appeared outside of the most affected countries—notably in Spain and the United States—and the disease will almost certainly continue in 2015 to threaten regional economic stability, security, and governance.

■ Antimicrobial drug resistance is increasingly threatening global health security. Seventy percent of known bacteria have acquired resistance to at least one antibiotic that is used to treat infections, threatening a return to the pre-antibiotic era. Multidrug-resistant tuberculosis has emerged in China, India, Russia, and elsewhere. During the next twenty years, antimicrobial drug-resistant pathogens will probably continue to increase in number and geographic scope, worsening health outcomes, straining public health budgets, and harming U.S. interests throughout the world.

■ MERS, a novel virus from the same family as SARS, emerged in 2012 in Saudi Arabia. Isolated cases migrated to Southeast Asia, Europe, and the United States. Cases of highly pathogenic influenza are also continuing to appear in different regions of the world. HIV/AIDS and malaria, although trending downward, remain global health priorities. In 2013, 2.1 million people were newly infected with HIV and 584,000 were killed by malaria, according to the World Health Organization. Diarrheal diseases like cholera continue to take the lives of 800,000 children annually.

■ The world's population remains vulnerable to infectious diseases because anticipating which pathogen might spread from animals to humans or if a human virus will take a more virulent form is nearly impossible. For example, if a highly pathogenic avian influenza virus like H7N9 were to become easily transmissible among humans, the outcome could be far more disruptive than the great influenza pandemic of 1918. It could lead to global economic losses, the unseating of governments, and disturbance of geopolitical alliances.

## Extreme Weather Exacerbating Risks to Global Food and Water Security

Extreme weather, climate change, and public policies that affect food and water supplies will probably create or exacerbate humanitarian crises and instability risks. Globally averaged surface temperature rose approximately 0.8 degrees Celsius (about 1.4 degrees Fahrenheit) from 1951 to 2014; 2014 was warmest on earth since recordkeeping began. This rise in temperature has probably caused an increase in the intensity and frequency of both heavy precipitation and prolonged heat waves and has changed the spread of certain diseases. This trend will probably continue. Demographic and development trends that concentrate people in cities—often along coasts—will compound and amplify the impact of extreme weather and climate change on populations. Countries whose key systems—food, water, energy, shelter, transportation, and medical—are resilient will be better able to avoid significant economic and human losses from extreme weather.

- Global food supplies will probably be adequate for 2015 but are becoming increasingly fragile in Africa, the Middle East, and South Asia. The risks of worsening food insecurity in regions of strategic importance to the United States will increase because of threats to local food availability, lower purchasing power, and counterproductive government policies. Price shocks will result if extreme weather or disease patterns significantly reduce food production in multiple areas of the world, especially in key exporting countries.
- Risks to freshwater supplies—due to shortages, poor quality, floods, and climate change—are growing. These problems hinder the ability of countries to produce food and generate energy, potentially undermining global food markets and hobbling economic growth. Combined with demographic and economic development pressures, such problems will particularly hinder the efforts of North Africa, the Middle East, and South Asia to cope with their water problems. Lack of adequate water might be a destabilizing factor in countries that lack the management mechanisms, financial resources, political will, or technical ability to solve their internal water problems.
- Some states are heavily dependent on river water controlled by upstream nations. When upstream water infrastructure development threatens downstream access to water, states might attempt to exert pressure on their neighbors to preserve their water interests. Such pressure might be applied in international forums and also includes pressing investors, nongovernmental organizations, and donor countries to support or halt water infrastructure projects. Some countries will almost certainly construct and support major water projects. Over the longer term, wealthier developing countries will also probably face increasing water-related social disruptions. Developing countries, however, are almost certainly capable of addressing water problems without risk of state failure. Terrorist organizations might also increasingly seek to control or degrade water infrastructure to gain revenue or influence populations.

## Increase in Global Instability Risk

Global political instability risks will remain high in 2015 and beyond. Mass atrocities, sectarian or religious violence, and curtailed NGO activities will all continue to increase these risks. Declining economic conditions are contributing to risk of instability or internal conflict.

- Roughly half of the world's countries not already experiencing or recovering from instability are in the "most risk" and "significant risk" categories for regime-threatening and violent instability through 2015.

- Overall international will and capability to prevent or mitigate mass atrocities will probably diminish in 2015 owing to reductions in government budgets and spending.
- In 2014, about two dozen countries increased restrictions on NGOs. Approximately another dozen also plan to do so in 2015, according to the International Center for Nonprofit Law.

## CRITICAL THINKING QUESTIONS

1. What criteria would you use to classify a foreign policy problem as a threat?
2. Construct a worldwide opportunity assessment.
3. Which of the threats identified is the United States in the best position to deal with? Which presents the most problems?

# 6

# China's New Calculations in the South China Sea

Yun Sun

In recent months, China's unilateral actions asserting its claims in the South China Sea (SCS) have driven regional tensions to a new high. China's well-calculated moves are motivated by multiple internal and external factors. These include boosting President Xi Jinping's prestige and authority for his domestic reform agenda, along with an assumption that the United States is extremely unlikely to intervene at this moment in time. Other than the overt actions to assert its claims in the SCS, official statements and legal studies analysis from within China also reflect a recalibrated determination to uphold the country's controversial nine-dashed line in the SCS.

From a Chinese perspective, the most transparent and direct explanation of China's rising assertiveness in the South China Sea is simple: China believes that its past unilateral restraint has done nothing to improve China's position regarding SCS disputes and these inactions have in fact resulted in other claimant countries strengthening their presence and claims. Therefore, for China to improve its position in the current climate or for future negotiations, it must first change the status-quo through all available means necessary. China prefers to utilize civilian and paramilitary approaches but does not reject military coercion if required. An advantaged position and certain exclusive privilege in the South China Sea are both believed to be indispensable for China's aspiration to become a "strong maritime power," a "key task" stipulated by the 18th Party Congress in 2012 and a policy personally endorsed by Xi. While China's aspirations for a "Blue Water Navy" and naval expansion face multiple choke points along its east coast from Japan down to the Philippines, the South China Sea is considered to offer China a much larger and less constrained maritime domain for naval maneuvers.

While the policy to change the status quo and pursue a strong maritime power status has existed for a few years, the particular timing of China's most recent actions is closely associated with Chinese domestic politics—President Xi needs a strong foreign policy posture in order to strengthen his domestic power base. Xi's ongoing reform agenda since his inauguration in 2013,

Yun Sun is a fellow with the East Asia Program at the Stimson Center. This piece was originally released as Asia Pacific Bulletin, No. 267, published by the East-West Center.

including "deepening economic reforms" and a strong "anti-corruption" campaign, have touched upon many sensitive issues related to existing interest groups and leadership politics in China. Therefore, Xi needs as much foreign policy credits as possible to build his strong-man image and defuse internal criticisms of his various domestic agendas. This does not necessarily suggest or prove that Xi personally does not endorse an assertive foreign policy, but it does add an additional layer of strong motivation to it.

Last but not least, China is behaving assertively in the South China Sea because it believes it *can*. This assessment is not only based on China's growing military capacity, which dwarfs the capabilities of perhaps all other Southeast Asian claimant countries combined, but also on a strong conviction in China that the United States will not use its hard power to counter Chinese actions. China has watched closely the U.S. hesitation about military intervention in Syria, and also in Ukraine, and draws the conclusion that the Obama administration does not want to involve itself in a military conflict. It is further believed that there is no desire within the Obama administration for a foreign policy legacy that includes a conflict with China. Having said that, China does recognize the difference between Ukraine, which is not a member of NATO, and the Philippines, which is a U.S. ally. However, when China seized control of Scarborough Shoal in 2012, the United States did nothing. Furthermore, as Madame Fu Ying, Chairperson of the Foreign Affairs Committee of the National People's Congress, pointed out recently at the Shangri-La Dialogue, the dispute between China and Vietnam "has nothing to do with US." The implied message is that Vietnam is not even a U.S. ally and the likelihood of U.S. military intervention on behalf on Vietnam is extremely remote, if not non-existent.

Other than taking unilateral actions to change the status quo, China is also strengthening the arguments behind its controversial "nine-dashed line" in the SCS. PLA Deputy Chief of Staff, General Wang Guanzhong made an unprecedented six-point elaboration on the legitimacy of the nine-dashed line at the Shangri-La Dialogue, a clear indication of Beijing's determination to uphold its controversial claims. This is in sharp contrast to a few years ago when the Chinese foreign policy and legal communities were still debating the validity of the nine-dashed line. Now Chinese analysts almost unanimously argue that China should unilaterally stick to the controversial claim.

China understands very well the contradictions between the nine-dashed line and the UNCLOS treaty, and has invested significantly in legal research to substantiate the "historic rights" argument. Some Chinese experts have found justification within UNCLOS itself, claiming that the treaty is "ambiguous" and "inconclusive" on the issue of historic titles. Therefore, in their view, the issue of historic rights is unresolved by UNCLOS and is an ongoing, open discussion. Other Chinese experts claim that the nine-dashed line would find no support from UNCLOS. Instead, they try to explore alternative justifications for it beyond UNCLOS from other international customary laws or codes of practices. Both schools argue that since the nine-dashed line predated UNCLOS for four decades and China's historical rights predated UNCLOS for even longer, therefore UNCLOS *cannot retroactively be applied* to supersede China's sovereignty, sovereign rights and maritime administrative rights formed throughout history.

China is also carefully calibrating what to claim within the nine-dashed line. The reason for its intentional "strategic ambiguity" is clear: to leave room and flexibility for future negotiations. Most Chinese analysts are inclined to see the waters within the nine-dashed line as a Chinese Exclusive Economic Zone, although the government is yet to openly endorse that position.

Many within the Chinese policy community clearly understand the weaknesses of these legal arguments. Nevertheless, having weak but legitimate justifications is better than having no justification at all, especially when such positions are backed by strong national power and the willingness to use it. In comparison, the reputational cost for China is believed to be manageable. In fact, in China's cost-benefit analysis, the real benefits of its coercive actions substantially outweigh the costs. After all, China has other ways—mainly economic—to improve ties with Southeast Asia while its claims in the South China Sea can hardly be achieved through any other method other than coercion. In addition, China does not accept the dispute settlement mechanism stipulated by UNCLOS. So even if the international tribunal supports the Philippines' claims, China will not accept the result and it will be very difficult, if not completely impossible, for the court to enforce its ruling.

Whether others like it or not, China is getting what it wants. The new developments in China's calculations and positions deserve accurate understanding and a timely response by the countries in the region, especially the United States.

## CRITICAL THINKING QUESTIONS

1. How should the United States respond to China's increased aggressiveness in the South China Sea?
2. Are there parallels between the maritime and security politics of the South China Sea and the Caribbean Sea?
3. What is the likelihood that China's new foreign policy will succeed? How might it produce unwanted results for China?

# 7

# How to Avoid a New Cold War

Samuel Charap and Jeremy Shapiro

This year, the tragedies and outrages of the Ukraine crisis have dominated headlines and thinking about Western relations with Russia. There can be little doubt that the United States and its European allies and partners need a response to the Russian annexation of Crimea, to the destabilization of eastern Ukraine, to the separatists' downing of a civilian airliner—and to the threat to global order that all of these actions represent. But the need for a response does not imply that any response will do. The response thus far has seemed more focused on punishing Russia and its leaders for their moral transgressions than on addressing the problems in Western-Russian relations that led to this impasse. A serious response should be grounded in a broader strategy that reflects the stakes in this critical relationship for regional stability and global order, as well as an understanding of how things went so terribly wrong.

In attempting to understand what went wrong, the Western press and Western policy makers tend to focus on the person of Russian President Vladimir Putin, and on his baleful influence on Western-Russian relations. This type of "great man" theory of history has the dual advantage of both simplicity of explication and clarity of response. If one man destroyed the relationship, then ridding ourselves of him will go most of the way toward righting it. Indeed, the targeting of European Union and U.S. sanctions against Putin's inner circle in recent months seemed designed to undermine his authority and set the stage for a palace coup.

However, focusing on the man at the top is a dangerous approach that has often (as with Saddam Hussein in Iraq, Muammar el-Qaddafi in Libya, or Bashar al-Assad in Syria) led Western policy astray. In the case of Russia, Putin is clearly a charismatic and important leader who exercises a great deal of control over policy. But his current policies, much as Western counterparts might find them distasteful, are hardly marginal in Russia; his approval rating stood at 85 percent in July and opposition to him—both within his system and

Samuel Charap is a senior fellow for Russia and Eurasia at the International Institute for Strategic Studies. Jeremy Shapiro is a fellow in foreign policy studies at the Brookings Institution. They both served on the Policy Planning Staff of the U.S. State Department in President Barack Obama's first term. Reprinted with permission from *Current History* magazine (October 2014). Copyright © 2015 Current History, Inc.

without—has been systematically neutralized. Moreover, the views he currently espouses are more a consequence than a cause of the problems in Russian-Western relations. Most importantly, if he were to disappear tomorrow, none of the fundamental problems would be resolved. Indeed, Putin's departure could well make those problems worse, since his successors might be yet more in tune with the nationalist and anti-Western strains so prominent in Russian political culture.

A broader strategy for addressing the problems in Russian-Western relations needs to move beyond Putin and revisit the arc of the relationship between Russia and the West in the post–Cold War period. The Ukraine crisis has sparked a debate about the enlargement of Euro-Atlantic institutions—NATO and the EU—after 1991 and the future of that process. On the one hand, there are those who blame the crisis on enlargement: It was Western encroachment, they claim, that precipitated Russia's moves, and thus they imply that the way forward is to provide Russia with guarantees that enlargement will cease. On the other hand, there are those who believe that enlargement cemented democratic gains in postcommunist Europe and protected vulnerable states from Russian aggression. They argue that the proper response to the crisis is to quickly grant membership in the Western institutions to Ukraine, Georgia, and any other Russian neighbors interested in joining.

Both groups are missing the fundamental issue: whether Russia ever can be a normal partner for the West. If one believes that the last 20 years demonstrate that Russia is innately hostile to the West and its values, and will never accept genuine partnership, then conflict becomes inevitable. Aggressive efforts to contain or confront Russia in light of the current crisis are therefore both necessary and without significant downside. By contrast, if instead one reads (as we do) the history of the post–Cold War period in a tragic light—as a series of miscalculations about the compatibility of continued institutional enlargement with a cooperative security relationship between Russia and the West—then there is a need to find a balance between sanctioning Russia for its recent transgressions of international norms and keeping the door open for better relations in the future.

## THIS TIME IS DIFFERENT

This dispute echoes a key historical debate—namely, whether the Cold War began due to fundamental contradictions between the West and the Soviet Union or due to a series of misunderstandings and miscalculations on both sides of the Iron Curtain. Yet even those historians who point to the latter set of causal factors do not deny that the contradictions existed. Indeed, the Soviet Union was an expansionist, ideological power with global ambitions and deep hostility to Western interests. Post-Soviet Russia is unpleasant, and has transgressed a number of key international norms in the past year, but it is not the Soviet Union.

In other words, despite the surface similarity between today's debate on Russia and the historical debate about the Cold War's origins, closer examination reveals the key difference: Fundamental incompatibilities cannot account for the current conflict. That 2014 would see outright confrontation between Russia and the West was an unexpected development for political leaders on both sides. As late as June 2013, Putin and U.S. President Barack Obama issued a Joint Statement on Enhanced Bilateral Engagement, which said: "The United States of America and the Russian Federation reaffirm their readiness to intensify bilateral cooperation based on the principles of mutual respect, equality, and genuine respect for each other's interests. Guided by this approach, today we reached an understanding on a positive agenda for relations between our countries. . . . This wide-ranging program of action requires enhanced engagement at all levels." Nine months later, Obama would introduce unprecedented sanctions on Russia for its actions in Ukraine.

While the current conflict might not have been inevitable, in the months and years leading up to the February 2014 invasion of Crimea, the Euro-Atlantic institutional architecture had increasingly become a source of friction between Russia and the West. That is not to say institutional enlargement caused the Russian invasion, as University of Chicago political scientist John Mearsheimer, among others, would have it. However, it is only possible to understand the Russian decision-making process on Crimea and Ukraine by situating it in the broader context of the post–Cold War order in Europe and its flaws. Equally, to understand the Western decision-making process on Ukraine, one must take into account the hugely significant achievements of that order.

## EASTERN PROMISES

The institutional enlargement path that the West embarked on in the mid-1990s has transformed much of postcommunist Europe for the better—an outcome that was far from inevitable in the early 1990s. But it is clear that this path had an inherent flaw from the start, primarily in how the West dealt with Russia and its neighbors. Ever since, the West has done its best to manage the consequences of that flaw. The Ukraine crisis put an end to the balancing act.

The story begins in the critical period of 1989–1991, when the post–World War II settlement was rejected in favor of a new Europe. The wildly successful decision to make the newly reunited Germany a full member of NATO and the European Community created a precedent for the rest of postcommunist Europe: enlargement, with slight modification, of the existing Euro-Atlantic institutions in order to facilitate the region's ongoing democratic and economic transformations.

The inherent flaw in this expansion was that NATO and the EU could never fully integrate Russia. Moreover, Russia would never accept integration on nonnegotiable Western terms. The alternative—a wholesale revision of the institutional order so that Russia could be comfortably accommodated within it—would have been a huge risk. Moreover, Russia was so weakened by its own postcommunist transformation that it could not block the enlargement process, and (until recently) it demonstrated no will to do so. In any case, after German reunification, Western decision makers were confident that the expansion of the status quo would pay quick dividends.

And it certainly did. Although there has been significant backsliding in recent years in Hungary, Bulgaria, and Romania, on the whole EU and NATO enlargement contributed to developing the secure and pluralistic market democracies we now see throughout Central and Eastern Europe. This was no foregone conclusion in the 1990s; indeed, as the Arab Spring demonstrates, such sudden transitions are usually much more fraught and frequently fail to produce consolidated, prosperous democracies. The stabilization of Central and Eastern Europe was a significant achievement of which Western statesmen are justifiably proud.

To achieve this geopolitical miracle, Western leaders naturally used the tools available: NATO and the EU. Although not designed for stabilization, these institutions turned out to be a good fit for that purpose. Postcommunist aspirants believed that membership would provide them with the levels of security and prosperity that the West enjoyed. Western policy makers in turn used the institutions to guarantee a root-and-branch reform of these countries' security sectors and domestic political economies.

Since the Central and Eastern Europeans greatly desired to join well-established organizations, there was no real negotiation over the terms of membership. NATO and EU officials were given free rein to roam the halls of former Warsaw Pact countries' ministries to impose Brussels's rules and recreate new structures in its likeness. Aspiring members had to adopt the existing rules in order to join the club.

## THREAT PERCEPTION

The use of these organizations for the stabilization of Eastern Europe did come at a cost, for which the reckoning is now coming due. Even if Russia had become a market democracy and sought membership (which, of course, it did not), NATO and the EU would not have been able to absorb such a large country with the multiplicity of economic, social, and security problems that would have come with it—unless the institutions were to change dramatically to accommodate that challenge. But the basic premise of NATO and EU enlargement was that the rules were not negotiable. Further, the use of the institutions for a stabilization program for all of postcommunist Europe except Russia created the impression that they were continuing their original purpose of containing Soviet/Russian influence through new, more modern means.

Because Russia could not be integrated like other postcommunist states, both sides pursued a policy of what might be called "partnership without membership." This policy did create a dense fabric of interaction between Russia and the West. It came in forms such as the NATO-Russia Council and the EU-Russia "strategic partnership," involving everything from twice-yearly summits at the presidential level to highly technical regulatory convergence efforts. There was also a wide variety of pan-European structures created in part to serve as a bridge to Russia: the Organization for Security and Cooperation in Europe (OSCE); the Conventional Forces in Europe Treaty; the Vienna Document (a confidence- and security-building regime); and the Open Skies Treaty, which provides for military transparency through observation flights. While these arrangements never fully satisfied either side, they formed, until the Ukraine crisis, a cornerstone of the European institutional order by providing multiple forums for increased dialogue, interaction, and cooperation with NATO's only potential adversary in Europe.

The goal of the partnership without membership model was easy to understand, though difficult to achieve. As its relationships with the Western institutions broadened and deepened, Russia would gradually develop into a globally integrated market democracy, and, crucially, it would no longer view the enlargement of these institutions as a threat. By increasing the quality and quantity of interaction with Russia, the West hoped Moscow would come to see the membership of its neighbors in Euro-Atlantic institutions as beneficial to Russia.

The risk inherent to the model was that it offered no contingency plan if things did not turn out the way its designers hoped. Initially, it seemed as though there was no need to plan for the worst during the period of increased cooperation and high hopes in the early years of the Putin presidency, and particularly following 9/11. The Putin of that period used rhetoric that might shock us if he were to use it today. Speaking to the BBC in March 2000, he said, "Russia is a part of European culture. I simply cannot see my country isolated from Europe, from what we often describe as the civilized world. That is why it is hard for me to regard NATO as an enemy. . . . We believe that it is possible to speak even about higher levels of integration with NATO. But only, I repeat, if Russia is an equal partner." Asked if Russia could join NATO, Putin responded, "Why not?"

Soon after that period, the relationship started to unravel. Russia's increasingly autocratic governance was a factor in this process, but far more important was the widening chasm in perceptions of regional integration. Even when the West and Russia were successfully cooperating on shared threats and challenges, from Afghanistan to nonproliferation to counterterrorism, Moscow still viewed Euro-Atlantic integration for Russia's neighbors as inherently threatening to its interests.

To Russia, this threat perception seemed uncontroversial—its neighbors were gradually being incorporated into political-economic and security blocs that Russia itself could not join. Regardless of the intentions of these countries or the blocs, such a move was bound to be threatening to the excluded state. But to the West, Moscow was denying its neighbors the right to make their own choices on foreign and security policy, which was disturbingly reminiscent of the Soviet Union's attitude toward the Warsaw Pact countries. This remains the fundamental chasm dividing the two sides: a regional integration project that, while not intended as an anti-Russian effort by its authors or the states that aspire to membership, Russia cannot (and does not desire to) join.

An action-reaction spiral set in, whereby EU/ NATO moves to the East and Russian countermoves would serve only to escalate the confrontation. In April 2008, NATO's Bucharest summit declaration proclaimed that Ukraine and Georgia "will become" members of the alliance. In August 2008, Russia invaded Georgia and recognized its two breakaway regions as independent states.

Later that year, the EU launched the Eastern Partnership, an enhanced economic and political offering to Moldova, Ukraine, Belarus, Georgia, Armenia, and Azerbaijan—but not Russia. Meanwhile, Russia championed its own regional security and economic integration projects, which took the form of the Collective Security Treaty Organization and the Eurasian Economic Union.

## NIGHTMARE SCENARIO

The Ukraine crisis began in the context of this contest for influence in what Europe and Russia used to call their "common neighborhood." In late November 2013, the Ukrainian government called off preparations to sign an Association Agreement with the EU, the key "deliverable" of the Eastern Partnership. Negotiations on these accords had closely conformed to the past practice of institutional enlargement, even if no immediate prospect of membership was offered in this case. Aspirant countries were expected to adopt EU norms and regulations wholesale in return for trade liberalization, visa facilitation, and closer political association. Instead, under pressure from Putin, President Viktor Yanukovych reversed his plan to sign the agreement, days before he was scheduled to do so at a major EU summit.

In the following days, several thousand Ukrainians came out to protest Yanukovych's about-face on Kiev's central Maidan Nezalezhnosti, or Independence Square. These peaceful, unarmed protests would likely have petered out had they been allowed to run their course. On the night of November 30, however, someone in the government—as yet unidentified—made the decision to use force against unarmed student protesters. The next day, upwards of 500,000 people rallied where there had been only 10,000 before. Despite the EU flags on the Maidan in November, the protests were now about overthrowing Yanukovych's corrupt authoritarian regime. Beginning with that first use of force, the government and the radical avant-garde of the protesters (mostly armed far-right nationalist groups) engaged in an escalatory spiral of violence.

On February 21, Yanukovych and opposition leaders signed an agreement, brokered by EU foreign ministers and Russia, intended to end the crisis. It called for returning to the 2004 constitution with limits on presidential powers, holding early elections, and ending the occupations of streets and buildings. However, the agreement collapsed immediately as Yanukovych fled the capital (and eventually left the country) while his government disintegrated. In these extraordinary circumstances, the parliament took extraconstitutional action and voted on February 22 to remove him from office and install a new government.

While the West celebrated a democratic breakthrough, the Kremlin saw these events as the latest in a series of regime change efforts meant to undermine its influence. These fears were reinforced by the composition of the new Ukrainian cabinet. A third of its top officials (ministers and above) came from the far-right and virulently anti-Russian Svoboda party, and 60 percent hailed from the four former Hapsburg provinces in the west of the country, the historical hotbed of Ukrainian nationalism. Putin and his inner circle seem to have concluded that the collapse of the February 21 agreement resulted at least in part from a Western plot to install a loyal government in Kiev—one that included far-right leaders who threatened to revoke Russia's basing agreement in Crimea, quickly move Ukraine toward EU and NATO membership, and cut the bilateral links on which Russia's energy and military-industrial sectors depend.

In the final days of February, when Putin decided to insert special forces, paratroopers, and other servicemen into Crimea, he sought to prevent a strategic setback in Kiev from becoming a strategic catastrophe: Russia's nightmare scenario of being completely pushed out of Ukraine by the West and its institutions. His decision was intended to secure the most important Russian physical assets in Ukraine, namely the Black Sea Fleet base at Sevastopol, and to coerce the new Ukrainian authorities into accommodating Moscow's broader interests in the country. That action and the subsequent efforts to destabilize eastern Ukraine were driven by a perceived need to guarantee that the nightmare scenario will not come to pass. As Putin himself put it during an interview in late May:

> I will reiterate: where are the guarantees that the coup d'état, this second color revolution that happened in Ukraine, won't be followed by NATO's arrival in Ukraine? Nobody has ever discussed this issue with us in the past two decades. I'd like to emphasize that nobody has conducted a meaningful dialogue with us on this. All we heard was the same reply, like a broken record: Every nation has the right to determine the security system it wants to live in and this has nothing to do with you.

While Russia's gambit in Ukraine has yet to play itself out as of this writing, its actions there have already relegated the partnership without membership paradigm in Western-Russian relations to the dustbin of history. A whole host of institutional arrangements involving Russia has been effectively gutted. Even if the conflict in Ukraine itself can be quickly ended, the confrontation between Russia and the West will remain. This presents serious risks for the stability of Europe.

## RAISING THE RISKS

The Ukrainian tragedy notwithstanding, the key question for European security remains what to do about the relationship with Russia. While it might be tempting to simply put aside the disputes of the past in the name of moving forward, these disputes are very much at the core of what divides Russia and the West today. They need to be addressed if we hope to avoid long-term confrontation.

In response to Russian actions in Ukraine, the emerging Western strategy is threefold: to assist and deepen integration with the new Ukrainian government and Russia's other vulnerable neighbors; to sanction and isolate Russia; and to reassure Central and Eastern European NATO members. Effectively, the West has doubled down on the institutional enlargement policy, reinforcing previous gains and expanding the institutions' reach farther East—Ukraine, Georgia, and Moldova have now all signed Association Agreements with the EU. It is clear that Russia will see these efforts not as a response to its actions in Ukraine but as an opportunistic continuation of the same post–Cold War policy that it has long decried as a threat to its security interests. This strategy has the benefit of being responsive to the politics of the moment and morally justified. However, it seems destined to deepen the confrontation. A newly assertive Russia is likely to continue to push back against enlargement, and the cycle of action and reaction will continue.

Under these circumstances, providing new NATO security guarantees or EU membership to ever more vulnerable states on Russia's borders raises the risks of a direct conflict with Moscow. And it is nearly impossible for the West to make good on security guarantees for these countries. Russia has made clear that it views keeping Euro-Atlantic institutions out of its neighborhood as a vital interest, while Europe and the United States do not view the security of Russia's neighbors as fundamental to their interests.

During the Cold War, many questioned whether the United States would sacrifice New York to defend Berlin. Today, few if any believe that it would do so for Kiev. In the event of a showdown, Washington would face a choice between transgressing heretofore sacrosanct security guarantees or risking war with a major nuclear power. Are the principles at stake—the right of every country to make its own foreign policy choices and freely choose its own alliances—really worth either of these outcomes? This question has been asked regarding previous rounds of enlargement; the difference today is that Russia has proved its willingness to act and thus demonstrated that this is no longer a rhetorical question.

Avoiding that unpalatable choice will require recognizing that the post–Cold War policy of institutional enlargement, despite its successes, has run its course. The West's continuing insistence that the only path to stability and security in Europe is for Russia's neighbors to be absorbed into Euro-Atlantic institutions is now begetting threats to stability and security in Europe.

## A NEW DEAL

Acknowledging that fact does not mean that the West must accept Russian domination of its sovereign neighbors. Instead, new arrangements are needed that are acceptable to both the West and Russia. Achieving such a deal is possible, but it will require both sides to compromise. The West would have to accept that the model that worked so well in Central and Eastern Europe will not work for the rest of the continent; institutional arrangements will have to be acceptable to Russia in order for them to succeed. Russia would have to strictly adhere to the limits such new arrangements would impose on its influence in the region, and forswear military intervention in the affairs of its neighbors.

Achieving such a bargain in the current atmosphere of mutual mistrust and recrimination will be extremely difficult. But it is not impossible. The first step is for the West to adopt a compromise along these lines as its long-term goal. The policy response to the current crisis should then be structured around achieving that goal. This does not mean that the West should simply accommodate Russian demands—the proposed bargain requires Russia to make difficult compromises too. Negotiations will likely have to be combined with elements of coercion in order to succeed. Such a strategy would offer Russia a path toward security in its neighborhood without confrontation with the West, but it would also entail isolation and confrontation if Russia refuses to agree to the new bargain.

In practical terms, sanctions must be accompanied by an offer to negotiate new institutional arrangements. Such an offer would not be unprecedented. In 2009, then–Russian President Dmitri Medvedev put forth a very similar proposal in the form of a draft European Security Treaty. The document was certainly flawed, but it was grounded in widely accepted principles such as respect for sovereignty, territorial integrity, and political independence, as well as the renunciation of the use of force.

The dismissive Western response to the proposal stemmed from concern that it was intended to undermine NATO and the EU. Even the relatively Russia-friendly German Foreign Minister Frank-Walter Steinmeier felt the need to emphasize that any discussion of European security could not challenge existing institutions. He declared, "[T]o avoid any possible ambiguity: The EU, NATO and the OSCE remain the cornerstones of European security. . . . What has taken us decades to build is not up for discussion." But it was specifically those cornerstones that Russia wanted to discuss. This time both sides will need to demonstrate a willingness to enter into negotiations without such taboos or other preconditions.

This is a policy of necessity, and so it is difficult for any Western leader to embrace publicly. It is abhorrent to many even to contemplate compromising the principles of enlargement that contributed to the successful transitions in Central and Eastern Europe. But the alternative is a confrontation with Russia that the West does not want, in order to uphold principles that it will ultimately be unwilling to defend.

## CRITICAL THINKING QUESTIONS

1. Can Russia be a normal partner?
2. How responsible was the United States and the West for the Ukraine crisis? How responsible was Russia?
3. How great is the danger of a new cold war?

# 8

# Fighting the Last War

*As president of Colombia, Álvaro Uribe triumphed over a fierce narco-insurgency. Then the U.S. helped to export his strategy to Mexico and throughout Latin America. Here's why it's not working.*

Elizabeth Dickinson

The sun was barely setting over a colonial villa in rural central Colombia as Álvaro Uribe Vélez, by any measure Colombia's most transformative modern president, recited lines of poetry to a small crowd beside a courtyard fountain. The former head of state, who left office in August 2010, projects the air of a financier in his official portraits. But today he was dressed like a *paisa*—with a traditional sombrero, a white handmade cloth draped over his shoulder, and a walking stick given to him by citizens of a nearby town.

On that perfect summer evening in early July, Uribe liked one particular verse—about a beautiful woman with enchanting eyes—so much that he recited it over and over to the dozens of locals seated in a circle around him. Also in the audience was the Colombian celebrity Catalina Maya, an actress and model, who sat perched on an armchair, her body twisted over its back to regard Uribe. Women and girls were crammed onto the villa's steps, and housemaids pretended to continue working as they peeked for glances at the ex-president, who every so often locked eyes with a new member of the crowd.

Álvaro Uribe is a well-loved man. During the eight years in which he led Colombia, he won the hearts of millions of his countrymen, from those in small villages to the most elite urban circles. And the reason why these millions adore Uribe largely boils down to one word: security. Uribe still casts a powerful spell over his former constituents because he used his time in office to smash a four-decades-old guerrilla insurgency with an overwhelming show of force—and in so doing made countless Colombians' lives immeasurably safer.

When Uribe took office in 2002, Colombia was the murder and kidnap capital of the world, the source of nearly all global cocaine, and an economic

Elizabeth Dickinson is a freelance journalist. She previously served as assistant managing editor of *Foreign Policy* magazine and Nigeria correspondent for *The Economist*.

weakling. The government had staggered through four decades of armed conflict with leftist rebels, most notably the Revolutionary Armed Forces of Colombia (FARC), and had tried everything—even negotiations—to end the strife. Nothing seemed to work until Uribe came along. Unlike previous presidents, Uribe believed—and managed to convince the country—that if Colombia fought with all its military might against the guerrillas, it could win. Determined to make a hard break from the past, he ended a fraught peace process that his predecessor had initiated with the rebels. Then he dispatched tens of thousands of troops to retake control of Colombian soil, focusing on securing the cities and highways. Uribe found an eager partner in the United States, which supplied state-of-the-art weapons and intelligence to aid in the dismantling of armed groups. Eventually, he also convinced the United Autodefense Forces of Colombia (AUC)—a private paramilitary force of some 30,000 fighters that had emerged to protect local elites and landowners from the guerrillas, only to become just as wrapped up in drugs and violence as its enemies—to demobilize.

By the time Uribe was reelected in 2006, a conflict that had long threatened to break the Colombian state suddenly seemed as if it might be drawing to an end. The murder rate had fallen by 45 percent, and the kidnapping rate—which hovered near 3,000 people per year in 2002—plummeted more than fourfold. Even drug interdictions were up to the point that traffickers started looking for alternative routes into the United States (through Mexico) and Europe (through West Africa). By the end of his second term, Uribe began talking about "the end of the end" of the guerrillas.

Colombia's incredible turnaround and the strategy credited with bringing it about have become not only a rare success story in the drug war, but also its most formidable brand and export. The governments of Mexico and several other Central American countries that have been plunged into violent confrontation with drug gangs have tried assiduously to replicate their South American peer's strategy. With U.S. support, Mexico has deployed troops, militarized its police, and fought tooth and nail to regain control of its farthest-flung states. Honduras, which has the world's highest murder rate, and Guatemala are flying in Colombian experts to advise them. Even in far-away conflicts such as Afghanistan, U.S. policy makers have looked for a model in the Andes.

There are two problems, however. The first is that none of these places, despite years of effort, has yet seen the kind of transformation that Uribe brought about in Colombia. In fact, so far, the momentum runs in the opposite direction. The case of Mexico is particularly striking; roughly 50,000 lives have been lost since the country's experiment with a Colombian-style militarized drug war began in 2006. The Citizen's Council for Public Security in Mexico recently estimated the kidnapping rate at three times that of Colombia's darkest days. Cartels are growing more sophisticated and violent, not less, despite the numerous leaders the government has picked off. By November 2011, 80 percent of the population polled by the public opinion firm Consulta Mitofsky said they believed security to be worse than just a year ago. A mere 14 percent believed that the government could beat the drug gangs.

The second problem is that, in Colombia itself, Uribe's strategy has reached a point of sharply diminishing returns. Having largely defeated what was, at bottom, a sweeping leftist insurgency against the state, and having decapitated a relatively cohesive paramilitary force, Colombia now faces a hydra-headed, apolitical, essentially criminal set of groups vying for turf and control over what's left of the drug trade. None of these groups is as powerful as its precursors, but nor do they seem to be susceptible to the same strategic countermeasures. And violence is starting to drift upward. "If you look at the trend lines on homicides and kidnapping, it looks like a backwards J," explains Adam Isacson, director of the Regional Security Policy Program at the Washington Office on Latin America. "They drop really sharply from 2002 to 2006, then there's a stagnation. In 2008 and 2009 several of those measures start to creep back up again."

The idea that sheer military might and political will can beat back the narcotics trade is a powerful one. Uribe's ideas and tactics have spread to every corner of the globe marred by the drug trade and nearly every institution that is fighting organized crime. Which means that if those ideas are misguided—or, perhaps more dangerously, misunderstood—then so too is nearly every fight in the drug war.

On the day of his visit to the countryside, Uribe woke well before dawn, driving off in his motorcade at six a.m. to make the three-hour trip from Medellín to a small mountain town called Támesis. On the winding road through alternating alpine coffee fields and orange trees in the tropical plains, Uribe pointed out the results of his time in office. "During the first years of my presidency, I received news twice a day about this road and kidnappings," he told me. "Eight years ago, it was impossible to cross."

Now almost sixty, Uribe speaks in a voice that is at once brash and familiar. When he talks—as he does almost constantly—his words come out as simple sentences, clean and well crafted without an extraneous word. His considerable charisma is of an austere variety. He doesn't smoke or drink, which is unusual in a country proud of its rabblerousing parties. He is famously demanding, but often refuses to delegate. While in office, he won a reputation for calling his force commanders' cell phones at five a.m. when he wanted an update. "Security policy needs strong direction," he told me as we drove.

Behind Uribe's sense of conviction, and his public persona, is a harrowing personal history. While most of Colombia's presidents have come from a small group of Bogota elite, Uribe came from the countryside, where his family lived in intimate proximity to the country's endemic violence. His father was killed by FARC guerrillas in 1983 on the family farm, not far from Támesis, when Uribe was thirty-one years old. Uribe dedicated his presidency to making sure the guerrillas paid for his loss—and the losses of so many of his countrymen. Many Colombians seem to regard him with the kind of gratitude you might reserve for someone who has pulled you back from the edge of a cliff.

As Uribe made his way by car from Medellín, hundreds of people from the countryside around Támesis were converging on a sniper-guarded gymnasium in the town, where the former president was scheduled to take part in a meeting of local civic leaders. Just after ten a.m., a tanned coffee farmer named Pedro Antonio Restrepo sat expectantly crouched near the edge of the bleachers there, his skin crinkled from years working outside in the sun. His eyes were wide with excitement. "I am an enemy of politics 100 percent," Restrepo told me. "But I had to come to see Uribe."

A decade ago, Restrepo lived under the gun. His land fell under the purview of the paramilitaries, which ran a mafia-like protection racket in the area. While their official name, the United Autodefense Forces of Colombia, suggested that these armed groups were a cohesive liberating force, freeing the countryside of the guerrillas that had pillaged, kidnapped, and massacred for so long, the paramilitaries had become as oppressive and dependent on the drug trade as FARC. Restrepo paid "taxes" to that local regime. If he didn't have the cash, the paramilitaries who knocked on his door would wait, guns in hand. "Go to town and sell a bag of coffee to get the money," they would tell him.

When Uribe came into office, his security strategy began with the recognition that the paramilitaries and guerrillas were taking advantage of the many spaces in his country—places like Restrepo's coffee-farming community—where the state simply didn't have a presence. If Uribe wanted to eliminate these illicit networks, Colombia needed to impose sovereignty over its own territories. It had to go in with troops, smash the rebel or paramilitary presence, and establish control. Then, with the rebels chased to the bush, the military assault would shade into a regime of police patrols and institutions—in a word, a state. He called his strategy "democratic security." (If he had crafted it later, after the U.S. wars in Iraq and Afghanistan, perhaps Uribe would have simply called it counterinsurgency, or COIN.)

The task Uribe had set before himself was essentially one of nation building, something he knew would be neither cheap nor easy. Making aggressive use of American aid was essential. Uribe's predecessor had already secured a $1.4 billion aid package from the United States as part of the Plan Colombia policy, a legacy of the Clinton era; the new president worked to make it his own. "Plan Colombia was essentially an antidrug policy," explains Michael Shifter, president of the Washington-based Inter-American Dialogue. "The trick in the Colombian case was to take aid intended to go after the drug war and to use it in a much more rational way: to build the strength of the state." The whole aid package eventually grew to the size of $8 billion.

Uribe found a willing and like-minded partner in George W. Bush, who often referred to the Colombian president as "mi amigo." A true coproduction of American aid and Colombian strategy, Uribe's "democratic security" became the centerpiece of the U.S. government's international counternarcotics plan. America supplied helicopters, weapons, intelligence equipment, expertise, and military trainers, and even footed some of the bill for gas. It also helped fund new military and police brigades created specifically to root out traffickers and interdict drugs. The military streamed into every corner of the country, burning cocaine labs and catching guerrilla leaders in its path. One of the biggest legacies of Uribe's time in office is sheer military manpower: today there are nearly 270,000 soldiers patrolling the country, as well as 162,000 police officers—meaning that the total number of security forces has been bumped up by more than 100,000 people since 2002.

As the aid poured in, Colombia reciprocated by going out of its way to cooperate with U.S. goals. In a move that would have made many South American governments squirm, Colombia let the United States vet and polygraph certain military recruits. Even more controversially, between 2002 and 2008 Colombia extradited 951 of its citizens to face criminal charges in the United States. Previous presidents had balked at foisting off their problems, and citizens, on a foreign justice system; Uribe embraced it. On American soil, the suspects often found themselves locked up on trafficking convictions with stiff sentences. Frequently, this was helpful for Uribe—his government was relieved of having to try some of its most contentious and despicable cases—but it also meant that many of the perpetrators of Colombia's worst human rights violations, including massacres, murders, and rapes, would likely never be held accountable for those crimes at home.

According to his critics, this wasn't the only compromise Uribe made on human rights in his all-or-nothing quest to quash the guerrillas. In October 2008, for example, it emerged that the Colombian military—under intense pressure to crack down on FARC—had been murdering civilians to boost its body count. (Declassified CIA files have since revealed that the practice of killing "false positives" dates back as far as a decade before Uribe's term.) In rural areas too, there were concerns that the military's all-out assaults on the guerrillas were displacing and killing far too many civilians. To this day, Colombia is home to the largest single population of internally displaced people—between 3.5 and 5 million in a population of 46 million. Union and community leaders have also been targeted by armed groups of every sort for their activism, and Uribe, in his brash style, often came off as complacent about this fact, or even complicit. "Uribe called us terrorists," remembers Franklin Castañeda, a spokesman for the country's National Victims' Movement. That kind of rhetoric made their activists targets of paramilitaries eager to weed out any potential leftist or guerilla influence. A number of U.S. senators and congressmen raised concerns about human rights abuses, and for five years they held up a free trade agreement with Colombia because of it. But others in the U.S. government were more interested in the dramatic reversal that Colombia seemed to be pulling off—and the example it might set for a world of newly troubled battlegrounds. By 2009, homicides in the country were down 40 percent, kidnappings were down more than 80 percent, and terror attacks were down 75 percent. "I know that Plan Colombia was controversial. I was just in Colombia, and there were problems and there were mistakes, but it worked," U.S. Secretary of State Hillary Clinton commented a month after Uribe left office. "And we need to figure out what are the equivalents for Central America, Mexico, and the Caribbean."

Today, Restrepo says that the paramilitaries in his area are gone—a fact he attributes to the former president's security policy. After I interviewed him at the gym in Támesis, he beseeched me to thank Uribe for him. "If there's any way that you can relay the message," he pleaded. When I later pointed him out in the crowd to Uribe, Restrepo's smile glowed with bashful pride.

Many of the Uribe government's admirers today are in Central America and the Caribbean, where a new front of the drug war is roaring, and again, U.S. counter-narcotics assistance is ratcheting up. There's a tremendous amount of interaction between Colombia and these countries, says Shifter of the Inter-American Dialogue. "If you talk to the ambassadors here, they'll tell you that there's just a lot of Colombians coming through and playing a helpful role."

For America's neighbor to the south, Uribe's success story is particularly of interest. Speak with Mexican analysts of almost any political stripe about the drug war these days, as I did on a recent trip to Mexico, and Colombia almost always comes up. Mexico, it is often said, is passing through the same difficult phase that its Andean peer overcame. "I do think it would be possible to lower the violence—look at what happened in Colombia," Arturo Borja, an economist at Mexico's Center for Economic Research and Instruction, told me. "In Colombia, they resolved the problem of violence and took away the power that the drug-trafficking organizations had. . . . [Colombia was] a fragile state in the 1980s and 1990s, but now they've turned things around."

In many ways, that sense of admiration has led to imitation. Indeed, when Mexico's president, Felipe Calderón, explained his strategy to the *New York Times* in October it read like a page straight from a "democratic security" handbook. "Essentially, our strategy has three main components," he said. "The first is to fight, debilitate, and neutralize armed groups. . . . [T]he second component is more important, which is the recuperation of the institutions of security and justice such as the police, the public ministers, the judges. . . . [T]he third element is the reconstruction of the social fabric [in a] society marked by a lack of opportunities."

The tactics are similar as well. Much as Uribe did with the Colombian military, over the last four years the administration of President Calderón has dispatched 50,000 soldiers across the country to break up organized crime. He has also upped extraditions to the United States and tried to rebuild the country's army and police forces. Colombia is even training Mexican policemen and prosecutors, based on their decades of experience fighting the war on drugs. The United States, keen on these changes, has begun to help Mexico in many of the ways it did Colombia: with intelligence, law enforcement expertise and training, and equipment.

On June 8, 2011, the governor of Chihuahua—Mexico's most violent state—welcomed Uribe to Ciudad Juarez, ground zero for the drug war, and vowed to follow the Colombian model in cracking down on organized crime. In office, Uribe was a vocal supporter of Mexico and Calderón; now he writes in their favor on his prolific Twitter feed. The two presidents signed an accord in 2009 affirming their commitment to ending organized crime.

And yet, for his trouble, Calderón has wound up with crashing public approval ratings and a growing protest movement that has questioned his tactics. It's not hard to see why. Elevating casualty figures have topped 50,000 over the last five years, and states that never saw significant cartels before are now falling like dominoes to the drug lords. The violence has also taken a particularly gruesome turn; bodies often turn up mutilated, bearing messages of warning for anyone who dares cross the assailants' paths, said Antonio Mazzitelli, head of the U.N. Office of Drugs and Crime in Mexico City. "In Mexico—and this is unique—those criminal organizations are using violence . . . with the aim of terrorizing and sending a clear message to everybody: 'Here we rule, and if you don't abide by my rule, this is what's going to happen to you.'" Journalists and human rights activists who ask troubling questions are often among the first targets for armed groups.

Why has Mexico's experiment in *Uribismo* fared so poorly? One way to answer that question is to take a closer look at how "democratic security" has worked out over the long run in Colombia—and, more importantly, how it hasn't.

Uribe left Támesis by midafternoon that day in July, stopping to make a surprise visit in another small town on the way back to the city. After nightfall, on the last leg of the drive back to Medellín in his motorcade, a radio report relayed the dispiriting news that FARC had just bombed a rural police station. The report was consistent with the group's newfound penchant for low-cost, high-impact terrorist attacks.

By the time Uribe left office, FARC had been forced to go back to the drawing board. Driven out of urban areas, short on manpower, and increasingly reliant on narcotics trafficking, the group's then leader, Alfonso Cano, decided that FARC couldn't contest the Colombian military anymore. So the group returned to its terrorist origins, undertaking high-profile attacks executed by small cells of guerrilla fighters called *pisa suaves*, or "light-treading" units. In other words, the government's all-out war on FARC was a success, but a qualified one. "It was very effective—democratic security and the U.S. assistance with Plan Colombia—against a guerrilla force made up of entities resembling an [army] battalion," says León Valencia, executive director of the Colombian think tank Nuevo Arco Iris, which released a study on FARC last August. Now the rebels have adapted—but the government's strategy largely has not. In the first six months of 2011, FARC undertook 10 percent more military operations than they did in the previous year, many of them headline-making massacres and bombings.

Still, setting FARC back by more than a decade, and sending it packing into the jungles, is undeniable progress. It is the vacuum created by the formal dissolution of Colombia's paramilitary force, the AUC, that has sent parts of the country into wrenching bouts of instability. In a complex demobilization process aimed at disbanding militias of some 35,000 men between 2003 and

2007, Colombia attained visible success in clearing out the upper ranks of the paramilitaries. Top leaders were often extradited to the United States to face tough, drug-related sentences. But when it came to draining the middle and lower ranks, the results were more murky. A significant number of the fighters, it is widely believed, simply returned to their work under new, criminal auspices. Others passed the reins to relatives or friends, leaving illicit networks essentially intact. What's clear is that Colombia, once riven by clashes between FARC and the AUC, has seen a wild proliferation of smaller violent groups that behave very differently from their forebears.

Where there was once a single, cohesive political entity representing paramilitary groups—the AUC—there are now innumerable criminal bands competing over the same objective: to terrorize their way into controlling the drug trade. Like the paramilitaries before them, they thrive when they can infiltrate local governments and become territorial barons. But unlike the paramilitaries, these new groups have neither political aims nor ideologies to control or direct their violence. They have even been known to make alliances with FARC when convenient.

In Medellín, I met a middle-aged woman named Doli Posada who described this new landscape. "There are so many people who are afraid to leave their neighborhoods these days," she told me, referring to the barrios that creep up from the mountainous city's high line. In the community where she lives, her neighbors are being asked, once again, to pay armed groups taxes to provide "security." After a few brief years of calm, today they feel anything but safe. According to many accounts, violence in the barrios took off when Medellín's once dominant crime boss, a former paramilitary known as "Don Berna" (his real name was Diego Fernando Murillo Bejarano)—was extradited to the U.S. in 2008. After Uribe's military had beaten back FARC, Don Berna had been able to solidify his control over the city and pacify it. Now that he's gone, new, smaller gangs have sprung up to fight over who gets to fill the vacuum. "By seriously crippling the competing guerrillas, the government had given a monopoly to Don Berna," wrote Francis Fukuyama and Seth Colby in a recent article in *Foreign Policy* magazine. "It was peace achieved through market dominance, not demilitarization."

And the problems are not just in Medellín. An hour's flight from Bogota, on the Pacific coast, the town of Buenaventura is reeling. During the height of summer, gangs held frequent gun battles to control several of the barrios that have access to the ocean in this seaside port town—the knotted creeks of the coastline are perfect for getting cocaine out of the country fast. In the licit markets too, prices here are much higher than in even the posh areas of Bogota, and the armed gangs control *every* market, from cocaine all the way to eggs, milk, and ripe plantains.

To make matters worse, many of these mid-level criminals with roots in the paramilitaries have a long history of infiltrating and co-opting local governments. For years, the paramilitaries' political aims conveniently aligned with those of the state: both groups wanted to defeat the guerrillas. So in many places, the price for security gains against FARC was a blind eye toward paramilitary criminal networks. By 2006, the AUC had become so powerful and so influential that its fingerprints were everywhere in the state itself. High-level representatives, including governors, congressmen, senators, and mayors, had all signed electoral pacts with the AUC that year, with the paramilitaries promising to guarantee a certain number of votes in exchange for influence with the new candidates in office. "When you have that level of penetration, demobilization isn't going to work completely," says Eduardo Salcedo-Albarán, a political scientist who worked as a consultant for an anti-corruption commission during Uribe's tenure and is coauthor of the forthcoming book *Drug Trafficking, Corruption, and States*. "You can't destroy all the relationships."

Officially, the government of Colombia doesn't buy into the story that remnants of the paramilitaries have become the new torment of the nation. The government calls the post-AUC groups "BACRIM" (an acronym for *"bandas criminales emergentes,"* or "emerging criminal bands")—a categorization that portrays them as separate from the past. Joshua Mitrotti Ventura, general manager of the current president's high council for reintegration, says that less than 10 percent of BACRIM members who have been apprehended can be traced back to the demobilization process: "The BACRIM don't necessarily correspond with the AUC; the majority are new people."

Yet Uribe saw the BACRIM coming, according to an American diplomatic cable released by WikiLeaks that recounts a conversation he had with the U.S. embassy back in 2004. "Uribe speculated that splinter groups of narcotrafficking organizations will follow in the wake of the paramilitaries," the document says. And when I asked him about the BACRIM in November, he acknowledged the link to demobilization in an e-mail: "In accordance with police reports, 11 percent of BACRIM members and 50 percent of kingpins come from demobilized people." Then and now, Uribe believed that the same military strategy could combat these new groups. "I consider that these organizations must be confronted the same as Colombia does against narco terrorist guerrillas," he wrote to me in November.

Yet a traditional military solution would seem profoundly ill-suited to this new threat. The Colombian research institute Indepaz estimates that the various BACRIM groups, which have emerged and multiplied at a rapid clip, claimed 7,100 fighters in 360 municipalities by the end of 2010. In cities like Buenaventura, the gang names are so numerous that residents have stopped trying to learn them. Worse, they are integrated into civilian populations, meaning that no blunt military instrument can flush them out. "The BACRIM have more access and ability to operate in population centers," explains the Washington Office on Latin America's Adam Isacson. "They are far more able to infiltrate at the local level."

Across many of Colombia's cities and towns, the violence looks less like the end and more like a new beginning of conflict. "Lots of people think that Uribe ended the paramilitaries, that narcotics trafficking went down," says Salcedo. "But when you look, it's really only been a reconfiguration [of the armed conflict]."

To be sure, this reconfiguration has been kind to many Colombians in many parts of the country, especially elites, who no longer fear that FARC is about to topple the state. But residents in parts of Medellín and Buenaventura, among other places, now say that the calm of the mid-2000s was little more than a cruel illusion. "There is permanent dispute for control" of the narcotics trafficking routes, says Victor Hugo Vidal, an activist for the Process of Black Communities working and living in Buenaventura. "When that fight for dominance is ongoing, the violence increases. And when someone becomes dominant, the violence goes down."

Colombia is still objectively less violent than it was ten years ago, but the statistics are beginning to slip. In the first three months of 2011, 8,245 people were displaced by fighting—1,000 more people than had been displaced in the entire previous year. Most of the displacement took place along the Pacific coast, increasingly the hub of drug trafficking, and hence armed group, activity. And Medellín's homicide rate has doubled since 2007. Among the most ghoulish indicators of new trouble in Colombia is the rate at which criminal gangs are picking off human rights defenders. The activists—or anyone who speaks out against crime—have become a nuisance to the armed groups. And their deaths are reminiscent of nothing so much as the slaughter of journalists, family members of victims, and other activists in Mexico.

At a very basic level, Colombia circa 2002 faced a very different set of problems than what Mexico faces today—and Uribe's "democratic security" strategy was tailored to the former. Drug trafficking was linked to an armed insurgency that, however corrupted over the years, still rested on an ideology and concrete political goals. FARC and the paramilitaries both cared about territory for its own sake. Mexican cartels, on the other hand, are less bothered by symbolic gains and are happy to operate near or even within state institutions.

The very natures of the two states are different as well. "Colombia had never been in control of its territory, so the real challenge was to assert state authority for the first time," explains Shannon O'Neil of the Council on Foreign Relations. "In Mexico, that's not the problem. The government has a presence in every small municipality; the question is, who do they report to? It's a very different challenge; Mexico's challenge is corruption."

Mexican institutions are hollowed out in a way that Colombia's never were. Colombia's police are national, and were never terribly corrupt. The 400,000-strong police force in Mexico is divided between federal, state, and local jurisdictions, and the closer to the ground you get, the more the drug cartels have been able to infiltrate. Often unpaid, underequipped, and terrified by the security situation, the local police take bribes or work as informants. "The infiltration of cartels is everywhere," says Walter McKay, a former Canadian policeman who has worked for the last three years as a consultant on security reform in Mexico. "It's not just in the police. The entire apple is rotten." When I corresponded with him in November, Uribe acknowledged Mexico's challenges on this front.

Indeed, while Colombia was building institutions from zero in many of its most desperate communities, Mexico urgently needs to cleanse its state—a task that is impossible when it's that very state that the government is trying to defend. "It's as if you are fighting with your enemy only to realize halfway that the arm you're using isn't working," explains Eduardo Guerrero, a political analyst and former advisor to the Mexican presidency. Calderón's response has been to circumvent these troubled institutions by creating a federal police force that is more than 30,000 strong and heavily vetted to be clear of illicit ties.

In recent months, Guerrero has produced striking evidence of the mechanics of why military tactics are failing to stop—and perhaps are even exacerbating—the conflict in Mexico. One of the major tactics of the Calderón administration has been to decapitate the cartels, much as Uribe did with major FARC and paramilitary leaders. Yet just as the paramilitaries did, the cartels have reacted to the loss of their leaders by fragmenting, rather than disappearing. In 2006, there were just six major cartels operating in Mexico; by 2010 that number had doubled, wrote Guerrero in *Nexos* magazine in June. Local trafficking organizations exploded during the same time frame, from eleven to 114. Unsurprisingly, nearly every crime indicator—from kidnapping to theft to murder—also went up during that time.

In other words, for all the differences between the problems Uribe faced when he took office in 2002 and the problems Calderón started tackling in 2006, the violent challenges that threaten both countries right now are increasingly similar. And in both places, these are the very threats that have proven resistant to military solutions. Yet at exactly the moment when this orgy of violence is spreading, the United States and Mexico are looking to up the ante on the current tactics. As America's role is winding down in Colombia, its role in security is being ratcheted up in Mexico, through the Merida Initiative, to fight the drug war there. The United States is training Mexican forces, providing them with helicopters, and helping with wiretaps. This summer, for the first time ever, officers from the Central Intelligence Agency started to work with the Mexican authorities—in Mexico—to organize and plan countercartel operations.

Perhaps this U.S. attention would be better appreciated if it were the only option. But many analysts insist that the Mexican drug war demands new approaches. It would go a long way if the United States itself would clean house; a U.S. Senate report concluded last June that nearly three-quarters of the weapons used in Mexico's conflict come from American dealers. Meanwhile, a recent report from the Washington Office on Latin America—which calls Colombia's experience a "cautionary tale" for Mexico—argues that the focus needs to shift from attacking the bad guys to protecting civilians. That means, first and foremost, more and better police. Underfunded, corrupt, and disempowered by the military, the police today provide only a veneer of pedestrian security. The latter investigate an appalling 8 percent of the crime reported—including the murders of victims the Mexican government is tallying as criminals. In 2010, the United States started to explore ideas like cleaning up the police force and strengthening the judicial system—but when those items were cut in the 2011 budget, the focus shifted back to the military.

None of this is to say that the experience in Colombia provides no lessons at all, argues Michael Shifter. In some ways, Mexico's failure to win with its Uribe-like strategy may have been partly a problem of misinterpretation, or mis-execution, rather than a refutation of the theory itself. Uribe, for instance, can truly claim credit for rallying national morale in Colombia around the country's existential struggle with FARC. As president, he made the case to Colombians that their country was facing a do-or-die scenario: fight back or become a narco-state. With his rhetoric and resolve, Uribe won support both from *paisas* and from the elites, who had for years been prone either to flee the country or to purchase their security from paramilitaries. Calderón, by contrast, is walking a tightrope—telling his citizens that there's a crisis while still reassuring tourists that there's nothing unsafe about Mexico—and he is fast losing his country's faith. "When they say in Washington, D.C., that Mexico should do what Colombia did," says Adam Isacson, "I think they are just nostalgic for this country whose elite was all on the same page as Washington."

On the morning of November 5, 2011, Uribe's successor made a long-awaited announcement: the main leader of FARC, nom-de-guerre Alfonso Cano, had been killed. Colombian troops had bombed the commander's location in the forested southern province of Cauca, an epicenter of the violence in recent months. His death was immediately hailed as the most significant blow to the organization in FARC's decades-long history. And it was particularly timely: the eccentric former anthropologist had been the brain behind FARC's recently updated strategy—the transition from army-like force to terrorist cells. (Fittingly, when Cano died, he appears to have been moving through the jungle with just a handful of fellow operatives.)

Ending Cano's dark legacy was also a symbolic coup for President Juan Manuel Santos, who had taken flak early in his term for being soft on security. In fact, for months before, Uribe—under whom Santos had served as defense minister—had backhandedly accused his successor of letting the country slip. "What I have found from moving from town to town is that there are many people with the idea that there are some symptoms of insecurity," Uribe told me in July. They felt "that instead of improving to some degree we are going a little bit backward from the point we had been."

If Colombia is backsliding, Uribe believes it can only mean one thing: that the country has walked away from "democratic security." I asked him if he thought Santos had done just that, and he hesitated to answer, saying that he needed to be diplomatic: "My impression is that they are the same [in their] determination but maybe they have changed some points."

But perhaps continuity was exactly the problem, as Santos has found out the hard way. When the new president came to office, he drafted a defense strategy that looked much like his predecessor's—as the electorate that elected him had come to expect. But as the indicators turned sour, the new president started to rethink. After a year in office, he swapped defense ministers and announced a new plan to combat the resurgent FARC. He named the BACRIM a primary enemy of the state, and created a new, more holistic defense plan that seeks to build up economic and social institutions in addition to security. He disbanded the national intelligence agency, which had been discredited by an earlier scandal that had revealed it was tapping the phones of journalists, opposition figures, and even then President Uribe. A victim's compensation law also won Santos praise—a first step, perhaps, in redressing years of suffering. Yet whether the new government can keep pace with the changes in this conflict is now more than ever open to question. And for the first time in almost a decade, Uribe might not be the best person to answer it. If FARC melts away even further, that may mean one thing: more BACRIM, fighting for market share. Colombia is still the source of 80 percent of the cocaine that arrives in the United States, according to the U.S. Drug Enforcement Agency. Should the guerrillas' trafficking machinery wither altogether, someone with a gun will inevitably pick up the slack. For the last several years, it has been not just the BACRIM but also the cartels to Colombia's north—in Mexico and the weaker states of Central America—that have stepped in to fill the void. These states will have to fight back, one way or another.

In its time and place, democratic security was an inspired strategy, albeit far from a perfect one. Until the demand for drugs dries up, Mexico, Guatemala, Honduras—even far flung narco-conflicts like those in Guinea-Bissau and Afghanistan—will have to find their own medicine.

Yet if there is a lesson to be learned, perhaps it is as much for the United States as it is for these theaters of the drug war: the violence won't stop until the narcotics trade does. Short of that, all that Washington—or anyone—can hope for is damage control. Off the main streets of Bogota and Mexico City, the damage is real. And not even Uribe knows the cure.

## CRITICAL THINKING QUESTIONS

1. How successful was the anti-narco-terrorism policy in Colombia?
2. What role should the United States play in dealing with narco-terrorist challenges to countries?
3. How would you define success in fighting narco-terrorism?

# 9

# U.S. and International Health Responses to the Ebola Outbreak in West Africa

## SUMMARY AND BACKGROUND

In March 2014, an Ebola Virus Disease (EVD) outbreak was reported in Guinea, West Africa. The outbreak is the first in West Africa and has caused an unprecedented number of cases and deaths. The outbreak is continuing to spread in Guinea, Sierra Leone, and Liberia (the "affected countries"); it has been contained in Nigeria and Senegal, and has been detected in Mali. As of October 22, 2014, more than 10,000 people have contracted EVD, more than half of whom have died.

Until October 2014, no secondary EVD cases had occurred outside of Africa. That month, health workers in Spain and the United States contracted EVD cases while providing care for Ebola patients. Other factors make this outbreak unique, including

- its introduction into West Africa;
- multi-country outbreaks occurring simultaneously;
- disease transmission within urban areas; and
- an unprecedented scale and pace of transmission.

In the aggregate, between 1976, when Ebola was first identified, through 2012, there were 2,387 cases, including 1,590 deaths, all in Central and East Africa. The number of Ebola cases in this outbreak is four times higher than the combined total of all prior outbreaks, and the number of cases is doubling monthly. The U.S. Centers for Disease Control and Prevention (CDC) and the World Health Organization (WHO) have projected an exponential increase in cases. WHO estimated that by the end of November, some 20,000 people may contract Ebola; CDC estimated that "without additional interventions or changes in community behavior," up to 1.4 million could contract EVD in Liberia and Sierra Leone by January 2015. CDC indicates, however, that the

Tiaji Salaam-Blyther is a specialist in global health with the Congressional Research Service. This is excerpted from Tiaji Salaam-Blyther, "U.S. and International Health Responses to the Ebola Outbreak in West Africa," Congressional Research Service, October 29, 2014.

outbreak may not reach such proportions since responses are intensifying. In Liberia, for example, improvements in burial practices have resulted in roughly 85 percent of all bodies being collected within 24 hours of being reported to national officials.

In an August 2014 report, WHO estimated that it would cost roughly $500 million to contain the outbreak by January. In September, international responses accelerated. The United Nations (U.N.) established the United Nations Mission for Ebola Emergency Response (UNMEER) "to utilize the assets of all relevant U.N. agencies" to address the health and broader social impacts of the outbreak. A proposed U.N. response would cost roughly $1 billion, about half of which would be aimed at addressing health impacts.

. . .

## Ebola Care and Treatment

There are no drugs proven to prevent or treat EVD, though efforts are underway to develop them. In October, press reports indicated that WHO planned to begin testing two Ebola vaccines in January on some 20,000 health workers and other volunteers. The organization also indicated that a treatment might be available for use in Liberia by early November. In the absence of specific treatments, health practitioners treat EVD symptoms with supportive care, which can reduce the fatality rate. Spread of the disease can be limited through the use of disease surveillance and containment measures. WHO has released manuals that outline appropriate patient care, management of contaminated objects, safe burial practices, and diagnostic protocol. These measures successfully contained all the previous Ebola outbreaks.

. . .

# U.S. RESPONSES TO PANDEMIC THREATS AND EBOLA

The United States is the leading funder of the international Ebola response and its financial support is continuing to rise. The U.S. Agency for International Development (USAID) reports that as of October 22, U.S. humanitarian funding for EVD responses totaled $344.6 million. In addition, the Department of Defense (DOD) is planning to spend more than $1 billion on containing the outbreak in support of U.S. EVD activities in West Africa, as described below.

On October 17, President Obama established an Ebola Czar to coordinate U.S. domestic and global responses to the Ebola outbreak. The U.S. Global Ebola strategy has four key goals:

1. control the outbreak,
2. mitigate second order impacts,
3. establish coherent leadership and operations, and
4. advance global health security.

U.S. global efforts focus primarily on Liberia, where the outbreak is most widely spread, although the United States is engaged in all three affected countries. As of October 25, nearly 900 U.S. Government personnel are stationed in the region, more than 700 of which are among the 4,000 military personnel who will be deployed to the region.

U.S. responses to the current Ebola outbreak are built on prior and ongoing efforts to build the capacity of foreign nations to prepare and respond to disease outbreaks—including Ebola. These activities are primarily implemented through USAID and CDC, though the U.S. Departments of Agriculture, Defense, and State also contribute to such efforts. Pandemic preparedness programs began in earnest after the 2005 avian flu outbreak and have experienced varying levels of congressional support. The section below briefly describes U.S. pandemic preparedness efforts, including Ebola outbreak responses, by agency.

## USAID Pandemic Preparedness Efforts

Since 2005, USAID has invested roughly $1 billion on helping countries detect, prepare for, and respond to outbreaks that originate in animals, such as Ebola, and that have the potential to cause pandemics. In FY2014, USAID spent $72.5 million on such efforts through the Emerging and Pandemic Threats (EPT) program, which operates in 18 countries in Africa and Asia. The program grew out of USAID's initial response to H5N1 avian influenza in 2005.

Congress appropriates funds directly to USAID for EPT. These funds have fluctuated between FY2005–FY2014. Related activities in 18 countries in East and Central Africa and South and Southeast Asia focus on:

- **viral detection**—identification of viruses in wildlife, livestock, and human populations that may be public health threats;
- **risk determination**—characterization of the potential risk and method of transmission for specific viruses of animal origin;
- **institutionalization of a "one health" approach**—integration of a multi-sector approach to public health (including animal health and environment);
- **outbreak response capacity**—support for sustainable, country-level response to include preparedness and coordination; and
- **risk reduction**—promotion of actions that minimize or eliminate the potential for the emergence and spread of new viral threats.

. . .

### USAID Ebola Responses

USAID has deployed a Disaster Assistance Response Team (DART) to West Africa to coordinate the U.S. Government's response to the Ebola outbreak. In coordination with other federal agencies, the team is overseeing the U.S.

response. Between March and October 2014, USAID has committed to provide more than $300 million for combating Ebola in West Africa. This included the provision of resources for 1,000 treatment beds, 130,000 sets of protective equipment for healthcare staff and outbreak investigators, as well as 50,000 hygiene kits, which include soap, bleach, gloves, masks, and other supplies to help prevent the spread of disease. USAID is also supporting the International Federation of Red Cross and Red Crescent Societies (IFRC) to raise public awareness of Ebola's mode of transmission, teach disease prevention practices to communities, train volunteers to detect Ebola symptoms and identify contacts of confirmed or suspected cases for further monitoring, and support safe burial and body management activities. USAID has reprogrammed funds from the Global Health and International Disaster Assistance accounts to fund these efforts.

## CDC Pandemic Preparedness Efforts

CDC funds its global pandemic preparedness efforts through a variety of accounts, including the Global Disease Detection (GDD) program, Emerging and Zoonotic Infectious Diseases, Global Health, Immunization and Respiratory Diseases, and Public Health Preparedness and Response. The Centers leverage resources from these and other program accounts to respond to global disease outbreaks—including Ebola. Appropriations for GDD have grown since 2003.

. . .

CDC has requested additional support ($45 million) in FY2015 to fund activities in support of the Global Health Security Agenda, which will accelerate activities to detect, prevent, and respond to global infectious disease threats like Ebola. CDC directly or indirectly supports pandemic influenza preparedness efforts in more than 50 countries. In some cases, CDC sends experts to work with WHO country offices or foreign health ministries, and at other times, CDC forms cooperative agreements with partners to support country efforts.

### CDC Ebola Responses

At the end of March 2014, CDC teams traveled to Guinea and Liberia to help those Health Ministries characterize and control the outbreak, identify and manage EVD cases, conduct contact tracing, and improve data management. Following an initial response, new cases flared up after appearing to decelerate for some time. CDC returned to the region and resumed technical assistance efforts. In addition to the activities discussed above, CDC is also training airport personnel and working with partners to display Ebola-specific travel messages for electronic monitors and posters at airports in the affected countries. CDC is not providing direct care of Ebola patients. As of October 22, 2014, CDC has committed more than $16.7 million for its Ebola responses.

## Department of Defense Ebola Responses

Until recently, DOD responses to the outbreak were focused on researching treatments and vaccines and providing laboratory diagnostic assistance to Sierra Leone and Liberia. On September 8, DOD announced that it would provide $22 million to set up a 25-bed field hospital in Liberia that would be used to treat EVD cases among healthcare workers. The Department of Health and Human Services (HHS) U.S. Public Health Service Commissioned Corps will deploy 65 officers "to Liberia to manage and staff the hospital." Military personnel will establish and supply the facility, but not provide direct medical care.

On September 16, President Barack Obama announced the launch of "Operation United Assistance." The operation is to be based in Monrovia, Liberia, will entail the deployment of roughly 4,000 U.S. military forces, and be overseen and coordinated by the DOD U.S. Africa Command. The operation will support:

- the coordination of U.S. and international relief efforts;
- the provision of medical personnel to train up to 200 health workers weekly; and
- the establishment of 12 treatment centers in Liberia, each with 100-bed capacity.

Operation-related efforts are underway. The first 22-bed ETC is expected to be completed by the end of October and three others are to be completed in November. More than 700 U.S. military personnel are in the region, including personnel from the U.S. Naval Medical Research Center who are operating three mobile medical labs for EVD testing. Congress has approved several DOD reprogramming requests to fund Operation United Assistance as well as other related activities, including those that supply personal protective equipment, laboratory inputs, and technical advisors to the region. Total DOD funding for the global Ebola response is expected to exceed $1 billion.

# POSSIBLE ISSUES FOR CONGRESS

The current Ebola outbreak has overwhelmed the governments of Guinea, Sierra Leone, and Liberia. Insufficient capacity to detect, treat, and prevent the spread of disease has enabled the virus to spread and has further weakened health systems that were already inundated and in dilapidated conditions. Congress has held several hearings on the outbreak and enacted legislation that urged expanding U.S. and international responses and that provided funds for U.S. responses. As the outbreak continues to spread, the Administration may request additional funds to contain the outbreak. This section describes issues Congress may consider as it assesses U.S. and international responses.

## Human Resource Constraints

At the end of August, WHO estimated that it would take 13,000 health workers to contain the Ebola outbreak. Although foreign governments and nongovernmental organizations are beginning to deploy medics and other health workers, their numbers are not sufficient to meet the human resource demands. Human resource constraints are most acute in Liberia, where access to Ebola care is the most limited. The United States has partnered with the Liberian government, WHO, and other groups to develop a Community Care Campaign (see "WHO Community Care Campaign"). Doctors Without Borders (known by its French acronym, MSF) has expressed concern about the Community Care Campaign, asserting that the CCCs could turn into "contamination centers" without strict infection control, adequate supplies, trained staff, regular supervision, the ability to diagnose and refer patients, and proper burial methods. WHO acknowledges that "any deficiencies in the quality of implementation could present major risk of virus transmission within the CCC thus exacerbating a situation it is set out to address." Key factors that may complicate safe implementation of the Community Care Campaign include:

- **Quality control.** Inconsistent adherence to infection control protocol is reportedly contributing to EVD cases among health workers. The inability to ensure disease infection, prevention, and control (IPC) protocols among trained health personnel calls into question whether non-governmental organizations, community health workers, and family members will adhere to IPC protocols. This concern is particularly acute for lay personnel (like family members) who may provide Ebola care in the CCCs.
- **Family care providers.** To avoid the possible spread of EVD from familial caretakers to other community members, WHO recommends that only one family member provide care for each patient for the duration of their stay in the CCCs. WHO specifies that the "family member providing supportive care to the patient must not go back and forth between the CCC and the community." However, collective familial care of and close community interaction with the ill is common in Liberia. It is unclear whether CCC supervisors will be able to curtail this custom and ensure that only one family member provides care. Other factors, including loss of income, separation of the caretaker from their uninfected family members, or emotional stress from being in a CCC, might also discourage compliance with WHO familial care guidelines.
- **Waste management and safe burial practices.** IPC protocol requires that those handling the soiled linen of EVD patients, cleaning the CCCs, or burying victims of EVD wear personal protective equipment (PPE). Further, in order to prevent the spread of EVD within CCCs, caretakers must follow strict protocol in using PPE and managing waste (using only designated areas for waste disposal and ensuring daily collection of human and PPE waste). The affected countries face deficiencies in waste management. In 2012, less than 20 percent of people living in the affected

countries had access to improved sanitation facilities. It may be a challenge ensuring strict adherence to IPC protocol among lay care takers without medical training, particularly if they lack access to sanitation themselves.

■ **Oversight.** According to WHO, "monitoring and supervision is critical in ensuring the success of the approach." Most of the "low level community health workers and members of the community" who will be tasked with providing care in CCCs have never done so before. The Community Care Campaign calls for once daily supervisory visits by at least one health care worker trained in IPC. It remains to be seen whether once daily visits are enough to ensure compliance with the IPC protocols, as well as others, including proper and consistent use of PPE by care takers, launderers, burial team, and sanitation workers.

■ **Supply chain management.** Due to poor supply chain management practices, many publicly funded health clinics in the affected countries face interruptions in medical supplies and often lack commodities such as gloves, masks, and gowns. A lack of protective equipment in ETUs and health clinics has been associated with EVD infection among health workers. Lapses in protective gear in CCCs can lead to unsafe practices, such as recycling or reusing existing PPE. It remains to be seen whether WHO and its partners will be able to ensure the continuous supply of commodities to disparate CCCs.

WHO recognizes the inherent risks of this effort and advises that Ministries of Health in the affected countries "embark on this approach in an incremental manner starting with a few pilots that are well monitored before taking it up to scale."

U.S. implementation of the Community Care Campaign is already underway. USAID is issuing grants to non-governmental organizations to oversee the management of Community Care Centers. The White House reports that the United States Government has already provided 9,000 community care kits in Liberia for use by individuals in their homes. NGOs generally have autonomy over the implementation of USAID grants, and USAID oversees implementation to ensure that program targets are met. Questions abound, however, about U.S. oversight and implementation of this campaign, particularly regarding U.S. government oversight of grantees managing CCCs and the standardization of quality control and IPC protocol.

## Leadership of the International Outbreak Response

Observers have criticized WHO leadership over the global Ebola response. Some critics have contended that budget cuts that began under WHO's reform efforts have made the Organization less effective and have limited its capacity to contain the outbreak. The 2014–2015 WHO program budget called for a 51 percent reduction in outbreak and crisis response activities from 2012–2013 levels. Some observers maintain that earlier budget cuts have also crippled the agency by reducing critical staff, causing the closure of the viral hemorrhagic fever unit, and undermining operational capacity. Beyond budgetary constraints, some critics contended that WHO's response has been stymied by bureaucratic bloat and undue influence of underqualified staff who attained their positions due to political relationships.

Weak health systems in the affected countries, inadequate capacity of WHO to carry out its own Ebola plans, as well as insufficient international responses to the outbreak have reignited debates about whether WHO should function primarily as an advisory body or maintain some form of operational capacity. Some analysts advocate for the establishment of a WHO-administered "Health Systems Fund," that could be used to both build long-term health system capacity, as well as address short-term crises like the ongoing Ebola outbreak. While supporting the need for a ready-to-deploy team of emergency health responders, others assert the "politics of sovereignty" would preclude WHO from leading such an effort.

## U.S. Support for Ebola Responses and Health Systems

The speed at which EVD is spreading across West Africa is attributable, in large part, to weak health systems in those countries. Donors have long grappled with how to address health emergencies in light of dysfunctional health systems. In the early 2000s, donors turned to disease-based funding and channeled health aid through non-governmental groups. Opponents of this approach argued that disease-specific programs exacerbate human resource shortages in the public sector and further weaken health systems when parallel bureaucracies are established and government authorities are bypassed. Supporters assert that disease-based funding strengthens oversight capacity and facilitates the monitoring and evaluation of the investments.

This debate intensified following the introduction of the President's Emergency Plan for AIDS Relief (PEPFAR). In an effort to curb the massive number of deaths that followed the introduction of HIV/AIDS, U.S. agencies provided funding to large non-governmental organizations and local partners who established care and treatment facilities outside of government networks. While the effort helped save millions of lives and averted millions more HIV infections, the United States became the sole supporter for millions of people worldwide whose lives would be at risk should U.S. funding be discontinued. In the second phase of PEPFAR (FY2009–FY2013), increasing portions of PEPFAR resources were used to support health systems in hopes of bolstering country capacity to assume ownership over HIV/AIDS programs. Now in its third phase, debate on the use of PEPFAR funds for building health systems has resumed. A 2013 GAO report noted that roughly 21 percent of PEPFAR funds were spent on capacity building projects under the "other" budgetary category. At her confirmation hearing, PEPFAR Country Coordinator Deborah Birx asserted that under her leadership, 50 percent of all PEPFAR resources, including those funded through other accounts, would be spent on care and treatment activities, as mandated. Health system advocates fear that budgetary reforms aimed at adhering to the law may imperil efforts to bolster health systems.

The U.S. Congress faces a similar dilemma with the current Ebola outbreak. The affected countries need focused support to contain and end this outbreak. If and when the outbreak is arrested, however, the countries may not be in any better position to detect, prevent, or respond to other potential disease outbreaks unless donors begin the arduous task of supporting the development of strong health systems. Ken Isaacs, Vice President of International Programs and Government Relations at Samaritan's Purse, described this dilemma at an August 2014 congressional hearing on Ebola, stating "While it should be the goal of the developed world to build capacity, the building of this capacity should not be the focus during times of an emergency crisis of a deadly disease that threatens the international community." USAID has reportedly established an Ebola Health Systems Strengthening working group to support the resumption of health care delivery and to bolster the health systems once the outbreak is contained.

Though PEPFAR and other U.S.-funded health programs have attempted to respond to calls for greater investment in health systems, no appropriations specifically targeting such efforts are provided. Language in appropriations and accompanying conference reports direct the majority of health aid to particular diseases, leaving minimal resources for broader activities to strengthen health systems. The inability of the affected countries to respond to an unforeseen health event may prompt Congress to review how global health funds are appropriated.

## Evaluating U.S. Responses

A variety of U.S. agencies are responding to the ongoing Ebola outbreak. The Department of State is leading diplomatic engagements; USAID is coordinating U.S. responses, including the provision of financial and material support; CDC is heading public health and medical response activities; and DOD is handling support for foreign armed forces. With the exception of USAID, the budgetary structure of each of these agencies enables them to respond to this unanticipated event by drawing from accounts that have flexible authorities. The Department of State's efforts to coordinate bilateral diplomatic engagements are conducted through existing channels (e.g., embassy contacts) and, as such, would not require additional, dedicated funding. Outbreak responses by the CDC can be financed through USAID disaster assistance accounts, as well as several CDC accounts that are used for domestic and international health efforts and for which there is not explicit congressional direction on their use. The DOD budget also supports an array of domestic and international health activities that do not receive detailed congressional direction.

Congress has established numerous directives over the years on how foreign aid funds are to be used. As the lead U.S. development agency, USAID often receives specific direction from Congress on how the bulk of its funds will be used through annual appropriations, leaving the agency with limited ability to address unanticipated events, like the current Ebola outbreak, without drawing from ongoing health efforts. According to USAID, it is currently reprogramming funds planned for preventing future outbreaks, as well as addressing ongoing outbreaks (including responses to H7N9 avian influenza in China and MERS-CoV in the Middle East), to address the current Ebola outbreak.

Supporters of the current appropriation structure see it as a tool for overseeing health programs and ensuring that congressional priorities are met. Opponents argue that congressional directives encumber the agility that is needed in the field and create artificial segmentation of health and development issues, thereby limiting the impact and sustainability of such efforts.

By their nature, disease outbreaks are often unpredictable, though with appropriate disease surveillance, detection, and response mechanisms, their impact can be minimized. At present, USAID pandemic preparedness efforts are focused on East and Central Africa, where previous Ebola and influenza outbreaks have occurred, as well as South and Southeast Asia. Now that Ebola has emerged in West Africa, another EVD outbreak may occur in the region; a scenario the affected countries may be ill-prepared to handle. The FY2015 budget request ($50 million) for pandemic preparedness is roughly 30 percent less than the FY2014 funding level ($73 million). Even if Congress funds USAID pandemic preparedness programs at the FY2014 funding level, one USAID official contends that it will not be enough to meet current demands.

## Addressing the Long-Term and Broader Effects of the Outbreak

Under the best of circumstances, experts predict that the outbreak can be contained by the end of January. In the meantime, the high death tolls are disrupting social structures and may cause broad, long-term effects in the region. MSF has reported that some affected villages in Sierra Leone have lost the majority of adult community members, leaving vulnerable populations—such as children and the elderly—without resources to cultivate agricultural land and procure food. Observers are also concerned about a growing number of children who are being orphaned from Ebola. This group is particularly vulnerable to marginalization due to overwhelming fear of the virus. Countries in West and Central Africa already had large orphan populations due to a variety of causes including armed conflict and HIV/AIDS. In 2012, some 28 million children were orphaned in the region, of whom more than 4 million lost one or more parent to AIDS. The outbreak is also hindering the capacity of these governments to address other health issues, such as obstetrical complications. Experts are concerned that child and maternal mortality rates, already high in the region, may further rise due to diminishing numbers of health personnel (caused both by Ebola deaths and abandonment of posts), diversion of limited resources to Ebola treatment centers, and public avoidance of health centers.

The full health effects of the Ebola outbreak may not be known until it is contained. An accounting of broader health and development needs will likely ensue and may rekindle debate over how U.S. global health assistance funds are apportioned. Congress is likely to face arguments from advocates from a variety of actors attempting to garner support for a bevy of health and development issues that will have likely worsened in the wake of Ebola, including maternal and child mortality, child vulnerability and orphanhood, poverty, food scarcity, and water-borne infections.

## CRITICAL THINKING QUESTIONS

1. From highest to lowest, rank the degree of success the United States has achieved in the four key goals of its Global Ebola strategy.
2. Select one of the issues that Congress might use to assess the United States and international response to the Ebola crisis. What grade would you give the United States? Why?
3. What is the primary long-term lesson of the Ebola crisis for U.S. foreign policy?

# 10

# ISIS and the Third Wave of Jihadism

Fawaz A. Gerges

In order to make sense of the so-called Islamic State (known as ISIS or ISIL, or by its Arabic acronym, Daesh) and its sudden territorial conquests in Iraq and Syria, it is important to place the organization within the broader global jihadist movement. By tracing ISIS's social origins and comparing it with the first two jihadist waves of the 1980s and 1990s, we can gauge the extent of continuity and change, and account for the group's notorious savagery.

Although ISIS is an extension of the global jihadist movement in its ideology and worldview, its social origins are rooted in a specific Iraqi context, and, to a lesser extent, in the Syrian war that has raged for almost four years. While al-Qaeda's central organization emerged from an alliance between ultraconservative Saudi Salafism and radical Egyptian Islamism, ISIS was born of an unholy union between an Iraq-based al-Qaeda offshoot and the defeated Iraqi Baathist regime of Saddam Hussein, which has proved a lethal combination.

## BITTER INHERITANCE

The causes of ISIS's unrestrained extremism lie in its origins in al-Qaeda in Iraq (AQI), founded by Abu Musab al-Zarqawi, who was killed by the Americans in 2006. The U.S.-led invasion and occupation of Iraq caused a rupture in an Iraqi society already fractured and bled by decades of war and economic sanctions. America's destruction of Iraqi institutions, particularly its dismantling of the Baath Party and the army, created a vacuum that unleashed a fierce power struggle and allowed non-state actors, including al-Qaeda, to infiltrate the fragile body politic.

ISIS's viciousness reflects the bitter inheritance of decades of Baathist rule that tore apart Iraq's social fabric and left deep wounds that are still festering.

Fawaz A. Gerges is professor of international relations and Middle Eastern politics at the London School of Economics and Political Science. His books include *The Far Enemy: Why Jihad Went Global* and, most recently, *The New Middle East: Protest and Revolution in the Arab World*. Reprinted with permission from *Current History* magazine (December 2014). Copyright © 2015 Current History, Inc.

America's bloody vanquishing of Baathism and the invasion's aftermath of sectarian civil war plunged Iraq into a sustained crisis, inflaming Sunnis' grievances over their disempowerment under the new Shia ascendancy and preponderant Iranian influence.

Iraqi Sunnis have been protesting the marginalization and discrimination they face for some time, but their complaints fell on deaf ears in Baghdad and Washington. This created an opening for ISIS to step in and instrumentalize their grievances. A similar story of Sunni resentment unfolded in Syria, where the minority Alawite sect dominates the regime of President Bashar al-Assad. Thousands of embittered Iraqi and Syrian Sunnis fight under ISIS's banner, even though many do not subscribe to its extremist Islamist ideology. While its chief, Abu Bakr al-Baghdadi, has anointed himself as the new caliph, on a more practical level he blended his group with local armed insurgencies in Syria and Iraq, building a base of support among rebellious Sunnis.

ISIS is a symptom of the broken politics of the Middle East and the fraying and delegitimation of state institutions, as well as the spreading of civil wars in Syria and Iraq. The group has filled the resulting vacuum of legitimate authority. For almost two decades, "al-Qaeda Central" leaders Osama bin Laden and Ayman al-Zawahiri were unable to establish the kind of social movement that Baghdadi has created in less than five years.

Unlike its transnational, borderless parent organization, ISIS has found a haven in the heart of the Levant. It has done so by exploiting the chaos in war-torn Syria and the sectarian, exclusionary policies of former Iraqi Prime Minister Nuri Kamal al-Maliki. More like the Taliban in Afghanistan in the 1990s than al-Qaeda Central, ISIS is developing a rudimentary infrastructure of administration and governance in captured territories in Syria and Iraq. It now controls a landmass as large as the United Kingdom. ISIS's swift military expansion stems from its ability not only to terrorize enemies but also to co-opt local Sunni communities, using networks of patronage and privilege. It offers economic incentives such as protection of contraband trafficking activity and a share of the oil trade and smuggling in eastern Syria.

## SECTARIAN WAR

Building a social base from scratch in Iraq, AQI exploited the Sunni-Shia divide that opened after the United States toppled Hussein's Sunni-dominated regime. The group carried out wave after wave of suicide bombings against the Shia. Zarqawi's goal was to trigger all-out sectarian war and to position AQI as the champion of the embattled Sunnis. He ignored repeated pleas from his mentors, bin Laden and Zawahiri, to stop the indiscriminate killing of Shia and to focus instead on attacking Western troops and citizens.

Although Salafi jihadists are nourished on an anti-Shia propaganda diet, al-Qaeda Central prioritized the fight against the "far enemy"—America and its European allies. In contrast, AQI and its successor, ISIS, have so far consistently focused on the Shia and the "near enemy" (the Iraqi and Syrian regimes, as well as all secular, pro-Western regimes in the Muslim world). Baghdadi, like Zarqawi before him, has a genocidal worldview, according to which Shias are infidels—a fifth column in the heart of Islam that must either convert or be exterminated. The struggle against America and Europe is a distant, secondary goal that must be deferred until liberation at home is achieved. At the height of the Israeli assault on Gaza during the summer of 2014, militants criticized ISIS on social media for killing Muslims while failing to help the Palestinians. ISIS retorted that the struggle against the Shia comes first.

Baghdadi has exploited the deepening Sunni-Shia rift across the Middle East, intensified by a new regional cold war between Sunni-dominated Saudi Arabia and Shia-dominated Iran. He depicts his group as the vanguard of persecuted Sunni Arabs in a revolt against sectarian-based regimes in Baghdad, Damascus, and beyond. He has amassed a Sunni army of more than 30,000 fighters (including some 18,000 core members, plus affiliated groups). By contrast, at the height of its power in the late 1990s, al-Qaeda Central mustered only 1,000 to 3,000 fighters, a fact that shows the limits of transnational jihadism and its small constituency compared with the "near enemy" or local jihadism of the ISIS variety.

Numbers alone do not explain ISIS's rapid military advances in Syria and Iraq. After Baghdadi took charge of AQI in 2010, when it was in precipitous decline, he restructured its military network and recruited experienced officers from Hussein's disbanded army, particularly the Republican Guards, who turned ISIS into a professional fighting force. It has been toughened by fighting in neighboring Syria since the civil war there began in 2011. According to knowledgeable Iraqi sources, Baghdadi relies on a military council made up of 8 to 13 officers who all served in Saddam Hussein's army.

## RATIONAL SAVAGERY

In a formal sense, ISIS is an effective fighting force. But it has become synonymous with viciousness, carrying out massacres, beheadings, and other atrocities. It has engaged in religious and ethnic cleansing against Yazidis and Kurds as well as Shia. Such savagery might seem senseless, but for ISIS it appears to be a rational choice, intended to terrorize its enemies and to impress potential recruits. ISIS's brutality also stems from the ruralization of this third wave of jihadism. Whereas the two previous waves had leaders from the social elite and a rank and file mainly composed of lower-middle-class university graduates, ISIS's cadre is rural and lacking in both theological and intellectual accomplishment. This social profile helps ISIS thrive among poor, disenfranchised Sunni communities in Iraq, Syria, Lebanon, and elsewhere.

ISIS adheres to a doctrine of total war, with no constraints. It disdains arbitration or compromise, even with Sunni Islamist rivals. Unlike al-Qaeda Central, it does not rely on theology to justify its actions. "The only law I subscribe to is the law of the jungle," retorted Baghdadi's second-in-command and right-hand man, Abu Muhammed al-Adnani, to a request more than a year ago by rival militant Islamists in Syria who called for ISIS to submit to a Sharia court so that a dispute with other factions could be properly adjudicated. For the top ideologues of Salafi jihadism, such statements and actions are sacrilegious, "smearing the reputation" of the global jihadist movement, in the words of Abu Mohammed al-Maqdisi, a Jordan-based mentor to Zarqawi and many jihadists worldwide.

## NEW WAVE

The scale and intensity of ISIS's brutality, stemming from Iraq's blood-soaked modern history, far exceed either of the first two jihadist waves of recent decades. Disciples of Sayyid Qutb—a radical Egyptian Islamist known as the master theoretician of modern jihadism—led the first wave. Pro-Western, secular Arab regimes, which they called the "near enemy," would be the main targets. Their first major act was the assassination of Egyptian President Anwar Sadat in 1981.

This first wave included militant religious activists of Zawahiri's generation. They wrote manifestos in an effort to obtain theological legitimation for their attacks on "renegade" and "apostate" rulers, such as Sadat, and their security services. On balance, though, they showed restraint in the use of political violence. Conscious of the importance of Egyptian and wider Arab opinion, Zawahiri spent considerable energy over the years trying to explain the circumstances that led to the killing of two children in Egypt and Sudan, and repeatedly insisted that his group, Egyptian Islamic Jihad, did not target civilians.

The first wave had subsided by the end of the 1990s. During the 1980s, many militants had traveled to Afghanistan to fight the Soviet occupation, a cause that launched the second jihadist wave. After the withdrawal of the Soviets from Afghanistan, bin Laden emerged as the leader of the new wave. The focus shifted to the "far enemy" in the West—the United States and, to a lesser degree, Europe.

To win support, bin Laden justified his actions as a form of self-defense. He portrayed al-Qaeda's September 11, 2001, attack on the United States as an act of "defensive jihad," or a just retaliation for American domination of Muslim countries. Baghdadi, by contrast, cares little for world opinion. Indeed, ISIS makes a point of displaying its barbarity in its internet videos. Stressing violent action rather than theology, it has offered no ideas to sustain its followers. Baghdadi has not fleshed out his vision of a caliphate but merely declared it by fiat, which contradicts Islamic law and tradition.

Ironically, Baghdadi—who has a doctorate from the Islamic University of Baghdad, with a focus on Islamic culture, history, Sharia, and jurisprudence—is more steeped in religious education than al-Qaeda's past and current leaders, bin Laden (an engineer) and Zawahiri (a medical doctor), who had no such credentials. Yet he surrounds himself with former Baathist army officers, rather than ideologues, and has not issued a single manifesto laying out his claim to either the caliphate or the leadership of the global jihadist movement. ISIS's brutality has alienated senior radical preachers who have publicly disowned it, though some have softened their criticism in the wake of U.S.-led airstrikes against the group in Iraq and Syria, which one ideologue described as "the aggression of crusaders."

Bin Laden said, "When people see a strong horse and a weak horse, by nature they will like the strong horse." Baghdadi's slogan of "victory through fear and terrorism" signals to friends and foes alike that ISIS is a winning horse. Increasing evidence shows that over the past few months, hundreds, if not thousands, of diehard former Islamist enemies of ISIS, including members of groups such as the Nusra Front and the Islamic Front, have declared allegiance to Baghdadi.

For now, ISIS has taken operational leadership of the global jihadist movement by default, eclipsing its parent organization, al-Qaeda Central. Baghdadi has won the first round against his former mentor, Zawahiri, who triggered an intra-jihadist civil war by unsuccessfully trying to elevate his own man, Abu Mohammed al-Golani, head of the Nusra Front, over Baghdadi in Syria.

## RECRUITING TACTICS

However, the so-called Islamic State is much more fragile than Baghdadi would like us to believe. His call to arms has not found any takers among either top jihadist preachers or leaders of mainstream Islamist organizations, while Islamic scholars, including the most notable Salafi clerics, have dismissed his declaration of a caliphate as null and void. In fact, many of these same renowned Salafi scholars have equated ISIS with the extremist Kharijites of the Prophet's time. ISIS also threatens the vital interests of regional and international powers, a fact that explains the large coalition organized by the United States to combat the group.

Nevertheless, ISIS's sophisticated outreach campaign appeals to disaffected Sunni youth around the world by presenting the group as a powerful vanguard movement capable of delivering victory and salvation. It provides them with both a utopian worldview and a political project. Young recruits do not abhor its brutality; on the contrary, its shock-and-awe methods against the enemies of Islam are what attract them.

ISIS's exploits on the battlefield, its conquest of vast swaths of territory in Syria and Iraq, and its declaration of a caliphate have resonated widely, facilitating recruitment. Increasing evidence shows that the U.S.-led airstrikes have not slowed down the flow of foreign recruits to Syria—far from it. The *Washington Post* reported that more than 1,000 foreign fighters are streaming into Syria each month. Efforts by other countries, especially Turkey, to stem the flow of recruits (many of them from European countries) have proved largely ineffective, according to U.S. intelligence officials. ISIS fighters have also highlighted the important role of Chechen trainers in developing the group's military capabilities. Some reportedly have set up a Russian school in Raqqa for their children, to prepare them for jihad back home.

Muslims living in Western countries join ISIS and other extremist groups because they want to be part of a tight-knit community with a potent identity. ISIS's vision of resurrecting an idealized caliphate gives them the sense of serving a sacred mission. Corrupt Arab rulers and the crushing of the Arab Spring uprisings have provided further motivation for recruits. Many young men from Western Europe and elsewhere migrate to the lands of jihad because they feel a duty to defend persecuted coreligionists. Yet many of those who join the ranks of ISIS find themselves persecuting innocent civilians of other faiths and committing atrocities.

## HEARTS AND MINDS

Now that the United States and Europe have joined the fight against ISIS, the group might garner backing from quarters of the Middle Eastern public sphere that oppose Western intervention in internal Arab affairs, though there has been no such blowback so far. More than bin Laden and Zawahiri, Baghdadi has mastered the art of making enemies. He has failed to nourish a broad constituency beyond a narrow, radical sectarian base.

There is no simple or quick solution to rid the Middle East of ISIS because it is a manifestation of the breakdown of state institutions and the spread of sectarian fires in the region. ISIS is a creature of accumulated grievances, of ideological and social polarization and mobilization a decade in the making. As a non-state actor, it represents a transformative movement in the politics of the Middle East, one that is qualitatively different from al-Qaeda Central's.

The key to weakening ISIS lies in working closely with local Sunni communities that it has co-opted, a bottom-up approach that requires considerable material and ideological investment. The most effective means to degrade ISIS is to dismantle its social base by winning over the hearts and minds of local communities. This is easier said than done, given the gravity of the crisis in the heart of the Arab world. The jury is still out on whether the new Iraqi prime minister, Haider al-Abadi, will be able to appeal to mistrustful Sunnis and reconcile warring communities. Rebuilding trust takes hard work and time, both of which play to ISIS's advantage.

Equally important, there is an urgent need to find a diplomatic solution to the civil war in Syria, which has empowered ISIS, fueling its surge after its predecessor, AQI, was vanquished in Iraq. Syria is the nerve center of ISIS—the location of its de facto capital, the northern city of Raqqa, and of its major sources of income, including the oil trade, taxation, and criminal activities. More than two-thirds of its fighters are deployed in Syria, according to U.S. intelligence officials.

In the short- to medium-term, it would take a political miracle to engineer a settlement in Syria, given the disintegration of the country and the fragmentation of power among rival warlords and fiefdoms, not to mention the regional and great power proxy wars playing out there. Until there is a regional and international agreement to end the Syrian civil war, ISIS will continue to entrench itself in the country's provinces and cities.

Yet even ISIS's dark cloud has a silver lining. Once Baghdadi's killing machine is dismantled, he will leave behind no ideas, no theories, and no intellectual legacy. The weakest link of ISIS as a social movement is its poverty of ideas. It can thrive and sustain itself only in an environment of despair, state breakdown, and war. If these social conditions can be reversed, its appeal and potency will wither away, though its bloodletting will likely leave deep scars on the consciousness of Arab and Muslim youth.

## CRITICAL THINKING QUESTIONS

1. Which of the historical forces that gave rise to ISIS is most important? Could ISIS have been prevented from occurring?
2. How effective a fighting force is ISIS?
3. What is the likely legacy of ISIS in victory and in defeat?

# Societal Influences on U.S. Foreign Policy

At one time a sharp distinction was made between the proper and improper place for societal influences such as public opinion, elections, and interest group lobbying in the making of foreign policy and domestic policy. Their influence was seen as normal and appropriate in domestic policy but this was not the case for foreign policy. Here their influence was seen as dangerous. A divided public or one united in its opposition to a president's foreign policy initiative could provide foreign governments with the hope that the United States might soon abandon its policy. The public voice also might be manipulated by foreign governments, providing them with a back door into the policy-making process. Another perceived danger was that societal forces might come to capture a foreign policy area in order to advance particular interests rather than the national interest. Nothing better captured this set of fears than the bipartisanship concept that "Politics stops at the water's edge" and President Dwight Eisenhower's warning against the influence of the "military-industrial complex" in his 1961 farewell address. Finally, for many, foreign policy was too important to be influenced or determined by an American public that knew very little about foreign affairs. Professionals and elected officials should make these decisions.

While many sought to restrict the influence of domestic politics on American foreign policy, this does not mean that societal influences were ever entirely absent. From the outset, thinking about the goals and conduct of American foreign policy was heavily influenced by the public's collective sense of who they were and what the United States stood for. Central to this self-image is a sense of exceptionalism that permeates John Winthrop's 1630 reference to the Massachusetts Bay Colony as a "city on the hill" and the concept of Manifest Destiny that emerged in the mid-1800s.

Attention to the underlying dynamics and content of America's self-image led commentators to develop the concept of national style as a central force in the making and conduct of American foreign policy. Early accounts spoke of the existence of a single American national style in foreign policy built around a sense of mission, the existence of a sharp distinction between war and peace, impatience, and an engineering strategic approach to solving foreign policy problems. More recent accounts have suggested that multiple and competing American national styles exist, each of which contains its own internal dynamics and holds different consequences for American foreign policy. Walter Mead, who has written widely on the American tradition in foreign policy, identifies four different American approaches to thinking about foreign policy: Madisonian, Hamiltonian, Jacksonian, and Wilsonian.

Today, along with studying underlying values and attitudes that shape U.S. foreign policy, a great deal of attention is also focused on the influence of interest group lobbying, public opinion, elections, political protests, and private institutions such as the media and think tanks. Research here shows a complex set of linkages between societal values, political forces, and U.S. foreign policy. For example, while the public does not appear to be well informed about foreign policy issues, it does seem to be predictable and rational in what types of policies it will support. And while an individual election may not change the course of American foreign policy, the four-year presidential electoral cycle of campaigning, primaries, and elections may have an impact on foreign policy decisions in unexpected ways, such as causing policy makers to avoid issues or to hurry to solve them. A far more complex view of interest group lobbying has also emerged. Interest group lobbying does not occur on a level playing field; rather, some groups are more powerful. Where once the focus of interest groups' foreign policy lobbying was almost exclusively on business and economic interests, the focus has now expanded to include ethnic groups, public interest groups, and foreign governments.

A moment's reflection brings forward a host of examples highlighting the extent to which societal influences are very much evident in the content and conduct of contemporary American foreign policy. Immigration policy divides Democrats and Republicans. Revelations of National Security Agency (NSA) secret surveillance on Americans as part of the war on terrorism divided not only liberals and conservatives but also the Republican Party, as Tea Party supporters opposed the program's continuation. Normalizing relations with Cuba was welcomed by business interests who saw new investment opportunities and markets. But it was opposed by many Cubans in Florida who either fled Cuba when Castro came to power or whose relatives did and who had long hoped to see the communist regime there fall. Public opinion polls, such as ones conducted by the Pew Research Center for the People and the Press, show that the media's role as an instrument of governmental oversight is viewed positively by about equal majorities of Republicans and Democrats

(August 8, 2013) but that its publication of the NSA surveillance program was not endorsed to the same degree, with only 47 percent voicing their approval (July 26, 2013). A Pew poll taken after Obama announced his NSA surveillance program reforms (January 24, 2014) showed that his speech made little impact on how the public viewed this issue.

The readings in this part provide examples of how both underlying societal attitudes affect the overall conduct of American foreign policy and how specific societal interests come into play in making specific foreign policy decisions. The foreign policy impact of energy and environmental considerations received attention in the Congressional Research Service's review of key issues in the Keystone XL Pipeline Project. This excerpt from their report highlights the extent to which foreign and domestic issues can both be present in a policy problem. Fredrik Logevall and Kenneth Osgood's "The Ghost of Munich: America's Appeasement Complex" illustrates the continuing influence that ideas (Munich and appeasement) can play in policy making long after the foreign policy problems that gave rise to them have passed. The Federation of Atomic Scientists presents us with a debate among representatives from think tanks from across the political spectrum on the impact and desirability of high levels of defense spending today. As we noted earlier, the issue of defense spending is a recurring one in U.S. foreign policy, raising questions about the importance of a healthy economy to U.S. foreign policy and who benefits by high levels of defense spending. In the final reading for part III, David J. Danelo argues, in "The Courage Crisis," that the domestic politics of the child refugee crisis that has become a focal point of the immigration debate reflects a lack of courage on the part of both Republican and Democratic Party leaders. Only by facing up to the geopolitical realities of the problem and embracing strategic common sense can it be solved.

## BIG PICTURE QUESTIONS

1. Make an argument for how American foreign policy could be improved if the public were given a larger voice in foreign policy matters.
2. What is the most effective avenue or means available to the public for making its voice heard in foreign policy?
3. At what stage in the decision-making process is the public's voice most important in policy making? When is it least important? Can (or should) this be changed?

## SUGGESTED READINGS

Karl Eikenberry, "Reassessing the All-Volunteer Army," *Washington Quarterly* 36 (Winter 2013), 7–24.

Brandon Fuller and Sean Rust, *State-Based Visas*, Cato Institute, Policy Analysis 748 (April 23, 2014).

Peter Gries, *The Politics of American Foreign Policy* (Stanford, CA: Stanford University Press, 2014).

Richard Haas, *Foreign Policy Begins at Home* (New York: Basic Books, 2014).

Pew Research Center, *Few See Adequate Limits on NSA Surveillance Program* (Washington, DC, July 26, 2013).

# 11

# Keystone XL Pipeline

## OVERVIEW AND RECENT DEVELOPMENTS

In May 2012, TransCanada (a Canadian company) submitted to the U.S. Department of State an application for a Presidential Permit authorizing construction and operation of pipeline facilities for the importation of crude oil at the U.S.-Canada border. The Keystone XL Pipeline would transport Canadian oil sands crude extracted in Alberta, Canada, and crude produced from the Bakken region in North Dakota and Montana to a market hub in Nebraska for further delivery to Gulf Coast refineries. A decision to issue the Presidential Permit would be conditioned on a State Department determination that the pipeline project would serve the national interest.

. . .

## DESCRIPTION OF THE KEYSTONE XL PIPELINE

In recent decades, the natural bitumen in oil sands, particularly deposits in Alberta, Canada, has been extracted to generate substantial quantities of crude oil. The Alberta deposits are estimated to be one of the largest accumulations of oil in the world, contributing to Canada's third-place ranking for estimated proven oil reserves (behind Venezuela and Saudi Arabia). In 2005, TransCanada announced a plan to address expected increases in Alberta oil production by constructing the Keystone Pipeline system. When complete, the system would transport crude oil from Alberta to U.S. markets in the Midwest and Gulf Coast. The pipeline system was proposed as two distinct phases—the Keystone Pipeline (now constructed and in service) and the Keystone XL Pipeline.

The Keystone XL Pipeline Project would consist of 875 miles of 36-inch pipeline and associated facilities linking Hardisty, Alberta, to Steele City, NE.

Excerpted from Paul W. Parfomak, Linda Luther, Richard K. Lattanzio, Jonathan L. Ramseur, Adam Vann, Robert Pirog, and Ian F. Fergusson, "Keystone XL Pipeline: Overview and Recent Developments," Congressional Research Service, January 5, 2015.

The pipeline would also include the Bakken Marketlink in Baker, MT—a pipeline lateral that could transport crude oil from the Bakken oil fields into Steele City (further discussed below). From Steele City, crude oil could be transported to the Gulf Coast via previously constructed TransCanada pipelines—the Cushing Extension and the Gulf Coast pipeline, both already operating [see map 11.1]. Both the Keystone XL and Gulf Coast pipelines would ultimately have a capacity of 830,000 bpd.

In 2012, TransCanada estimated the capital cost of the U.S. portion of the Keystone XL Project would be $5.3 billion. However, this figure has reportedly risen to $8 billion during the permit review. Currency swings, changing regulatory requirements, the cost of materials, and legal expenses could be factors contributing to the increase in project cost.

. . .

# PRESIDENTIAL PERMIT APPLICATIONS

Federal agencies ordinarily have no authority to site oil pipelines, even interstate pipelines. This authority generally would be established under state law. However, the construction of a pipeline that connects the United States with a foreign country requires executive permission conveyed through a Presidential Permit. Executive Order 13337 delegates to the secretary of state the president's authority to receive applications for Presidential Permits. Issuance of a Presidential Permit requires a State Department determination that the project would serve the "national interest." The term is not defined in the executive orders or elsewhere. The State Department has asserted that, consistent with the president's broad discretion in the conduct of foreign affairs, it has discretion in deciding the factors it will examine in making a national interest determination.

## Consideration of Environmental Impacts under NEPA

As part of its Presidential Permit application review, the State Department must identify and consider environmental impacts within the context of the National Environmental Policy Act (NEPA). NEPA requires federal agencies to consider the environmental impacts of a proposed action, such as issuing a permit, before proceeding with them and to inform the public of those potential impacts. To ensure that environmental impacts are considered before final agency decisions are made, an environmental impact statement (EIS) must be prepared for every major federal action that may have a "significant" impact upon the environment. With respect to the Presidential Permit application submitted by TransCanada for Keystone XL, the State Department has concluded that approval of a permit requires the preparation of an EIS.

. . .

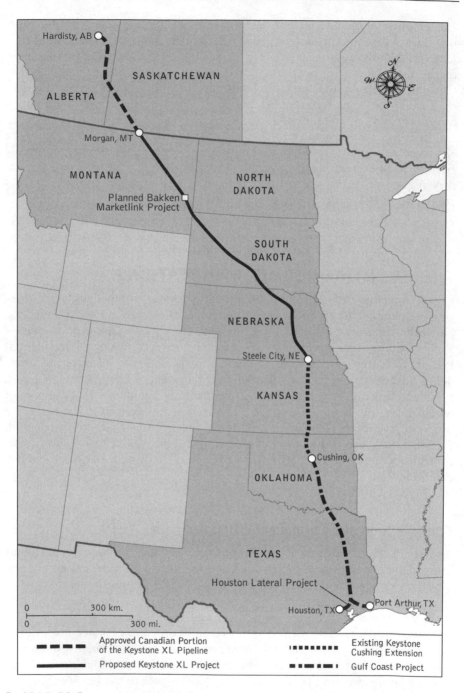

## MAP 11.1

Proposed Keystone XL Project and Associated Projects

*Source:* Based on figure 1.2-1 from the U.S. Department of State's *Final Supplemental Environmental Impact Statement for the Keystone XL Project,* January 2014.

## The National Interest Determination

Generally, after a final EIS is issued, a federal agency may issue a final record of decision (ROD) regarding the permit application of a proposed project. However, for a Presidential Permit, issuance of the final EIS represents the beginning of a public review period during which the State Department gathers information from those necessary to inform its national interest determination. Ultimately, a decision regarding issuance of a Presidential Permit for a pipeline project would be reflected in a combined "Record of Decision and National Interest Determination," issued by the State Department as required under elements of both NEPA and Executive Order 11424.

The process of determining a project's national interest illustrates the distinctly different yet interrelated requirements applicable to the NEPA process and the Presidential Permit application process. Under NEPA, the State Department (or any other federal agency considering an action) must fully assess the environmental consequences of an action and potential project alternatives *before* making a final decision. However, NEPA does not prohibit a federal action that has adverse environment impacts; it requires only that a federal agency be fully *aware of* and *consider* those adverse impacts before selecting a final project alternative. NEPA is intended to be part of the decision-making process, but not dictate a particular outcome.

. . .

## State Siting and Additional Construction Requirements

As noted above, the federal government does not currently exercise siting authority over oil pipelines within the United States. Instead, pipeline siting for the Keystone XL Project must comply with any applicable state law—which varies from state to state. South Dakota, for example, required TransCanada to apply for a permit for the Keystone XL Project from the state public utility commission, which issued the permit on April 25, 2010.

At the time of TransCanada's initial application for a Presidential Permit, Nebraska did not have any permitting requirements that applied specifically to the construction and operation of oil pipelines, although a state statute did include a provision to grant eminent domain authority to oil pipeline companies unable to obtain the necessary property rights from landowners. However, due to the controversy surrounding the Keystone XL Project, Nebraska held a special session of its legislature in 2012 to enact legislation authorizing the governor to approve oil pipeline siting. The governor approved Keystone XL's route through the state in 2013. However, in 2014, a Nebraska District Court ruled that the 2012 statute violated the Nebraska Constitution, nullifying the governor's pipeline siting approval. If the decision holds up on appeal, Trans-Canada will have to petition the Nebraska Public Service Commission for approval of the pipeline's planned route through the state.

In addition to state *siting* requirements, there are numerous local, state, tribal, and federal requirements applicable to oil pipeline *construction, operation, and maintenance*. For example, the 2013 draft EIS for Keystone XL lists major permits, licenses, approvals, and consultation requirements for the proposed project that would be required by federal, state, and local agencies prior to its implementation. These include water and wetlands-related permits from the Army Corps of Engineers; Environmental Protection Agency review and issue of National Pollutant Discharge Elimination System permits; Bureau of Land Management temporary use permits on federal lands; Fish and Wildlife Service consideration of impacts to endangered species; and multiple state/county agency consultations or permits for projects that cross navigable waters or state highways, or involve work potentially affecting state streams, cultural resources, or natural resources.

. . .

# KEY FACTORS RELEVANT TO THE NATIONAL INTEREST

There are numerous policy considerations potentially relevant to the national interest determination for Keystone XL. The following are brief introductions to key issues in ongoing congressional debate: energy security, environmental impacts, economic impacts, the Canada-U.S. relationship, and Keystone XL in the context of U.S. energy policy, broadly.

## Energy Security

The United States and Canada maintain extensive trade in crude oil and petroleum products. Canada is the single largest foreign supplier of crude oil and petroleum products to the United States—and the United States is the dominant consumer of Canada's exports. Of the 7.7 million barrels per day (Mbpd) the United States imported in 2013, Canada supplied 2.5 Mbpd (33 percent), more than the combined imports from the next two largest suppliers—Mexico and Saudi Arabia. Keystone XL would bring Canada's total petroleum export capacity to the United States via pipeline to over 4.1 Mbpd, enough capacity to carry more than 48 percent of U.S. crude petroleum imports in 2012. Given that Canada actually supplied the United States with 2.5 Mbpd in 2013, large increases in Canadian supply via pipeline could ultimately be possible, although much of the increased crude supply, while refined domestically, could be destined for foreign markets in the form of petroleum products such as diesel fuel.

Increased energy trade between the United States and Canada is viewed by some pipeline proponents as a major contributor to U.S. energy security. Most notably, TransCanada's Presidential Permit application argues that the pipeline will allow U.S. refiners to substitute supply from Canada—a stable, friendly neighbor—for other foreign crude supply and to obtain direct pipeline access to growing Canadian crude output. Such energy security arguments have taken on additional weight for some proponents in light of the recent geopolitical tensions in Venezuela, as well as in other oil-producing countries in the Middle East and North Africa.

With expanded pipeline capacity extending to the U.S. Gulf Coast, Alberta crude may compete with other heavy crudes such as those from Mexico, Venezuela, and elsewhere. It is difficult to predict precisely how this competition would play out, but it could take place through shifting discounts or premiums on crude oils from various sources. Thus, it could be possible for Canadian oil supplies to effectively "push out" waterborne shipments from other countries, although this would depend on a wide range of market conditions. If Keystone XL is not permitted, the absence of the pipeline may encourage Alberta producers to increase shipments by rail and to find an alternate pipeline export route through either the Canadian East or West Coast. Thus, Canadian supplies may displace heavy oil supplies in overseas markets and potentially lead to relatively more overseas imports coming into the U.S. Gulf Coast.

. . .

## Economic Impacts of the Pipeline

The economic impacts of the Keystone XL pipeline have been the subject of considerable debate. In light of the ongoing recovery from the recent U.S. economic recession, a particular focus has been the prospect of new jobs directly associated with the pipeline's construction and operation, as well as jobs that may be created indirectly or otherwise induced due to the pipeline's construction or due to an increase in crude oil supplies. Other economic considerations include property tax revenues to local jurisdictions, although they are more straightforward. Regarding economic impact, the State Department's Final EIS for the Keystone XL Project application concludes:

> During construction, proposed Project spending would support approximately 42,100 jobs (direct, indirect, and induced), and approximately $2 billion in earnings throughout the United States. . . . Construction of the proposed Project would contribute approximately $3.4 billion (or 0.02 percent) to the U.S. gross domestic product (GDP). The proposed Project would generate approximately 50 jobs during operations. Property tax revenue during operations would be substantial for many counties, with an increase of 10 percent or more in 17 of the 27 counties with proposed Project facilities.

Because job projections, in particular, involve numerous assumptions and estimates, the State Department's job estimates for Keystone XL have been a source of disagreement. One challenge to State's analysis is that different definitions (e.g., for temporary jobs) and interpretations can lead to different numerical estimates and "fundamental confusion" about the Final EIS numbers. Consequently, it may be difficult to determine what overall economic and employment impacts may ultimately be attributable to the Keystone XL pipeline or to the various alternative transport scenarios if the pipeline is not constructed. It is beyond the scope of this report to try to evaluate specific job calculations and methodology. Nonetheless, stakeholders and analysts have asserted lower and higher job estimates in support of their positions regarding the pipeline.

. . .

## Global and Regional Environmental Impacts

Debate about the environmental impacts of the Keystone XL pipeline have focused largely on its potential to induce greater oil sands crude production and associated emissions of greenhouse gases. However, concerns about oil spills from the pipeline, and the impact of pipeline construction in environmentally sensitive areas along the route, have also been important.

. . .

Each mode of oil transportation involves some risk, and each has historically resulted in oil spills. Although pipelines and oil tankers transport the vast majority of oil within the United States, other modes of transportation have increased in recent years. In particular, the volume of crude oil carried by rail increased from approximately 4 million barrels in 2010 to approximately 87 million barrels in 2013, a 20-fold increase. Some portion of the recent increase is related to the increase in Canadian oil sands crude production and pending status of the Keystone XL pipeline.

. . .

Although some might equate rejection of the Keystone XL permit with avoiding oil spills, a more accurate tradeoff would be the risk of spills from this particular pipeline compared to spills from other modes of oil transportation which may be used as alternatives. Keystone XL Pipeline proponents and opponents, including those in the rail industry, have cited their own interpretations of spill data to argue that one transportation mode is significantly riskier than others. However, any such conclusion is open to debate.

. . .

## Canada-U.S. Relationship

Oil production and exports are a major source of economic development and revenue for Canada. Continued expansion of Canada's oil production is, therefore, a high national priority for Prime Minister Stephen Harper's government, although not all Canadians share this view. As Canada's largest crude oil customer, the United States has anchored Canada's energy trade. Historically, the energy relationship between the United States and Canada, while intertwined, has been straightforward—taking the form of a steadily growing southward flow of crude oil to U.S. refineries. Energy products have been traded freely back and forth between the two countries under the North American Free

Trade Agreement (NAFTA) and energy transportation infrastructure generally has been constructed as needed with little fanfare. But the U.S. permitting process for the Keystone XL Pipeline has greatly complicated that energy relationship, creating new tensions between the U.S. and Canadian governments as well as within Canada.

. . .

## Keystone XL and U.S. Energy Policy

Beyond the debates about the proposed Keystone XL Pipeline's impacts on oil sands production and greenhouse gases, some stakeholders have expressed a broader concern about whether the approval or denial of the project could set a precedent for U.S. energy policy. They argue that while many of the decisions that may affect the development of the oil sands will ultimately be made by the market and the national and provincial governments of Canada, the choice of whether or not to approve the permit for the project is an opportunity for the U.S. government to signal its future direction.

Some stakeholders have pushed for a national energy policy that moves the United States away from a reliance on fossil fuels. They see the decision to build the proposed pipeline as a 50-year-long commitment to a carbon-based economy and its resulting GHG emissions. Some observers contend that with meaningful action on climate policy slowed or stalled in Congress, the courts, and, to some extent, the regulatory agencies (i.e., local, state, and federal environmental and land use agencies), the sole remaining outlet to leverage a low-carbon energy policy is case-by-case action on such items as infrastructure permits. Some of these stakeholders have actively opposed the permit for the project believing that it may set a precedent. If the pipeline is allowed to go forward, they say, it may be the case that no future infrastructure project would be held accountable for its incremental contribution to cumulative GHG emissions.

Others recognize that the project could affect U.S. energy policy by setting a precedent and sending a signal, but they reach a different conclusion. Many regard the project as one element of a revitalized energy production sector in North America and urge that U.S. policy should support investment in such infrastructure for economic and national security reasons. In this view, since Canadian oil sands will be developed regardless of the transportation mode used, the public policy interest lies in supporting North American energy suppliers rather than those overseas.

## CRITICAL THINKING QUESTIONS

1. What is the proper balance between domestic and foreign policy concerns in making decisions on matters that touch on both policy areas? Is that balance present in the Keystone XL Pipeline controversy?

2. Who should make the decision on an issue such as this that involves domestic and foreign policy interests: the president, Congress, or the State Department?
3. What topics or questions should be looked at in the National Interest Determination the State Department must make? Are these the same for all issues that have both foreign and domestic policy considerations?

# 12

# The Ghost of Munich

## AMERICA'S APPEASEMENT COMPLEX

Fredrik Logevall and Kenneth Osgood

T he annual Values Voter Summit might seem an unlikely place to get a preview of the 2012 presidential debate on foreign policy. True, the gathering of several thousand conservative activists, sponsored by the Family Research Council, typically features a parade of Republican stars, many of them hoping for a shot at the top spot on the GOP ticket. But the attendees tend to focus on domestic issues that matter to social conservatives: religious freedom, protection of marriage, and abortion. The breakout sessions during the 2009 summit, held last September in Washington, featured topics like "The Threat of Illegal Immigration," "Countering the Homosexual Agenda in Public Schools," and "Global Warming Hysteria: The New Face of the 'Pro-Death' Agenda."

Yet Minnesota Governor Tim Pawlenty used his evening plenary address to launch a blistering attack on President Obama's foreign policy. Although relatively new to the national stage, Pawlenty secured his place as an early contender for the Republican nomination by delivering a rousing speech that garnered four standing ovations and landed him a strong showing in the Values Voter straw poll that always accompanies the summit. Strength, Pawlenty said, was one of the values under attack in the current political environment: "Not only did the president abandon missile defense, but he is opening negotiations with Iran and North Korea. The lessons of history are clear: Appeasement and weakness did not stop the Nazis, appeasement did not stop the Soviets, and appeasement did not stop the terrorists."

By leveling the "appeasement" charge, Pawlenty tapped into a central theme that is sure to figure in both the 2012 presidential race and the upcoming midterm elections. But in selling his foreign policy bona fides to the Republican

Fredrik Logevall is a professor at Cornell University and coauthor of *America's Cold War: The Politics of Insecurity*. Kenneth Osgood is a professor at Florida Atlantic University and author of *Total Cold War: Eisenhower's Secret Propaganda Battle at Home and Abroad*. "The Ghost of Munich: America's Appeasement Complex," Fredrik Logevall and Kenneth Osgood, *World Affairs* 173, no. 2: 13–26 (July/August 2010). Copyright © 2010. Reprinted with permission of the World Affairs Institute, www.WorldAffairsJournal.org.

faithful, Pawlenty also summoned the most commonly used, widely accepted, and poorly understood historical analogy in American politics.

The reference to appeasement, of course, evokes the memory of the notorious Munich Pact of 1938. With the world on the brink of war, British Prime Minister Neville Chamberlain sought to find a way out by meeting Adolf Hitler on his own turf, at the Bavarian city of Munich, nerve center of the Nazi Party. There Chamberlain made his infamous deal with the devil, allowing Hitler to annex a large chunk of Czechoslovakian territory in return for a pledge of peace. Chamberlain returned to a hero's welcome in England. Carrying the black umbrella that would later become a symbol of shame, and waving the Munich agreement in his hands, he proclaimed that his appeasement policy had produced "peace in our time." Less than a year later, Europe was at war. From that moment on, Munich would symbolize the ultimate folly of making agreements with dictators.

Although the United States was not party to the 1938 agreement, Americans have nonetheless fixated on it for seven decades. "Munich" and "appeasement" have been among the dirtiest words in American politics, synonymous with naïveté and weakness, and signifying a craven willingness to barter away the nation's vital interests for empty promises. American presidents from Harry Truman on have feared the dreaded "Munich analogy"—and projected an air of uncompromising toughness lest they be branded as appeasers by their political opponents.

For a time, Vietnam seemed to challenge Munich, providing a counter narrative about the danger of avoiding diplomacy; but the specter of appeasement never really went away, and now it is back with force. As a candidate, Barack Obama virtually invited the Munich ghost to return when he signaled his willingness to meet with the leaders of Iran, Syria, and other so-called pariah states without preconditions. This set off a firestorm from the right, with then President Bush leading the charge. "We have an obligation to call this what it is," Bush declared in a speech before the Israeli Knesset, "the false comfort of appeasement, which has been repeatedly discredited by history." The drumbeat continued steadily following Obama's inauguration. Scores of conservative commentators and politicians bludgeoned the new president for scrapping the missile defense plans for Eastern Europe, thereby allegedly caving to Moscow, and for trying to engage Tehran and Pyongyang. Obama had taken "another move straight out of the Neville Chamberlain foreign policy playbook," Congressman Steve King charged. Newt Gingrich, the former House speaker who harbors presidential ambitions, sounded the same theme, asserting that "patterns of appeasement and avoidance . . . are the heart of this administration."

We have, of course, heard these arguments before. For the better part of the last century, Americans looked at the Soviet Union in much the same way as they now look at Iran, North Korea, Syria, Venezuela, and other "rogue states": as dangerous, cunning, and above all devious. Americans assumed that the men in the Kremlin were motivated more by their Marxist-Leninist ideology than by the traditional interests of the Soviet state. Because of their very nature, they could not be trusted. Negotiations were pointless. Munich and the 1930s seemed to offer a clear-cut lesson, as Truman put it in 1948: "Appeasement leads only to further aggression and ultimately to war."

As the current debate over U.S. foreign policy again turns on the lessons of the past, Americans would do well to take a closer look at the country's long wrestling match with Munich's ghost. Such an examination would show, first, that "Munich" has retained its power in American political discourse for more than seventy years largely because of electoral calculations. Second, contrary to the prevailing wisdom, the success or failure of American foreign policy since the 1930s has to a great extent hinged on the willingness of presidents to withstand the inevitable charges of appeasement that accompany any decision to negotiate with hostile powers, and to pursue the nation's interests through diplomacy. Sometimes these negotiating efforts failed; sometimes the successes proved marginal. But those presidents who challenged the tyranny of "Munich" produced some of the most important breakthroughs in American diplomacy; those who didn't begat some of the nation's most enduring tragedies.

When considering the Munich accord and its legacy, we should remember that Franklin Roosevelt initially greeted the pact with equanimity—and that it infuriated Hitler. Like many informed Americans (and Europeans), Roosevelt suspected that Britain and France were unready for war at the time, and he knew that the American public had no desire to enter into another European conflict. Negotiations seemed the best course to take. "Good man," FDR famously cabled Chamberlain after the conference, even as he privately acknowledged that the Briton was "taking very long chances." Hitler, meanwhile, wanted war in 1938. He was angry that he had let himself be maneuvered into a diplomatic agreement that bought the democracies time. For Chamberlain, Munich indeed represented a tactical victory of sorts. It provided England with a breathing spell to build its strength in preparation for the likely showdown with the Nazi juggernaut. As a result, Chamberlain won broad support for his efforts among his informed countrymen, who understood he had few cards to play.

When war came the following year, however, "Munich" instantly became a symbol of diplomatic naïveté. By the time Chamberlain died in November 1940, his reputation was in tatters. "Few men can have known such a tremendous reverse of fortune in so short a time," he remarked not long before his death.

In short order, Roosevelt articulated the new meaning of Munich. "Normal practices of diplomacy . . . are of no possible use in dealing with international outlaws," he said over and over again as he tried to convince an isolationist Congress and a fretful public of the need for war. With dictatorship and tyranny, there could be no negotiated settlements, no deals, only capitulation. This led logically to the policy of "unconditional surrender," announced at Casablanca in 1943. Roosevelt's notion of total victory sat well with Americans—perhaps too well. For years to come they would expect a similar form of moral clarity and unambiguous triumph in all their dealings with foreign adversaries. But unconditional surrender is, in fact, rarely achieved—and never without tremendous cost, as the sixty to seventy million dead from the Second World War make clear.

The slide into the Cold War solidified the role of "no more Munichs" as a cornerstone of American political discourse. From the start in 1946, America's containment strategy envisioned little room for diplomacy with Moscow, at least until such a time as the Soviet system fundamentally transformed, or the balance of power tilted decisively in the direction of the United States and the West. The "lesson of Munich" seemed to suggest that negotiations with Joseph Stalin and his Kremlin associates would be pointless, if not dangerous. And domestic politics merely accentuated the danger. Following the success of the Chinese Communist revolution in 1949, Republicans berated the Truman administration for "losing" China, and Senator Joseph McCarthy ratcheted up the pressure by charging the Democrats with "twenty years of treason."

These partisan attacks cast a long shadow over American foreign policy. A generation of politicians learned a simple lesson: A Communist gain anywhere, on anyone's watch, would be met with charges of appeasement—now equated not just with spineless gullibility, but treacherous disloyalty. This heated atmosphere narrowed the range of acceptable policy choices available to presidents and sent diplomacy out into the cold.

Thus the United States took a somewhat paradoxical stand in the immediate postwar years; it proved largely unwilling to negotiate even though it was in the strongest position to do so. In the 1940s and throughout the 1950s, the American strategic arsenal surpassed that of the Soviet Union in all but one category—the number of men under arms. In terms of nuclear warheads, missiles, bombers, submarines, warships, military bases, points for logistical support—to say nothing of its vastly superior economic strength and ideological appeal—the United States far surpassed the Soviet Union.

What's more, Washington knew it. Publicly, however, politicians and government officials articulated a different line: that the threat was as great as ever, that Moscow's ambitions were global, its capabilities immense. That was the smart message in terms of domestic politics, both to maintain support for a vigilant U.S. posture on the world stage and to win and hold elected office. Negotiation still carried the stench of appeasement, and to advocate it was to run the risk of being called the Neville Chamberlain of a new, more dangerous era.

An abiding faith in the Munich analogy became one of the few things that was truly bipartisan in postwar American politics. In the years that followed Chamberlain's fateful trip to Bavaria, Democrats and Republicans alike displayed a common understanding of the dangers of appeasement, and a common belief in the political value of using the Munich analogy to undermine the other party. Indeed, the analogy has most often been evoked on two kinds of occasions: when the country is preparing for a war overseas, as with Korea, Vietnam, and Iraq, and during election seasons. Thus the Republican Party platforms in 1948, 1952, and 1964, for example, included stark condemnations of "appeasement." In those years, and in 1956 and 1960 as well, the major presidential candidates almost ritualistically smeared their opponents as "weak," as insufficiently vigilant, as likely to give away the store to the wily and cunning Soviets. Republicans did it; Democrats did it. Truman holds the dubious distinction of using the word "appeasement" in a public setting more often than any other American president—much of the time while selling the war in Korea or campaigning for Adlai Stevenson.

Yet it was Democrats who came to feel the sting most acutely, starting with Truman himself after the "loss" of China. A decade later, John F. Kennedy endured withering Republican attacks for his decision to negotiate with Soviet leader Nikita Khrushchev during and after the Cuban Missile Crisis. Kennedy's vice president and successor, Lyndon Johnson, paid due attention. When he announced a massive escalation in Vietnam, for example, in July 1965, he referred confidently to the lessons of history: "We learned from Hitler at Munich that success only feeds the appetite for aggression. The battle would be renewed in one country and then another country, bringing with it perhaps even larger and crueler conflict, as we have learned from the lessons of history."

As the war dragged on, Johnson's reading of the past would fall under painful scrutiny. After more than half a million men and overwhelming firepower failed to win the war, Americans came to accept a new historical lesson—one that stressed not the utility but the futility of force. The ghost of Munich now had to contend with the ghost of Vietnam.

American involvement in Southeast Asia transformed the politics of appeasement. Up until this point, liberals and moderates had both played the game, or some variation of it, as diligently as their conservative counterparts. Vietnam exposed an essential and tragic flaw of the Munich analogy, forcing the left to start shying away from the comparison. This opened them up to political attack, however, because for the right the power of Munich had not diminished. Savvy Democrats understood this, and remained wary of risking the charge of appeasement by appearing too eager to negotiate with Communist foes. This political reality produced a paradoxical outcome: henceforth it would be easier for Republicans to pursue negotiations with adversaries.

Hence, as the saying goes, only Nixon could go to China. Only a Republican with strong anti-Communist credentials—and Richard Nixon's were second to none—could stand up to the charges of weakness that would come from conservative hard-liners. Democrats had already paid their pound of flesh for losing China; they wouldn't do it again.

And so it was that Nixon—the man who had blasted Truman and Stevenson, and then Kennedy and Johnson, for being muddle-headed appeasers—made the first big breakthrough in Cold War diplomacy. Announcing in his 1969 inaugural address a new "era of negotiation" to replace the old one of "confrontation," he not only helped repair two decades of frozen relations between Washington and Beijing, but he and his national security adviser, Henry Kissinger, presided over détente, a relaxation of Cold War tensions that fostered, among other things, a productive round of arms control agreements and the Anti-Ballistic Missile (ABM) Treaty. These moves showed that diplomacy with adversaries could work.

The opening of China led to the beginning of a vital commercial relationship that, despite occasional tensions, has served the American economy well over the years and also acted as a force for liberalization within China itself, gradually easing Mao Zedong's repressive structures. Much the same could be said about the impact of détente within the Soviet Union. The 1975 Helsinki Accords, finalized by Nixon's successor, Gerald Ford, provided a mechanism for advancing human rights within the Soviet bloc. Historians now realize that Helsinki sowed many of the seeds for change that would bear fruit a decade later under Mikhail Gorbachev's *glasnost*.

Still, détente did not sit easily with the right wing of the Republican Party. Nixon's seeming acknowledgment of the Soviet Union as an equal, and his tacit recognition of Kremlin domination of Eastern Europe, smacked too much of a pact with the devil. Grassroots conservatives attacked détente and the China opening fiercely. The firebrand Phyllis Schlafly, a leading voice of the New Right, led an assault on Nixon's leadership of the GOP. "Civilized people don't dine with murderers and criminals," she said, as she compared Nixon to—who else?—Neville Chamberlain, and condemned the ABM Treaty as yet another Munich. "The delusion that America can be defended by treaties instead of by weapons is the most persistent and pernicious of all liberal fallacies," Schlafly declared.

Such arguments gained traction as the years went on. It was Jimmy Carter who paid the biggest political price for the new turn in relations with Moscow. He entered the White House determined to build on the détente policy engineered by Nixon and continued under Ford. But embracing the policies of his Republican predecessors opened him up to attack from, oddly enough, his Republican opponents. Neoconservative intellectuals such as Norman Podhoretz complained about a "culture of appeasement" that was encouraging Soviet adventurism in the third world and turning a blind eye to Russia's growing strength. Ronald Reagan sensed an opportunity. He focused his quest for the White House in large part on wooing grassroots conservatives by attacking détente and playing up the present danger. Asked what he thought of détente, Reagan quipped, "Isn't that what a farmer has with his turkey—until Thanksgiving?"

Carter defended himself by toughening his foreign policy accordingly, setting in motion, Americans often forget, the arms buildup, the secret war in Afghanistan, and other tough policies now generally ascribed to his successor. Prodding Carter along was the hawkish Zbigniew Brzezinski, who repeatedly lectured his boss on the politics of national security. "It is important that in 1980 you be recognized as the president both of *peace* and of *resolve*," Brzezinski advised in April 1979. "For international reasons as well as for domestic political reasons," he later elaborated, "you ought to deliberately toughen both the tone and the substance of our foreign policy."

In the end, Reagan played to the Brzezinski script better than Carter did, riding his message of hard-hitting anti-Communism and unquestioning patriotism into the Oval Office. In part he did so by reframing the lessons of Munich to link them to a new interpretation of the meaning of Vietnam. "There is a lesson for all of us in Vietnam," he announced in the summer of 1980. "If we are forced to fight, we must have the means and the determination to prevail or we will not have what it takes to secure the peace." In virtually the same breath, Reagan spoke of World War II, which came about, he asserted, "because nations were weak, not strong, in the face of aggression." One war began because of weakness; another was lost because of it. Both taught the very same lesson: the importance of standing firm in the face of aggression.

Yet in time Reagan would show a different side. He entered office sounding very much like the antithesis of Carter; by the time he left, he looked more like Carter than either liberals or conservatives today care to admit. His anti-Communism did not diminish, but his sense of how to best contend with Soviet power certainly evolved. Negotiations, formerly anathema to him, came to hold promise, particularly after Gorbachev rose to power in 1985. Reagan reached out to him, and the two men initiated a series of stunning diplomatic breakthroughs that laid the groundwork for the end of the Cold War. Thus in 1987 they signed the Intermediate-Range Nuclear Forces (INF) Treaty, banning all land-based intermediate-range nuclear missiles in Europe. As bilateral relations warmed, Gorbachev also unilaterally reduced his nation's armed forces, helped settle regional conflicts, and began withdrawing Soviet troops from Afghanistan.

Reagan had come to see what other U.S. leaders have always found when they break free of the never-negotiate straitjacket: that diplomacy can be a vital tool for enhancing American interests. Although Reagan had once attacked détente for perpetuating the Kremlin's immoral rule, as president he came to realize that by relaxing tensions, he could actually destabilize the Soviet regime's grip on power. As he jotted in his diary, "If we opened them up a bit, their leading citizens would be braver about proposing changes in their system." By negotiating with him, Reagan gave Gorbachev the sense of security he needed to move ahead with his domestic reforms, measures that ultimately paved the way for the Soviet Union's demise.

The more Reagan talked with Soviet leaders, the more he came to understand "something surprising," as he later recalled: "Many people at the top of Soviet hierarchy were genuinely afraid of America and Americans. Perhaps this shouldn't have surprised me, but it did." He realized he could accomplish more by giving the Soviets fewer reasons to fear American power and more reasons to cooperate. As Reagan once said about negotiations: "You're unlikely to get all you want; you'll probably get more of what you want if you don't issue ultimatums and leave your adversary room to maneuver; you shouldn't back your adversary into a corner, embarrass him, or humiliate him; and sometimes, the easiest way to get things done is for the top people to do them alone and in private."

Conservatives in his own party didn't see it that way. Like Nixon, Johnson, Kennedy, and others before him, Reagan came under fire for his alleged appeasement. The Conservative Caucus pulled out the stops, running a full-page newspaper ad juxtaposing photos of Reagan and Gorbachev with photos of Chamberlain and Hitler. The conservative icon William F. Buckley Jr. chimed in, alleging that Reagan fundamentally misunderstood the Gorbachev regime: "To greet it as if it were no longer evil is on the order of changing our entire position toward Adolf Hitler." As early as 1983, when Reagan was embarking on the largest peacetime military buildup in U.S. history, Norman Podhoretz compared Reagan to Chamberlain and complained that "appeasement by any other name smells as rank, and the stench of it now pervades the American political atmosphere." Reagan had become a "Carter clone," Podhoretz later griped, warning—less than two years before the fall of the Berlin Wall—that "the danger is greater than ever."

Viewed from the perspective of history, what seems most striking about these critiques is how utterly and completely wrong they were. Declassified documents from Soviet and American archives reveal that it was the deep structural problems in the Soviet system, more than Reagan's military buildup, that paved the way for the USSR's collapse. These same documents demonstrate that the president's willingness to engage Gorbachev diplomatically only hastened that process. Soviet documents also reveal something counterintuitive: Gorbachev became more open to negotiating with the West not because of Russia's military weakness, but in fact because of its strength. He came to realize that he could accept deep cuts in his nuclear arsenal, and loosen his grip on Eastern Europe, because Soviet military power remained sufficient to guarantee his country's security.

If such hard-liners as Richard Nixon and Ronald Reagan could embrace diplomacy and trumpet the value of negotiations, why then has the Munich analogy continued to exert such a pull on American politics? Why is it that since 1939 every American politician who advocated engaging an adversary felt obliged to declare that talking was not the same thing as appeasing? Why are Americans so comfortable with the use of force but so uncomfortable with negotiations? And, even more curiously, why has the Munich analogy gained so much traction in the United States, which didn't experience firsthand the terrible consequences of appeasement, but not in Europe, which did?

Part of the answer stems from historical experience. In contrast with Europeans, whose experience living cheek by jowl with powerful neighbors taught the necessity of compromise and living with imperfect solutions, Americans for a century after the War of 1812 felt no such imperative. The Great Powers of the nineteenth century were far away, and the nation was to a large extent protected by two oceans that functioned as vast moats. Later, during the era of the two world wars, U.S. power grew quickly just as that of many other large states declined. In short order, the United States went from being a junior member of the Great Power club to possessing informal hegemony over a sizable part of the globe. Neither before nor after attaining immense international clout, therefore, did Washington have to negotiate and compromise continually to prosper.

Intellectually, too, Americans have found it hard to accept the inevitability of failures in world affairs, to acknowledge the need to occasionally make the best of a bad bargain. Imbued with a moralistic sense of mission, they have tended to view international rivals not as competing states with competing interests, but as evil, demonic, and impervious to reason. The veteran diplomat George F. Kennan once observed: "We Americans like our adversaries wholly inhuman; all powerful, omniscient, monstrously efficient, unhampered by any serious problems of their own, and bent only on schemes for our destruction. Whatever their real nature, we always persist in seeing them this way. It is the reflection of a philosophic weakness—of an inability to recognize any relativity in matters of friendship and enmity."

So it has been since the days of the Revolution. Americans have repeatedly ascribed their difficulties to the malevolent workings of a single demonic figure, the very personification of evil. Thomas Jefferson, Samuel Adams, Thomas Paine, and other revolutionaries set the tone, casting all the colonists' problems at the feet of King George. Reading beyond the first idealistic passage in the Declaration of Independence—the immortalized part about inalienable rights—one finds a tedious and exaggerated litany of King George's abuses. He was responsible for all manner of "injuries and usurpations," from blocking trade to inciting Indian massacres. In writings from this era, George is a "tyrant of the earth" and a "monster in human form," his aides "apostate sons of venality," "execrable parasites," and "first-born sons of Hell."

Later conflicts would likewise be blamed on lone evil-doers: the Spanish "butcher" in Cuba in 1898, the "beast of Berlin" in 1917, and a host of other monsters: Hitler, Stalin, Ho Chi Minh, Manuel Noriega, Saddam Hussein. Add to this the list of Mideast madmen who have made America's enemies list: Ayatollah Khomeini, Gamal Abdel Nasser, Abdul Kareem Qassim, Muammar el-Qaddafi, and Mahmoud Ahmadinejad. Many of these rulers fully earned the title "tyrant," of course, especially for their repressive policies at home. But only one was Hitler.

The propensity to view all adversaries as equally wicked and degenerate has usually rendered negotiations morally suspect a priori. Disputes were not about managing interests, for which agreements could be made, but about vanquishing evil, for which one could give no quarter. Diplomatic disputes became holy crusades. Americans came to see international difficulties primarily as military problems, with no foreseeable solutions except through confrontation and force.

Add to this the particular nature of American domestic politics, where the game often turns on which contestant appears the toughest. Nixon, whose political antennae were as well tuned as any White House occupant's over the past half century, summarized the prevailing political wisdom when he reminded Reagan, in 1987, that Americans responded better to toughness than to pragmatism and compromise. "Many people felt my popularity had gone up because of my trip to China," Nixon said. "In fact, it had only improved slightly. What really sent it up was the bombing and mining of Haiphong."

Yet as Reagan came belatedly to understand, and as Nixon had once argued himself, it makes little sense to assume that talking to adversaries jeopardizes American security. Like any other tool of statecraft, diplomacy is subject to failure and to unrealizable expectations, but it can also bring sustainable success. Although the record shows that Americans have been profoundly suspicious of negotiations with adversaries, those presidents who have managed to free themselves from the shackles of "No More Munichs" have often achieved real and lasting national security gains—and, in the process, bolstered their historical reputations.

Conversely, leaders who have chosen the alternative of relying on ultimatums, on threats and "comply-or-else" bluster, have too often painted themselves into corners—their bluffs called, they feel intense pressure to take the next step, to escalate confrontation, often culminating in a resort to major military force (Exhibit A: LBJ and Vietnam). Ultimatums can work in international politics, but the risks for disaster are immense (Exhibit B: George W. Bush and Iraq). As presidents from both parties have come to understand, maintaining maneuverability by broadening the range of options is usually a much better way to get what you want.

As the debate over Obama's foreign policy continues, we would do well to remember that those who scream "appeasement" the loudest are those that understand its meaning the least. MSNBC's *Hardball* offered a taste of this two years ago when Chris Matthews hosted conservative radio personality Kevin James for a discussion about Bush's "appeasement" remark before the Knesset. As James echoed this charge, angrily denouncing Obama's foreign policy platform as tantamount to appeasement, Matthews interrupted to ask, "I want you to tell me now, as an expert, what did Chamberlain do wrong?" For almost five full minutes, James dodged the question, unable to articulate anything that happened at Munich in 1938 beyond that "Neville Chamberlain was an appeaser." Finally, Matthews got James to admit the sad reality: "I don't know." Matthews then answered his own question: "What Neville Chamberlain did wrong, most people would say, is not talking to Hitler, but giving him half of Czechoslovakia in '38."

Matthews got it right. And it's a simple history lesson we should keep in mind should the debate about U.S. foreign policy continue to revolve around a shaky understanding of what actually happened in 1938: Chamberlain's mistake was not in going to Munich; it was what he agreed to when he got there.

For nearly five decades, American presidents faced an adversary that was far more dangerous, and far more powerful, than all of today's "rogue states" combined. And yet every Cold War president came eventually to understand that diplomacy could be a vital instrument for advancing U.S. interests and preventing nuclear war. Indeed, many would say, the weakness of American diplomacy was not that it engaged the enemy too much, but that it did so too rarely and too cautiously, that it missed too many opportunities to resolve, or at least to de-escalate, the Cold War conflict.

"Let us never negotiate out of fear," Kennedy declared in 1961, summoning up some Rooseveltian rhetoric during one of the tensest moments of the Cold War, "but let us never fear to negotiate." Barack Obama, more than his predecessors (including Kennedy himself), seemed in his first year to grasp the penetrating wisdom of those words, and to shape his foreign policy accordingly. Will he stand his ground as another election approaches and the phantom of Munich again stalks the halls of power in Washington? It remains to be seen.

## CRITICAL THINKING QUESTIONS

1. Why are foreign policy ghosts so hard to defeat? Are there any "good" ghosts in American foreign policy?
2. What other countries have foreign policy ghosts?
3. What recent foreign policy undertakings by the United States might produce foreign policy ghosts? What would they be?

# 13

# Debate: Should the United States Increase or Decrease Its Spending for Defense?

The word "sequestration" is on everyone's lips this election season, at least those connected with the defense apparatus. Sequestration raises larger issues regarding the appropriate amount to spend on defense. Two issues stand in the foreground: America's growing debt and a multipolar world of evolving threats. Currently, President Barack Obama plans to reduce discretionary funding by 1 percent with $525.4 billion for FY 2013. Is this too much? Is this not enough?

Ms. Mackenzie Eaglen of the American Enterprise Institute (AEI), the Project on Defense Alternatives, and Mr. Christopher Preble of the Cato Institute debate below whether the U.S. should increase or decrease its spending for defense.

## DEBATE

### Mr. Carl Conetta, Mr. Charles Knight, and Mr. Ethan Rosenkranz, Project on Defense Alternatives*

The U.S. national security budget has experienced massive growth over the past decade, more than doubling in size since 1998. While some in Washington

Information courtesy of the Federation of American Scientists (www.fas.org). First published November 15, 2012. http://fas.org/policy/debates/20121115_defense_budget .html. Last accessed March 17, 2015.
*Carl Conetta is director of the Project on Defense Alternatives (PDA). Formerly he was a Research Fellow of the Institute for Defense and Disarmament Studies (IDDS) and also served for three years as editor of the IDDS journal *Defense and Disarmament Alternatives*, and the *Arms Control Reporter*. Charles Knight is Senior Fellow at the Project on Defense Alternatives and cofounded the project with Carl Conetta in 1991. In 1989 he founded the Ground Force Alternatives Project at the Institute for Defense and Disarmament Studies where he was a Research Fellow at the time. Ethan Rosenkranz joined the Project on Defense Alternatives in 2011 after more than four years on Capitol Hill where he handled a diverse portfolio of issues, including Appropriations, Budget, Economy, Energy, Taxes, and Veterans' Affairs. Mr. Rosenkranz was also one

have bemoaned recent "cuts to defense," in fact real cuts have been trivial since 2010—and not much is planned for future years. The oft-cited $487 billion reduction in the Pentagon budget is derived from past aspirational planning, not current reality. President Barack Obama's FY13 budget request sets a 10-year "base budget" spending level that is only a couple of percentage points below the Fiscal Year 2012 enacted spending levels, projected for ten years and adjusted for inflation.

To put today's defense spending in context, analysis conducted by the Project on Defense Alternatives shows that the United States spends 42 percent of the world total. Moreover, the United States and its allies have a four-to-one spending edge on potential adversaries. During the Cold War, this ratio was much closer to parity.

Despite the heated rhetoric in this election year, there is broad bipartisan support for cutting the deficit by more than $2 trillion as demonstrated by the passage of the Budget Control Act in 2011. Unfortunately, the current panic about the pending "sequester" discourages clear thinking. A 2013 sequester of $55 billion in security spending will be a precipitous reduction for the Pentagon—bringing the base defense budget back down to the size it was in 2007.

The new Congress will face the challenge of enacting long-term deficit reduction legislation that avoids both institutional disruption and the economic pain associated with deep cuts to government spending—a matter of real concern while the economy remains weak.

In order to achieve budget savings and set the Pentagon's budget on a sustainable path forward, America's defense posture must reset in light of new strategic challenges and circumstances to achieve a better balance between military power and other elements of national strength.

Due to current economic and fiscal realities, we must take a more cooperative approach to achieving security goals—one in which responsibilities, burdens, and authorities are proportionately shared among allies and the broader community of nations. It is imperative that the United States prioritize those threats that pose the greatest danger, tailor war capabilities, and force modernization efforts to a more realistic assessment of current and emerging military challenges.

President Obama's FY13 budget plan proposes spending $5.76 trillion on national security over the next ten years. The Project on Defense Alternatives recommends spending $5.2 trillion over ten years for savings of $560 billion or nearly 10 percent.

Under this plan, the size of the active-component military would be reduced from more than 1.4 million troops today to 1.15 million by the end of 2016—a 19 percent reduction in military personnel. Combat troops and units would be reduced by only 17 percent, however—more for the ground

---

of the principal architects of the Congressional Progressive Caucus (CPC) alternative budget resolutions for Fiscal Years 2011 and 2012, incorporating much of the defense savings outlined by the Sustainable Defense Task Force.

forces, less for the air forces. The reduction in National Guard and Reserve personnel would also be less: only 11 percent. Once this drawdown is complete, the annual Defense Department base budget would stabilize at approximately $455 billion (2012 dollars), which is 14 percent below the Fiscal Year 2012 budget.

While the prospects for long-term deficit reduction remain tenuous, real savings can be achieved in the national security budget this year: in fact, the Project on Defense Alternatives has identified at least 18 programs in the Pentagon's budget that could be safely reduced or eliminated for $17–20 billion in savings this year. For example, by doubling the proposed reduction in U.S. troops stationed in Europe, and enacting commensurate reductions in end strength, the United States could save $500 million in Fiscal Year 2013. By reducing investments in strategic nuclear systems and missile defense, the Pentagon could achieve almost $6 billion in savings.

Short-term and long-term savings options outlined above would bring defense expenditures down to a level close to that required by the sequestration provisions of the Budget Control Act. However, unlike the cuts mandated by sequestration, the proposed reductions would be introduced gradually over a period of five years, thus mitigating the near-term stress on both the armed services and the American economy. And, notably, these options would achieve substantial savings without reducing military personnel wages or benefits. The additional savings realized by adopting the defense posture outlined above can be used to bolster non-military security accounts, revitalize the American economy, and reinvest in international diplomacy and development. In this way, our military efforts can be reconciled with the long-term preservation of national strength and global influence.

## Ms. Mackenzie Eaglen, American Enterprise Institute (AEI)*

Determining what our defense capabilities can do for the nation, our allies and peace and stability around the world is the lens through which our military budget should be evaluated. Like all federal spending, military investment must be analyzed both quantitatively and qualitatively. While numbers tell an important story, they are but a part of the whole picture. Consequently, any analysis of the defense budget must answer the question of what is the return on that spending.

### Cashing a "Peace Dividend" without the Peace

America's defense budget is set to decline by every metric: in real terms, as a percentage of the federal budget and relative to the size of our economy. In

---

*Mackenzie Eaglen has worked on defense issues in the U.S. Congress, both House and Senate, and at the Pentagon in the Office of the Secretary of Defense and on the Joint Staff. She specializes in defense strategy, budget, military readiness and the defense industrial base. In 2010, Ms. Eaglen served as a staff member of the congressionally mandated Quadrennial Defense Review Independent Panel, a bipartisan, blue-ribbon commission established to assess the Pentagon's major defense strategy.

nominal terms, defense spending in 2017 is projected at $567 billion, a little over 12 percent of the federal budget and 2.8 percent of America's expected GDP. Since 1940, America has spent only 2.8 percent of its GDP on defense twice: in FY 1999, and FY 2001. When those budgets were constructed, the world looked far different than it does today.

This would place defense spending at a post-WWII historic low by both of these metrics. The U.S. is already ranked 23rd in the world for the size of our defense budget relative to our economy. Worse, the decline in defense spending is based on projections that do not include sequestration, which would cut another half trillion dollars from the military over the next decade. In FY 2021, the final year of sequestration, defense spending would be a little more than 2.3 percent of GDP—close to the NATO floor of 2 percent of GDP.

In real terms, the military's budget is losing ground to inflation and falling faster in purchasing power than numbers alone indicate. All of these trends are worrisome because this is not your grandfather's defense budget, demands on U.S. forces are not falling significantly alongside mission reductions in Iraq and Afghanistan, and the world is increasingly unsettled.

## Budget Growth Consumed by Consumables

Much of the current debate about the size of the defense budget is driven by the perception that the post-9/11 era's large military spending increases mirrored previous build-ups. But defense budget growth after 2001 generated little cushion. The increases have largely been consumed by current operations, not on future preparedness.

Adding to the budget strain was the fact that combat operations in Iraq and Afghanistan were undertaken without any prior mobilization. Much of the corresponding growth in military spending over the last decade was largely hollow as increased health care costs and urgent war-related priorities took precedence over longer-term priorities like modernization.

This year, the cost of people now comprises a full 50 percent of the defense budget. As health care costs continue to rise, this share will only grow in the coming years. For instance, DoD health care costs were $17.4 billion in 2000. Since then, health care costs have ballooned by 144 percent to $42.5 billion in FY 2013.

One illustrative way to look at the problem are the fourteen programs—representing just 1 percent of line items—that constitute 21 percent of procurement spending. Collectively, these programs represent most of each service's key procurement objectives from the past decade of spending.

Unsurprisingly, the wars in Iraq and Afghanistan meant that ground forces and related systems received priority funding. Examples include the Bradley and Stryker fighting vehicles, mine resistant ambush protected vehicles (MRAPs), Abrams tank upgrades, Predator and Reaper RPVs, as well as the Global Hawk system. Yet an emphasis on these programs meant that systems designed for other contingencies fell as priorities. Navy and Air Force money went largely to existing programs of record like the DDG-51, C-17, and F/A-18E/F.

The reality is that many of the services' most critical next-generation programs were terminated, deferred or trimmed over the past decade—putting the U.S. military further out of reach from an upgraded arsenal after ten years of budget growth.

### The "Next Generation" Is Now Here

America's decade of largely hollow defense increases unfortunately has left the military unready for the multitude of challenges of the 21st century. The arsenal of new equipment acquired for counterinsurgency operations over the past decade would be critical in a future land engagement but is poorly suited for many other threats that may emerge in maritime or air-dominated domains.

As advanced technologies proliferate to other states and entities, America's military edge is shrinking as many high-tech modernization programs are continuously foregone. As senior Air Force leaders have testified, "Legacy fourth-generation aircraft simply cannot survive to operate and achieve the effects necessary to win in an integrated, anti-access environment."

The services need new and innovative solutions to defeat enemy air defenses and anti-access and area-denial technologies. Part of the solution is stealth, including the Air Force's nascent new bomber and the fleet of F-22 fighters. Another part of the solution includes the integration of electronic, sensor, space and cyber attack capabilities. But whatever the solution or, more likely, the basket of solutions—it is wholly unaffordable under current budget projections.

The level of investment needed in order to finance a credible deterrent posture, maintain robust overseas presence, and at the same time invest in new capabilities that can survive in contested environments is incompatible with ongoing and projected cuts to defense spending. The U.S. simply cannot sustain a global military and superpower posture under current plans.

## Mr. Christopher Preble, Cato Institute (Cato)*

### The Bottom Line on Sequestration

There is bipartisan opposition in Washington to sequestration, the automatic spending cuts mandated by last year's Budget Control Act—passed, inconveniently enough, by many of the same people who now rail against it. But the cuts are modest: over the next decade, the federal government will spend about $44 trillion with sequestration, $45 trillion without. And few people are considering the beneficial effects that even those modest cuts could have, both in reducing the nation's debt, and in stimulating economic activity.

---

*Christopher A. Preble is the vice president for defense and foreign policy studies at the Cato Institute. He is the author of three books, including *The Power Problem: How American Military Dominance Makes Us Less Safe, Less Prosperous and Less Free*, which documents the enormous costs of America's military power, and proposes a new grand strategy to advance U.S. security.

In truth, however, neither Democrats nor Republicans are committed to reducing government spending, and both sides have chosen to focus on possible cuts in the military to score political points. President Obama's party hopes to convince Republicans to agree to higher taxes to spare the Pentagon's budget. Such cuts, Secretary of Defense Leon Panetta has said, would be akin to "shooting ourselves in the head." Members of the GOP, for their part, have attempted to protect the Pentagon by appealing for more cuts in domestic spending, although some have signaled a willingness to abandon the "no new taxes" pledge in order to keep the money flowing.

But the most persistent line of argument against sequestration, beyond whether the cuts will undermine the nation's security, is the contention that they will wreck the economy and cast hundreds of thousands into the ranks of the unemployed. In his speech to the Republican National Convention, Mitt Romney claimed that "trillion dollar cuts to our military will eliminate hundreds of thousands of jobs," while the GOP platform predicts that sequestration would accelerate "the decline of our nation's defense industrial base . . . , resulting in the layoff of more than 1 million skilled workers."

Where do Romney and the GOP get their statistics? From the Aerospace Industries Association (AIA), the trade group representing some of the nation's largest defense contractors. According to the AIA's studies, authored by George Mason University Professor Stephen Fuller, defense cuts under sequestration would result in a decline of about $86.5 billion in GDP in 2013, and the loss of 1,006,315 full-time, year-round equivalent jobs. Fuller even broke the job losses down state by state, providing convenient talking points for politicians in the heat of an election year. Virginia will lose 122,800; Florida will shed 39,200. And so it goes.

Several scholars have challenged the AIA's conclusions. The Brookings Institution's Peter Singer noted that only 1 out of every 70 American workers were involved in aerospace and defense, and no more than 3.53 million jobs—direct, indirect, and induced—were sustained by that industry. How then, he asked, could a 10 percent reduction in defense spending result in the loss of one third of all defense-related jobs? The Mercatus Center's Veronique de Rugy was equally skeptical that sequestration would upend the fragile economy. "I understand that catastrophic job losses make a convenient case against sequestration," she wrote at the blog for the conservative *National Review,* "but that doesn't make them true."

Economist Benjamin Zycher showed why they weren't. In a study published by the Cato Institute, Zycher documented how Fuller's study (and others like it) grossly exaggerated the harmful economic effects of spending cuts. Military spending has historically contributed very little to GDP growth, and Zycher therefore concluded that cuts would have little long-term impact on GDP in the future.

But the AIA's approach to spending cuts, and particularly to Pentagon cuts, reveals a deeper conceptual flaw: they ignore the beneficial effects that would result from shifting resources from the military to more productive sectors of the economy. Pentagon spending cuts can be expected—all other factors being equal—to generate greater economic activity elsewhere.

Such transitions are certainly difficult for the workers directly affected. But that applies equally to booksellers or music stores as to jet fighter machinists. Competition from Amazon and Kindle drove Borders out of business. The iPod killed Tower Records. In a similar vein, unmanned aerial vehicles and improvements in radar and missile technology may be most responsible for the obsolescence of the F-22 fighter.

The bottom line on sequestration? The Pentagon cuts currently under consideration are small relative to its gargantuan budget, and consistent with those of past post-war draw downs. The United States will maintain a substantial margin of military superiority over any conceivable combination of rivals even if it spends far less than it does today. And cuts in military spending should pay dividends for the economy over the long run.

---

## CRITICAL THINKING QUESTIONS

1. Which of the three think tanks presented the strongest argument on defense spending?
2. How important is the level of defense spending to U.S. national security? Does more spending mean more security?
3. How would a defense contractor, a human rights advocacy group, a multinational oil corporation, and a local government view the notion of a "peace dividend?"

# 14

# The Courage Crisis

*The children's refugee "crisis" on the U.S.-Mexico
border is but a symptom of the real crisis: denial and
cowardice among U.S. politicians of both parties.*

David J. Danelo

Most Americans have been surprised as well as dismayed by the "child
refugee crisis" that erupted, seemingly from thin air, on the U.S.-
Mexico border in the spring and summer of this year. I was dismayed, but not surprised.

In May 2007, I made my first visit to the political demarcation that sepa-
rates Mexico from the United States. For a month I traveled the 1,952 miles of
*la linea* from east to west, starting at Boca Chica Beach near Brownsville,
Texas, where the Rio Grande empties into the Gulf of Mexico, and ending at
the iconic fence separating San Diego and Tijuana. Stories about Mexico's
drug violence, which then-new President Felipe Calderón was taking unprecedented steps to address, were regular news staples. President George W. Bush's
proposed immigration reform bill had taken center stage politically (very temporarily, as it turned out), even as Representative Tom Tancredo (R-CO) and
CNN broadcaster Lou Dobbs thundered about the "illegals" onslaught.

My border exploration began as an interesting freelance assignment from
*Parade* magazine but evolved into a defining professional experience. I wrote
a book about the U.S.-Mexico border in 2008 and later traveled extensively in
northern Mexico on a research project. In June 2011, the Obama Administration, through former Commissioner Alan Bersin, appointed me to direct policy
and planning for U.S. Customs and Border Protection within the Department
of Homeland Security. At 60,000 employees, Customs and Border Protection
is the largest law enforcement organization in the Federal government. I left
just over a year later, concerned about the Administration's policy compass.

David J. Danelo is the director of field research at the Foreign Policy Research Institute.
From June 2011 to July 2012, he served in the Obama Administration as Executive
Director, Office of Policy and Planning, U.S. Customs and Border Protection. Reprinted
by permission of *The American Interest* 10, no. 2 (October 27, 2014). Copyright ©
2014 by The American Interest LLC.

Drugs. Violence. Immigration. "Illegals." Little appears to have changed along the border in seven years, even as the region has dominated recent headlines in a somewhat novel way. At the center of the 2014 "crisis" are waves of Central American refugees, a great many of whom happen to be children seeking asylum in the United States. Although the migrants are refugees seeking asylum, the overheated politics surrounding immigration have only increased the political inconvenience of their exodus.

Like the Bush Administration before it, President Obama has asked a divided Congress to pass legislation that will bring systemic, structural immigration reform into law. He has been answered for the most part with a mixture of confusion, venality, and, above all, irresponsibility. Unlike George W. Bush, whose plan also fell into the maw of congressional dysfunction, Obama poised himself to go further on his own, issuing a series of Executive Orders—some of which he has stayed until after the 2014 midterm elections—that prescriptively define which immigration rules the Departments of Homeland Security, Justice, and Defense will and will not enforce.

But that has not, and cannot, really fix the problem. The tension in the border "crisis" hearkens back to geopolitical dilemmas with more enduring roots than can be captured in emotional, media-driven debates. And while there have been consistent flaws in this Administration's policy tactics, the far more troubling failures involve the absence of strategic common sense, creativity, and, above all, courage.

Why does courage matter in policymaking? Isn't that more appropriate for measuring combat valor than metering conference room debates? Courage is an intangible; it cannot be fed into a database or revealed by a statistical analysis. Yet courage is relevant because it defines the limits of action. Leaders with courage can expand the realm of the possible, as FDR once did, when he reminded us that the only thing we have to fear is fear itself. Without it, would-be leaders spread malaise and leave the public paralyzed in a crisis of confidence.

The presence or absence of this mystical quality is especially crucial when there is compelling evidence for both sides of an issue. And if we do not see "it" in a president, we refuse to accept his administration's bold policies on contentious issues like border security and immigration reform. No matter how convincing or urgent the logic for action becomes on our teeming shores, we steadfastly refuse to hand our chief executive the keys to our golden doors unless we detect a stout heart guiding his outstretched hand. President Bush's immigration reform proposal was brave in one sense: He went against his party base to proffer it. President Obama's immigration policy, on the other hand, has only served to heighten the partisan divide.

In the United States, border security and immigration reform occupy a strange category in that they are simultaneously foreign and domestic policy concerns. There are practical threats to public security that border security must address, and there are issues of economic prosperity that border management must encourage. From terrorists to narcotics to Ebola, border authorities are charged with preventing people or things from entering the United States that could cause the public harm. At the same time, from tourists to supply chain components to customs revenues, authorities must speed the passage of people and things into the United States that bring benefit. These dueling requirements are imposed on customs authorities at every U.S. port of entry, and they are woven into the fabric of the immigration laws those officials must enforce.

But as our divided Congress illustrates, the American public does not know how to handle the geopolitical challenge presented over the past three decades through our recent immigration waves, whether those waves take the form of legal guest workers who overstay employment visas, illegal migrant women hiking through deserts to give birth, or young children from Honduras, El Salvador, and Guatemala emerging on our South Texas shoreline. When we talk about a "crisis" on national and international media, we are not just referencing that moment's events along the southern border. We are really talking about a much broader question: What kind of nation will we become?

In 2005, the renowned political scientist Samuel Huntington proposed one explanation for the existing geopolitical tension in his final book, *Who Are We? The Challenges to America's National Identity.* The immigration wave from Latin America over the past three decades, Huntington said, is incompatible with the core of American identity and threatens the very fabric of Western civilization. "All societies face recurring threats to their existence, to which they eventually succumb," Huntington wrote in the book's foreword. "Yet some societies, even when so threatened, are also capable of postponing their demise by halting and reversing the processes of decline and renewing their vitality and identity." Huntington's prescription is straightforward: "Americans should recommit themselves to the Anglo-Protestant culture, traditions, and values that for three and a half centuries have been embraced by Americans of all races, ethnicities, and religions." In short, Huntington argued for constraining the Latin American migration wave lest the power and promise of what it means to be American be lost forever.

Fortunately for migrant advocates, there is an alternative geopolitical argument. Robert Kaplan, in his 2010 book *The Revenge of Geography: What the Map Tells Us about Coming Conflicts and the Battle against Fate,* argues that we need not fear the threat of Latin American migration into the United States because it is necessary—even beneficial—for the two societies to merge. "The organic connection between Mexico and America—geographical, historical, and demographic—is simply too overwhelming," Kaplan wrote.

America, I believe, will actually emerge in the course of the twenty-first century as a Polynesian-cum-mestizo civilization, oriented from north to south, from Canada to Mexico, rather than as an east to west, racially lighter-skinned island in the temperate zone stretching from the Atlantic to the Pacific.

Kaplan welcomes migration and sees tremendous benefits to bridging the national divide.

Which viewpoint best suits the American interest? Which prescription should we use to frame policy? This is not an insignificant question. For Team Huntington, no policy on immigration reform that reduces controls or quotas for any Latin American country is welcome. No policy proposal passes muster if it specifies insufficient punishment for "criminal illegals" or inadequate funding for border security. It matters not whether migrants are legal guest workers who fail to speak adequate English and overstay their visas, or eight-year-old orphans fleeing abusive and violent communities. "Illegals" denote not just people who have broken a law but people whose very presence endangers the American way of life. "Illegals" take American jobs. "Illegals" are people who only the naive think can be assimilated. Team Kaplan sees all these issues from the opposite perspective.

The fact that the battle lines in this debate have hardened around partisan bases makes the situation that much worse. In successive elections, the Democratic National Committee has presented the Republican position as racist and xenophobic. This is an unfortunate line, for, inflammatory adjectives aside, Huntington's overall analysis is correct: The wave of Latin American migration over the past three decades into the United States, driven largely (as hundreds of migration scholars have illustrated) by increasingly restrictive U.S. border controls, is unlike any that has happened before in American history. The Democratic Party's denial of this truth only hardens Republicans, who look at immigration reform and see only a mounting siege on American culture and partisan calculations.

The irony of Huntington's case, and of the resulting political divide, is that the most obstructive U.S. immigration policies (many of which remain part of our legal code today) originated from the Democratic side of the aisle. For the first century of the country's existence, there were no restrictions at all on immigration into the United States. It was not until 1882 that a Democratic-controlled Senate and Republican-led House of Representatives united to assert that a specific group of immigrants could not be assimilated. After they passed the bill, Republican President Chester A. Arthur signed the Chinese Exclusion Act. It became America's first migration ban.

The anti-migration position continued during the next four decades regardless of which party held power, even hardening during several Democratic administrations. Congress passed anti-Japanese, anti-European, and anti-illiterate laws. Public sentiment driving these policies came not only from Huntington's "Anglo-Protestant culture" but from labor unions, self-styled progressives, and eugenicists. Woodrow Wilson vigorously opposed welcoming migrants, making the same policy case that Huntington did—albeit with a eugenics subtext.

Not everyone supported restrictive policies. Then, as now, immigration supporters included industrialists who sought to profit from an expanded labor pool, religious advocates who viewed migration as a human right, and undocumented migrants themselves, who banded together politically as Germans, Irish, Chinese, Italians, Czechs, Jews, Arabs, Poles, and Japanese, asserting that no matter their native language, they too were entitled to pursue the American dream.

Today, these migrants are Asian and Latin American, and the political argument for their rights remains the same. For Asians, the issue appears less contentious. But for Latin Americans in general, and Mexicans in particular, their historically huge numbers challenge America's idea of its own culture. And if migrants, whether legal or illegal, perceive one political party as fundamentally opposed to their ethnic origins, culture, and "unassimilable" way of life, then such a wave also challenges the existing political landscape—especially near an election.

The Huntingtonians' ultimate fear is not merely a bifurcation of American culture but a split of U.S. territory. "Demographically, socially, and culturally, the *reconquista* of the Southwest United States by Mexico is well under way," Huntington claimed in 2004. But Huntington made a mistake by conflating migrants seeking work with an eccentric professor's political ideals. That professor, the University of New Mexico's Charles Truxillo, a widely quoted Chicano studies activist, believes that, by 2080, the U.S. Southwest and Northern Mexico will secede from their respective countries and form a *República del Norte*. "There is a growing fusion, a reviving of connections," Truxillo said in a fall 2000 interview. "Southwest Chicanos and Norteño Mexicanos are becoming one people again."

Unfortunately for Truxillo's dreams of reviving a mythic Aztlan empire (another moniker for the feared *República* to come), little public support exists on either side of the border for overthrowing the legacies of their English and Spanish colonial oppressors. Truxillo stokes Huntingtonian suspicions of a Mexican *reconquista* by asserting that Northern Mexico and the U.S. Southwest represents a "spiritual homeland" for migrants from Mexico and other Latin American countries.

But in Northern Mexico, deep in the heart of this supposed spiritual homeland, an interesting Anglo re-conquest has unfolded over the past two decades. In 2009 and 2010, I traveled extensively throughout this region, visiting all six Mexican states bordering the United States as well as Sinaloa. From Monterrey, in Mexico's northeast to Tijuana in the west, I saw increased trade and economic activity (a NAFTA legacy), as well as bumper stickers supporting every branch of the U.S. military (presumably from family connections). Every Mexican I met knew someone living in the United States. Many Mexicans apologized to me—in their own country—for not being able to speak English. American culture has seeped south as Mexicans and their culture have migrated north. Salsa, barbecue, Corona, and *beisbol* are now equally popular in both countries.

For Truxillo's political vision of a *reconquista* to bear fruit, both southwestern Americans and northern Mexicans would need to believe they would benefit more from creating a new nation than from simply allowing the tensions between their two countries to evolve, and dissolve. They would have to conclude, by a commanding majority, that assimilating both cultures each into the other would weaken the two states instead of strengthening them. Few on either side of the border appear to believe these things. Even Truxillo recognized this in 2000, saying that those who have achieved positions of power or otherwise are "enjoying the benefits of assimilation" of Hispanic, Latino, or indigenous ethnicity are likely to oppose a new nation. That fits the description of most people living in the region we are discussing.

As Kaplan argues in *The Revenge of Geography*, while Mexicans migrating to and from the United States may feel a cultural duality, this has not translated into secessionist energy or political violence. Northern Mexico has endured criminal strife, but it is not because the Sinaloa Cartel is bankrolling the *reconquista*. Quite the contrary, most borderland residents of Mexican origin describe a situation of ongoing exile, feeling not quite at home in either country. "I am Mexican, but I do not think any of the terms apply to me," a Mexican-born San Antonio high school student told sociologist Harriett Romo, responding in Spanish to a question of whether he identified as Hispanic, Latino, Chicano, or Mexican-American. "*Yo soy quien soy*" ("I am who I am"), he said.

By virtue of being present in the United States, this young man—undoubtedly lacking legal documentation—may hope to eventually call himself an American. While he may not assimilate as quickly as Huntington would like, I doubt Truxillo would be able to draft this student into his *República del Norte* army simply because he speaks Spanish. "I guess my more personal side is Mexican," an American woman of Mexican origin told Romo, "but I don't think I can define my ties to Mexico. We have double identities. Half of my papers are Mexican. Half of the other ones are American. Sometimes I feel I don't belong anywhere." Such migrants are not likely to find meaning or opportunity by fighting for the *reconquista*, unless perhaps there is a very plush revolutionary payroll to tempt them.

Despite Professor Truxillo's assertions (and Professor Huntington's fears), few in either Northern Mexico or the U.S. Southwest will have any more interest in reclaiming the *República* in 2040 (or 2080) than they have today. In Europe, Scots and Catalans, like stressed tectonic plates, are ready to rumble at any moment, but both Mexicans and Americans are mixtures of migrant races and, at least at some level, they know it. Who needs the hassles of a third set of papers from yet another constructed nationality? *Yo soy quien soy.*

Unfortunately, the simplicity of just being who you are turns out to be less achievable on the Potomac these days than on the Rio Grande. Although the flow of unaccompanied Guatemalan, El Salvadoran, and Honduran children arriving at the U.S. border started more than two years ago, it only emerged as a "crisis" when the Administration could no longer prevent news organization from documenting the deplorable conditions these minors lived in while detained. The politics surrounding the child refugees—which represent an actual, not theoretical, humanitarian crisis—are colored by the racial, ethnic, and political overtones of the Huntington/Kaplan debate. What else can one call a situation in which children are either sent back to war zones or allowed to roam around the United States without adequate shelter or food because our legal system cannot process their cases quickly enough, with the rest detained in varying degrees of squalor while awaiting their day in court?

First, some blunt facts. In most of Guatemala, El Salvador, and Honduras, nobody really knows who is in charge. For more than a decade, over half of Guatemala's territory has been listed by all reputable security analysts as "ungoverned space." The governments of El Salvador and Honduras have equally questionable writ over their regions. Traveling through these chaotic spaces, Catholic Refugee Services workers report endemic violence, intimidation, and poverty that is just as likely to come from policemen or soldiers as from gangs or cartels. Honduras has the highest murder rate in the world today (if you don't count the Syrian government murdering its own people *en masse*), and El Salvador and Guatemala are not far behind. In both El Salvador and Guatemala, policemen and military members told researchers from the Immigrant Policy Center that they had sent their own children north to seek U.S. asylum, saying their lives were at risk if they remained anywhere in their home country.

The United States has not been the only receiving country of refugees fleeing these three failed states. According to the United Nations High Commissioner for Refugees, asylum requests in Belize, Costa Rica, Nicaragua, Panama, and Mexico have increased 432 percent over the past year. Even in Nicaragua, one of the region's poorest countries, asylum requests increased between 2012 and 2013 by 240 percent; one suspects this is so because it is a lot closer as a destination, rather than for its bucolic weather and scenic charms.

Instead of addressing the refugee crisis with direct, engaged leadership, both major American political parties have exploited the border situation to appeal to the worst instincts of partisan extremes—instincts that, with Republicans in particular, are rooted in fears of miscegenation rather than sound, humane policy. The House GOP's position borders on immoral. Rather than seeking to stabilize the situation, in keeping with U.S. experience with past refugee crises (Vietnamese refugees following Saigon's fall, for example), the GOP wants to turn the United States into one large Anglo-Protestant gated community. Many of the same voices who now call for sending thousands of destitute children back to war zones and for changing a competent and rational 2008 law aimed at protecting human trafficking victims once excoriated Janet Reno for sending Elián González back to Fidel Castro's Cuba at gunpoint. What *reconquista* are your constituents afraid of? One led by orphans with coloring books, or 13-year-olds forced into prostitution?

But if the House Republicans appear to lack a heart, then President Obama seems to be missing a spine. The Administration's domestic policy agenda on immigration has been so inconsistent and opaque that it has been exceptionally difficult to discern the real reason, outside of ubiquitous partisan political considerations, why it does anything at all. Whether they are artificially inflating deportation statistics or advocating amnesty workarounds (and stoking the smuggling rumor mill) through the prosecutorial discretion and

Deferred Action for Childhood Arrivals policies, Obama Administration officials have been so inconsistent and haphazard with their Executive Orders that they have increased, rather than reduced, uncertainty for migrants. In so doing, the president's policies create voter dependency around race and ethnicity in small doses, and the Democrats seem to expect their base to keep coming back for more. Unfortunately, this form of political heroin offers no protections beyond momentary fixes.

As Exhibit A, consider the Administration's net response to the child refugees. On the one hand, Administration officials seem intent on "changing the enforcement culture" of immigration and border management authorities; on the other, they fail to recognize that, by law, enforcement is exactly what the American taxpayers have hired them to do. And although migrant advocates have hammered President Obama as the "Deporter in Chief," his Administration has inflated the deportation numbers significantly by adding Voluntary Returns at the U.S.-Mexico border as deportations in 2012. These were never counted as deportations before, and they have made the data difficult to track from previous years.

But what has the president's response been to a legitimate *refugee* crisis? Deportations. Security enhancements. Prison funding. Instead of leading, the president needs to get his base jonesing for that post-election policy fix, an Executive Order pardoning millions of undocumented workers "because Congress won't act." Unfortunately, a future president could just as easily rescind Obama's order, leaving millions of migrants in dangerous limbo. Democrats appear more concerned about being seen as political salvation swamis than about making sound and internally coherent policy.

The most dynamic changes poised to occur in U.S. migration policy in the next decade may not be in the United States, but rather in Mexico. The historic wave of Mexican migration into the United States appears to have slowed dramatically, if not altogether ended. In 2011, the net flow of migrants from Mexico to the United States fell to zero. Since then, more Mexicans have left the United States than have arrived. "Looking back over the entire span of U.S. history, no country has ever seen as many of its people immigrate to this country as Mexico has in the past four decades," the Pew Research Center reported in 2012, illustrating why Huntington was both right and wrong. "However, when measured not in absolute numbers but as a share of the immigrant population at the time, immigration waves from Germany and Ireland in the late 19th century equaled or exceeded the modern wave from Mexico."

Huntington correctly identified the Mexican wave as historic. But he incorrectly concluded that this wave would not recede or that it was incompatible with advancing the American interest in the 21st century. In August 2014, Mexico's Congress, which has been running circles around our own, passed President Enrique Peña Nieto's long-awaited energy reform bill, ending 75 years of state control over the energy sector. As migration flows indicate, Mexico is slowly but steadily evolving into a middle-class country. "The result of that will be a sea change in its relations with the United States, which will finally see Mexico not as a problem but as a partner," predicts Fareed Zakaria, echoing Robert Kaplan. "Once they do, North America—the United States, Mexico and Canada—will become the world's most important, vibrant and interdependent economic unit."

Unfortunately for Republicans (and, of course, for Professor Truxillo), most migrants who have become U.S. citizens and are now "enjoying the benefits of assimilation" can only find a political home among Democrats. But rather than exert moral authority through patient, deliberate leadership, President Obama has exploited the border challenges for political gain. The lack of candor and direct engagement from both sides is shameful. Americans should demand better; we should expect at least a scintilla of courage from our leaders. In the meantime, the kids just keep on coming.

## CRITICAL THINKING QUESTIONS

1. Why is courage lacking?
2. Is there a lack of courage in dealing with other foreign policy problems?
3. Whose position provides a better starting point for thinking about the immigration problem: Samuel Huntington's or Robert Kaplan's?

# Institutions and U.S. Foreign Policy

A merican foreign policy making is often pictured as taking place in a series of concentric circles. The further a person or institution is placed from the center, the less influence it has. In the innermost circle are the president, key foreign policy advisors, and the National Security Council. One step removed is Congress, with its elaborate committee system that passes legislation and oversees the bureaucracy. Just beyond it is the third circle, containing the national security bureaucracies and officials led by the State Department, Defense Department, and organizations comprising the intelligence community. Beyond this core set of foreign affairs bureaucracies is found yet another circle, containing the judiciary and other bureaucracies whose foreign policy influence on occasion may be considerable but who generally are not active participants in foreign policy making. Elections, interest groups, public opinion, the media, and political protests are generally placed in the outermost circle, although, as we discussed in the last part, this is not uniformly the case for all foreign policy issues.

Our concern in part IV is with the institutions in the innermost circles: the presidency, Congress, and the foreign affairs bureaucracy. In judging their influence, scholars have turned their attention to four factors. The first is the character, personality, or operating style of those who lead these organizations, with the president receiving the most attention, although no consensus exists as to how best characterize key personal traits such as their personality, operating styles, and beliefs about the nature of world politics. The second is organizational structure. Common concerns here are lines of jurisdiction, the nature of standard operating procedures, and the patterns of interaction or lack thereof among organizations. One of the key reforms put forward after 9/11 was the need for greater information sharing among intelligence agencies and the need to break down the "silos" within which these organizations operated.

A third concern is with the organizational culture that shapes the behavior of organizational members. Foreign Service officers, for example, have long been criticized for being overly cautious and risk averse in their decision making. Finally, attention has been directed at the manner in which these individuals and organizations interact to make and implement foreign policy decisions. In keeping with the classical realist model of international relations, early decision-making theories were built around the principle of rational choice. According to it, people make decisions by weighing the costs and benefits of different lines of action and choose the one with the highest rewards at the lowest acceptable cost. It has since been recognized that to effectively understand how individuals and organizations interact to make decisions, more varied and complex models are needed. Among the most prominent today are those focusing on small groups, bureaucratic bargaining, and the psychological traits of key individual decision makers.

Accounts of Obama's foreign policy have addressed all four of these concerns to varying degrees. A great deal of attention has been directed at Obama's decision-making and managerial style, with most characterizing it as overly analytical and detached, resulting in a foreign policy some label as pragmatic and others as undisciplined. He is seen as having anchored foreign policy decision making in the White House more forcefully than any president since Richard Nixon. Obama and Congress have also sparred frequently over the extent to which the president has exercised or overreached in his exercise of presidential powers in pursuing the war on terrorism, immigration reform, blocking the Keystone XL Pipeline, and normalizing relations with Cuba. For its part, Congress continued to deny the president trade promotional authority that would accelerate the signing of international trade agreements and pass additional economic sanctions against Iran, bringing forward threats of presidential vetoes, and it held investigations of high-profile foreign policy missteps such as the attack on the American diplomatic post in Benghazi. The Benghazi attack (2012), revelations about the NSA's secret domestic surveillance program (2013), and recurring problems with treatment of women in the military are prominent examples of continuing concern for how bureaucracies implement foreign policy.

Our first reading is an excerpt from the first State Department "Quadrennial Diplomacy and Development Review" (QDDR). Based on a similar exercise conducted by the Defense Department, the QDDR seeks to highlight the role the State Department and the U.S. Agency for International Development can and should play in American foreign policy along with the changes that need to be made to make this a reality. Ken Gude, in "Understanding Authorizations for the Use of Military Force," provides insight into perhaps the most controversial manner in which Congress can exercise its authority. Using the authorization for a military campaign against ISIS, he examines both the legal and historical bases for congressional action. In "National Insecurity: Can Obama's Foreign Policy Be Saved?" David Rothkopf presents a critique of the administration's foreign policy that focuses on the manner in which President Obama makes foreign policy decisions and manages the foreign policy decision-making process. He suggests that Obama might learn from the manner in which George W. Bush, his predecessor, reformed his decision-making style late in his term as president. The final reading, "Reforming the NSA," by Daniel L. Byman and Benjamin Wittes, takes up the question of how to reform the National Security Agency in the aftermath of the well-publicized revelations by Edward Snowden. Byman and Wittes argue that these revelations were not the case of a bureaucracy run amok but of an inherent conflict between the need to provide security and be accountable and transparent at the same time.

## BIG PICTURE QUESTIONS

1. What is the proper relationship between the president and Congress in making foreign policy? Does it matter what the issue is or what countries are involved?
2. Rank the State Department, Defense Department, Central Intelligence Agency, National Security Agency, and Commerce Department for their roles in American foreign policy today. What do you think the ranking will look like in ten years?
3. Which matter most: the people making decisions or the organizations that provide them with information and implement the decisions reached?

## SUGGESTED READINGS

Gordon Adams and Shoon Murray (eds.), *Mission Creep* (Washington, DC: Georgetown University Press, 2014).

Michael Allen, *Blinking Red* (Washington, DC: Potomac Books, 2013).

Robert Jervis, "Do Leaders Matter and How Would We Know?" *Security Studies* 22 (2013), 153–79.

David Kaye, "Stealth Multilateralism," *Foreign Affairs* 92 (July 2013), 113–24.

Jon Kyl et al., "War of Law," *Foreign Affairs* 92 (September 2013), 115–25.

# 15

# The First Quadrennial Diplomacy and Development Review

The vanguard of civilian power are the American diplomats and other officials based in 271 posts around the world. They perform five core civilian missions. They prevent, resolve, and end conflicts. They counter threats that cannot be addressed through U.S. military force alone. They address and solve global political, economic and security problems that directly affect the United States and cannot be solved by the United States alone. They advance a positive U.S. political, economic, development, environmental, and values agenda in the world. And they connect Americans to the world and the world to America by assisting American citizens who travel and live abroad while serving as the front line of our border security.

Civilian power is equally the power of development professionals from USAID and other agencies working in more than 100 countries to fulfill a strategic, economic, and moral imperative for the United States. This dedicated corps of experts—many of whom are veterans of decades spent in some of the world's poorest and most challenging places—also carry out core civilian missions. They strengthen the regional partners we need to address shared threats and challenges, from climate change to global criminal networks. They help governments transform their countries from islands of poverty to hubs of growing prosperity, generating new sources of global demand. They advance universal rights and freedoms. And they prevent conflicts and reduce humanitarian suffering in times of crisis.

. . .

The scope and nature of civilian power has also changed over the past half-century. It is more and more operational: civilian agencies and private groups of all kinds are increasingly able to deploy resources on the ground in countries around the world. This operational dimension of civilian power is evident in the work that USAID and many other agencies, including the Peace Corps, have done in developing countries for decades. It is also evident today when diplomats and development professionals partner with one another. Embassies

Excerpted from "Leading Through Civilian Power: The First Quadrennial Diplomacy and Development Review," United States Department of State, 2010.

around the world also create the political space and provide the logistical platforms for civilian programs, projects, and initiatives with the government officials and the people of the host country.

. . .

When U.S. civilian power is aligned, it can help to reduce, prevent, or ameliorate conflict. By deploying integrated teams of experienced mediators, negotiators, and early-responders that draw not only from State but also from USAID, the Department of Defense, the Department of Justice, and the Department of Homeland Security, the U.S. government can help to prevent armed conflict from breaking out and reduce the likelihood that United States or other forces will be required. Where U.S. forces are deployed, civilian experts in governance, economic development, infrastructure, health, education, and other basic services are the "closers" who, with their local counterparts, can ensure the transition from conflict to stability to long-term development. On the other hand, when civilian agencies deploy personnel and resources to achieve specific objectives in a fragile state or conflict zone without a strategic framework and a long-term plan, the whole can be less than the sum of the parts.

. . .

## ADAPTING TO THE DIPLOMATIC LANDSCAPE OF THE 21ST CENTURY

The classic diplomacy of grand capitals is the business of managing relationships between states, bilaterally and regionally. Classic diplomacy was born within a rigidly prescribed set of formal relations between countries—a world of international demarches, communiqués, and negotiated agreements of every sort. Indeed, the word "diplomat" comes from diploma, an instrument of formal accreditation issued by a government to envoys officially designated to represent another nation. The world of classic diplomacy still exists and remains central to the success of our foreign policy.

But the diplomatic landscape of the 21st century now extends far beyond classic diplomacy. It features a more varied set of actors: many more states capable of and intent upon pursuing independent diplomatic agendas; a variety of U.S. government agencies operating abroad, and transnational networks of many different kinds—corporations, foundations, non-governmental organizations, religious movements, and citizens themselves. These actors interact in multiple spaces far beyond foreign ministries: multilateral organizations, interagency processes, boardrooms, chatrooms, town halls, and remote villages. This landscape features a new range of issues on the diplomatic agenda. Advancing industrialization and increasing populations have exacerbated shared challenges that include environmental degradation, climate change, pandemic disease, and loss of biodiversity.

Effective U.S. diplomacy in the 21st century must adapt to this landscape. It must also be prepared to reshape it. In particular, our diplomats must be prepared to respond to—and effect change in—three domains where evolving trends require new ways of doing business:

1. Because a wide array of our government agencies increasingly engage with their counterparts abroad, our diplomats have to be prepared to lead the implementation of global civilian operations and to pursue whole-of-government diplomatic initiatives;
2. Because new transnational forces are increasingly challenging the capacity of 20th century institutions, and emerging centers of influence are changing the geopolitical landscape, our diplomats have to be prepared to build new partnerships and institutions and reshape old ones at both the regional and global level; and
3. Because a wide range of non-state actors are growing in reach and influence, our diplomats have to be prepared to go beyond the state to engage directly with new networks, from the private sector to the private citizen.

Our efforts in these three domains will become core missions for the State Department. The new diplomatic landscape will not adapt to us; we must develop our capabilities, channel our resources, and organize our structures to operate effectively within it. As we do so, we must remain committed to excellence in the essential work we are already doing—from treaty negotiations to consular services to political reporting.

. . .

## ELEVATING AND TRANSFORMING DEVELOPMENT TO DELIVER RESULTS

President Obama and Secretary Clinton have launched a new era in American foreign policy by committing to elevate development alongside diplomacy and defense as an equal pillar of American foreign policy. In a world shaped by growing economic integration and diffused political power; by the persistent weakness of fragile states; by the tensions wrought by globalization and risks from transnational threats; and by the challenges of hunger, poverty, disease, and global climate change, development progress is essential to promoting America's national security and economic interests, as well as our values.

Successfully incorporating development as a third pillar of our foreign policy requires not merely elevating development, but engineering a new strategy for its pursuit and undertaking the institutional reforms and partnerships necessary to succeed.

The Administration has already begun charting this new approach to development; in September 2010, President Obama issued the first national development policy since President Kennedy created the United States Agency for International Development in 1961. In launching USAID, Kennedy defined a new vision for the role of development in promoting American values and advancing global security. He pronounced a new commitment and a new approach that would match the realities of the post-war world. Responding to current realities, President Obama's 2010 Presidential Policy Directive on Development (PPD) focuses U.S. development efforts on broad-based economic growth, democratic governance, game-changing innovations, and sustainable systems for meeting basic human needs. It defines an approach based in partnership—not patronage—and sets the goal of putting ourselves out of business by putting countries on a path to self-sustaining progress.

Consistent with the PPD, we will focus our efforts in six development areas where the U.S. government is best placed to deliver meaningful results: food security, global health, global climate change, sustainable economic growth, democracy and governance, and humanitarian assistance. Throughout each of these, we will elevate and refine our approach to women and girls.

The Administration has launched Presidential Initiatives in three of these areas: the Global Health Initiative (GHI), the Global Hunger and Food Security Initiative—Feed the Future (FtF), and the Global Climate Change Initiative (GCCI). Launched by President Obama, FtF is the U.S. component of a global initiative aimed at promoting a comprehensive approach to food security by accelerating economic growth, raising individual incomes, and reducing poverty. Building on the important foundation of the President's Emergency Plan for AIDS Relief (PEPFAR), the President's Malaria Initiative, and other long-standing programs, GHI expands U.S. global health commitment by focusing on five vital areas in which we can deliver meaningful results: disease prevention and treatment, health systems, maternal and child health, neglected tropical diseases, and increased research and development. And GCCI responds to the profound threat climate change poses to development by spurring global greenhouse gas emission reductions in energy sectors and promoting adaptation in vulnerable countries and communities.

. . .

## PREVENTING AND RESPONDING TO CRISIS, CONFLICT AND INSTABILITY

Internal violent conflict, weak or failed governance, and humanitarian emergencies in numerous states around the world have become a central security challenge for the United States. The State Department is committed to preventing and resolving crises and conflicts of many kinds—interstate wars and aggression, coups, insurgencies, proliferation, and countless others. Our diplomats mediate state conflicts and bring pressure to bear against rogue action, resolving conflicts from the former Yugoslavia to Northern Ireland. Our military assistance helps allies defend themselves and ward off attacks while deepening their relations with the United States. But one of the principal challenges identified by the QDDR is the need for the State Department and USAID to substantially improve our ability to address the crises and conflicts associated with state weakness, instability, and disasters, and to support stability and reconstruction following conflict.

Such conflicts have rarely been simple, but today they are defined by their complexity. They often involve multiple factions within states and are driven by a mix of religious, ethnic, ideological, political, economic, and geographic factors. They are ignited or sustained by the actions of governments, insurgent groups, criminal organizations, and terrorist networks. Increasingly, we see the effects of climate change, urbanization, growing youth populations, food insecurity, and natural disasters providing a spark to long-simmering grievances. International experts in conflict prevention and response use terms like "complex political emergencies" and "complex peace operations" to describe their field. And humanitarian emergencies—ranging from earthquakes to floods—continue to cause massive human suffering. More than ever before, effective solutions to the range of crisis, conflict, and instability require us to reach across agencies as well as beyond government to apply policies and programs that advance reconciliation, security, good governance, rule of law, and provision of basic human needs.

Despite their complexity, patterns emerge in the causes and enabling conditions of these conflicts. The link between internal conflict and weak governance stands out. Fragile states are unable to provide physical security and basic services for their citizens due to lack of control over physical territory, massive corruption, criminal capture of government institutions, feudal gaps between rich and poor, an absence of social responsibility by elites, or simply grinding poverty and the absence of any tradition of functioning government. States and peoples compete for scarce resources, territory and power. When the United States is called upon to prevent or respond to crisis or conflict, that response must address these links in ways that require new knowledge, skills, and tools.

. . .

Yet too often our reaction has been both *post hoc* and *ad hoc*. We have not defined and resourced the problems of conflict and crisis as a central mission of our civilian toolkit or developed adequate operational structures to support U.S. and multi-partner responses. We have responded to successive events without learning lessons and making appropriate institutional changes to provide the continuity and support. Too frequently, we:

- Miss early opportunities for conflict prevention;
- React to each successive conflict or crisis by reinventing the process for identifying agency leadership, establishing task forces, and planning and coordinating U.S. government agencies;
- Scramble to find staff with expertise in conflict mitigation and stabilization, pulling personnel from other critical roles to send them to crisis zones with limited preparation;
- Rush to compile resource requests and reprogram within limited budgets;
- Turn to embassies that are not equipped to house or execute complex, multilayered responses or to operate amidst significant instability;

- Leave it to our civilian and military teams in the field to figure out how best to work together;
- Rely on traditional diplomatic and development strategies rather than build new tools (embedded in on-going institutions and processes) tailored to conflicts and crises;
- Coordinate poorly with multilateral institutions, foreign governments, and nongovernmental partners in our response;
- Delay bringing conflict, humanitarian, terrorism, law enforcement, intelligence, and military communities into the same policy and planning process for emerging crises, missing opportunities for synergy, shared intelligence, and integrated solutions; and
- Fail to adequately understand and plan for the unintended consequences of large-scale operations and assistance, which can inadvertently intensify corruption and breed local cynicism towards our efforts.

It is time for a new approach. We start by embracing crisis and conflict prevention and resolution; the promotion of sustainable, responsible, and effective security and governance in fragile states; and fostering security and reconstruction in the aftermath of conflict as a central national security objective and as a core State mission that must be closely supported by USAID and many other U.S. government agencies. We will define this mission by building on the expertise acquired over the past two decades by personnel throughout the U.S. Government, as well as the experience of other countries and partners. We will treat the knowledge and skills necessary to address these problems as a distinct discipline. We will develop the flexible, innovative approaches required for linkages to longer term development. And we will organize ourselves to carry out this mission most effectively.

We have learned from what has succeeded and failed in the past. Going forward, we will:

- Adopt a lead-agency approach between State and USAID based on clear lines of authority, a complementary division of labor, joint structures and systems, and standing agreements with other agencies;
- Bring together a cadre of personnel experienced in this discipline within a new bureau, fill out a standing interagency response corps that can deploy quickly and flexibly in the field, and provide broader training for diplomats, civil servants, and development professionals;
- Develop a single planning process for conflict prevention and resolution, sustainable governance, and security assistance in fragile states, including planning to address potential intended consequences of our assistance and operations;
- Develop standing guidance and an international operational response framework to provide crisis and conflict prevention and response that is not dependent on individual embassies;
- Create new ways and frameworks for working with the military to prevent and resolve conflicts, counter insurgencies and illicit actors, and create safe, secure environments for local populations;

- Coordinate and integrate assistance to foreign militaries, civilian police, internal security institutions, and justice sector institutions to promote comprehensive and sustainable security and justice sector reform; and
- Strengthen our capacity to anticipate crisis, conflict, and potential mass atrocities and raise awareness of emerging governance problems.

. . .

## WORKING SMARTER

The urgent and critical nature of State and USAID missions—to secure the conditions abroad that ensure American security and prosperity at home—demands excellent, accountable management in support of high rates of success. Every dollar spent in building our workforce and carrying out our policies and programs is provided by U.S. taxpayers, and they rightly demand a return on their investment. We owe it to the American people to ensure that our personnel have the skills and training to match their missions, that we make smart choices about what we do with their resources, that our choices are transparent, and that we deliver results. We will seek to utilize the strengths of all U.S. government agencies and not seek to duplicate established relationships, personnel and mechanisms, but coordinate the most effective agencies to carry out the work.

## CRITICAL THINKING QUESTIONS

1. Compare the threats and evolving global system identified in the QDDR with that presented in Obama's West Point speech and the intelligence community's "Worldwide Threat Assessment." How similar are they? What accounts for any differences?
2. Which holds the greater potential for addressing the global problems identified here: public civilian power or private civilian power?
3. What should the role of the ambassador be at an embassy and in the making of U.S. foreign policy?

# 16

# Understanding Authorizations for the Use of Military Force

Ken Gude

Since President Barack Obama laid out his strategy to degrade and ultimately defeat the Islamic State of Iraq and al-Sham, or ISIS, the debate has turned to whether he has sufficient legal authority to carry out that strategy or whether he needs a new congressional authorization for this mission. This is now even more pressing as U.S. and coalition air forces began striking ISIS targets in Syria this week, expanding U.S. military action to a second country. While the Obama administration has asserted that it has sufficient legal authority for this mission, many legal scholars and some elected officials on both sides of the aisle disagree.

There are multiple potential sources of authority in U.S. law for military action. As commander in chief, the president derives authority to use military force in certain circumstances from Article II of the Constitution. Congressional authorizations for the use of military force allow the president to lead a military campaign consistent with the scope defined by Congress. The War Powers Resolution was an attempt to restore the original constitutional balance on war powers between the legislative and executive branches. But in practice, it has afforded the president greater latitude to use military force at the outset of a conflict.

Regardless of the merits of the various legal claims, the best path forward is for President Obama and Congress to work together on a new authorization for the campaign against ISIS. This new authorization should be exclusively directed at ISIS, prohibit the large-scale deployment of U.S. ground combat troops, and include both a geographic limitation and a resolution clause based on agreed criteria for ending the military phase of the fight against ISIS.

Ken Gude is a senior fellow with the National Security and International Policy team at the Center for American Progress. This piece was originally published by the Center for American Progress in September 2014. Reprinted with permission from the Center for American Progress.

# THE PRESIDENT'S LEGAL AUTHORITY FOR MILITARY ACTION

The Constitution divides the power to declare war and the power to conduct war between the legislative and executive branches. Article I of the Constitution invests Congress with the authority to declare war and to raise and maintain military forces. Article II of the Constitution establishes the president as commander in chief of the U.S. military and gives that office the authority to lead American military forces and prosecute armed conflicts. In this system, Congress decides whether to fight, and the president as commander in chief manages the fight authorized by Congress.

## THE ROOTS OF WAR POWERS

The division of power between the legislative and executive branches was initially intended to address two very specific experiences and concerns. First, the Founding Fathers feared unilateral decisions to initiate military actions that were common to monarchs with absolute rule; giving Congress the authority to initiate military action broke with European norms and would be a check on reckless military adventurism. Second, they recognized that collective decision making during war, as many had experienced during the American Revolution, was ineffective. Granting the president the sole responsibility for leading the military ensured unity of command. It also enabled the president to respond to immediate threats under Article II.

The limitations of declaring full war became apparent early in American history during the XYZ Affair, also known as the Quasi-War, when the French government began to seize American merchant ships in 1798. Rather than declare war, Congress authorized the president to "acquire, arm, and man no more than twelve vessels, of up to twenty-two guns each" and then authorized public U.S. vessels to capture armed French vessels. From that time, both declarations of war and other authorizations for the use of military force have provided congressional sanction for war.

# HISTORICAL CONGRESSIONAL AUTHORIZATIONS OF FORCE

More than half of all the congressional use of force authorizations—18 of 35—came in the first 30 years after independence. These ranged from large wars, such as the War of 1812, to small engagements to fight naval piracy. It was also relatively common for Congress to restrict the president to the use of specific types of armed force. This was the case in the Quasi-War, which even limited the number of naval ships that could be used. Even though it was a long time ago, the only time this congressional power was tested in the Supreme Court, it was upheld unanimously.

Congressional authorizations have grown much less frequent over time, with only nine occurring in the nearly 100 years since the United States entered

World War I. The last actual declaration of war under Article I was for World War II. Congressional authorizations in the 20th century have often been for major military actions such as World Wars I and II, the Gulf War, the Iraq War, and the response to the 9/11 attacks. The 2001 authorization for the use of military force, or AUMF, directed at the perpetrators of the 9/11 attacks is the longest continuously used congressional use of force authorization.

## THE PRESIDENT'S ARTICLE II POWERS

The Korean and Vietnam Wars are notable exceptions to seeking congressional authority. President Harry Truman claimed the Korean War was a "police action" and did not require congressional authorization. President Lyndon B. Johnson exploited the vaguely worded Gulf of Tonkin Resolution as justification for pursuing the armed conflict in Vietnam. These significant examples show how war powers have shifted toward the executive branch since the early days of American history.

Recent presidents of both parties and in different contexts have concluded that it is lawful for the president to use military force without congressional authorization in a wide range of circumstances. Generally, since the Korean War, presidential use of military force without congressional authorization has rested on two criteria. First, the military action is intended to defend U.S. persons, property, or national interests. Second, the military operation is clearly short of the traditional understanding of war. The Obama administration relied on this interpretation of its Article II authority to undertake the bombing campaign in Libya in 2011 and the initial deployment of U.S. forces to Baghdad and airstrikes targeting ISIS in August.

In reaction to the continued prosecution of the Vietnam War without specific congressional authorization, Congress passed the 1973 War Powers Resolution, or WPR, to re-establish congressional prerogatives. In cases of legitimate military action in self-defense, the president must notify Congress within 48 hours and obtain congressional authority within 60 days of deploying American military forces into hostilities. This can be extended another 30 days if requested by the president. The common interpretation of the WPR has created a 60-day or 90-day window during which the president has a virtually free pass to use force. This is often referred to as the "sixty-day clock."

## WAR POWERS AND THE CONFLICT WITH ISIS

The Obama administration claims that both the 2001 AUMF in response to 9/11 and the 2002 Iraq War AUMF provide the necessary congressional authorization for its military campaign against ISIS. Since it has not yet put forward a formal legal rationale, it is not clear whether the Obama administration is relying on both Article II and this statutory authority or if it has dropped its Article II claim. The interpretation that the 2001 and 2002 AUMFs cover the current conflict with ISIS has caused considerable controversy among legal scholars and elected officials and raised concerns that it has, at a minimum, stretched those AUMFs beyond their originally intended use.

Regardless of the legal controversy, proceeding without a new and clear authorization to use force against ISIS will undermine President Obama's previously stated desire to establish a durable legal framework for the fight against terrorist groups. Without congressional action, future presidents would likely follow this precedent and apply an expansive interpretation of existing authority to take military action against terrorist groups and limit Congress' appropriate role in such actions.

In order to avoid such a precedent, the Obama administration and Congress should work in concert to develop a specific congressional authorization for the conflict with ISIS that builds on the strategy the president presented to the nation earlier this month. Congress is in recess until after the election, but it will reconvene for a lame duck session in November and should enact an AUMF focused on ISIS at that time.

## WHAT AN ISIS AUMF SHOULD LOOK LIKE

The United States has the experience of nearly 13 years of armed conflict against Al Qaeda, which can inform any process for a new use of force authorization against ISIS. As Sen. Tim Kaine (D-VA) said yesterday at the Center for American Progress Action Fund, enacting "the 2001 AUMF with no geographic limitation and no temporal limitation was a serious mistake."

Rather than simply extend the 2001 AUMF to include ISIS and more groups, a new AUMF directed at ISIS should provide clarity of mission and purpose and sufficient authority to achieve those objectives. This could be a step toward the durable legal framework President Obama wants to leave to his successor.

### Targeting ISIS

First, the new AUMF should explicitly name ISIS in the operative portion of the authorization. There must be enough flexibility to account for the frequent name changes and splintering of terrorist groups: ISIS is on its third name just this year, evidenced by President Obama's references to the group as the "Islamic State of Iraq and the Levant," or ISIL, and the group shortening its own name to simply the "Islamic State."

ISIS presents a unique set of challenges: It is operating across a former international border with sanctuary in ungoverned spaces in both Iraq and Syria; controls large amounts of cash, military equipment, and foreign fighters; and has access to oil fields and other substantial sources of revenue. The AUMF should focus on these challenges and how to combat them, as outlined in the recent CAP report "Supporting the Syrian Opposition."

## Determining the Extent of Military Engagement

Second, Congress is within its power to define the nature of U.S. military engagement against ISIS. President Obama has repeatedly pledged that no U.S. ground troops would be involved in this military campaign. To ensure that no large-scale U.S. combat forces are deployed, the AUMF could authorize President Obama to deploy specific capabilities against ISIS. These would most likely involve air power and special operations forces for specific missions such as assisting airstrikes, training and advising local forces, or providing support to protect Americans who are directly threatened by ISIS forces. Congressional approval for these missions should include a requirement that the president seek additional authority for the long-term deployment of regular ground forces. This would be distinct from last week's vote in Congress to authorize the U.S. military to provide training and military equipment to the Syrian rebels in their fight against ISIS and the Assad regime.

Additionally, the AUMF should include a geographic scope placing boundaries on the areas where the president is permitted to use force. When combating a nation-state, the geographic limits are understood, but a non-state actor such as ISIS can slip across multiple international borders. Consequently, Congress should define a geographic scope in Iraq and Syria to provide clarity about the military mission to the American people. It should acknowledge that ISIS could move across another recognized border and allow for use of force in areas outside of Iraq and Syria with congressional notification within 30 days. At that point, Congress can determine whether it is necessary to amend the original scope of the authorization to include the new area of operation.

## Determining a Conclusion to Military Action

Finally, the AUMF should include a clause that determines the conclusion of military action against ISIS. Again, unlike in conflicts between nation-states, there will be no potential peace treaty or cease-fire agreement negotiated between the two sides. In such situations, determining when the conflict is over is extremely difficult and fraught with political risk, but simply allowing the authority to continue carries little such risk. Without agreeing to terms that define the conditions necessary to shift to normal law enforcement and intelligence in the fight against ISIS, this authorization could create the kind of permanent state of war that President Obama has rightly decried.

This mechanism should establish a set of criteria for President Obama and Congress to agree on the point when the armed conflict with ISIS is over. White House Chief of Staff Denis McDonough recently said on *Meet the Press*, "Success looks like an ISIL that no longer threatens our friends in the region, no longer threatens the United States. An ISIL that can't accumulate followers, or threaten Muslims in Syria, Iran, Iraq or otherwise."

Building on that starting point, the criteria should include a determination that ISIS is no longer capable of threatening the U.S. homeland, does not control territory, and is diminished to the point that local military and law enforcement can manage the threat. This could allow a transitional period akin to examples in which the United States has helped countries reduce and manage the threat from insurgencies so that local governments can handle them on their own. Despite the ongoing challenges in countries such as Afghanistan, Pakistan, Yemen, and Somalia, it can and has been done successfully in Colombia and the Philippines. With consistent and targeted assistance from the United States, those two countries have experienced a significant reduction in violence and reached a level of stability and economic growth that few thought possible a decade ago.

To evaluate the status of this conditions-based approach to the conflict, the president would be required to submit an annual report assessing the capabilities of ISIS against the agreed criteria. If the president determines that ISIS is degraded to the point that the criteria have been met, Congress would then vote to either accept or reject those findings, with an affirmative vote concluding the authority of the AUMF.

## CONCLUSION

President Obama should seek an authorization for the use of military force, or AUMF, that is explicitly and exclusively directed at ISIS, prohibits the large-scale deployment of U.S. ground combat troops, and includes both a geographic limitation and a resolution clause based on agreed criteria for ending the military phase of the fight against ISIS. This will set up a rational and durable framework for fighting terrorism.

## CRITICAL THINKING QUESTIONS

1. Is a new authorization needed for the military mission against ISIS?
2. Is a new War Powers Act needed to cover all cases involving the use of force?
3. How is the situation facing Congress today different from that in the past?

# 17

# National Insecurity

## CAN OBAMA'S FOREIGN POLICY BE SAVED?

David Rothkopf

Y ou're still a superpower," a top diplomat from one of America's most
dependable Middle Eastern allies said to me in July of this year, "but
you no longer know how to act like one."

He was reflecting on America's position in the world almost halfway into
President Barack Obama's second term. Fresh in his mind was the extraordi-
nary string of errors (schizophrenic Egypt policy, bipolar Syria policy), mis-
steps (zero Libya post-intervention strategy, alienation of allies in the Middle
East and elsewhere), scandals (spying on Americans, spying on friends), half-
way measures (pinprick sanctions against Russia, lecture series to Central
Americans on the border crisis), unfulfilled promises (Cairo speech, pivot to
Asia), and outright policy failures (the double-down then get-out approach in
Afghanistan, the shortsighted Iraq exit strategy).

The diplomat with whom I was speaking is a thoughtful man. He knew
well that not all of these problems are the result of the blunders of a single
really bad year or the fault of any one president. The reality is that any president's foreign policy record depends heavily on luck, external factors, cyclical
trends, and legacy issues. And, to be sure, Obama inherited many of his greatest challenges, some of the biggest beyond his control.

Obama's presidency is largely a product of a moment in history that likely
will be seen someday as an aberration—the decade after 9/11, during which a
stunned, angry, and disoriented America was sent spinning into a kind of
national PTSD. Call it an age of fear, one in which the country and its leaders
were forced to grapple with a sense of vulnerability to which they were unac-
customed. The response of George W. Bush's administration—entering into
the long, costly wars in Iraq and Afghanistan, remaking U.S. national security
policy around the terrorism threat—led to a backlash that ushered Obama into

David Rothkopf is CEO and editor of the FP Group. His book *National Insecurity:
American Leadership in an Age of Fear* published in October 2014. This article was
originally published in *Foreign Policy* (September/October 2014): 45–51. Reprinted
with permission of *Foreign Policy*.

office with a perceived mandate to undo what his predecessor had done and avoid making similar mistakes.

The problem is that in seeking to sidestep the pitfalls that plagued Bush, Obama has inadvertently created his own. Yet unlike Bush, whose flaw-riddled first-term foreign policy was followed by important and not fully appreciated second-term course corrections, Obama seems steadfast in his resistance both to learning from his past errors and to managing his team so that future errors are prevented. It is hard to think of a recent president who has grown so little in office.

As a result, for all its native confidence and fundamental optimism, the United States remains shaken and unsteady more than a decade after the 9/11 attacks. Many of its problems have only grown dangerously worse: Its relative influence has declined; the terrorism threat has evolved and spread; and U.S. alliances are superannuated, ineffective shadows of their former selves. Compounding this is such gross dysfunction in Washington that, on most issues, the president is presumed to be blocked by Congress even before he has had the opportunity to make a move.

If the nation is to recover fully, Obama must not only identify and attempt to reverse what has gone wrong, but he also must try to understand how he can achieve new gains by the end of his second term. That is to say that huge challenges remain unaddressed and rising to them requires a hard look at himself—his responses, his messages, his management, and his team.

He must start by devoting special attention to the instances that knocked his foreign policy off the rails. And one stands out, even in the minds of some of the president's most prominent loyalists.

On Aug. 20, 2012, Obama met with reporters to discuss the crisis in Syria. When pressed to respond to the growing chaos and human toll there, the president replied as he had since the onset of Syria's war: He blended tough rhetoric with assiduous avoidance of risky American commitment to helping any of the parties to the conflict. But in an unscripted moment, he suggested that he would take action against the Syrian regime if it used chemical weapons, saying, "We have been very clear to the Assad regime, but also to other players on the ground, that a red line for us is we start seeing a whole bunch of chemical weapons moving around or being utilized. That would change my calculus."

Despite intelligence reports of multiple violations of that red line, the White House managed to ignore or sidestep the issue—that is, until exactly one year later, when, on Aug. 21, 2013, a major chemical-weapons attack claimed the lives of an estimated 1,429 people in Ghouta, a Damascus suburb.

The tripwire strung by the president himself had been clearly and unmistakably tripped. Now, his credibility was at stake.

Three days later, Obama met with his national security team and indicated that he was inclined to strike Syria, ordering naval vessels, with the capacity to deliver cruise missiles against Syrian targets, into position in the Mediterranean Sea. The planned attack would be small, be delivered from afar, and pose essentially no risk—beyond the reputational—to the United States or its allies. Even so, Obama did not want to be seen as acting alone. Lacking many close relationships with European or other world leaders, he called one of the few he thought he could count on: British Prime Minister David Cameron, who suggested he was ready to help with military action. The two moved rapidly in seeking a quick response from the British Parliament. But Obama, Cameron, and their teams would soon discover that they had moved too quickly and had badly miscalculated. To many members of Parliament, the leaders' one-two punch evoked the George W. Bush–Tony Blair misadventure in Iraq. The scars hadn't quite healed from that experience. Shockingly, to the White House and to the prime minister's office, Parliament rejected Cameron's call to arms.

This coincided with the U.S. Congress's growing doubts about the action. Some, perhaps most, of this was politics. The Republican Party had long before embraced obstructionism as a principal strategy in its efforts to damage the Democratic president. Obama asked his top national security advisors, Secretary of State John Kerry, Secretary of Defense Chuck Hagel—both former senators—and National Security Advisor Susan Rice to help persuade Congress to offer support. (Unlike some of his more effective predecessors, Obama had little appetite to work to personally build congressional backing, whether by horse-trading, intimidation, working the phones, or otherwise harnessing the power of the bully pulpit.) More skeptical than ever after the British vote, however, neither the Republicans nor the Democrats could see the wisdom of supporting the president's red-line statement.

Despite these headwinds, by the afternoon of Aug. 30, 2013, the White House appeared set to follow through on the limited-attack option. Kerry was sent out to deliver an impassioned set of casus belli remarks to the public, laying out the rationale for action, and commanders expected to receive their orders the next day.

But later that afternoon, the president went on a walk around the South Lawn of the White House with his chief of staff, Denis McDonough, a longtime loyalist whose relationship with the president dates back to just prior to the 2008 campaign. McDonough was not just a chief of staff—he was a member of the president's tightly knit innermost circle and a former deputy national security advisor. McDonough had also long been one of the voices urging that America not get involved in Syria, often stiffening the commander in chief's resolve to keep out of the crisis when pressure came from others, such as first-term Secretary of State Hillary Clinton, who thought Washington ought to do more to support moderate opponents of Syrian President Bashar al-Assad. It was during their 45-minute stroll that Obama shared with McDonough his concerns about following through on his Syria plan.

Afterward, when the two joined a small group of top advisors in the Oval Office, Obama reportedly announced, "I have a big idea I want to run by you guys," and then segued into his new plan to put action on hold until he could get a formal vote of congressional support. Many in the group were stunned by the news, including Rice, who reportedly argued that it would send a message of vacillation and would set a bad precedent of deferring to Congress on such issues.

Notably, the group did not include several key national security principals. Obama called Hagel to let him know about the decision to punt. Absent as well was Kerry, whom Obama later privately informed about his change of mind. The secretary of state's team felt he had been treated badly, having been asked to play the role of front man on this issue just hours before.

"This was the real turning point for the administration's foreign policy," a former senior Obama advisor told me. "This was when things really started to go bad."

With Syria festering for more than two years amid pleas to the United States for leadership and support from longtime regional allies, the media was primed to respond, and many critics immediately assailed the president for being indecisive. It was a charge that, despite the president's tough decisions on issues such as launching the raid that killed Osama bin Laden, had not bubbled up overnight.

It was clear from the outset that Congress would never approve the president's request and that, in asking for it, he was effectively seeking to be denied—as if to say, "Stop me before I take a risk I really don't want to take." It also set a precedent that would seemingly require the president to seek congressional approval for future military actions, even though the War Powers Resolution explicitly notes that he does not require it.

Fortunately for Obama, an opportunity soon arose—thanks to a proposal from the Russians and some swift action by Kerry—to negotiate a deal in which the Syrians would agree to give up their chemical weapons. This was more than a fig leaf. It eliminated a serious threat to the Middle East. However, the embrace of that deal led to further unintended consequences: It made Assad look more reasonable and required him to be in place in order to get rid of the weapons. This only pressured the Syrian president less, while providing an excuse for continued U.S. inaction in support of Syria's moderate opposition.

A year later, the world is witnessing the Hydra-headed worst-case scenario in which Assad is stronger, according to Obama's own top intelligence advisor, retired Lt. Gen. James Clapper, and Assad's most dangerous radicalized opponents, now called the Islamic State, have also gained considerable ground. The group has not only seized much of Syria, but it also has spread its mayhem into Iraq, raising the prospect of the emergence of a new extremist state straddling what was once the Syria-Iraq border.

The tensions around the Syria crisis had other knock-on costs that were themselves symptomatic of a misfiring process and team. For example, on the edges of the G-20 summit in St. Petersburg, Russia, which took place Sept. 5 and 6, 2013, Washington continued to push for international support of military action as it had been doing ineffectively since late August. In one meeting, Rice pressed the German delegation relentlessly for leadership within the European Union. The Germans sought more time and consultation with other EU member states, frustrating Rice to the point that she lost her cool and reportedly launched into a profanity-filled lecture that featured a rare diplomatic appearance of the word "motherfucker." Germany's national security advisor,

Christoph Heusgen, was so angered that he told an American confidante it was the worst meeting of his professional life.

(Rice's bluntness and hot temper have undercut her effectiveness throughout her career. In July 2014, *The New Republic* reported that she once confronted Palestinian President Mahmoud Abbas outside the Oval Office, saying, "You Palestinians can never see the fucking big picture." A U.N. ambassador of one of the world's major powers told me that he didn't "understand what she thinks she is achieving by talking to us like a longshoreman." The brusqueness hasn't helped with her interpersonal relationships within the administration or with her staff, either. It is a particularly frustrating Achilles-heel for someone who is well known among her friends as having the capacity to be very warm, humorous, and engaging.)

The timing of the dust-up with Germany was particularly bad. Within a few weeks, revelations that Washington had been spying on the German leadership added a further chill to the relationship. When Rice's counterpart called her prior to German Chancellor Angela Merkel's first call with Obama on the issue, Rice compounded her past action with something even worse: She offered a defense that suggested Obama was either incompetent or a liar. That is, she told the Germans that the president did not know about the spying.

Rice's relationship with the Germans had deteriorated so significantly by the summer of 2014 that when Washington sought to repair the bilateral strain over surveillance issues, it was apparent to those who knew the history that it might be counterproductive to have Rice head the U.S. delegation visiting Germany to patch things up. Instead, McDonough—in a rare diplomatic mission for a chief of staff—led the team that met with Heusgen and others. (Needless to say, given Germany's centrality to the Atlantic alliance, bad blood hasn't helped during the Ukraine crisis, either.)

McDonough's trip framed still other questions about the sometimes-blurry structure and discipline of the White House's national security process. As national security advisor, Rice had already begun to breed resentment at the State Department for playing a high-profile role usually reserved for the secretary of state. Now, with the Germany mission, Obama's chief of staff had undertaken, on the president's behalf, a function that traditionally would have been handled by the State Department (or quietly by the national security advisor). What's more, the structure of the mission sent the message that McDonough might become something like a second national security advisor—or, at least, that he might assume somewhat greater national security responsibilities than many of his predecessors had. (Kristie Canegallo—one of McDonough's deputies, who, like her boss, also has National Security Council experience—has as one of her stated duties oversight of issues associated with the war in Afghanistan.)

This crossing of lines led one former national security advisor from a Democratic administration to tell me, "If it had been me and they tried to do that, I would have quit."

A weak point of the Obama White House has always been management style and structure. The problem begins with the fact that, as with five of the past six U.S. presidents, Obama had very little foreign policy experience before he was elected. But of those five, Obama was unique in that he lacked any executive-management experience of any sort: Jimmy Carter, Ronald Reagan, Bill Clinton, and George W. Bush had all been governors. Furthermore, he had only four years of Washington experience and a personality that was "much more that of the lawyer than the CEO," according to a senior administration official.

As a result, Obama has been deliberative to a fault and an inveterate seeker of the middle ground. He also has not been inclined to develop strong bonds with most of his cabinet members or to empower them or agency heads, which is essential in a sprawling U.S. government that is the world's largest and most complex organization.

Compounding the management problem was the president's own undermining of his system. During National Security Council (NSC) and other staff meetings, for example, he was known for going around the room and asking for everyone's views (often putting subordinate aides in the awkward position of undercutting or deviating from the views of their bosses). Typically, such meetings would end without the president making a decision. He would later reveal whatever conclusion to which he had come to a handful of close White House aides, often the small group with which he met each morning to review the latest intelligence. This took transparency out of the process and overly empowered his inner circle.

The hope was that, in his second term, the president might address some of these issues. But by all reports, the situation has gotten worse. On the foreign policy side, this has meant that "the true believers"—as one first-termer called McDonough, Rice, Deputy National Security Advisor Ben Rhodes, and U.N. Ambassador Samantha Power, among others—have moved up and gained power, periodically being supported by Obama's closest political advisors. Many of the people who often offset their views—such as Hillary Clinton, former CIA Director Leon Panetta, and former Defense Secretary Robert Gates—have moved on.

Kerry and Hagel are strong personalities with good ties to the president, but they don't have the ready access of those who work just down the hall from the Oval Office. They aren't the ones who interact with the president in the side conversations, morning intelligence briefings, and other exchanges that occur through Obama's day—and the NSC process has simply not been effective in offsetting that disparity of influence. Moreover, Kerry and Hagel are largely consumed with agendas that keep them away from the White House and primarily within the orbit of their agencies or on airplanes.

Henry Kissinger once told me that in the U.S. government, as in real estate, the same three things matter: "Location, location, and location." This is truer than ever in this administration, where if your office is not in the complex at 1600 Pennsylvania Avenue, regardless of your title, you are often out of the loop.

As Obama's bubble has gotten smaller, the president has reportedly become frustrated with criticism too, compounding his famous aloofness with a more defensive attitude. The most notable example of this unfolded during his Asia visit in April 2014—a trip made largely with the intent of communicating to regional leaders that the United States was not abandoning its international leadership role. In the Philippines, Obama described, with barely concealed anger, his approach to foreign policy as one of seeking modest outcomes: "You hit singles; you hit doubles," he said—a far cry from his "audacity of hope" days and his speeches about transforming the world that marked his first year in office.

Immediately after this speech, he continued his explanation when he lectured the press corps aboard Air Force One. It was during this second unburdening that Obama sought to drive home the point that his mantra on international issues was, in his own words, "Don't do stupid shit." (An infelicitous turn of phrase, it has since engendered such a negative reaction, including criticism from Hillary Clinton, that it has itself become a prime example of doing stupid shit.) While the comment certainly had the effect of lowering expectations, it was also seen as a fit of pique and as further proof to the skeptical that this administration is content to sit on the world's sidelines—despite allies asking, as one Middle Eastern leader put it, that the United States be "not a player, just a coach."

More than at any time in the past, Obama's administration has chosen, in a very deliberate way, to concentrate more power within the White House. Although the NSC has continuously increased in power since it was formed in 1947, under Obama its staff has grown to around 370 people, roughly 10 times the size it was during the 1970s and almost twice as large as it was during the early Bush years. (It grew in part because it absorbed Bush's Homeland Security Council.) More importantly, the White House staff has taken the lead on key issues from the outset, so much so that many D.C.-based ambassadors now habitually bypass the State Department in order to speak to those in the West Wing or in the NSC offices in the Eisenhower Executive Office Building.

But even the bloated NSC staff is not big enough to replace the cabinet agencies it often edges out of the picture. And when it tries to be operational (witness Rice-led delegations to address the transition in Afghanistan or to negotiate with Israeli Prime Minister Benjamin Netanyahu), it eats into its ability to do its core jobs: coordinating the development and implementation of foreign policy and providing advice to the president.

This is a costly approach. Concentrating power in the White House increases the likelihood of groupthink, especially in second terms like this one, when many of the stronger and diverse voices in the administration have left and have not been replaced by equally strong and diverse successors. Groupthink in an environment in which the leader is a cautious lawyer and his closest aides have campaign histories can lead to an overly tactical approach to problems. And if there is one great void that has dogged this administration, particularly in its second term, it is in the area of strategy.

Part of the shift to White House centrism no doubt has to do with Obama's personality—he can be cool, somewhat closed, and wary—and his history of managing the small staff of a senator. But some of it, as Obama's former national security advisor, Tom Donilon, told me, has been deliberate. Donilon pointed out that when one wants to use all the tools in the administration's toolbox, one needs to run things out of the NSC. Consequently, on many issues, foreign leaders want to know where the president stands and deal primarily with those perceived as close to him.

Although there is a certain logic to this, recent history suggests that the impulse needs to be held in check.

It is easy, and perhaps natural, to conclude that the president can do little to improve his performance. But that is not true. In fact, some useful insights into how to get the president's national security act together come from what many in the White House—not to mention the general public—might see as the unlikeliest of sources: George W. Bush's administration.

Admittedly, the idea that Bush finished strong in office is not part of the common narrative of a presidency much more defined by its actions in the wake of 9/11, the errors associated with the Iraq invasion, the rendition and torture of prisoners, Guantánamo, Abu Ghraib, and the related alienation of important allies worldwide. But during his second term, Bush and his team produced another, underappreciated story. On the national security and foreign policy side, this included the stabilization of Iraq via the surge, the introduction of the "light footprint" approaches to combating terrorism that were ultimately adopted by Obama (including the use of drones and special operations), the ramping-up of America's cyber-capabilities and cyber-defenses, and the advancement of the Millennium Challenge Corporation's work in Africa and of PEPFAR. There was also an important nuclear deal with India and stronger relations with Brazil, European allies, and moderate Arab states, among others. What's more, Bush's response to the financial crisis was courageous and made an enormous contribution to the speed with which the United States recovered, a speed much greater than in most other impacted countries, such as those of the European Union.

Several factors contributed to Bush's second-term turnaround. One was simply the experience of being in office. But not only did Bush and his team grow more effective, they also became more adaptive to the world around them.

The 9/11 attacks were a shock. Perhaps for the first time in U.S. history, a conflict began not with a speech or a headline, but with a moving, horrifying, indelible image that virtually every individual in the United States saw. It was more than a visceral jolt or a trauma, however: It also presented Americans with the idea that there were new dangers in the world that the country was ill-prepared to face. "In the aftermath of 9/11, we were essentially just reacting," former Secretary of State Condoleezza Rice told me in her Stanford University office after she ended her tenure in Foggy Bottom. "It took some time before we could stop, catch our breath, and make a critical reappraisal of what we were doing."

Reflection eventually followed, including for principals such as Rice and Stephen Hadley, her deputy national security advisor during Bush's first term who replaced her as national security advisor when she moved to the State Department. Hadley was deeply thoughtful and understood the NSC as well as anyone in Washington. Indicative of the evolution in his thinking—and that of the team—was a willingness to return to core assumptions. After his time at the White House, for example, Hadley told me, "Thinking back, I now wonder if our mistake may have been in not considering whether the reason Saddam Hussein was so secretive about his weapons of mass destruction capabilities was not because he had the weapons and wanted to conceal them, but because he did not have them and he wanted to hide that."

"From the Iranians," he posited. "From us."

Beyond traveling up the learning curve of a new, challenging period in U.S. foreign policy, Bush realized his team needed to change and began making both subtle and significant changes. Rice went to Foggy Bottom, and immediately the relationship between the secretary of state and the national security advisor improved from the sometimes-difficult one that existed between Rice and Colin Powell in Bush's first term.

"There's no doubt that going to State with the experience of having been national security advisor and having seen some of the problems State had been having was an advantage," Rice told me. "And it helped, of course, to have Steve Hadley at the NSC, who was a way better national security advisor than I was because he was the right personality for it. And I think I was the right personality to be secretary of state. I always laughingly say, 'We finally got into the right positions.'"

Rice knew that there was another factor that would shape the new national security team: Bush himself. He was no longer a neophyte president. In Rice's words, "The president had grown."

She saw evidence of this particularly in his newfound ability to corral the Defense Department. He would "demand things from the Pentagon. He was so much more confident, for instance, in putting together the surge than he was in the questions he would ask of the military going into Iraq." And as Bush took a firmer hand on Iraq policy, he gradually dialed back or offset the influence of his vice president, Dick Cheney (whom one senior Bush NSC official described as continuing to want to "keep breaking china"). At this point, according to Rice, Bush didn't want to do anything militarily with North Korea or Iran. "He wanted to engage in diplomacy," she said. "The president was in a different place."

Rice is clearly protective of the former president, but many top officials, some of whom went on to serve Obama, support her viewpoint. So too do the actions of the administration: Other than the surge within Iraq, there were no new major confrontations during Bush's second term, even in the face of provocations such as the deteriorating situation in Afghanistan or Russia's 2008 aggression into Georgia. Wherever possible, diplomatic responses—or much more limited and, ideally, covert military responses—were sought. This established the trend of treading more lightly, which Obama seized upon and then, in the eyes of his critics, carried too far.

Bush also strengthened his team. He brought in a new White House chief of staff, Joshua Bolten, who helped the president secure a new treasury secretary, Henry Paulson, who was to play a central foreign policy role and take the lead on China matters. (Paulson would also have a vital leadership role during the financial crisis that followed.) Bolten was a master manager, experienced in the ways of the executive branch but also deft and content to remain behind the scenes guiding events with a firm but sensitive touch. The freelancing, ego-driven, creative but disruptive Defense Secretary Donald Rumsfeld was gone by 2006, replaced by Robert Gates, one of the most respected professional national security civil servants the United States has produced in the past three decades. And though Cheney remained influential, Bush became more hands-on, and his new team was all the more dedicated to working with the formal national security process, not via backdoors as had been the wont of Cheney and Rumsfeld during Bush's first term.

Given Hadley's decades of experience within and around the NSC apparatus, he had a clear philosophy of his job as national security advisor. The interagency process, he observed, was run in two ways. The domestic side, he said, was "very White House staff-focused." The staff would talk with the president and then design policy initiatives. Once a policy "was essentially cooked or well along," he said, the cabinet secretaries then joined to move forward on implementation.

Things were usually different on the national security side, where there was a more "principle-centric process" in developing policy "with the national security principals, the secretary of state, defense, you know, the chairman of the Joint Chiefs, intelligence folks," Hadley said. "And then collectively, we brought our recommendations and choices to the president." (In an aside, Hadley said that in his view, the Obama administration often adopted the White House–driven domestic-policy approach for use on a wide range of national security and foreign policy issues.)

Noticeably, Bush changed course on key issues. Not only did he show courage on some of those changes—adding troops for the surge was hugely unpopular, for example—but he also showed a willingness to get personally involved to try to make things work. In some ways, this meant that he simply rolled up his sleeves and did the work of a manager. For example, he instituted weekly videoconferences with his team in Iraq, as well as regular exchanges with Iraqi Prime Minister Nouri al-Maliki.

With benefit of hindsight, of course, the world now knows that the stabilization that occurred during the surge—and as a result of this period of attention—would not last and that Maliki was a slippery, dangerous character. But it is also clear that for the last two years of Bush's tenure, Iraq perhaps achieved its post-invasion high point. It is telling to note that when asked whether Obama would maintain regular interactions with Maliki, one of his aides reportedly suggested the president was disinclined to engage in that kind of "micromanagement" of such situations.

Bush saw himself as the coach of his team, with an obligation to lead and personally connect with his cabinet. During tough moments, I was told, he would play a vital role bucking up spirits during cabinet or one-on-one meetings. One former top official who served in both the Bush and Obama administrations spoke of a moment when Bush put his hands on the shoulders of a cabinet member, particularly distraught during the financial crisis, and attempted to "talk him off the ledge." This nonpartisan, experienced actor said, "If people could have seen those 20 minutes as I did, they would have thought they got their money's worth from Bush as president."

For Obama, much can clearly be learned from studying how Bush managed to remake his team, his own role, and his foreign policy in ways that, while not offsetting the errors of his first term, advanced U.S. interests substantially. The solution was not complicated: It necessitated a sound process, the right team, an engaged president, and a willingness to acknowledge errors and seek to correct them. It required a belief that management actually matters and that much could still get done in the administration's last couple of years.

To be sure, Obama has shown that it is within him to implement at least some of these changes. During his first term, after a shaky start, Obama's NSC process improved with the appointment of Donilon as national security advisor and McDonough as his deputy. The new team, with a respect for process discipline and a willingness to play a primarily behind-the-scenes role, enabled the president to more effectively engage a diverse, strong-minded group of national security principals. On critical issues, such as the bin Laden raid and dozens of other tactical decisions like it, the president played a strong leadership role and showed great character and courage. More recently, on matters like the National Security Agency scandal, Obama has begun to acknowledge and address some of his administration's errors.

It isn't too late for the president to build on these successes and undertake the broad reassessment that's needed—and Americans can hope that his recent policy reversal that has led to limited intervention in Iraq may be a sign of a new willingness to do so. But challenges remain in the composition of his team; the structure of the administration; its risk-averseness and defensiveness; its tendency to be tactical and focused on the short term, rather than strategic in its approaches to problems; and the president's seeming unwillingness to devote more of himself to working with peers worldwide to shape and lead action on many big issues.

In short, Obama needs to take a page out of his predecessor's book—and where that change must begin is crisply suggested by the old joke: How many psychotherapists does it take to change a lightbulb? Just one. But the lightbulb itself has to really want to change.

# CRITICAL THINKING QUESTIONS

1. Does a good decision-making process guarantee a good policy decision will be made?

2. What lessons should the next president take away from the management and decision-making styles of Bush and Obama?
3. What are the dangers of the decision-making style advocated in this reading? Are they greater than those found in the Obama administration's current decision-making style?

# 18

# Reforming the NSA

## HOW TO SPY AFTER SNOWDEN

Daniel L. Byman and Benjamin Wittes

The long-running debate over the tradeoffs the United States should make between national security and civil liberties flared up spectacularly last summer, when Edward Snowden, a National Security Agency contractor, handed journalists a huge trove of heavily classified documents that exposed, in excruciating detail, electronic surveillance programs and other operations carried out by the NSA. Americans suddenly learned that in recent years, the NSA had been acquiring the phone and Internet communications of hundreds of thousands of U.S. citizens, as well as collecting massive volumes of bulk telephone records known as "metadata"—phone numbers and the time and length of calls. Along with the rest of the world, Americans found out that the NSA had broken common forms of online encryption, tapped the phones of various foreign heads of state, and monitored global communications far more aggressively than was previously understood.

Howls of outrage erupted. Brazilian President Dilma Rousseff, who learned from the Snowden leaks that the NSA had been monitoring her personal conversations, described the NSA's activities as a "violation of human rights and civil liberties," decrying the "disrespect to national sovereignty." In the United States, both ends of the political spectrum denounced the NSA's activities. Rand Paul, a Republican senator from Kentucky, called them "an all-out assault on the Constitution," and the former Democratic vice president Al Gore said they were "obscenely outrageous."

Proposals for reform are now legion. Soon after the leaks, President Barack Obama appointed an independent group of experts to examine the issue. The group's report, published last December, recommended more than 40 far-reaching reforms, including ending the government's bulk collection of telephone metadata and restricting surveillance on foreign leaders. The panel

Daniel L. Byman is the director of research and a senior fellow in the Center for Middle East Policy at Brookings. He is also a professor at Georgetown University's Security Studies Program. Benjamin Wittes is a senior fellow in governance studies at The Brookings Institution. He is cofounder and editor-in-chief of the *Lawfare* blog and is a member of the Hoover Institution's Task Force on National Security and Law. Reprinted by permission of *Foreign Affairs* 93, no. 3 (May/June 2014). Copyright © 2014 by the Council on Foreign Relations, Inc., www.ForeignAffairs.com.

suggested that telephone providers or a private third party, not the government, should hold the metadata and give officials access to it only when ordered to do so by the secret Foreign Intelligence Surveillance Court. The panel also recommended requiring the FBI to obtain judicial approval before issuing a "national security letter," a form of administrative subpoena the government uses to obtain phone numbers, e-mail addresses, and financial transaction records. Congress is also mulling action. Last October, Patrick Leahy (D-Vt.), chair of the Senate Judiciary Committee, and James Sensenbrenner (R-Wis.), former chair of the House Judiciary Committee, proposed a major rollback of the NSA's programs. At the same time, the Senate Intelligence Committee put forward a modest bill that tinkered with, but largely validated, the current legal status quo.

Obama responded to the public outrage and various calls for reform with a major speech and a presidential policy directive in January. Obama defended the NSA, emphasizing the necessity of intelligence and noting that nothing he had learned "indicated that our intelligence community has sought to violate the law or is cavalier about the civil liberties of their fellow citizens." Yet Obama also warned that given the NSA's power, the U.S. government has a "special obligation" to scrutinize the agency's activities. He acknowledged that non-U.S. citizens overseas have privacy interests that the United States must respect. He also restricted the NSA to obtaining specific records only with an order from the Foreign Intelligence Surveillance Court and only on targets that are two steps removed from the phone number of a suspected terrorist, rather than the previous three steps. Obama also declared a "transition" to end the government's collection of bulk telephone metadata; two months later, as this article went to press, the administration was reportedly proposing to change the system so that phone companies would store the metadata, rather than the government.

Although bold on principles, Obama's plans for reform have been vague on some important details. In January, he said that the United States would still spy on non-U.S. citizens, including foreign leaders, if "there is a compelling national security purpose"—quite a caveat. And he called for working with Congress—not exactly a sure-fire source of action—on national security letters, but he did not mention requiring the FBI to obtain judicial consent before demanding records.

The proposed reforms and Obama's less than full embrace of them reflect a fundamental clash when it comes to what the American public demands of its intelligence community. The real problem that Snowden's revelations brought to light was not a government agency run amok: the NSA never meaningfully exceeded the writ given to it by the White House, Congress, and the courts, at least not intentionally. Rather, those revelations highlighted a basic conflict between two things that U.S. citizens and their government demand from their intelligence agencies: a high, if not perfect, level of security, on the one hand, and strict privacy protections, accountability, and transparency, on the other. Those imperatives were never easy to reconcile and are even harder to resolve today. Indeed, Snowden's revelations demonstrated how the implicit bargain that has governed the U.S. intelligence community since the 1970s has broken down.

For four decades, U.S. intelligence work was predicated on a compromise. Covert spying was allowed—including, at times, against U.S. citizens—so long as it was subjected to formal, albeit secret, oversight and a sharp distinction was maintained between domestic and foreign targets. Today, however, thanks to both technological developments and the NSA's increased role in counterterrorism after 9/11, that boundary has become hard to uphold. Meanwhile, the U.S. government's decreasing ability to keep its own secrets has exposed the flaws in the intelligence compromise.

But that does not mean that the U.S. government should abandon its quest for good intelligence. As communications technologies spread and the overall volume of communication increases, the NSA's role is growing even as the political space the agency enjoys has shrunk. The question really underlying all the fevered talk of reform is whether the NSA can win back the public's trust, or at least its acquiescence.

In recent months, a new consensus on intelligence gathering has begun to emerge among a wide swath of the U.S. political establishment, although it excludes critics on the civil liberties left and the libertarian right. The NSA should retain many of its powerful capabilities, but it needs to change the way it thinks about its interactions with the American people and become more open about its operations. While still keeping their collection methods secret, officials have begun—and need to continue—to publicly disclose far more about the categories of people the NSA targets for surveillance and how the agency collects and uses information. Officials have also started to accept more public oversight of such activities and the reality that many of the NSA's secrets about the information it targets, the technology it penetrates, and the rules that govern its activities will inevitably be revealed.

As a result, the NSA will have to determine whether a new program's benefits really outweigh the potential costs of exposure. Such decisions will come at a price. The new limits on NSA surveillance will at times leave the U.S. government less informed about threats and opportunities. So U.S. policymakers and citizens alike will have to consider how much security and diplomatic advantage they are willing to forgo in exchange for greater restraint from the intelligence community.

## THE GREAT COMPROMISE?

The NSA claims that its activities have helped prevent numerous terrorist attacks at home and abroad since 9/11. Such claims are difficult to verify without access to classified data. More important, they rely on an inappropriate measure of success. The agency's true remit goes beyond just stopping attacks: the NSA seeks to identify terrorists, understand their organizations, and anticipate and disrupt their activities. On that broader set of tasks, the agency has accomplished a great deal in recent years. But however important, the NSA's data collection is rarely the only factor in effective counterterrorism. Such operations are the result of coordination and cooperation among many different intelligence organizations.

Additionally, the recent debate over the NSA has focused too narrowly on counterterrorism. That attention is understandable: U.S. government officials know that the easiest way to defend the agency after Snowden's disclosures is to invoke its role in preventing terrorist attacks. Moreover, the collection of bulk telephone metadata—the most controversial program Snowden revealed—happens to be a counterterrorism program. But the NSA does vital day-to-day work in the realms of diplomacy and cybersecurity as well. By accessing the communications of foreign leaders and officials, particularly of U.S. adversaries, the NSA provides U.S. policymakers with insights into when a state might go to war, break a treaty, or otherwise make a dramatic (or subtle) policy shift.

NSA activities allow U.S. officials to negotiate more effectively by tipping them off to the positions of foreign officials. That advantage applies even to relationships with allies, with whom the United States maintains extensive intelligence-sharing arrangements. The intelligence gathered by the NSA can confirm the accuracy of information that allies voluntarily share with Washington. Even friendly states sometimes choose to shade the facts or share partial information with Washington in an attempt to avoid embarrassment or shape U.S. policy.

In order to accomplish its missions, the NSA has built up a vast array of collection capabilities—too vast, say the agency's many critics at home and abroad. Americans do have good historical reasons to be suspicious. In the 1960s and 1970s, the NSA, along with other U.S. intelligence agencies, conducted abusive surveillance of journalists; members of Congress; Martin Luther King, Jr., and other civil rights leaders; and prominent opponents of the Vietnam War, such as Muhammad Ali and Benjamin Spock. After the Watergate scandal, journalists and congressional investigators eventually exposed such snooping, which led to widespread distrust of government surveillance and secrecy. (Some of the names and details of specific targets, however, were not disclosed until last year, in declassified NSA documents.)

To guard against future abuses while also preserving the confidentiality that intelligence agencies require, in the late 1970s, Congress devised a series of oversight committees and other mechanisms that relied on two overarching concessions. First, the new rules granted legislators and judges more oversight over the intelligence agencies but required nearly all their reviews to take place in secret. Second, the 1978 Foreign Intelligence Surveillance Act (FISA) allowed the FBI (the NSA was not permitted to operate domestically) to target the communications of people inside the United States, including U.S. citizens, but required it to obtain approval for doing so from the secret Foreign Intelligence Surveillance Court, staffed by federal judges appointed by the chief justice of the United States. Other rules required the NSA to discard U.S. citizens' communications inadvertently swept up by dragnets aimed at overseas targets, unless the agency concluded that the data had foreign intelligence value.

Beginning around the same time, the White House and the Department of Justice also increased their oversight of the intelligence community. The net result of all these changes was a system in which the NSA could use its vast powers only in certain circumstances and only under the supervision of a lot of minders. Throughout the 1980s and 1990s, this system seemed to work well. The agency was careful not to target U.S. citizens illegally and avoided using even its limited powers to their fullest extent. As a consequence, the NSA mostly stayed out of major controversies and behind the scenes, its operations at once robust but very much subject to the law.

## THREAT ASSESSMENT

In recent years, however, two major changes have deeply upset the status quo, empowering the NSA in the short term but undermining its longer-term support from and legitimacy with the American public. The first change was the profound shift in national security priorities provoked by the 9/11 terrorist attacks. The failure to stop the attacks led to criticism in the media and Congress that U.S. intelligence agencies had been too passive in the face of the growing jihadist threat. Critics charged that the NSA, chastened by the revelations of its abuses in the 1970s, had interpreted its powers too conservatively and had too often hesitated to collect information that might have involved U.S. citizens—even when those Americans were in contact with suspected terrorists overseas.

In response to such pressure, legislators and officials inside and outside the NSA pushed for more aggressive surveillance measures as counterterrorism, long just one part of the agency's portfolio, became its priority. President George W. Bush's warrantless wiretapping program, initiated shortly after 9/11, circumvented FISA procedures and safeguards altogether and, when revealed, led to significant changes in the law itself—changes that confirmed the agency's authority to conduct surveillance without individualized warrants on non-U.S. citizens or residents overseas whose communications the NSA collected when they passed through the United States. (The changes made clear, though, that the surveillance had to be limited to those communications and that the NSA still had to have individualized warrants when targeting U.S. citizens or residents abroad.) The post-9/11 quest for more and better intelligence also led to a huge increase in the NSA's budget, which, according to the *Washington Post,* totaled almost $11 billion last year, up by over 50 percent since 2004.

The second change was more akin to a tectonic shift: advances in technology began permanently blurring the distinctions between domestic and foreign surveillance and between U.S. citizens and foreign nationals. The Internet and the spread of mobile and wireless devices have vastly increased the extent of international communications by people in the United States, who now frequently interact with people of other nationalities over the Internet.

These technological changes have made it much more difficult to separate domestic and foreign communications. In the 1970s, foreign communications involved large phone circuits and satellite feeds that were largely distinct from domestic communications infrastructure. Today, the data streams have become hopelessly entangled. Messages between Internet users in the United States sometimes travel to and from sites and facilities in Europe or Asia, even if the final destination is an office next door. Foreign communications often go through the United States, a byproduct of the centrality of U.S. companies and infrastructure to the Internet's technical architecture. When the NSA taps online communications from foreign nationals abroad, it often ends up capturing messages sent between U.S. citizens in the United States. If the agency excluded U.S. sites from its coverage, it might miss out on foreign communications that are routed through or stored on U.S. servers.

These changes have created major technical challenges for the agency—and a huge boon. The NSA can access people's Facebook messages, Skype feeds, financial documents, e-mails, and stored computer documents, allowing it to learn exponentially more about a target than it could have in the pre-Internet age. These days, in fact, the NSA's biggest technical problems involve not collection but analysis. The NSA estimates that it "touches" (without specifying what that means) a cache of information from the Internet equivalent to 580 million file cabinets of documents every single day. The agency can only hope to analyze a tiny fraction of this enormous haul.

These changes also test the limits of the 1970s compromise. Thanks to Snowden's leaks, a significant portion of the American public now doubts that the NSA truly focuses on overseas communications and has little faith in the government's oversight mechanisms. The NSA, of course, struggles to keep its own secrets under wraps. The agency can rightly blame leakers for this problem. But given the number of people who have access to NSA documents (more than a million people have "top secret" clearance), such leaks seem almost inevitable.

The agency has thus begun working even harder to keep its secrets. In an interview with one of us last December, Lonny Anderson, the NSA's chief technology officer, said that the agency has begun to more closely monitor its employees' use of agency resources, limit the amount of data that their terminals can access, and centralize its data storage in its internal cloud. Such changes will make the NSA less agile, and at the end of the day, Anderson conceded, "You can never stop someone who's determined, who . . . has got all the right badges, [and who has] some technical skills."

Indeed, Washington should now expect that its allies and adversaries, not to mention the general public, will occasionally gain access to at least the general patterns of U.S. intelligence collection. At times, they will even gain access to the specifics. The impact of such revelations will vary. U.S. enemies assume that Washington listens to them, so they are unlikely to be shocked by revelations. But U.S. allies claim to have different expectations—or at least they did until Snowden's revelations angered foreign leaders such as Rousseff and Germany's Angela Merkel, who found out that their personal communications had been intercepted.

## SPY GAME

Although some of the foreign outrage was manufactured, the Snowden revelations have hurt the United States' relations with its allies in two vital ways. First, they surprised and angered publics in allied countries, forcing leaders such as Merkel and Rousseff to respond to—or exploit—that anger. Second, the United States has now lost some of the moral high ground it had occupied in debates over cybersecurity and Internet governance. After years of protesting Chinese cyber-intrusions into U.S. systems, Washington now looks hypocritical. In fact, the Snowden documents suggest not just that the United States, like China, engages in cyberspying but that the United States is really good at it.

The revelations have also threatened U.S. technology firms, which many critics now suspect cooperate voluntarily with the NSA and thus essentially operate as an arm of the U.S. government. A presidential policy directive that accompanied Obama's speech in January acknowledged the risks that such perceptions pose to the country's "commercial, economic, and financial interests, including a potential loss of international trust in U.S. firms" and "the credibility of our commitment to an open, interoperable, and secure global Internet." Yet Obama offered technology companies mostly rhetoric, rejecting the review panel's call for the NSA to stop undermining encryption standards. Major U.S. Internet companies have begun openly contemplating the adoption of more sophisticated encryption methods.

Meanwhile, foreign countries have toyed with the idea of requiring Internet companies to provide local data-storage services to their citizens. Some foreign governments and companies may turn to domestic firms for their technological needs; such firms will be sure to emphasize that their U.S. competitors will not keep foreign data secure. But these efforts may ironically make the NSA's job easier, since the agency is less constrained by laws or oversight in accessing data stored abroad.

For their part, NSA officials are deeply concerned about the impact of the revelations on U.S. companies. Anne Neuberger, who acts as the agency's top liaison to the domestic private sector, said in an interview with one us last December that they "feel a sense of responsibility to look at" the damage to Silicon Valley's reputation after Snowden's leaks. The NSA simply cannot function without industry cooperation. But as Obama's speech showed, the administration does not have that much to offer the technology industry in the way of new restraints without seriously inhibiting the NSA's data collection. The most important gesture to the industry in Obama's speech was the repeated reference to respecting the privacy of non-Americans, which was designed to reassure overseas individuals about using U.S. software and Internet services.

U.S. intelligence officials shoulder some of the blame for the lack of public confidence in the NSA, since they have not always been completely honest in their public statements. James Clapper, the director of national intelligence, told the Senate in March 2013 that the NSA does "not wittingly" collect data on U.S. citizens. But less than three months later, the massive metadata collection program was revealed, leaving Clapper to lamely claim that his original statement had been the "least untruthful" one he could give at the time. Journalists have also done their part to diminish the public's trust, sometimes publishing misleading claims, as when the Norwegian daily *Dagbladet* reported last November that the NSA had collected Norwegian phone conversations—only to have Norway's intelligence service turn around and disclose that it had done the spying itself.

## THE CHAMBER OF SECRETS

Whatever the cause, the fact is that the NSA, and by extension the Obama administration, now faces a big public relations problem. One response would be to further increase secrecy in the hopes of preventing more embarrassing leaks. Another would be to accept that much more information about U.S. intelligence work is likely to become public in the future and thus to conduct that work more visibly. Washington's best approach, however—and the direction the government seems to be stumbling toward—would be to combine these responses by making hardheaded judgments about what secrets the agency really needs to keep and working even more rigorously to protect them but also adopting a much more open posture toward less sensitive forms of intelligence collection.

Above all, any scaling back of secrecy must be well planned and should proceed according to a coherent theory of how civil liberties can best coexist with surveillance and how transparency can coexist with espionage. That does not seem to be happening now: the intelligence community is currently rolling back surveillance programs and disclosing thousands of pages of classified documents (including dozens of Foreign Intelligence Surveillance Court opinions and orders) that offer information on the telephone metadata collection program and on the targeting of foreigners, all without a clear strategy or, at least, without a strategy that has been explained in public. The process seems mostly reactive, an impulsive response to bad press and to blowback from individual foreign governments.

As it contemplates more disclosures and reforms, the U.S. government needs to answer some basic questions about what kinds of surveillance its intelligence agencies currently refrain from and what kinds of surveillance they should conduct more openly. It is not clear how intelligence officials should react if new restraints prove harmful to U.S. security. Nor is it clear whether U.S. officials and the American public would be willing to accept the results of less effective surveillance programs in the name of greater transparency. Obama has begun answering these questions. But some of his answers, such as those related to the technology industry and the privacy of non-U.S. citizens, have left too many details undetermined.

To set a clearer agenda for reform, the NSA should begin by dividing its activities into three broad categories. First, the agency should identify what it really must keep secret. In truth, only a fraction of the NSA's current activities—penetrating new technologies, for example, or monitoring supposedly secret systems of U.S. rivals, such as China—are so sensitive that the mere revelation of their existence would damage U.S. interests.

The NSA needs to work harder to keep those programs hidden by granting far fewer people access to them. Anderson said that stricter controls on access are already in the works, with a system to tag each piece of data that the NSA collects and each user. Data and user tags could then be matched depending on the user's privileges. Keeping access to the most important secrets limited to a smaller circle of confidants would make it more likely that they stayed secret.

But a push for more secrecy will provoke new fears of future abuses. Keeping fewer people in the loop would also increase the risk that important dots could go unconnected. Anderson acknowledged this risk, saying the agency is currently erring on the side of data security at the expense of effectiveness. There is no way to resolve that dilemma: to preserve secrecy, the NSA will have to forgo the benefit of having lots of eyes on a problem. But this tradeoff is sometimes worthwhile, since it ensures that the most important programs are privy to only a select group of analysts.

When it comes to the agency's less sensitive work that has not yet been exposed, the NSA should be prepared to abandon it if the benefits do not outweigh the costs of disclosure. Some spying on allies, for example, should be reconsidered, as Obama has already committed to doing. The practice in itself is not wrong, and it often yields valuable findings. But just as often, the benefits are not worth the price.

Third, the NSA must lift the veils over certain programs it means to continue. Because of Snowden's leaks and subsequent disclosures and declassifications, the metadata collection program, for example, is not a secret—and so even if some version of it continues, it makes sense to err on the side of openness going forward. More generally, the NSA should disclose more information to the public about the scope and scale of politically sensitive surveillance, where possible, and even more specifics to Congress. Bringing in civil liberties groups to discuss the parameters of some programs involving the surveillance of U.S. citizens would also help. The NSA is not likely to convince such groups to take the agency's side, but it could still explain to them its procedures for minimizing intrusions.

Becoming more open will require a shift in the institutional culture of the NSA and in the intelligence community more generally. But that shift is already taking place. In 2012, the NSA's then deputy director, John Inglis, quipped that the agency is "probably the biggest employer of introverts" in the federal government. But over the past few months, the country's most powerful introverts have begun speaking out publicly to an unprecedented degree. Last December, senior NSA officials even agreed to participate in a lengthy series of podcasts with one of us on the future direction of the agency.

Ultimately, increasing the transparency of the NSA and boosting oversight of its activities will have serious operational consequences. Those changes may at times slow down surveillance or make the agency more hesitant to acquire data that, in hindsight, would have been useful for counterterrorism or other essential operations. But conducting intelligence in public, at least to a certain degree, will help preempt scandals and allow the NSA to educate policymakers and journalists about what it does and why.

Despite Snowden's leaks, much of the public still misunderstands how the NSA works and what it does. In the past, the agency has welcomed this ignorance, since it helped the government keep its secrets secure. But now that the cat is out of the bag, the NSA, mindful of the value of public trust, needs to recalibrate its operations in order to increase public understanding of how it works. The necessary reforms will, to one degree or another, require Americans to take on more risk—a decision that will lead to political criticism should another terrorist attack occur on U.S. soil. If done well, however, the reforms will also make the agency more sensitive to public concerns while preserving its necessary core capabilities.

## CRITICAL THINKING QUESTIONS

1. What is the proper balance between civil liberties and national security? Must a trade-off exist between the two?
2. Must NSA reforms lead to more risks?
3. Write a presidential order establishing a new set of rules for the NSA to operate by.

# Responses

J ust as challenging as the task of identifying foreign policy problems is that of constructing effective responses to them. Traditionally, the primary instrument of foreign policy, especially as conducted by the great powers of an era, is through the use of military force. Depending on the circumstances, military power has been used to protect countries from foreign threats through supporting a policy of isolationism, defeating an opponent, deterring another state from taking an unwanted course of action, compelling an opponent or hesitant ally into taking a given course of action, or providing reassurance to an ally. These multiple uses often lead policy makers into the trap of thinking that military power is the equivalent of an international currency that can be used effectively for any policy goal under any circumstance, just as money can be used to purchase any commodity in any store with equal effectiveness.

Reality is quite different. Time and again the limits of military power have proven to be real, as captured by the often repeated phrase "winning the war and losing the peace." To be effective, military power as a resource must be translated into a coherent strategy and effectively implemented in a specific context. Inevitably, "friction" occurs as plans on paper run into the human and bureaucratic realities of putting them into place and the ability of other states to take unanticipated countering action. There is also the constant potential for "blowback" where actions taken have unanticipated effects that undermine the effectiveness of one's policy and even create new foreign policy problems.

The initial solution to the overreliance on military power as an instrument of foreign policy was to stress the need for delving into the full tool kit of policy instruments available to policy makers, running the gamut from public and private diplomacy to economic aid and sanctions to covert action. Additionally, unilateral, bilateral, and multilateral delivery methods had to be explored. The result was an unwieldy set of options, each of which had their supporters and detractors, that eventually led to calls for a "portfolio review" of American foreign policy assets.

Recently attention is being given to more structured and systematic ways of judging the merits of different potential responses to a foreign policy problem. One of the most frequently proposed strategies for doing so is a variation on SWOT analysis that was developed to aid businesses in their planning. SWOT stands for Strengths, Weaknesses, Opportunities, and Threats. Each of these categories is divided into internal factors (those relating to the United States) and external factors (those relating to the problem and/or countries and nonstate actors involved in the problem). Using SWOT analysis, policy makers are required to address the questions of what strengths or advantages the United States has in addressing the problem, what weaknesses or disadvantages it confronts, what opportunities might exist for the United States to exploit or manipulate in trying to achieve its goals, and finally what threats might be encountered that could lead to failure or greatly increase the cost of success. Properly used SWOT analysis is repeated as the response progresses in order to incorporate changing conditions into foreign policy calculations.

Advocates of this type of analytic approach to selecting responses to foreign policy problems argue that it does more than help identify an appropriate response. First, it will highlight points of agreement and disagreement. State and Defense Department officials, for example, may not see the similar set of strengths and weaknesses. All too often it is assumed that everyone sees the world the same way. Especially important is incorporating the perspective of other countries into the analysis. What does a SWOT analysis look like from their perspective? Second, it also helps determine the goals to be pursued. If on balance the analysis indicates that available responses are not likely to achieve the desired goal, the goals being pursued need to be reexamined.

In spite of calls to broaden the set of policy tools used in formulating responses to foreign policy problems, military power remains the response of first choice. The continuing central role played by military power in American foreign policy thinking is very much evident in critiques of Obama's foreign policy. Obama is simultaneously criticized for continuing to follow in George W. Bush's footsteps and over rely on its use and for being reluctant to use military force in such matters as the use of drones to target terrorist leaders, removing Libyan leader Muammar Gaddafi from power, and dealing with the crises in Syria and Ukraine. Looking beyond the use of military power to advance U.S. foreign policy goals, Obama's administration has come in for criticism for its lack of progress in obtaining a nuclear arms control agreement with Iran and in promoting trade, environmental, and human rights.

One of the most challenging aspects of formulating responses to foreign policy problems is that they rarely emerge in isolation from one another. Sometimes they emerge sequentially. A problem is solved, and another appears. Other times they occur together and overlap, making formulating a response difficult. Our first selection illustrates this point by bringing together three of Obama's speeches on U.S. foreign policy toward the crisis in Syria, beginning with is reference to a "line in the sand" regarding chemical weapons and ending with his announcement of a military response to ISIL. In the second selection, a 2015 speech given by Gareth Evans, former prime minister of Australia, our focus shifts to another complex problem that intersects with the challenges the Unites States faces in formulating a Syria policy: how to think about and implement the concept of Responsibility to Protect (R2P), which is intended to prevent genocide, war crimes, and crimes against humanity. Evans suggests four different benchmarks to use in evaluating R2P's past and future. He concludes that while many challenges lie ahead there is reason for optimism.

One of the more pressing foreign policy problem areas facing the United States is cybersecurity, as Franklin Kramer and Melanie Teplinsky assert in "Cybersecurity and Tailored Deterrence." The authors recommend moving from a defense-only approach to defending American cyber communication networks to an approach that builds around sanctions, active defense, international agreements, and increased standards for protection of electric power companies and financial firms.

Next, Clyde Prestowitz directs our attention to trade policy. In "A Tale of Two Trade Deals" he argues that, contrary to what many believe, trade agreements with Asia are of less importance to the United States than are those with Europe and we need to redirect our energies in this direction. Our final reading, "The Trouble with Sanctions," deals with a different dimension of trade policy. Here, Bijan Khajehpour, Reza Marashi, and Trita Parsi argue that neither economic sanctions nor the diplomacy component of the administration's dual track policy toward stopping Iran's pursuit of nuclear weapons have been very effective. To understand the trouble with sanctions the authors examine the stated objectives of economic sanctions against Iran and the internal politics of Iran over how to respond to them. Without an understanding of how Iran views these sanctions and their options, there is little hope that they can succeed.

## BIG PICTURE QUESTIONS

1. Pick a contemporary problem in American foreign policy and use SWOT analysis to select a policy goal and response.
2. Rank the four dimensions of SWOT by their degree of importance to the success of American foreign policy.
3. Make an argument for why military power should remain the key element of power in the conduct of American foreign policy.

## SUGGESTED READINGS

Lawrence Friedman, "Ukraine and the Art of Crisis Management," *Survival* 56 (May 2014), 7–42.
Michael Froman, "The Strategic Logic of Trade," *Foreign Affairs* 93 (November 2014), 111–18.

Paul Pillar, "We Can Live with a Nuclear Iran," *Washington Monthly* (March/April 2012), 13–19.

David Shorr, "Think Again: Climate Treaties," *Foreign Policy* 204 (March 2014), 38–43.

Dov Zakheim, "Abandon Nation Building," *National Interest* 131 (May 2014), 38–45.

# 19

# President Obama's Remarks on American Foreign Policy toward Syria, 2012–2014

## REMARKS BY THE PRESIDENT TO THE WHITE HOUSE PRESS CORPS*

Q: Mr. President, could you update us on your latest thinking of where you think things are in Syria, and in particular, whether you envision using U.S. military, if simply for nothing else, the safe keeping of the chemical weapons, and if you're confident that the chemical weapons are safe?

. . .

THE PRESIDENT: On Syria, obviously this is a very tough issue. I have indicated repeatedly that President al-Assad has lost legitimacy, that he needs to step down. So far, he hasn't gotten the message, and instead has double downed in violence on his own people. The international community has sent a clear message that rather than drag his country into civil war he should move in the direction of a political transition. But at this point, the likelihood of a soft landing seems pretty distant.

What we've said is, number one, we want to make sure we're providing humanitarian assistance, and we've done that to the tune of $82 million, I believe, so far. And we'll probably end up doing a little more because we want to make sure that the hundreds of thousands of refugees that are fleeing the mayhem, that they don't end up creating—or being in a terrible situation, or also destabilizing some of Syria's neighbors.

The second thing we've done is we said that we would provide, in consultation with the international community, some assistance to the opposition in thinking about how would a political transition take place, and what are the principles that should be upheld in terms of looking out for minority rights and human rights. And that consultation is taking place.

I have, at this point, not ordered military engagement in the situation. But the point that you made about chemical and biological weapons is critical. That's an issue that doesn't just concern Syria; it concerns our close allies in the region, including Israel. It concerns us. We cannot have a situation where chemical or biological weapons are falling into the hands of the wrong people.

---

*The White House Office of the Press Secretary, August 20, 2012.

We have been very clear to the Assad regime, but also to other players on the ground, that a red line for us is we start seeing a whole bunch of chemical weapons moving around or being utilized. That would change my calculus. That would change my equation.

Q: So you're confident it's somehow under—it's safe?

THE PRESIDENT: In a situation this volatile, I wouldn't say that I am absolutely confident. What I'm saying is we're monitoring that situation very carefully. We have put together a range of contingency plans. We have communicated in no uncertain terms with every player in the region that that's a red line for us and that there would be enormous consequences if we start seeing movement on the chemical weapons front or the use of chemical weapons. That would change my calculations significantly.

# REMARKS BY THE PRESIDENT IN ADDRESS TO THE NATION ON SYRIA*

Over the past two years, what began as a series of peaceful protests against the repressive regime of Bashar al-Assad has turned into a brutal civil war. Over 100,000 people have been killed. Millions have fled the country. In that time, America has worked with allies to provide humanitarian support, to help the moderate opposition, and to shape a political settlement. But I have resisted calls for military action, because we cannot resolve someone else's civil war through force, particularly after a decade of war in Iraq and Afghanistan.

The situation profoundly changed, though, on August 21st, when Assad's government gassed to death over a thousand people, including hundreds of children. The images from this massacre are sickening: Men, women, children lying in rows, killed by poison gas. Others foaming at the mouth, gasping for breath. A father clutching his dead children, imploring them to get up and walk. On that terrible night, the world saw in gruesome detail the terrible nature of chemical weapons, and why the overwhelming majority of humanity has declared them off-limits—a crime against humanity, and a violation of the laws of war.

. . .

If we fail to act, the Assad regime will see no reason to stop using chemical weapons. As the ban against these weapons erodes, other tyrants will have no reason to think twice about acquiring poison gas, and using them. Over time, our troops would again face the prospect of chemical warfare on the battlefield. And it could be easier for terrorist organizations to obtain these weapons, and to use them to attack civilians.

If fighting spills beyond Syria's borders, these weapons could threaten allies like Turkey, Jordan, and Israel. And a failure to stand against the use of chemical weapons would weaken prohibitions against other weapons of mass

---

*The White House Office of the Press Secretary, September 10, 2013.

destruction, and embolden Assad's ally, Iran—which must decide whether to ignore international law by building a nuclear weapon, or to take a more peaceful path.

This is not a world we should accept. This is what's at stake. And that is why, after careful deliberation, I determined that it is in the national security interests of the United States to respond to the Assad regime's use of chemical weapons through a targeted military strike. The purpose of this strike would be to deter Assad from using chemical weapons, to degrade his regime's ability to use them, and to make clear to the world that we will not tolerate their use.

That's my judgment as Commander-in-Chief. But I'm also the President of the world's oldest constitutional democracy. So even though I possess the authority to order military strikes, I believed it was right, in the absence of a direct or imminent threat to our security, to take this debate to Congress. I believe our democracy is stronger when the President acts with the support of Congress. And I believe that America acts more effectively abroad when we stand together.

This is especially true after a decade that put more and more war-making power in the hands of the President, and more and more burdens on the shoulders of our troops, while sidelining the people's representatives from the critical decisions about when we use force.

. . .

So let me answer some of the most important questions that I've heard from members of Congress, and that I've read in letters that you've sent to me.

First, many of you have asked, won't this put us on a slippery slope to another war? One man wrote to me that we are "still recovering from our involvement in Iraq." A veteran put it more bluntly: "This nation is sick and tired of war."

My answer is simple: I will not put American boots on the ground in Syria. I will not pursue an open-ended action like Iraq or Afghanistan. I will not pursue a prolonged air campaign like Libya or Kosovo. This would be a targeted strike to achieve a clear objective: deterring the use of chemical weapons, and degrading Assad's capabilities.

. . .

I don't think we should remove another dictator with force—we learned from Iraq that doing so makes us responsible for all that comes next. But a targeted strike can make Assad, or any other dictator, think twice before using chemical weapons.

. . .

Finally, many of you have asked: Why not leave this to other countries, or seek solutions short of force? As several people wrote to me, "We should not be the world's policeman."

I agree, and I have a deeply held preference for peaceful solutions. Over the last two years, my administration has tried diplomacy and sanctions, warning and negotiations—but chemical weapons were still used by the Assad regime.

However, over the last few days, we've seen some encouraging signs. In part because of the credible threat of U.S. military action, as well as constructive talks that I had with President Putin, the Russian government has indicated a willingness to join with the international community in pushing Assad to give up his chemical weapons. The Assad regime has now admitted that it has these weapons, and even said they'd join the Chemical Weapons Convention, which prohibits their use.

It's too early to tell whether this offer will succeed, and any agreement must verify that the Assad regime keeps its commitments. But this initiative has the potential to remove the threat of chemical weapons without the use of force, particularly because Russia is one of Assad's strongest allies.

I have, therefore, asked the leaders of Congress to postpone a vote to authorize the use of force while we pursue this diplomatic path. I'm sending Secretary of State John Kerry to meet his Russian counterpart on Thursday, and I will continue my own discussions with President Putin.

## STATEMENT BY THE PRESIDENT ON ISIL*

My fellow Americans, tonight I want to speak to you about what the United States will do with our friends and allies to degrade and ultimately destroy the terrorist group known as ISIL.

As Commander-in-Chief, my highest priority is the security of the American people. Over the last several years, we have consistently taken the fight to terrorists who threaten our country. We took out Osama bin Laden and much of al Qaeda's leadership in Afghanistan and Pakistan. We've targeted al Qaeda's affiliate in Yemen, and recently eliminated the top commander of its affiliate in Somalia. We've done so while bringing more than 140,000 American troops home from Iraq, and drawing down our forces in Afghanistan, where our combat mission will end later this year. Thanks to our military and counterterrorism professionals, America is safer.

Still, we continue to face a terrorist threat. We can't erase every trace of evil from the world, and small groups of killers have the capacity to do great harm. That was the case before 9/11, and that remains true today. And that's why we must remain vigilant as threats emerge. At this moment, the greatest threats come from the Middle East and North Africa, where radical groups exploit grievances for their own gain. And one of those groups is ISIL—which calls itself the "Islamic State."

Now let's make two things clear: ISIL is not "Islamic." No religion condones the killing of innocents. And the vast majority of ISIL's victims have been Muslim. And ISIL is certainly not a state. It was formerly al Qaeda's affiliate in Iraq, and has taken advantage of sectarian strife and Syria's civil war to gain territory on both sides of the Iraq-Syrian border. It is recognized

---

*The White House Office of the Press Secretary, September 10, 2014.

by no government, nor by the people it subjugates. ISIL is a terrorist organization, pure and simple. And it has no vision other than the slaughter of all who stand in its way.

In a region that has known so much bloodshed, these terrorists are unique in their brutality. They execute captured prisoners. They kill children. They enslave, rape, and force women into marriage. They threatened a religious minority with genocide. And in acts of barbarism, they took the lives of two American journalists—Jim Foley and Steven Sotloff.

So ISIL poses a threat to the people of Iraq and Syria, and the broader Middle East—including American citizens, personnel and facilities. If left unchecked, these terrorists could pose a growing threat beyond that region, including to the United States. While we have not yet detected specific plotting against our homeland, ISIL leaders have threatened America and our allies. Our Intelligence Community believes that thousands of foreigners—including Europeans and some Americans—have joined them in Syria and Iraq. Trained and battle-hardened, these fighters could try to return to their home countries and carry out deadly attacks.

. . .

Our objective is clear: We will degrade, and ultimately destroy, ISIL through a comprehensive and sustained counterterrorism strategy.

First, we will conduct a systematic campaign of airstrikes against these terrorists. Working with the Iraqi government, we will expand our efforts beyond protecting our own people and humanitarian missions, so that we're hitting ISIL targets as Iraqi forces go on offense. Moreover, I have made it clear that we will hunt down terrorists who threaten our country, wherever they are. That means I will not hesitate to take action against ISIL in Syria, as well as Iraq. This is a core principle of my presidency: If you threaten America, you will find no safe haven.

Second, we will increase our support to forces fighting these terrorists on the ground. In June, I deployed several hundred American servicemembers to Iraq to assess how we can best support Iraqi security forces. Now that those teams have completed their work—and Iraq has formed a government—we will send an additional 475 servicemembers to Iraq. As I have said before, these American forces will not have a combat mission—we will not get dragged into another ground war in Iraq. But they are needed to support Iraqi and Kurdish forces with training, intelligence and equipment. We'll also support Iraq's efforts to stand up National Guard Units to help Sunni communities secure their own freedom from ISIL's control.

Across the border, in Syria, we have ramped up our military assistance to the Syrian opposition. Tonight, I call on Congress again to give us additional authorities and resources to train and equip these fighters. In the fight against ISIL, we cannot rely on an Assad regime that terrorizes its own people—a regime that will never regain the legitimacy it has lost. Instead, we must strengthen the opposition as the best counterweight to extremists like ISIL, while pursuing the political solution necessary to solve Syria's crisis once and for all.

Third, we will continue to draw on our substantial counterterrorism capabilities to prevent ISIL attacks. Working with our partners, we will redouble our efforts to cut off its funding; improve our intelligence; strengthen our defenses; counter its warped ideology; and stem the flow of foreign fighters into and out of the Middle East. And in two weeks, I will chair a meeting of the U.N. Security Council to further mobilize the international community around this effort.

Fourth, we will continue to provide humanitarian assistance to innocent civilians who have been displaced by this terrorist organization. This includes Sunni and Shia Muslims who are at grave risk, as well as tens of thousands of Christians and other religious minorities. We cannot allow these communities to be driven from their ancient homelands.

So this is our strategy. And in each of these four parts of our strategy, America will be joined by a broad coalition of partners. Already, allies are flying planes with us over Iraq; sending arms and assistance to Iraqi security forces and the Syrian opposition; sharing intelligence; and providing billions of dollars in humanitarian aid. Secretary Kerry was in Iraq today meeting with the new government and supporting their efforts to promote unity. And in the coming days he will travel across the Middle East and Europe to enlist more partners in this fight, especially Arab nations who can help mobilize Sunni communities in Iraq and Syria, to drive these terrorists from their lands. This is American leadership at its best: We stand with people who fight for their own freedom, and we rally other nations on behalf of our common security and common humanity.

## CRITICAL THINKING QUESTIONS

1. How many Syria foreign policy problems are there? Is this unique or typical of foreign policy problems?
2. Which is preferable: a consistent statement of goals, objectives, and strategies or one that changes as situations change?
3. Looking back at the readings in part I, how would Robert Kagan, David Unger, and Barry Posen evaluate Obama's polices as contained in these speeches?

# 20

# R2P

## LOOKING BACK, LOOKING FORWARD

Gareth Evans

In November 1975, seven months after the Khmer Rouge had marched into Phnom Penh and commenced its reign of genocidal slaughter, U.S. Secretary of State Henry Kissinger famously said to Thai Foreign Minister Chatichai: "Tell the Cambodians that we will be friends with them. They are murderous thugs, but we won't let that stand in our way".

It was essentially to make politically as well as morally impossible that kind of response—born of Cold War **realpolitik**—to genocide and crimes against humanity that the concept of the responsibility to protect (R2P) was born.

R2P was also created to make both politically and morally impossible the kind of response we heard to Rwanda in 1994—"just black African tribes chopping each other up as they have been doing since time immemorial". And to make impossible the kind of response we so often heard in the 1990s in the Balkans—"just the fires of old nationalist and religious hatred burning themselves out".

The whole point of the R2P doctrine, in the minds of those of us who conceived it, was above all to change the way that the world's policymakers, and those who influence them, thought and acted in response to emerging, imminent and actually occurring mass atrocity crimes.

It was to generate a reflex international response that genocide, other crimes against humanity and major war crimes happening behind sovereign state walls were everybody's business, not nobody's.

It was to create a new norm of international behaviour which states would feel ashamed to violate, compelled to observe, or at least embarrassed to ignore.

It was to stimulate the creation of new institutional mechanisms, national and international, that would help translate that sense of moral and political obligation to protect into effective action.

Keynote Dinner Address by Professor the Honorable Gareth Evans AC QC, Former Foreign Minister of Australia and Co-Chair of the International Commission on Intervention and State Sovereignty, to APR2P/GCR2P/Stanley Foundation/ICRtoP Conference on *The Responsibility to Protect at 10: Progress, Challenges and Opportunities in the Asia Pacific*, Phnom Penh, Cambodia, 26 February 2015.

The bottom line was always to change behaviour: to ensure that global policymakers would never again have to look back, in the aftermath of yet another genocidal catastrophe, and ask themselves how they could possibly have let it all happen again.

R2P was designed for pragmatists rather than purists. Its intended contribution was not to international relations theory but political practice. It was designed not to create new legal rules but rather a compelling new sense of moral and political obligation to apply existing ones.

Those of us gathered at this important conference approach R2P from multiple different perspectives. We come from different geographic regions; some of us are academics, some practitioners; some of us are more focused on prevention, others more on reaction; some of us instinctively approach problem-solving top-down, others bottom-up.

But what I hope all of us can recognize is that the core motivation that drove R2P from the beginning, and must still be at the heart of the enterprise today, is that mass atrocity crimes are a totally unacceptable assault on our common humanity, and that whatever else we mess up in the conduct of international affair, we must never again be found wanting as an international community when it comes to halting or averting another Cambodia, Rwanda or Srebrenica.

This is the context, and these are the benchmarks, against which R2P's success or failure over the last decade should be measured, and its likely future over the next decade and beyond should be assessed. There are four big things that R2P was designed to be: a normative force, an institutional catalyst, a framework for preventive action and a framework for reactive action. So, looking back, what has R2P achieved so far and, looking forward, what will it achieve in the future, in each of these four areas?

## R2P AS A NORMATIVE FORCE

It may be too big a call to say, as the British historian Martin Gilbert did two years after the 2005 World Summit, that acceptance of the responsibility to protect is "the most significant adjustment to sovereignty in 360 years", but it is certainly true to say that R2P, evolving as it has through successive stages since the original ICISS report, has gained over the last decade much more worldwide normative traction than most observers had thought possible, and certainly did so in a way that remains unimaginable for the concept of "humanitarian intervention" which it has now almost completely displaced.

The best evidence of this is in the annual debates on R2P in the General Assembly, even in the aftermath of the strong disagreements over the Libyan intervention in 2011which have had many sceptics pronouncing its death rites. Certainly there is less general comfort with the third pillar than the first two, and there will always be argument about what precise form action should take in a particular case, but the basic principles are under no threat. In the most recent annual General Assembly debate on R2P in early September 2014, in which statements were made by or on behalf of 81 states from every regional group, there was overwhelming support for all the basic R2P principles.

Further evidence of the acceptance achieved by R2P lies in the record of the Security Council. For all the continuing neuralgia about the Libyan intervention and the paralysing impact of that on its deliberations on Syria, the Security Council, which had before 2011 passed only four resolutions mentioning R2P, *after* its March 2011 decisions on Cote d'Ivoire and Libya, by the end of 2014 had endorsed 22 other resolutions directly referring to the responsibility to protect, including measures to confront the threat of mass atrocities in Yemen, Libya, Mali, Sudan, South Sudan and the Central African Republic, and had authorised another twelve Presidential Statements employing that language.

While none of these have authorized a Libyan-style military intervention, and a great many references are in pillar one terms, referring to states bearing the primary responsibility to protect their own populations, they make clear that the Council is comfortable with both the language and substance of the doctrine in all its dimensions.

With the weight behind it of a unanimous General Assembly resolution at head of state and government level, and with all the further UN member-state acceptance it has acquired since, as described above, R2P can certainly be described in moral and political terms as a new international *norm—and, moreover, not just an "emerging" one.* It does not create more legal obligations than already exist under international law in relation to genocide, other crimes against humanity and war crimes, but it does amount a new standard of behaviour, and a new guide to behaviour, generally accepted as such, for every state.

All that said, there is more work to do to consolidate R2P's normative force. There are still significant differences evident across the world in the nature and degree of individual state policymakers' commitment to R2P—intellectually, morally and emotionally—and it is important that these be minimized in the years ahead if the new norm is to further consolidate and flourish, and be the framework within which atrocity crime issues are effectively addressed in practice.

Of course if a norm is aspirational, rather than just boringly descriptive of universal existing practice, getting it fully embraced in principle is not going to guarantee effective implementation in practice. But if norm consolidation is not a sufficient condition for practical delivery, it is certainly a necessary one.

The major task for R2P advocates in the near future is to encourage a *mindset* convergence in this respect among the states, and groups of states, that will matter most in the world of the 21st century—not just the United States, China, European Union and Russia, but emerging major powers like the other "BRICS" states, India, Brazil and South Africa. My judgement, for what it's worth, is that we are not as far away from achieving that as is sometimes assumed, but more persuasion and pressure from other state actors and civil society, of the kind that many participants in this conference are engaged in mobilising, will certainly still be required.

As to the *United States*, there is little risk of it engaging in the general adventurism and militarisation of R2P of the kind feared by so many of its critics, particularly in the global South: at least since the end of the George W. Bush presidency, getting the United States started looms as a bigger concern than stopping it. While its military response to the Islamic State, or Da'esh, in Syria and Iraq might be thought to be an exception to the much more cautious trend of recent years, there has been a clear R2P justification for it in the terrible atrocities perpetrated by the militants (separate and distinct from the more problematic homeland-terrorism rationale), the scale of the operations has been modest, and they have been undertaken with the express or implicit support of the governments of the states involved.

Generally the United States has been a strong supporter of the R2P norm in a UN context, and has played a leading role in developing early warning and response preparedness, and nuanced military response strategies, that have been useful models for other states. The only really disappointing, and frustrating, aspect of the U.S. commitment, from an R2P norm entrepreneurship perspective, is the deliberate decision of the Obama administration to refrain, other than in an in-house UN context, from actually using "responsibility to protect" terminology: the main privately stated reason being a domestic political one, viz. not to stir up those many forces in the country deeply sceptical of any terms associated with national or international legal obligations. Those of a more sceptical cast of mind might be minded to think it another example of something not made in the United States not existing. Either way, the reluctance has not been helpful.

In the case of the *UK* and *France*, the enterprise of achieving greater international consensus around the application of R2P would benefit from a rather more cautious approach to the use of coercive military force than they have tended to exercise so far, certainly when they overreached in Libya in 2011: sentimental attachment to "humanitarian intervention" in the UK, and Bernard Kouchner's "*droit d'ingerence*" in France, is still somewhat evident. But they do both get it about R2P, and their leadership in Europe continues to be necessary. The other major EU power, Germany, continues for obvious historical reasons to be almost painfully unwilling to use military power in any context: if that position were to prevail, R2P would lose the cutting edge it will always needs to be a completely effective atrocity-curbing tool.

*China*—contrary to many expectations—did not play any kind of spoiling role in the debate leading up to the World Summit debate which embraced R2P in 2005, and has not been the strongest obstructive voice since. It did not oppose the initial Resolution 1973 on Libya, and has framed its subsequent objections not absolutely but in terms of the need to use "extreme caution" in authorizing the use of force to protect civilians, and to "fully and strictly" implement Security Council resolutions and not 'wilfully misinterpret' them: it has expressed strong support in that context for the concept, initiated by Brazil, of "Responsibility While Protecting" with its two key elements of close attention by the Security Council to agreed prudential criteria like last resort and proportionality before granting any military mandate in atrocity crime cases, and close monitoring of the implementation of any such mandate during its lifetime.

Beijing is becoming increasingly outspoken on international relations issues, but at the same time is increasingly visibly self-conscious about China's need to be seen to be playing a constructive, responsible role in international affairs. It should not be assumed to be instinctively unresponsive to the need for sometimes quite robust cooperative responses to mass atrocity crimes.

The remaining P5 member, *Russia*, was in the lead-up to 2005, and has been since, a more obdurate opponent of robust action, but in the event opposed neither the World Summit Outcome Document, nor the 2011 Libya resolutions, nor many other Security Council resolutions and Presidential Statements referring to R2P. It in fact explicitly *relied* on R2P to justify its own military invasion of Georgia in 2008 but this generated a strongly negative international response, and R2P was not in fact invoked—although many had expected it to be—in its equally unhappy annexation of Crimea in 2013 and continuing intervention in Ukraine.

Russia has been the main blocker of any effective resolution in Syria, particularly in the early months when a united Security Council front could have made a big difference. Its intransigence has been primarily driven by the *realpolitik* of its close and long-standing economic and strategic relationship with Damascus and the Assad regime has constantly prevailed, and it is not to be assumed that its intransigence will be as complete in other contexts in the future if the tensions over Ukraine which are currently poisoning relationships with the U.S. and EU countries can be resolved. Russia's stated objections to R2P in recent years have been much more directed to the way in which R2P was applied in Libya ('double standards dictated by short term circumstances or the preferences of particular states') than to its inherent normative content. Senior officials have shown serious interest in the "Responsibility While Protecting" concept as a way of re-establishing broader Security Council consensus.

Of the remaining BRICS threesome (India, South Africa and Brazil), *India*'s position is the most relevant for this region. India was the last significant state to be persuaded to join the 2005 consensus, and has remained a generally unenthusiastic supporter of R2P since (save in the context of the Sri Lankan issue in 2009, when Foreign Minister Pranab Mukherjee called on the Colombo government to exercise its responsibility to protect its own citizens). It has generally focused not on opposing military force so much as setting conditions for its exercise, including that it 'be the measure of last resort and be used only when all diplomatic and political efforts fail' and that Security Council mandates be closely monitored: it has been a strong supporter in this respect of "Responsibility While Protecting".

India has wanted to be seen internationally as a champion of human rights and democracy, but at the same time to maintain its noninterventionist credentials with the Non Aligned Movement (NAM), a difficult balance to maintain (as, comparably, is its position as simultaneously a global champion and national resister of nuclear disarmament). It seems reasonable to assume that as Delhi looks more and more to assuming a global leadership role, it will contribute to bridge-building on these issues in a more active and systematically constructive way: again it is crucial that the P3 and others be responsive to its concerns about the potential misapplication of military force in R2P contexts.

## R2P AS AN INSTITUTIONAL CATALYST

All the normative consolidation in the world will not be of much use if R2P is not capable of delivering protection in practice. The continued evolution of institutional preparedness, at the national, regional and global level, is absolutely crucial if R2P is to move beyond rhetoric to effective practical implementation, particularly at the crucial stages of early prevention, and early reaction to warning signs of impending catastrophe.

Although much more needs to be done, the story in this respect so far has been reasonably encouraging. Particular effort is going into the creation of "focal points" within key national governments and intergovernmental organizations, namely high-level officials whose designated day-job it is to analyse mass-atrocity risk situations and to energise an appropriately swift and early response within their own systems and in cooperation with others. The joint NGO-government initiative led by the Global Centre to establish a global network of such focal points had seen by the end of 2014 over 40 states signed up, from every region of the world, although Asian countries has been slower than those in other regions to sign on.

Although in some cases cosmetics need to be matched by more substance, the reality is that from Uruguay to the United States, from the DRC to Cote d'Ivoire, from Lithuania to New Zealand—as well as in the UN itself with the Joint Office of the Special Advisers for the Prevention of Genocide, and R2P—there is a large and growing group of states building a real community of commitment.

More institutional response capacity is needed in the civilian sphere in the form of the organization and resourcing of civilian capability able to be utilized, as occasion arises, for diplomatic mediation, civilian policing and other critical administrative support for countries at risk of atrocity crimes occurring or recurring: commitments to develop that capability have to date been more often rhetorical than real.

But probably the most crucial institutional need for the future is to create a culture of effective support for the International Criminal Court and the evolving machinery of international criminal justice, designed to enable not only trial and punishment for some of the worst mass atrocity crimes of the past, but potentially providing an important new deterrent for the future.

In the military sphere, the main need is to have in place properly trained and capable military resources available both for rapid 'fire-brigade' deployment in Rwanda-type cases, and for long-haul stabilization operations like those in the Congo and Sudan, not only in no-consent situations, but where vulnerable governments request this kind of assistance. And although the establishment of effective military rapid reaction forces on even a standby basis remains more an aspiration than a reality, key militaries—again with the United States playing a prominent role—are devoting serious time and attention now to debating, and putting in place, new force configuration arrangements, doctrine, rules of engagement and training to run what are now being increasingly described as 'Mass Atrocity Response Operations' (MARO).

Here as elsewhere, regional organizations can be expected to play an ever more important role, exercising the full range of the responsibilities envisaged for them in Chapter VIII of the UN Charter. So far, although both the European and African Unions have shown occasional willingness to act collectively, only ECOWAS in West Africa has so far shown a consistent willingness to respond with a full range of diplomatic, political, economic and ultimately military strategies in response to civilian protection crises.

But regional and sub-regional organizations in Latin America, and above all here in Asia, have lagged a long way behind. I hope very much that this conference, and the work of the Asia-Pacific Centre which has contributed so much to our deliberations, will generate some new momentum in this respect.

One important point that has emerged from our discussions is that in the future we may need to broaden our focus beyond the formal institutional players in national governments, and in regional and global intergovernmental organizations. Non-state actors in civil society are going to be ever more significant drivers, in this context as in many others. And Ed Luck has made the interesting suggestion that, given the role that individual citizens—and officials—have so often played as participants in genocidal bloodshed or as passive bystanders, there is a case for developing and promoting, in parallel with the R2P, the idea of the "Individual Responsibility to Protect".

# R2P AS A PREVENTIVE FRAMEWORK

The credibility of the whole R2P enterprise has depended from the outset on giving central importance to prevention, in three different contexts. First, long before any atrocity crime has occurred or been threatened, but when ethnic or religious or other tensions, unresolved economic or other grievances, or manifest governance inadequacies, or all of the above, suggest there may be a serious problem in the making unless these underlying issues are systematically addressed. Second, when warning signs—like overt hate propaganda—begin to accumulate, and more rapid and focused preventive responses have to be mounted if catastrophe is to be averted. And third, in a post-violence situation, where the crucial need is to rebuild the society in a way which seriously addresses all the underlying causal issues, and ensures that the whole ugly cycle does not recur.

It needs to be acknowledged, in talking about this dimension of R2P, that at least when one is talking about prevention in the long-term structural senses described above, aiming at stopping the original occurrence and subsequent recurrence of catastrophe by addressing underlying causes, the R2P mission is for the most part indistinguishable from two or three others—the *conflict prevention* mission, the general *human rights violation-avoidance* mission, and to some extent the *development* mission as well. But the point that matters here is that while structural prevention may not be an exclusive R2P concern, it is unquestionably R2P core business, and we ignore it at our peril. Some states may be more comfortable than others in talking about long-term structural prevention in R2P terms: but what matters is that, whatever frame of reference they choose, they just get on with the task.

The good news about prevention is that the toolbox of relevant measures at all preventive stages—across the whole spectrum of political and diplomatic, economic and social, constitutional and legal, and security strategies—is well known, and as experience accumulates, and lessons-learned literature proliferates, there is an ever more detailed and sophisticated understanding by professionals of the detailed strategies that are likely to be most effective, and cost-effective. One theme strongly emphasized in commentary from the global South, and emerging from hard experience on the ground, is the critical need for more sensitive attention to be paid by external interveners and assisters to local social dynamics and cultural realities, and the perceptions of their own requirements by local populations at all levels.

It is also encouraging that, stimulated by the reports of the Secretary General to member states, prepared by Jennifer Welsh, in 2013 on "State responsibility and prevention" and 2014 on "International assistance and the responsibility to protect", recent General Assembly Interactive Dialogues on R2P have placed renewed attention on both the preventive toolbox generally, and capacity-building and other preventive strategies in the context of the Pillar Two "assistance" responsibility.

The less good news is that while there is a long tradition of regular lip-service being paid to the need for effective prevention, in both national and international debates, the record of practical delivery is not stellar. Part of the problem of getting sufficient resources to engage in successful atrocity, or conflict, prevention is the age-old one that success means that nothing visible actually happens: no-one gets the kind of credit that is always on offer for effective fire-fighting. And it's an iron law of politics that it is like bathing a very recalcitrant dog to get anyone excited about supporting something for which he or she is unlikely to get any recognition.

## R2P AS A REACTIVE FRAMEWORK

This is where the rubber hits the road. What do we *do* if a state, through incapacity or ill-will, has failed to meet its Pillar One responsibilities? What do we do if prevention has manifestly failed, and mass atrocity crimes are actually occurring or imminently about to occur?

R2P from the outset has involved a whole continuum of both non-coercive and coercive responses, and is absolutely *not* about coercive military interventions alone, notwithstanding that these have taken over so much of the ongoing debate.

Those reactive responses include diplomatic peacemaking, political incentives as well as political sanctions, economic incentives as well as economic sanctions, offers of amnesty as well as threats of criminal prosecution, the jamming of radio frequencies by non-forceful means, arms embargoes as well as the use of arms, and various kinds of peacekeeping falling short of full scale peace enforcement. And the application of coercive military force can of course take the form of Pillar Two assistance rather than invariably more controversial Pillar Three intervention—when done at the invitation of the government unable to deal alone with a mass atrocity situation not of its own making. All this is not as well understood by policymakers and commentators as it should be, and needs to be constantly reinforced.

But however much one may seek to preference non-military solutions, the reality is that in some R2P situations—classically Rwanda—only coercive military force would have halted the atrocities. And some of these situations will allow little or no time for systematically exhausting options short of military force: where large scale killing is occurring or manifestly imminent, a quick judgement may have to be made that no lesser action is capable of halting or averting the harm.

One hears from some academics (and nervous officials) that there are a whole set of intractable structural problems involved in *any* coercive military intervention designed to halt an actual or avert an imminent mass atrocity crime, including mixed motives (interveners will often have self-interested as well as altruistic aims), the counterfactual problem (the impossibility of *proving* that any given number of people would have died without the intervention), the conspicuous harm problem (there is bound to be at least some collateral civilian damage), the end-state problem (how to leave after an intervention without the harm recurring), and the inconsistency problem (how can you intervene anywhere if you can't do so everywhere you ideally should).

My practitioner-focused response to these anxieties, however, is straightforward: welcome to the real world. Any decision-making in any real crisis almost invariably involves hard judgment calls, weighing and balancing considerations that almost never all point conveniently the same way. R2P is a framework for action for pragmatists, not purists, and this is very well understood by those who have to apply it, not just write about it.

Because of the degree of sensitivity and difficulty involved in any decision to use coercive military force—against the will of the government of the state concerned—it has been assumed from the outset by most R2P advocates, certainly me, that it would only be in the most extreme and exceptional circumstances that it will be authorised by the Security Council. And so it has proved to be, with only the Cote d'Ivoire and Libya cases in 2011 giving rise to such a mandate. It is impossible to know how many thousands of lives were saved in Benghazi by that initial intervention in Libya, but certainly possible to argue that had the UN Security Council acted anything like as swiftly and robustly in the 1990s, 8000 men and boys in Srebrenica, and close to 800,000 men, women and children in Rwanda, would still be alive today.

But of course the Libya case, as already noted, whatever the initial lack of controversy has subsequently proved desperately divisive, because of the widespread perception—certainly among the influential BRICS group members—that the P3 members unacceptably transformed a limited civilian protection mandate into an open-ended regime change one. If R2P is to have a future in all the ways that it needs to—if we are not, in the face of extreme mass atrocity situations, to go back to the bad old days of indefensible inaction as with Cambodia, or Rwanda, or Bosnia, or of otherwise defensible action taken in defiance of the UN Charter, as in Kosovo—then a solution simply has to be found to the current post-Libya stand-off. The good news, I believe, is that a solution is in sight should agreement be able to be reached on some variant of the "Responsibility While Protecting" proposal originally put on the table by Brazil, in which Russia, China and India, among others, have all shown interest.

Overall, while there are certainly plenty of challenges ahead for R2P, there are many grounds for optimism about its future of R2P over the next decade and beyond. It is important to emphasise again that the disagreement now evident in the UN Security Council *is* really only about how the R2P norm is to be applied in the hardest, sharp-end cases, those where prevention has manifestly failed, and the harm to civilians being experienced or feared is so great that the issue of military force has to be given at least some prima facie consideration. There is much more to the R2P project than just these extreme late-stage situations, and much to indicate that its other preventive, reactive and rebuilding dimensions all have both wide and deep international support.

Policymakers now around the world do understand the stakes, and the imperative for cooperative action, much better than they used to. I don't believe that anyone really wants to see a return to the bad old days when appalling crimes against humanity committed behind sovereign state walls were seen by almost everyone as nobody else's business.

And I think we can be optimistic enough to believe that R2P principles are already so internalised and embedded that no leader knowing of such crimes will ever say again to a counterpart what Kissinger did to Chatichai in 1975. I may be wrong but we must all hope that I'm right, and together work like hell to ensure that I am.

## CRITICAL THINKING QUESTIONS

1. What evidence exists that R2P has been accepted or rejected by global leaders as an important concept?
2. In order of importance, rank the four benchmarks put forward for evaluating R2P. Explain your reasoning.
3. Suggest two important additions or changes in R2P that are needed for it to reach its full potential as an international norm.

# 21

# Cybersecurity and Tailored Deterrence

Franklin D. Kramer and Melanie J. Teplinsky

Cyber has become the new conflict arena. It ranks as one of the greatest national security challenges facing the United States for three reasons. First, as the revelations about the National Security Agency's (NSA's) activities suggest, cyber offense has far outpaced cyber defense. Second, cyber capabilities are prevalent worldwide and increasingly are being used to achieve the strategic goals of nations and actors adverse to the United States. Third, it is highly unlikely that cyber espionage and other cyber intrusions will soon cease. While the NSA disclosures focus on the United States and the United Kingdom, there is little doubt that China, Russia, Iran, North Korea, and others are engaged in significant cyber activities. The fundamental question is whether the cyber realm can, consistent with the national interest, be made more stable and secure.

This paper proposes that a critical step in the establishment of such a stable and secure cyberspace will be the development of a tailored deterrence approach to cyber that reduces the national security threat from cyber adversaries. Tailored deterrence will not be sufficient in and of itself to stabilize and secure cyberspace. For example, it will not resolve fundamental issues—laid bare by the reaction to the NSA revelations—regarding the relationship of the U.S. government to its citizens and companies as well as to its close allies. Norms of behavior and requirements of law will need to be reviewed. But tailored deterrence can serve as a key element of a cybersecurity strategy designed to reduce adversarial intrusion into U.S. private, commercial, and governmental networks.

Despite over a decade of U.S. government and private sector investment in network defenses designed to reduce our vulnerability to cyber intrusion,

Franklin D. Kramer is a distinguished fellow and member of the board at the Atlantic Council and a former assistant secretary of defense for international security affairs. Melanie J. Teplinsky is on the advisory board for CrowdStrike, Inc., is an adjunct professorial lecturer at American University's Washington College of Law, and previously counseled on cybersecurity while in private practice at Steptoe & Johnson LLP. This piece was originally published as an issue brief by the Atlantic Council in December 2013. Reprinted with permission of the Atlantic Council.

the two key national security threats from cyber adversaries—cyber espionage and cyberattack against critical infrastructure—are increasingly severe. Evidence of this trend includes mounting reports of ongoing nation-state sponsored campaigns of intellectual property (IP) theft against major U.S. corporations and defense industrial base companies; the escalating spate of attacks on U.S. financial institutions over the past two years; and the 2012 cyberattack against Saudi Aramco—one of the most destructive attacks on the private sector to date—which destroyed over 30,000 computers at the world's largest energy company.

Neutralizing the cyber threat will take more than redoubled efforts to defend our networks. Hardening networks certainly will prevent some attacks, but it will not prevent them all. It is not only the NSA which has significant cyber capabilities, and a defense-only strategy will fail against nation-state actors and other determined adversaries who have the time, motivation, and resources to defeat even sophisticated defenses. Moreover, if history is any guide, a defense-only cyber strategy is unsustainable in the long term because it will saddle U.S. government and private organizations with escalating costs for enhanced—but ultimately imperfect—network defenses that adversaries will defeat for a fraction of the cost.

For these reasons, this paper recommends that the United States shift from a defense-only paradigm to a hybrid model of cybersecurity based not only on defense, but also on tailored deterrence, with a heavy emphasis on raising the costs of, and reducing the benefits from, cyber attacks. Tailored deterrence can be a key part of a strategy to provide a stable, secure cyberspace. This paper provides a brief overview of the concept of tailored deterrence and recommends the following four critical actions designed to increase attacker costs, deny attackers the benefits of their attacks, mitigate key consequences, and extend the breadth of those efforts into the international arena so we need not "look back years from now and wonder why we did nothing in the face of real threats to our security and our economy":

1. **Cyber Sanctions:** Authorize both governmentally imposed sanctions for cyber espionage and civil remedies, including treble damages and forfeiture, in order to deter cyber threat actors by imposing costs, or the threat thereof.
2. **Certified Active Defense:** Authorize a limited number of certified private entities to work with government to take active defense measures focused on attribution, initially to protect critical information within the defense industrial base. Active defense measures directed toward attribution will deter adversaries by raising the costs and risks associated with cyber espionage.
3. **Focused Standards for Protection and Resilience—Electric Grid and Finance:** Reduce critical infrastructure vulnerability and enhance resilience by developing differentiated mandatory standards, initially for the most critical electric power and financial companies. Reducing

vulnerability bolsters our defenses and increasing resilience enhances deterrence by mitigating the consequences of any successful intrusions.

4. **Agreement Among Like-minded Nations:** Expand protection against espionage and critical infrastructure vulnerability via agreement among like-minded nations. Common international approaches can extend and amplify deterrent effects and could be achieved initially through agreement among the United States, Australia, Canada, France, Germany, Japan, the Republic of Korea, the United Kingdom, and perhaps the European Union, to create a Cyber Stability Board.

Because several of these recommendations involve new approaches, this paper proposes that they be undertaken on a pilot-program, or other limited basis, which can be evaluated and expanded if proven effective and desirable.

To maximize their effectiveness, these recommendations can and should be implemented in tandem while maintaining the United States' drive for an open Internet and its commitment both to preserve and enhance personal privacy and to protect civil liberties. None of the recommendations above implicates any of the programs made public in the recent revelations of the activities of the National Security Agency (NSA), but privacy and civil liberty considerations should still be reviewed in connection with their adoption and implementation.

# 1. TAILORED DETERRENCE

Tailored deterrence recognizes that adversary calculations can be affected by more than the threat of simple retaliation through attack. Increasing costs to adversaries through methods other than attack as well as denying adversaries the benefits of an attack (e.g., "deterrence through denial"), including through consequence mitigation, can have significant deterrent effects on an adversary and should be utilized as part of an effective cybersecurity strategy.

Tailored deterrence most clearly entered official United States doctrine in the 2006 *Quadrennial Defense Review* (QDR), though, of course, elements of the analysis had long been part of strategic thought. The concept has since regularly been reaffirmed including in the President's 2012 strategic defense review which provides that "[c]redible deterrence results from both the capabilities to deny an aggressor the prospect of achieving his objectives and from the complementary capability to impose unacceptable costs on the aggressor."

Tailored deterrence previously has been applied to asymmetric warfare issues in a manner that has application to cyber. In a 2012 analysis of tailored deterrence and terrorism, Matthew Kroenig and Barry Pavel wrote:

> Deterrence is a strategic interaction in which an actor prevents an adversary from taking an action that the adversary otherwise would have taken by convincing the adversary that the cost of taking that action will outweigh any potential gains. To achieve deterrence, therefore, an actor can

shape the adversary's perception of the costs or benefits of a particular course of action. . . .

When considering deterrence, many analysts think solely in terms of deterrence-by-retaliation, but deterrence theorists also advanced a second type of deterrence strategy: benefit denial, or deterrence-by-denial, strategies which contribute to deterrence by threatening to deny an adversary the benefits of a particular course of action. . . . If actors believe that they are unlikely to succeed or reap significant benefits from a certain course of action, they may be deterred from taking it.

Kroenig and Pavel make clear that while defense and deterrence by denial overlap, there is an important distinction:

Deterrence is distinct from other strategies such as defense. There is a fine line between deterrence-by-denial and defense because defensive postures can have deterrent effects and deterrent capabilities can aid in a defensive operation. To distinguish between these approaches, we follow previous scholarship in defining defensive policies as those that are designed primarily to fend off an opponent in the event of an attack, and deterrence policies as those that are intended to convince an adversary not to attack in the first place.

In the discussion below, deterrence theory is applied to cyber in nontraditional manners; that is, by raising costs through other than threat of attack and by denying the benefits of cyber attack to adversaries. Such actions would not encompass the full spectrum of a cyber strategy, however. There still are reasons for strong defenses and, in the context of actual warfare, the threat of retaliation. The discussion herein, however, significantly broadens cyber strategy by making deterrence a feasible effort short of all-out retaliation.

## 2. CYBER SANCTIONS

The United States has long utilized sanctions against individuals, entities, and countries in pursuit of counterterrorism, nonproliferation, and other policies. Cyber sanctions could be used in a comparable fashion to meet the growing challenge of cyber industrial espionage. Cyber sanctions will deter cyber espionage by raising costs, or the threat thereof, and therefore are essential to the broader cybersecurity strategy recommended in this paper.

Cyber sanctions would have three critical benefits to the United States. First, they would raise the cost to malicious hackers. Second, they would send a strong geopolitical signal to countries that encourage or actively support malicious hacking. Third, if done properly, they could authorize and encourage private initiatives, which would then supplement the government's capability to respond to malicious hacking.

Sanctions could be of two types. They could be governmental, akin to nonproliferation or counterterrorism sanctions, or they could provide civil remedies, which would be a new approach.

Governmental sanctions could be implemented by the President under existing law, or new authorities could be created by the Congress. Under existing law, the President already has the authority to impose targeted sanctions against cyber threat actors. Specifically, under the International Emergency Economic Powers Act (IEEPA), the President can declare a "national emergency" where there is an "unusual or extraordinary [foreign] threat" to the United States' "national security, foreign policy, or economy." The President would then have broad authority under the IEEPA to address the cyber threat through financial sanctions, including freezing the U.S.-based assets of, and blocking financial transactions with, individuals, private organizations, and governments contributing to the threat. The already substantial effect of these actions would be amplified by the fact that financial institutions throughout the world "often refuse to do business with sanctioned entities."

Alternatively, Congress could establish a cyber sanctions regime through legislation. Two separate bills currently are pending. The Senate bill, the Deter Cyber Theft Act (DCTA), requires the President to block imports of products containing or similar to stolen U.S. technology or made or exported by a company that the director of national intelligence identifies as having benefited from theft of U.S. technology or proprietary information.

The House bill, the Cyber Economic Espionage Accountability Act (CEEAA), requires the President to identify—and make public (unless inconsistent with national security)—a list of foreign government officials or agents stealing IP via cyber espionage. Under CEEAA, such persons would be ineligible for U.S. visas and would be listed on the Office of Foreign Assets Control's Specially Designated Nationals and blocked persons list. Moreover, CEEAA authorizes the President to exercise all authorities granted under IEEPA to freeze the assets of such persons.

Cyber sanctions also profitably could be extended by providing civil remedies to corporate victims of cyber espionage. One of the differences between cyber and other areas is the significant economic impact on private entities. General Keith Alexander, head of U.S. Cyber Command, recently characterized the volume of IP theft that the United States experiences as "astounding" and publicly stated that, in his opinion, it is the "greatest transfer of wealth in history," although more recent analysis has reduced the probable size of the loss. Given that situation, authorizing private entities to seek legal remedies against malicious hacking entities could be beneficial.

As a general matter, 'private attorneys general' support public policy ends in many arenas. Empowering private sector cyber espionage victims to seek monetary damages could substantially raise the costs of, and thereby deter, cyber espionage. A private attorneys general approach potentially would have significant value if affected firms were allowed to collect punitive damages, perhaps treble damages, as in antitrust suits or specified statutorily authorized damages for circumstances in which the specific determination of compensatory damages would be difficult.

The viability of a 'private attorneys general' approach rests, in part, on successful attribution. The private sector has made great strides in addressing the attribution problem, which generally was viewed as intractable just a few short years ago. Effective attribution via nongovernment sources is now possible in at least some cases, as evidenced by the February 2013 Mandiant Report, which offered extensive evidence—including actual video of intrusion activities—of the role that China's People's Liberation Army played in a years-long cyber espionage campaign against companies in the United States. This capability paves the way for private litigants to obtain meaningful remedies for cyber espionage.

Several potential avenues exist for private litigants to obtain civil remedies for cyber espionage. First, the EEA could be amended to include a federal civil cause of action for economic espionage, including (1) treble damages for any losses arising out of economic espionage; and (2) a statutory penalty and/or a civil forfeiture provision. The availability of treble or statutory damages would encourage victimized corporations to sue EEA violators, redounding to the nation's benefit.

While a judicial remedy could be useful, an alternative would be to utilize an administrative proceeding in which government would both expedite and support private claims for loss/damage from cyber espionage and cyber attacks. Private and governmental efforts could be combined as is done in the government contracting context when a contractor initiates a bid protest challenging the propriety of a contract award. To initiate a proceeding, a private entity would file its claim with an administrative body of the government, just as bid protests are filed with the Government Accountability Office. The government then would be responsible for reviewing all evidence (classified and unclassified) in its possession and preparing for the private litigant an unclassified "report" including such evidence. After any necessary administrative adjudication to resolve disputed issues of fact or law, the record would be complete, and the administrative agency would issue a decision. If the agency determines that a foreign government or foreign actor was responsible for the cyber espionage or cyber attack that the private litigant alleged, administrative sanctions could be imposed on those entities. This would be new ground but given the magnitude of the cybersecurity problem, such an approach is worthy of serious consideration.

Once a private litigant has obtained a judgment against a foreign actor, a civil forfeiture provision should be an integral part of any statutory remedy. Such a provision would give the courts the authority to order the seizure of property used to commit, facilitate or owned by a company benefitting from the commission of the violation. Seizure of a foreign actor's property offers a way to attack the economic base of cyber threat actors.

A second enforcement mechanism would be to block imports of products benefitting from cyber espionage, as proposed in the Senate bill referenced above. This would provide relief in the competitive arena and also generate grounds for the offending entity to change its practices and settle with the harmed party.

Sanctions should not be looked on as a panacea in and of themselves as they generally are most effective as part of a comprehensive effort. Sanctions—both governmental and through private attorneys general—would, however, raise adversaries' costs of engaging in cyber attacks and, in conjunction with the steps outlined below, could play a pivotal role in the effort to address the growing cyber threat.

## 3. CERTIFIED ENTITIES AND ACTIVE DEFENSE

For over a decade, the cornerstone of U.S. cybersecurity policy has been vulnerability mitigation—strengthening cyber defenses to reduce vulnerability to attack. But there is a growing understanding that defense—particularly in the face of concerted adversaries focused on a specific target—will be most successful if it includes "active" components that serve a deterrent function, beyond passive protection alone. Accordingly, this paper recommends limited active defense measures as one element of a broader deterrence-based strategy.

Active defense received its first significant notice when the Department of Defense (DoD) published its 2011 strategy for operating in cyberspace. Although the term "active defense" is not specifically defined in the DoD cyber strategy, it has since been associated with a broad spectrum of activities.

This article is not advocating broad authorization for the private sector to engage in active defense, concerns about which have been spelled out in detail elsewhere, nor is it advocating private sector retaliation, vigilantism, or hackback. Rather, this paper recommends, as a starting point, authorizing those limited active defense measures that contribute to better (1) assurance (including better detection of intrusions and malicious activity across the supply chain); and (2) attribution (i.e., identification of threat actors). Such measures will raise adversaries' costs and risks, thereby serving a deterrent function essential to the success of the proposed hybrid cybersecurity model.

A new legal framework authorizing *certified* private sector cybersecurity providers to take limited, but meaningful steps under proper supervision likely would be an important element of tailored deterrence. A way to begin would be to create a framework to help protect the nation's most significant secrets maintained in the defense industrial base. Such a framework would set forth the requirements for "certification," and would require cybersecurity providers to meet certain standards, register with the government, and/or satisfy bonding requirements. To ensure adequate oversight, transparency, and accountability, the legal framework also would require certified cybersecurity providers to describe in advance and subsequently report their participation in certain activities to law enforcement. The use of private actors in such situations has a strong historical basis.

Such efforts would need to be carefully constrained. The economic and political ramifications of the use of certain active defense techniques on globally interconnected networks may require the type of judgments that governments ordinarily make. Moreover, engaging in active defense potentially implicates U.S. domestic law at both the federal and state levels, and, given the global reach of the Internet and cyber adversaries, active defense may involve actions or effects outside U.S. borders, potentially implicating the domestic law of other nations. On the other hand, a limited number of entities certified by the government in their expertise and working with government could add to the government's capabilities to address extensive cyber intrusions through the application of active defense. Such certified private sector entities acting under government supervision could be authorized to take limited steps to capture the attribution evidence necessary to raise the costs to—and thereby deter—cyber adversaries whether through sanctions, civil litigation, criminal prosecution, or a "name and shame" strategy.

Finally, recognizing that even the best-regulated program potentially could result in harm to innocent third parties, the proposed legal framework should provide for government compensation if authorized active defense measures cause such harm. Such a framework would permit a limited group of certified private sector actors to engage, with oversight, in socially beneficial actions while ensuring the availability of compensation should innocent actors suffer any damage as a result.

# 4. FOCUSED STANDARDS FOR PROTECTION AND RESILIENCE—ELECTRIC GRID AND FINANCE

Cyber standards also have a potentially important role to play in the proposed hybrid model of cybersecurity. Cyber standards could be of significant value if clearly delineated and made mandatory in limited sectors where the public interest is very substantial. Standards should focus not only on protection, but also on resilience, since it cannot be assumed that networks will not be penetrated. Resilience, by denying the benefits of an attack, would have deterrent impact, as would stronger defenses in the arenas where an adversary could potentially create the most harm to the nation.

In the cyber arena, most firms' evaluation of risks generally coincides with the national risk. However, in the case of key critical infrastructures—particularly electricity and finance—that certainly is not the case. For example, the harm from the loss of electric power, especially for an extended time, goes far beyond one firm's loss of revenue. Duke Energy, PG&E Corporation, and other major electric power firms are in a different category than, by comparison, Walmart or Ford Motor Company or Pizza Hut. This is equally true for major banks and financial institutions.

Accordingly, mandatory standards could be limited to a very few key critical infrastructures—as suggested, a good starting point would be electric power and finance—and only the most significant entities in those fields. It probably makes sense to start initially only with the largest companies in each field, say no more than the top 50 and perhaps fewer. Those firms would have the capacity to implement mandatory standards and their experience could provide a model for others. It would further make sense, and indeed only be fair, to expect those firms to receive compensation for the cost of implementing the standards since the requirements would be mandatory for the national interest, not for market reasons.

An important question regarding mandatory standards is whether standards can be clearly delineated. In fact, there are a series of fundamental actions that would greatly improve cybersecurity. On the protection side, it would be entirely possible to create a standard that required patching within forty-eight hours, whitelisting, use of least privilege, and continuous monitoring. These are equivalent to the so-called "Australian top 4," which the Australian government has publicly stated could have mitigated at least 85 percent of the targeted cyber intrusions to which its Defence Signals Directorate responded in 2010. Other well-known and effective measures include programming in so-called safe languages, using operational systems with limited capabilities, encryption of key data streams, and authentication with cryptography.

Enhanced protection, while highly desirable, cannot immunize operational systems against penetration. Resilient systems are therefore necessary. Standards that enhance resilience will not prevent an attack but will improve our ability to mitigate the consequences of successful attacks, and therefore play an important role in the proposed hybrid cybersecurity strategy.

While a good deal of analytic work has been done on resilience, there are far too few actual capabilities available. A two-pronged approach is required. Longer-term, a significant research and development effort needs to be undertaken. More immediately, resilience can be enhanced through integrity, segmentation, and the capacity to fight back and regain control of infected networks.

Integrity capabilities exist in the market and essentially allow a potentially infected network to be reset to a known status. Requiring electric power control networks and key financial networks to have that capacity is important. Segmentation dissociates certain parts of the network from others, thereby helping isolate sources of infection. Segmentation could be complemented by redundancy—not of complete networks but of key portions. Fighting back to regain network control can be necessary if the intruder seeks to keep out the network operator, which is potentially likely in a significant conflict. Fighting back will require human efforts: highly trained "white hat counterhackers." Generating such teams could be a combined government–private sector effort. Much as the government provides some key elements in disaster relief and other elements come from the private sector, government funding and training could help create and support underlying capabilities that take advantage of private sector human capital and organization. One approach might be a "Cyber Guard" modeled on the National Guard but which could allow some greater private sector organizational efforts.

None of these proposed remedies is perfect, of course, just as no set of standards can protect against accidents or failures in other arenas. What they can do, however, is make things significantly better. In brief, there is a short list of well-known approaches that would have high value for cybersecurity. All of these could be included in a cyber standard.

Of course, it is important not to "freeze" bad solutions into regulations. One of the primary concerns associated with mandatory regulatory regimes is that "imposing rigid regulatory requirements—requirements that by their nature will be unable to keep up with rapidly evolving technologies and threats—would require industry to focus on obsolete security requirements rather than facing the actual threat at hand, effectively making systems less secure." A mandatory regulatory regime for limited sectors could be designed to ameliorate such concerns. Regulations could focus on outcomes and companies could be left with the freedom to choose the technologies used to achieve those outcomes. To prevent companies from focusing on compliance with "obsolete" regulatory requirements, companies could be deemed to comply with regulations when they achieve an outcome equal to, "or better" than, that specified in the regulations.

In short, mandatory cyber standards limited to key critical infrastructure would allow a focused effort that takes account of national interest beyond that which the market alone would generate and are therefore an important element of the hybrid cybersecurity strategy described herein.

# 5. LIKE-MINDED NATIONS

The Internet is structurally and operationally international, and it would seem to follow that cybersecurity would be enhanced through cooperation among like-minded nations. There already have been some steps including the Budapest Convention, which is focused on cyber crime; some coordination through military and other security arrangements such as in NATO; and more generalized discussions in fora such as the Association of Southeast Asian Nations (ASEAN) Regional Forum (ARF), the Asia-Pacific Economic Cooperation Organization (APEC), and the Organization for Economic Cooperation and Development (OECD).

What has not yet happened, however, is an effectively coordinated effort to deal with cyber espionage and critical infrastructure vulnerability to prevent serious economic and national security consequences for the United States and its close partners. A significant attack on electric power, telecommunications, or finance could have very consequential economic results not only for the country being attacked but also for its economic partners. Likewise, on the security side, militaries are heavily dependent on electricity, telecommunications and finance to maintain their operational effectiveness. Allies and close partners that expect to work together and rely upon one another have an interest not only in their own cyber systems but also those of their allies and partners.

An international entity dealing with both espionage and critical infrastructure vulnerability would be of great value. For example, a "Cyber Stability Board, along the lines of the financial stability board established by nations for financial issues under the Basel agreements, could be created." Nations that could effectively do this include Australia, Canada, France, Germany, Japan, the Republic of Korea, the United Kingdom, the United States, and perhaps the European Union.

There is no likelihood of creating such a board unless the issues presented by the NSA revelations focusing on spying among countries are resolved in some satisfactory form. As is well known, the United States has a "Five Eyes" agreement with the United Kingdom, Canada, Australia, and New Zealand concerning espionage. The countries named above that are not included in the Five Eyes—France, Germany, Japan and the Republic of Korea—are all close treaty allies of the United States. It should be possible to organize a common approach to espionage—both military and industrial—and cyber security with such countries since each is a full democracy with common interests. To be sure, there would have to be changes in behavior, not only on the United States' part but also by others—for example, there are numerous media reports of French industrial espionage. On balance, the gains from a common approach to cyber security appear to outweigh any significant loss from curtailing espionage especially given the close working relationships generally found among these countries.

Assuming that the geopolitical obstacles to creating such a board could be surmounted, such a board could coordinate multiple international cybersecurity efforts, increasing defenses and enhancing deterrence. First, focusing on cyber espionage, nations could establish governmental cyber sanctions along the lines suggested above. As noted, sanctions work best as part of a coordinated effort, including on an international level, and the board could help develop common approaches to sanctions.

Second, the board could facilitate common approaches to the use of active defense by certified private sector actors. Certified actors would be more effective if operating under a common international legal regime. As noted above, creating a legal regime that allows private entities to engage in limited active defense measures focused on attribution may require significant legal changes. Coordinating multiple national laws would be a task for the board.

Third, the board could help develop a coordinated operational approach. Cooperative action by like-minded nations—including sharing data, analysis, and tools concerning threats and remediation, as well as undertaking combined operations—could significantly enhance the operationalization of self-defense and resilience efforts.

Fourth, in order to ensure that militaries can operate as required, common standards should be established between and among this group of like-minded countries for key critical infrastructures upon which militaries depend. All of these nations are treaty allies with the United States and have worked closely on multiple military standards-setting activities. Ensuring that there is good coordination between military requirements and civilian-run cyber structures could be a function of the board.

Fifth, international agreement could help enhance effective public-private partnerships. The involvement of private entities is at a minimum very valuable and often indispensable to cybersecurity. As has previously been recommended,

> One key element will be to create a network of strategic decision-makers—including from the private sector—who could be identified in advance to deal with attacks on critical infrastructure. There is no virtue in having an ad hoc approach to such a significant problem, and organized procedures would be of great value.

An international approach also would benefit critical infrastructure providers, many of which operate on a multinational basis.

Sixth, while it would not be the only place to do so, a board could harmonize national approaches to the key cyber offenders. A common front to the intrusions will enhance the effectiveness of response.

Seventh, an international board could harmonize privacy and civil liberty approaches. These issues are raised clearly in both international and domestic terms by the NSA revelations. While, as this article has suggested, the United States, along with its allies, has the opportunity to fundamentally shift the odds in its favor in the long-running cyber fight, that needs to be done while preserving the commitment to innovation, an open Internet, personal privacy, and the protection of civil liberties.

There are clear differences in approach to privacy and civil liberties in the transatlantic context and, more generally, among the United States and its allies. Those considerations need to be dealt with, and while our recommendations do not implicate personal privacy in most instances, data privacy may come into play to the extent that Internet Service Providers (ISPs) and/or private cybersecurity providers in the course of network monitoring collect data that could be considered personally identifiable information. In these instances, ISPs and other private companies should be required to handle (e.g., collect, use, disclose) such information consistent with the fair information practice principles, and appropriate oversight/accountability measures should be in place to ensure that any monitoring system is used in the way promised; that appropriate data destruction/retention policies are in place; and that information is not misused (e.g., improperly shared with government or shared in violation of stated privacy policies).

Finally, it should be recognized that a deterrence approach is not necessarily a one-way street. Nations adversely affected by cyber sanctions or other deterrence measures designed to curb economic espionage can take steps of their own to respond. As will be recalled, in the Cold War it was "mutual" assured destruction. While mutuality is not likely to be the case, it would not be impossible to expect China, for example, which states that it is the object of significant international cyber intrusions, to create a mirror-like regime (or even an asymmetric response) to deal with such activities (likely with less due process). Policymakers would need to evaluate this prospect, but the overall benefit of an organized international approach to creating a more stable, secure cyberspace appears to counsel strongly in favor of undertaking the steps recommended above.

## CONCLUSION

Cybersecurity is of fundamental concern to the United States and its allies and partners, but there is no silver bullet. To achieve the necessary degree of security, it is imperative to reject a defense-only cyber strategy and embrace a hybrid strategy that relies not only on defense but also on tailored deterrence to reduce overall cyber risk. Toward this end, this paper recommends simultaneously raising the costs to cyber offenders; increasing the private sector's ability to complement the government's efforts to achieve security; and developing standards and other approaches that focus on resilience as well as protection, take into account the international nature of cyber, and simultaneously are fair to companies on whom additional burdens are placed. Through the targeted actions described in this issue brief, all of these goals can be achieved and a more secure cyberspace created.

## CRITICAL THINKING QUESTIONS

1. Which of the four proposals put forward is the most valuable as a tool for deterring cyber threats?
2. Can cyber deterrence work when the aggressor is unknown?
3. Should the United States adopt an offensive cybersecurity strategy?

# 22

## A Tale of Two Trade Deals

*Never mind Asia, time to pivot to Europe.*

Clyde Prestowitz

While Washington is consumed by political furor over how to get the federal budget deficit under control, strangely few people are talking about its troublesome twin sister. Unlike the budget deficit, the half-trillion-dollar U.S. trade deficit does nothing to stimulate the economy even in the short term. Rather, it is sucking jobs out of the country year in and year out while also raising doubts about America's ability to maintain its global security commitments. Taking sensible measures to reduce our chronic imbalance of trade would require neither austerity nor tax increases, and is the key both to creating jobs and to restoring confidence in America.

So what, you might ask, is the administration's policy on trade? Right now its primary focus is on a deal known as the Trans-Pacific Partnership, or TPP, which President Obama wants finished up by October. If concluded according to plan, the TPP will include the United States, Canada, Mexico, Peru, Chile, New Zealand, Australia, Brunei, Singapore, Malaysia, and Vietnam, with the possibility that Japan and Korea might also join. The treaty would also be open for other countries to join if they could meet the required standards.

Beyond this, as Obama announced in his State of the Union address, the White House is looking for a deal gazing in the opposite direction. Known as the Transatlantic Free Trade Agreement (TAFTA), it would tie the United States and the European Union into the world's largest trading block.

As with most trade deals, both the TPP and TAFTA have geopolitical as well as economic significance. Indeed, one reason the administration is placing strong priority on the TPP is because it sees the deal as an important part of its larger foreign-policy "pivot to Asia." With the rise of China and recent U.S. emphasis on Iraq, Afghanistan, and the Middle East, some Southeast Asian and East Asian countries have been looking for assurances that the U.S. will

Clyde Prestowitz is the founder and president of the Economic Strategy Institute. He formerly served as counselor to the secretary of commerce in the Reagan administration, as vice chairman of President Bill Clinton's Commission on Trade and Investment in the Asia-Pacific Region, and on the advisory board of the ExIm Bank. His most recent book is *The Betrayal of American Prosperity.*

remain engaged in the region and provide a countervailing power. So along with stationing 2,500 Marines and increasing the U.S. naval presence in Australia, opening a drone base in the Cocos Islands, increasing naval visits to Singapore and other Asian ports, and raising the U.S. naval presence in the western Pacific to 60 percent of all U.S. ships, the administration is seeking special economic ties with the nations noted above—which, of course, do not include China.

A potential trade deal with Europe also has economic and geopolitical implications, but it has not yet generated the same level of expectation, commentary, and lobbying. This is partly because it is not as far advanced as the TPP, but it is also because few imagine that Europe will be a source of either major opportunities or major threats. Why place bets on an aging, stagnant Europe, goes the conventional thinking, when this is likely to be the century of Asia?

Yet the geopolitical case for the TPP is not nearly so strong as the administration argues, and the agreement is certainly not worth the cost the U.S. is likely to have to pay. Meanwhile, the economic case for forging closer trading ties with Europe is comparatively much stronger. It's time to look deeper at how these two trade deals fit into America's grand strategy.

In early 2011, Deputy National Security Advisor for International Economic Affairs Mike Froman invited me and a few other trade experts to the White House to request suggestions and support for the TPP.

Froman made two basic arguments. The first was geopolitical: the TPP, Froman explained, was the administration's way of demonstrating to our Asian friends and allies that we are back and committed to them. The second was economic: the deal would further open some important markets to American business, he argued, and, most importantly, would serve as a template for negotiating much broader and purer global free trade deals in the future.

To understand the administration's reasoning, it is necessary to have a little background. In 2001, the World Trade Organization (WTO), the 158-nation body that attempts to govern global trade, launched the so-called Doha Round (after Qatar's capital city, which hosted the launch meeting). The purpose of these negotiations was to achieve a dramatic increase in global trade liberalization. By 2008, however, the talks had gone nowhere and American frustration was at the boiling level.

In response, the Bush administration developed a theory of competing free trade agreements, or FTAs. The idea was that by concluding a series of special bilateral and regional trade deals, the U.S. would eventually force reluctant countries to sign on to Doha for fear of being frozen out of preferred access to key markets. While such FTAs were permissible under WTO rules, they were anathema to free trade economists because they inevitably distort trade and welfare by granting preferential treatment to favored partners.

As a test of the theory, the Bush White House announced in the fall of 2008 that it was joining an existing, largely ignored regional trade agreement among Singapore, Brunei, New Zealand, and Chile. After this, however, not much happened until the Obama administration committed to its "pivot to Asia." That put crafting a much larger "Trans-Pacific" deal on Washington's front burner, as Forman explained.

This reasoning struck me at the time, and still strikes me, as dubious at best. Let's start with the geopolitical calculation.

There is no doubt that the growth of China's power does unnerve other Asian nations. A Singaporean minister for foreign affairs expressed the concern succinctly to me over dinner one night. "As an ethnic Chinese myself," the minister said, "I know that China views the world hierarchically—with a particular position, either up or down but not equal, for each country. Furthermore, I know the place the Chinese are likely to have for Singapore, and I don't want to be in it in a Chinese-dominated world. So we need America to prevent Chinese domination."

Yet if the rise of China makes Singapore and other Asian nations feel insecure, it's hard to see how the TPP should make them feel better. It won't halt the rise of China nor the relative decline of the U.S. And in any case, the United States has hardly abandoned Asia. The Pentagon maintains 100,000 troops in East Asia and the Pacific and keeps the Seventh Fleet patrolling the western Pacific as it has for nearly seventy years. We have security treaties with Japan, Korea, the Philippines, and Australia and quasi-security arrangements with Singapore.

We have done this despite no longer having to worry about the Soviet Union or the spread of world communism. We have done it despite China's lacking any motive to interrupt its trade with us, and any desire to attack us. Meanwhile, most of the Asian countries benefiting from our security umbrella pursue industry targeting and strategic trade policies that have contributed to the chronic U.S. trade deficit and the offshoring of millions of U.S. jobs even as our Navy dutifully patrols the trade lanes. Geopolitically, the question should not be what we can do for prospering Asian countries made anxious by the growth of China. Rather, it should be what they can do to help relieve *us* of the economic burden of our continuing military commitment.

Then what about the economic case for the TPP? The Peterson Institute for International Economics has done an analysis showing that the TPP might result in a 0.0038 percent increase in GDP for the U.S. by 2025. In actuality the economic benefits, if any, are likely to be still less.

The agreement would virtually abolish tariffs. It also has provisions for liberalizing textile trade, and for reducing agricultural subsidies and barriers. It would ensure that state-owned enterprises compete fairly with private industry, and provide for stronger protection of intellectual property and investment rights. And it would reduce barriers to entry in a variety of service industries, including telecommunications and environmental goods and services.

No doubt, many multinational companies headquartered in the U.S. would benefit from these provisions. Companies such as Apple and General Electric, for example, would find it easier and safer to offshore R&D and production and to avoid U.S. taxes by keeping profits in Asia.

But whether it will be good for the U.S. economy as a whole is doubtful. That's because the TPP ignores the most important drivers of global trade and investment. For example, it has no provisions for dealing with currency manipulation, even though several of the countries in the negotiation, and others that are likely to join later, routinely drive down the cost of their exports and drive up the cost of their imports by keeping their currencies artificially low.

The effects of this easily negate any benefits that might result from lowering trade barriers. For example, new Japanese Prime Minister Shinzo Abe's first policy action to restart the Japanese economy was to devalue the yen by about 20 percent versus the dollar. That is a multiple of Japan's average tariff level.

Nor does the TPP address the many structural issues that lock foreign producers out of Asian markets. Consider the Japanese car market, for example. Because of the strong yen and high wages, Japan has become a high-cost location for automobile production. At the same time, the United States has become a low-cost production center, thanks to the recent restructuring of its industry and the stagnation of American wages. One would expect that in view of its high costs, Japan's imports of foreign cars would be soaring and Japan's producers would be closing factories as U.S. and European producers have done under similar circumstances.

But none of that is happening, despite the fact that Japan imposes no tariffs on imported cars. So what else is at work? Complex Japanese rules and taxes that favor its domestic industries, plus a dealer network designed to exclude foreign-built cars. Joining with Japan in the TPP would not fix any of that. Indeed, by reducing the 2.5 percent U.S. tariff on cars built in Japan, it would help Japanese automakers to avoid having to reduce their costs.

Nor does the TPP deal with the problem of investment incentives. These are the packages of tax holidays, free land, state-financed worker training, regulatory exemptions, and capital grants that countries use to attract investment in production, R&D labs, and other facilities by global companies.

For example, Intel recently opened a new plant in China to make Pentium chips, the microprocessors that drive most of the world's computers. Why China? Chip fabrication is highly automated, making labor costs insignificant. In the absence of distorting subsidies, the low-cost places to produce Pentiums would be Intel's facilities in New Mexico and Arizona. But Intel CEO Paul Otellini has pointed out that the financial incentives offered by China are not available in America, and that they are worth about $100 million in annual Intel profits. These kinds of incentives are far, far more important as drivers of trade, production, and jobs than anything the TPP is talking about.

An additional problem is how the TPP would destroy the Caribbean Basin Free Trade Agreement (CAFTA) and poke big holes in the North American Free Trade Agreement (NAFTA). For example, under both agreements, textile producers in the Caribbean and Mexico who use U.S. yarn receive duty-free access to the U.S. market for textiles and apparel. The U.S. struck these deals partly in response to the discriminatory trade and industrial policies of some

Asian countries that were distorting markets and causing the loss of U.S. jobs. A second objective was to help create jobs in Mexico and the Caribbean and thereby reduce the number of undocumented immigrants from these countries while also providing an alternative to employment in the drug-trafficking trade.

By removing tariffs on textile imports from Vietnam, the TPP would displace an estimated 1.2 million textile workers in the Caribbean Basin and Mexico along with about 170,000 in the United States, according to Mary O'Rourke, an industry analyst. Some see that as simply the price of achieving true free trade and optimizing the planet's division of labor. But Vietnam is dominated by state-owned enterprises and is far from being a market economy. Furthermore, under a situation of true free trade, it would be China, not Vietnam, that would take most of the textile business, because China has gigantic excess capacity in textiles, as it does in just about everything else.

Meanwhile, it isn't even clear that the TPP will change trading patterns within Asia to the advantage of the U.S. economy. Beijing is now pushing its own Regional Comprehensive Economic Pact, and so far all ten member countries of the Association of Southeast Asian Nations, plus Japan, Korea, Australia, New Zealand, and India, have signed up. This China club has more members—and more *important* members—than the American TPP club. Indeed, all the TPP members except those from the Americas are also in the China club.

None of this is to suggest that the United States couldn't prosper from a deeper trading relationship with Asia if it were done on the right terms. Indeed, imagine if the U.S. went for the whole enchilada and proposed something like a trans-Pacific European Union? Take the advanced democratic economies of the Pacific—Canada, the U.S., Mexico, New Zealand, Australia, Japan, and Korea—and make them one integrated economy with a common antitrust regime, a common set of employment and environmental standards, one banking system, and eventually one currency—call it the Yollar or the Yelarso or the Denso. Make the union open to new entrants if and when they reform their economies enough to qualify for membership.

That entity would be the world's biggest, richest economy. It would eliminate the structural impediments to U.S. exports in much of Asia, and bring most of the world economy under a true free trade standard. With this kind of a union there would be much less currency manipulation and much less (if any) need for "pivots" and more U.S. military in Asia. But, alas, Washington isn't even thinking about anything like this, even though it would be a game-changing economic and geopolitical move.

So if the TPP looks like a lose-lose situation for the United States, what about a deal with Europe?

This notion was first voiced at a high level in 1995 when then Secretary of State Warren Christopher proposed a joint effort to better bridge the Atlantic. In November of that year, I was with 100 European and American CEOs when they met in Seville, Spain, and proposed a far-reaching agenda to increase trade and investment in the European and American markets. The following December, Washington and Brussels agreed to conduct a joint study on how to reduce tariff and non-tariff barriers. In a book at the time, I cited analysis by my own Economic Strategy Institute estimating that a TAFTA would boost U.S. GDP by 1.6 to 2.8 percent while raising EU GDP by 1 to 1.9 percent.

Nevertheless, objections were raised. Because it would be so large, some feared that a U.S.-EU deal might destroy the newly created WTO. Because the markets were already highly integrated, the likely gains from the deal might be small. A formal negotiation might actually worsen U.S.-EU relations by bringing contentious issues, like subsidies to our respective aircraft manufacturers, brutally to the fore. Some also said it would really be the rich, white guys ganging up against the rest of the world. So nothing happened. Eventually the WTO launched the aforementioned Doha Round, in which important parts of the rest of the world thumbed their noses at the European and American visions of free trade.

This experience is one reason why TAFTA deserves a second look, but there are also others. First is the need for growth in an age of high debt and austerity. Neither the U.S. nor Europe is politically prepared to stimulate its economy through any significant increase in deficit spending. That means growth must come from some other source, and the efficiencies that would come from further integration of European and American economies are a plausible answer.

Labor unions in the EU are strong and wages are high, so there will be no race to the bottom. And the EU and the U.S. largely share a commitment to free markets, free trade, and democracy. Much of what has gone wrong with the WTO derives from systemic conflicts between the U.S. and the EU on the one side and the more interventionist and authoritarian political economies of the rest of the world on the other.

The biggest economic gain from TAFTA would be from harmonizing regulation. Inconsistencies in regulation raise the costs of transatlantic trade in automobiles, for example, by 27 percent, and by 6.5 percent in the electronics sector alone. The United States and Europe both have safe headlights, for instance, but EU cars exported to America must have different headlights than those sold in Europe and vice versa. That non-tariff barrier inhibits exports while raising costs by forcing producers to keep extra stocks of different headlights. The same holds true for electronics and most other products. Mutual recognition of essentially equivalent standards and removal of similar non-tariff barriers would boost U.S. GDP by 1 to 3 percent ($150 billion to $450 billion), according to a 2005 study by the Organisation for Economic Cooperation and Development.

Beyond this, there are also significant economic gains to be had by eliminating non-tariff barriers to trade in services. More than 70 percent of the GDP in both markets derives from provision of services. Yet service trade is highly restricted by non-tariff barriers, such as differing rules and conflicting standards that bar the integration of cell phone service in the U.S. and Europe.

Meanwhile, although tariffs between the two economies are already low, there would also be significant immediate economic gains from tariff elimination. These potential gains range from 1 to 1.3 percent of GDP ($135 billion to $181 billion) for the United States. The European Commission has estimated that a comprehensive deal would result in a 50 percent increase in overall transatlantic trade. Putting all this together suggests that TAFTA would add 2 to 4 percent to U.S. GDP.

There is also a strong geopolitical case for TAFTA. For one, it would help contain the centrifugal forces in the EU that are gaining strength. British Prime Minister David Cameron wants to renegotiate the UK's membership and submit the results to a referendum. This creates a real threat of a UK exit from the EU that might take others along. TAFTA would provide glue to hold Europe together, something that is a major long-term U.S. geopolitical and economic objective for the very good reason that the EU is not only a zone of peace and democracy but also America's major partner in dealing with Russia, the Middle East, and Africa. It is also, of course, America's biggest economic partner by far.

To those who view Europe as a demographic and economic backwater compared to Asia, it may be surprising to know the facts. Yes, Europe faces an aging population. But birth rates have plunged far deeper and faster in East Asia than in Europe, and as a result East Asia's population is aging far more quickly. Fully 30 percent of Japan's population will be over sixty-five by 2030, and its working-age population has been shrinking since the mid-1990s. China's workforce is shrinking now too, thanks to its one-child-one-family norm. Demographers expect China to soon experience hyper-aging unlike anything in the cards for Europe. South Korea, Singapore, and Taiwan are already experiencing the same fate. The United Nations projects that by 2030, France and South Korea will each have the same proportion of elders in their population.

Europe also remains, despite its slow recovery from the Great Recession, the world's largest economy and a powerhouse that is vital to the United States. Americans sell three times more merchandise exports to Europe than to China, while the EU sells the United States nearly twice the goods it sells China. Transatlantic trade generates $5 trillion in sales annually and employs fifteen million workers. It accounts for three-quarters of global financial markets and more than half of world trade. No other commercial artery is as integrated. Roughly $1.7 billion in goods and services cross the Atlantic daily, equaling one-third of total global trade in goods and more than 40 percent in services.

Finally, far from destroying the prospects for a global economy based on true free trade, TAFTA may be the only thing that can get China and other mercantilist nations on board. Given that the U.S.-EU economies constitute more than half of the global economy, TAFTA would tend to set global standards, and along lines affirming the fundamental precepts of free trade.

The conclusion is clear. The TPP is lose-lose for the U.S., both geopolitically and economically. The White House should drop and the Congress oppose it while we focus on the vast promise of a stronger transatlantic partnership that will benefit the whole world.

## CRITICAL THINKING QUESTIONS

1. Identify a trading agreement entered into by the United States in the post–World War II era. Evaluate the role played by diplomatic, economic, and security interests in setting it up. How does this compare with the trade agreements discussed in this article?
2. Present an argument for creating an African or Western Hemisphere free trade system.
3. Do geopolitical and economic conditions today continue to support Prestowitz's argument?

# 23

# The Trouble with Sanctions

*American policy is devastating Iran's economy—and increasing the risk of war.*

Bijan Khajehpour, Reza Marashi, and Trita Parsi

S anctions on Iran have taken on a life of their own as the relationship between Washington and Tehran has steadily deteriorated. Sanctions were initially imposed nearly thirty-four years ago in response to the Iran hostage crisis—when revolutionaries seized the U.S. embassy in Tehran and held diplomats hostage for 444 days. Today, the U.S.-Iran conflict has expanded into numerous areas, but the United States and many of its allies insist on a core focus: they believe that the Iranian regime seeks to develop the technical capability and material to build nuclear weapons on short notice—though U.S. intelligence believes that Tehran has not yet made the political decision to weaponize its nuclear capability. For its part, Iran has long insisted that its nuclear program is for strictly peaceful purposes. In an effort to blunt Iran's presumed nuclear—and some would argue, regional—ambitions and increase its leverage vis-à-vis Tehran, Washington has spearheaded a potent barrage of unilateral and multilateral sanctions. Together with on-again, off-again negotiations under the auspices of the United Nations Security Council, Washington has pursued a carrot and stick strategy—now known as "dual track"—utilizing primarily negative inducements to convince Iran to change its nuclear policy.

Neither the sanctions nor the diplomacy component of the dual track policy has produced satisfactory results thus far. As of June 2013, seven meetings between Iran and the permanent members of the United Nations Security Council plus Germany (the P5 + 1) have taken place over a four-year span. In contrast with most negotiation processes, the two sides actually came closest to a deal in their first meeting, in October 2009. Since then, diplomacy has steadily devolved into an exchange of ultimatums and mutual escalation—with

Bijan Khajehpour is a managing partner at Atieh International. Reza Marashi is research director at the National Iranian American Council. Trita Parsi is the founder and president of the National Iranian American Council and an expert on U.S.-Iranian relations, Iranian foreign politics, and the geopolitics of the Middle East. This essay originally appeared in the Summer 2013 volume of the *Cairo Review of Global Affairs*.

Washington and Tehran taking turns not being able to take "yes" for an answer.

As in any negotiation, the devil is in the details—and there are many to discuss. But one detail stands out above all else: What kind of relationship does Washington want with Tehran? Over the duration of the Obama administration, America's preference has been to work towards small confidence-building measures—without clarifying its long-term objectives. This is better than nothing, but due to the lack of trust between Washington and Tehran, small tactical steps are unlikely to work—and to date, they have not worked. If the Obama administration, together with its allies, does not decide on an end game—that is, a detailed vision for normal relations with Iran—it cannot clearly communicate to Tehran the goal of diplomacy, sanctions, cyber warfare, secret assassination, and any other form of pressure. This is rarely addressed. Unless Washington and Tehran can see the same light at the end of the tunnel, the reluctance to take risks for peace will likely remain. And they will be more likely to continue escalating the conflict toward a military confrontation that both sides would independently seek to avoid.

With strategic clarity lacking in both Washington and Tehran, investment in the coercive instrument of sanctions has grown significantly over the past four years—the severity of U.S.-led sanctions enforced over the past eighteen months has even taken veteran Iranian officials by surprise. The combination of sanctions on Iran's oil and banking sectors is estimated to have cut Tehran's oil revenues by as much as 50 percent—from $100 billion in 2011 to approximately $50 billion in 2012.

Rather than attempting to impose a blanket economic embargo on Iran, the United States has instead used its massive leverage over the international financial system to create a new model for sanctioning Iran. It also laid the foundation for creating international buy-in through the three rounds of sanctions at the United Nations. Upon entering the White House, Barack Obama retained the same priorities, policy vehicles, and many of the same personnel on Iranian sanctions as his predecessor. Over the duration of his first four years in office, Obama signed into law the most comprehensive unilateral sanctions framework in history, led efforts to secure new multilateral sanctions at the United Nations Security Council, and played an instrumental role in convincing the European Union (EU) to implement its own set of unilateral sanctions.

Unilateral American sanctions have arguably inflicted the most pain on Iran during Obama's presidency. In July 2010, he signed into law the Comprehensive Iran Sanctions, Accountability, and Divestment Act, which updated the Iran Sanctions Act of 1996 with an array of punitive measures—two of which stand out: the sanctioning of providing gasoline and other fuels to Iran, and banning the sale of equipment and services that would help Iran increase its gasoline production capabilities. As these sanctions caused Iran's imports to fall, the country was faced with potential fuel shortages, thereby forcing it to domestically produce gasoline that has caused the chronic pollution in Tehran to reach even more deadly levels.

With the U.S.-Iran conflict no closer to a peaceful resolution after nearly three years in office, Obama authorized what has been brashly described by American officials as the "nuclear option" in Washington's financial war against Tehran, by way of the National Defense Authorization Act of 2011 (NDAA). These sanctions restrict the access of foreign banks to the U.S. financial system if they process petroleum transactions with Iran's central bank. Less than a year later, with congressional pressure unrelenting, Obama signed the Iran Threat Reduction and Syria Human Rights Act (ITRSHRA). Building on the NDAA sanctions, ITRSHRA cuts off access to the U.S. market for companies that do business with Iran's energy sector and freezes the U.S. assets of persons, insurers, and lenders that facilitate repatriation of Iranian oil revenues and/or do business with the National Iranian Oil Company and the National Iranian Tanker Company. Gary Ackerman, a Democratic Party congressman from New York, describes the intent of this mixture of unilateral American sanctions: "The goal . . . is to inflict crippling, unendurable economic pain [in Iran]. Iran's banking sector—especially its central bank—needs to become the financial equivalent of Chernobyl: radioactive, dangerous, and most of all, empty."

With Tehran now facing what many consider the most draconian sanctions regime in history, does this mean sanctions are working? Have sanctions increased the likelihood of a compromise in the nuclear standoff? Or, are sanctions causing hardliners in Tehran and the West to dig in their heels and eschew the compromises that will be necessary for a peaceful resolution to the crisis?

Iran sanctions are a highly politicized issue, with domestic political ramifications in Washington and Tehran, as well as in Tel Aviv and Brussels. Though sanctions have been the primary policy tool used by the West since concerns about Iran's nuclear ambitions intensified in 2002, thus far they have failed to alter Tehran's nuclear policy. The question remains: Why? To better understand how sanctions have played out over the years, it is useful to deconstruct the stated objectives of sanctions, the internal state of play in Iran in response to sanctions, and the effect that sanctions have (and do not have) on the diplomatic process.

## IRAN'S CALCULUS

The Obama administration has made sanctions the center of its Iran policy since the first round of negotiations with Tehran collapsed in November 2009, although its motivations for doing so and its public pronouncements about the objectives have varied. Perhaps the most commonly stated objective is changing Iran's nuclear calculus, with sanctions being the primary tool used to raise the cost of Iran's nuclear pursuits. The overarching goal is to make the cost of continuing Tehran's nuclear path too high to bear, thereby leading to a change in its nuclear policy. The strategy envisions a three-part scenario in achieving this goal: devastate the Iranian economy with a tacit understanding that civilian Iranians will be hurt in the process; as sanctions take root and permeate

Iranian society, civilians together with various stakeholders will pressure the government and potentially create regime-threatening protests; with the economy weakened—and new fissures created within Iranian society *and* among Iranian stakeholders—the Islamic Republic's regional and international strategic objectives become too costly to continue at current levels.

A subset of changing Iran's nuclear calculus is getting Tehran back to the table and negotiating in good faith. This logic supposes that sanctions will force key stakeholders in Tehran to believe that returning to negotiations and seeing them through is the only avenue for ending the forms of pressure that threaten their domestic, regional, and international priorities.

Another key driver of sanctions involves domestic politics in the United States and in Europe. One of the objectives, say some sanctions advocates, is to strengthen the credibility and leverage of pro-engagement camps, thereby providing political cover for politicians who favor non-military solutions to the conflict between Iran and the West. In the United States and within the European Union, sanctions serve as a shield against political attacks from neoconservatives who label negotiations with Tehran as a demonstration of weakness and naiveté. In Tehran too, sanctions indirectly support the engagement camp also, by reminding citizens of the consequences of hardline policies, and providing leverage for factions favoring détente with the West.

Some Western officials also present sanctions as an alternative to an American or Israeli attack on Iran, by helping delay Iran's nuclear program and thereby adding more time for diplomacy. Rhetoric within the Obama administration has stressed a preference to resolve differences over Iran's nuclear program diplomatically, while also emphasizing "all options are on the table"—including war—to prevent Iran from acquiring a nuclear weapon. American and European officials further believe that effective sanctions may help dissuade Israel from launching a unilateral strike on Iran; Israel has laid down numerous red lines over the past decade in an effort to demarcate specific developments in Iran's nuclear program that would trigger an Israeli attack.

Political signaling is another key driver of sanctions, with the signals intended to reach three key audiences: to show political constituents in the United States that Washington is increasing pressure on Tehran to unprecedented levels; to show Middle Eastern allies and foes that America is still in charge and make an example of Iran for its challenge to Pax Americana in the region; and thirdly, to show the world that Iran is paying such a heavy price for its nuclear pursuits that no country should seek to emulate Tehran's path to nuclear capability.

In order to maintain and increase the heavy price that Tehran pays, a special emphasis is given to maintaining unity within the P5 + 1. This logic infers that Washington must seek to maintain a multilateral approach toward Iran regarding the nuclear issue—because Tehran is highly adept at exploiting rifts in the international community. Sanctions are the baseline tactic that the P5 + 1 can agree on in an effort to maintain international unity around diplomatic efforts to place red lines on Iran's nuclear program.

While these motivations for sanctions are not mutually exclusive, the central objective is to change Iran's nuclear calculus and force it to agree to a deal that it otherwise would refuse or has already refused. Since that specific objective has not been achieved thus far, sanctions cannot be deemed to have been successful. This begs another question: Why haven't Iranian stakeholders capitulated in some way under the pressure of severe sanctions?

## THE WESTERN ANIMOSITY NARRATIVE

Sanctions have had a devastating impact on the Iranian economy. Numerous regime stakeholders openly acknowledge this, although they also blame Iran's economic decline on a number of other factors such as subsidy reforms, varying degrees of mismanagement, and long-standing corruption.

Representatives from the Iranian Chamber of Commerce have said that 50 percent of the economic predicament is a direct consequence of sanctions and the other 50 percent is due to failed economic policies. Mohsen Rezaei, secretary of the Expediency Council and former commander of the Iranian Revolutionary Guard Corps, believes that 40 percent of the current economic problems are due to sanctions, blaming the rest on mismanagement as well as corrupt networks that are "trying to benefit from the current chaotic situation in the economy." The deputy speaker of the Iranian Majles, Mohammad Reza Bahonar, has said that external sanctions are causing 50 percent of the current economic difficulties, with the rest being the consequence of weak political decisions and structural issues.

Supreme Leader Ayatollah Ali Khamenei is steadfast in his defiance of sanctions. The escalation of sanctions has enabled him to strengthen a powerful pre-existing narrative that portrays Western powers as a brutal, immoral group of governments out to "get" Iran, and that their core interest is to keep Iran underdeveloped and dependent. This narrative serves to maintain unity in a fragmented power structure by sustaining the image of an unrelenting enemy. This in turn justifies a feared security apparatus—to counter that enemy—and mobilizes the support of a minority segment of society that can be paraded as "popular support" when needed—on the anniversary of the revolution, during elections, etc.

As long as the narrative of Western animosity remains in place, Khamenei will justify the empowerment of his military-security apparatus as a necessary instrument for countering threats against the Islamic Republic. In January, he commented that "the sanctions are meant to strain the people's patience, incite the people to oppose the Islamic Republic, and increase the pressure on Iranian officials in order to alter officials' calculations"—in other words, he continues to promote the image of a strong external enemy and the imperative "not to give in." Khamenei's formula for countering the sanctions—which he describes as "economic warfare"—has been dubbed the "economy of resistance," a vague term for a greater degree of protectionism, support for domestic industry, and lowering the Iranian economy's dependency on oil exports.

Khamenei may be the supreme leader, but his position on nuclear policy is not immovable. There are Iranian domestic interests and structures that can challenge his narrative, and create counter narratives enabling a policy course correction. But they are unlikely to do so in the absence of clear, tangible, and positive potential outcomes in the event of an Iranian nuclear policy shift. To provide some degree of flexibility, Khamenei allows experiments, but does not commit to them until he gets a sense of security about the initiatives—an Iranian version of "leading from behind." Indeed, the supreme leader can hide behind an array of institutions when he needs to justify or delay a decision. So, a critical question is how key constituencies read the current state of play, especially those layers of power that are closer to Khamenei.

## WAITING FOR SANCTIONS FATIGUE

While there is wide acknowledgement in Iran that sanctions have created economic and social costs for the country, individuals close to the core of Iran's power structure are relishing the narrative of resistance. According to this line of thought, while Iran suffers economically, it is also gaining newfound respect on the international stage due to its refusal to succumb to Western pressure. "Those who are witnessing how Iran is managing its enormous challenges develop a new level of respect for Iran, and that has given Iran a new credibility on the international stage," one influential parliamentarian remarked. "Iran has become a role model for developing countries and there is a greater willingness among developing nations to work and trade with Iran." While the idea that Iran is viewed as a role model or with greater respect is certainly debatable, it is an argument that is frequently cited by officials as a vindication of their narrative.

Moreover, this narrative contends that as long as Iran stands firm, global sanction fatigue—including in Europe—will ultimately cause the collapse of this policy. A senior decision-maker in Tehran spoke confidently of the belief that Europe cannot stomach a return to sanctions-based policies reminiscent of those imposed on Saddam Hussein's Iraq. This in turn will slowly unravel the coalition against Iran. "The sanctions—and especially the continuation of these sanctions—have exposed Washington's true character to many international players, including Western countries," he said. "I believe that the Europeans won't continue to blindly support the U.S. strategy, and the time will come when the EU or some of the European countries will go a different path and Iran will wait for that break." A Majles deputy close to Speaker Ali Larijani echoed this sentiment, expressing a degree of skepticism regarding Europe's dedication to sanctions: "In the Majles presiding board, there is an understanding of what the U.S. is doing. We understand that they have a strategy to antagonize Iran. However, the big puzzle is the EU's behavior. It seems as if the Europeans have fallen into an American-Israeli trap and they don't know how to come out of it. If they continue this way, they will lose more and more of their economic foothold in Iran."

Iranian regime officials—aiming to bolster Khamenei's hardline narrative—seek to politically capitalize on the negative impact of sanctions in order to influence the Iranian populace's attitudes towards the West. Rather than denying the negative impact of sanctions, decision-makers in Tehran increasingly acknowledge them to vindicate their claims of Western hostility towards Iran. "It's true that the sanctions are imposing an economic cost on the Iranian people and the regime, but they are also imposing a social cost on the U.S.," one influential policymaker said. "The Iranian people are learning more about the hypocrisy and the true image of the West. I believe that the Iranians are becoming more and more anti-Western and that will have long-term costs for the Western countries in our region." Although it is unlikely that sanctions will turn the entirety of Iran's population against the West, Iranians inside Iran have increasingly voiced their displeasure with both the government *and* the sanctions that create new hardships. A senior Iranian diplomat echoed as much: "The society has become nuanced in its political awareness. It can analyze to see how far the current economic conditions are a result of Western pressure and Western double standards and to what extent it is the doing of the Iranian government." Accurate polling is questionable in Iran, yet a long series of studies—including a recent scientific poll conducted by Gallup—supports the notion that a strong plurality of the Iranian population tends to put the blame for the economy on the U.S. rather than on the Iranian government. If this trend holds, the regime will find more opportunities to strengthen its narrative of resistance and blame the West for Iran's deteriorating economy as the duration and bite of sanctions intensifies.

Overall, the strategic outlook of Iran's supreme leader is to maintain a clear distance from the United States. However other stakeholders have developed alternative agendas. Some segments of the Iranian power structure view a good relationship with the West as a prerequisite for Iran's economic and technological progress. Others believe that Tehran should ease tensions with the West to provide a greater degree of peace and tranquility in the region. However, as long as the antagonistic policies of Western countries remain in place, the Khamenei discourse will continue to dominate.

## UNDERMINING REFORM

A critical step for sanctions to succeed in changing Iran's nuclear calculus is to create room for the emergence of a competing narrative that paves the way for a shift in policy. Though the repressive nature of the Iranian regime and its efforts to eliminate any public debate about the nuclear issue renders the emergence of such a public narrative next to impossible, this does not necessarily hold true for narratives within the inner circles of the regime. Thus far, however, no such counter narrative appears to have emerged among influential elements of the Iranian elite.

"Even though regime members outside the core can have a voice and influence, it is sad to say that none of them actually has a strategy on how to amend the national security policy," a regime insider explained. "Therefore, the core around Ayatollah Khamenei is not only the most powerful, but also the only group that has a strategy, i.e., the 'strategic distance and antagonism' to the U.S." At present, there is no discernible competing strategy to the current narrative favored by Khamenei and the layers of power closest to him. While mainstream conservatives may be more amenable to negotiations and a nuclear compromise, they have not formulated a strategy accordingly, as they feel that the dominant narrative will hold firm. The other reason for the lack of a counter narrative can be found in the failure of Western countries to craft and communicate an alternative scenario. In Iranian eyes, there are no indications of how the dynamics of nuclear negotiations would change if Iran indeed changed its policy. These interest groups do not seem impressed by offers of the removal or suspension of some sanctions. Consequently, the core narrative is not only unchallenged during internal debates, it is further consolidated by continued external antagonism.

A former high-level diplomat and foreign ministry official described the result of this trajectory: "The status of being in an 'economic war' means that a lot of the actual issues in the country cannot be debated, which is also impeding the political development of the country. The situation has undermined the position of the reformists and empowered the hardline elements."

Iranian intellectuals critical of the regime—even though they have diverging views on whether the Iranian government should show more flexibility or whether Western countries should adopt a new policy—tend to agree that sanctions only reinforce the dominant anti-Western narrative, thus making it very difficult for any other perspectives to emerge. There is also agreement with the notion that sanctions have undermined the domestic process of democratization, which in turn has aided longstanding efforts by hardline forces to dominate Iranian politics.

A former mayor of Tehran points out that neither Iran's elite nor its society at large wish to see the destruction of Iran. Therefore, he says, any internal or external push that would bring Iran to the brink of "economic destruction" will be met with a harsh reaction. The problem, he adds, is that most Iranian elites have not decided whether the West or their own regime is primarily responsible for the country's sanctions predicament.

## REGIME CHANGE?

Stark divisions over foreign and domestic policy among the Iranian elite are unmistakable. However, those divisions do not appear to have affected regime cohesion around the nuclear issue or on the response to sanctions. And if elite insiders are to be believed, sanctions have helped strengthen cohesion rather than intensify rifts. A serving senior minister articulated his view accordingly: "The main objective of these sanctions has been to impose regime change or at least to weaken the Iranian regime. They have failed in that objective and in fact, they are strengthening the core of the Iranian regime, because they have regime constituents." The minister says that the main result of sanctions is their socio-economic costs including the negative impact on Iran's economic development. Another current official with influence over Iran's economic policies shared this sentiment: "Western governments thought that Iran would collapse economically after the central bank sanctions. Well, now they know that they have failed. If they continue this way, it will just strengthen Iran's resolve to confront the West."

Naturally, regime officials will tend to toe the party line, which does obscure a clear picture of the thinking inside the system. However, when cross-checked with former regime officials and regime-critical intellectuals, a similar sentiment emerges. A former deputy foreign minister candidly describes a line of thinking that exists beyond the supreme leader's inner circle: "It was obvious to us that the sanctions' pressure will increase and it was also clear to us that the main target was to weaken the regime, but that compelled us to stay strong, work together, and prove the Western strategy wrong." A former senior Iranian diplomat shared this sentiment, saying that he believes continued sanctions will further harden Iran's position in future diplomatic negotiations. It is reasonable to believe that beyond these statements of bravado, a more conflicted situation exists. The critical question, however, is whether those internal divisions are having an impact on the strategic calculations of the regime.

## PRIVATE SECTOR PRESSURE

For its part, the private sector is unhappy about the current state of affairs, especially the negative impact of sanctions—and government policies—on private sector activity. But in their private lobbying campaigns, rather than pushing for a different foreign policy, they have tended to focus on lobbying the government to secure concessions for the private sector, thereby acknowledging that they do not have the necessary political influence to change nuclear policy. The main forum for such lobbying has been regular sessions titled "Dialogue between the Iran Chamber of Commerce and the Government," which involve the president of the chamber (Mohammad Nahavandian) and key ministers (finance, commerce and industry, agriculture, petroleum, etc.). Ayatollah Khamenei's decision to declare the current calendar year as the "Year of Domestic Capital and Domestic Industry" is likely related to these lobbying efforts.

Thus far, the private sector has secured a number of concessions. Numerous product categories of imports have been included in the currency exchange priorities so that such companies can use favorable currency exchange rates for their imports. The implementation of the second phase of subsidy reform has been delayed (this was achieved through direct interaction between the private sector representatives and the Majles). A decree by the Expediency Council on "Drive to Self-Sufficiency in Industry, Agriculture, Defense, and Security" has been finalized—a document to promote local industry and local production. This was also the result of lobbying with the Expediency Council. Permits have been issued for private sector companies to participate in the exportation of petroleum (including crude oil) and petrochemical products.

In February 2013, Ayatollah Khamenei signed a decree on "General Policies on Domestic Production and Protection of Iranian Labor and Capital." The latest evidence that domestic industry is lobbying to improve the investment environment manifested itself when the supreme leader's decree highlighted twenty-three new benefits to Iran's private sector, including but not limited to: promotion and protection of the production of strategic goods, as well as goods that are required for domestic manufacturing; completion of the value chain of raw materials and products, and an end to the sale of raw materials; promotion of producing goods in the domestic market, the competitive production of which will lead to net hard currency revenue for the economy; management of hard currency resources emphasizing the needs for domestic production and entrepreneurship aiming at maintaining the value of the national currency; an increase in the role of the private sector and cooperative sectors in domestic production; and the breaking of all monopolies in production, commerce, and consumption.

While it is correct to say that a number of these initiatives will also benefit the quasi-governmental sector, the central point is that the Iranian business community (private or quasi-governmental) is mainly focused on improving its own operational and investment climate rather than lobbying for a change in nuclear strategy. Moreover, while Western intelligence suggests that the Iranian business community has put pressure on Khamenei to shift his nuclear stance, no publicly available information has been able to confirm this. In spite of the bite of sanctions, Khamenei's narrative of resistance continues to dominate, and key stakeholders seem more intent on seeking concessions from the government rather than pressing for a change in its nuclear policy.

## TALKING TO AMERICA

While there was greater diplomatic activity in 2012 and 2013 compared to 2011, there are no signs that sanctions have compelled Tehran to "come back to the table" in the manner that the sanctioning states desire. Meetings over the past year have failed to produce a compromise. Tehran signaled openness to halting the production of medium enriched uranium (MEU) at the 19.75 percent level—a level of enrichment needed to produce medical isotopes for cancer patients, but also an important step closer to the 90 percent level required for nuclear weapons. However, Iran resisted calls to cease activities at its heavily fortified underground enrichment facility in Qom and ship out its stockpile of MEU. In return, Tehran sought the lifting of sanctions and/or upfront recognition of its right to enrich—demands the U.S. and its allies rejected. Tehran dragged its feet in scheduling the most recent meetings, either seeking to create the perception that it is in no hurry, or truly believing that it could afford to play for time—or perhaps seeing little benefit in coming to the table at all. In any case, there are no signs yet that the sanctions noose around Tehran's neck, as State Department Spokesperson Victoria Nuland has put it, has softened the Iranian negotiation position.

Some foreign policy hands in Tehran contend that in spite of increasingly uncontrollable infighting within the regime, viewpoints among various political factions have converged on the nuclear issue. Even influential foreign policy experts, who were sidelined by President Mahmoud Ahmadinejad and later joined opposition leader Mir-Hossein Moussavi's presidential campaign in 2009, believe that "succumbing under pressure only invites more pressure," and have even privately circulated proposals such as withdrawing from the Nuclear Non-Proliferation Treaty (NPT). Though Iranian officials no longer deny the immense impact of sanctions on the Iranian economy, Khamenei has reinforced his refusal to allow sanctions to affect Iran's nuclear policy. Iran won't negotiate "with a gun held to its head," he stated on February 7, 2013, in response to Vice President Joe Biden's call for direct U.S.-Iran talks. In a speech on February 16, he expanded on his reasoning with a direct reference to sanctions and the notion that Tehran will react positively to incentives as opposed to pressure:

> Sanctions are painful and they are a nuisance, but there are two ways to react to such pain: One group are those who start begging for forgiveness, but a brave nation like Iran will try to mobilize its inner resources and to pass through the "danger zone" with determination and courage. . . . The Americans should show that they don't want to bully us, that they won't engage in evil acts, show us that their words and deeds are not illogical and that they respect the rights of the Iranian people, show that they won't push the region into further confrontations and that they won't interfere in the internal affairs of the Iranian people—they will see that the Islamic Republic has good will and the people are logical. This is the only way to interact with the Islamic Republic.

The sanctions have, however, achieved one outcome: There is an elevated and intense debate in Tehran on the issue of talking to America for the purpose of establishing a better relationship with Washington. It is in this context that Khamenei's statement is so critical, as he is not rejecting the argument that Iran should establish relations with Washington, but rather the notion that it should do so while facing escalating economic pressure orchestrated by the United States. Khamenei is in essence declaring that the conversation about establishing relations with the U.S. (by first accepting the invitation for bilateral talks) will not translate into real action until Washington's sanctions-based approach is ended.

Although the deep-seated distrust between the United States and Iran has also been heightened by sanctions and the crisis over Tehran's nuclear program, these are only two of many issues dividing them. However, the nuclear program remains the top priority for U.S. policymakers working on Iran—

often to the detriment of more important issues, such as the deteriorating human rights situation in the Islamic Republic.

An Iranian nuclear bomb is neither imminent nor a foregone conclusion. The sixteen U.S. intelligence agencies judge with high confidence that Iran has conducted no nuclear weapons-related experiments since 2003, that it currently has no nuclear weapons program, and that it has not made the political decision to pursue nuclear weapons.

In theory, this provides ample political space for Obama to pursue a sustained process of diplomacy dedicated to ensuring that Iran's nuclear program remains verifiably peaceful. In practice, however, we often see the opposite from Washington—self-imposed time limits on diplomacy, unprecedented coercive measures, and sensationalistic government-fed journalism about an imminent Iranian nuclear weapon. Why the disconnect?

At present, Iran is pursuing a strategic middle ground called nuclear latency: It aims to build a nuclear energy program that would allow for the production of a nuclear weapon on short notice if an existential threat came to the fore. This is often referred to as the "Japan option"—after the country that has made significant investments in peaceful nuclear energy without developing key expertise to produce a nuclear weapon or its corresponding delivery systems. Like Japan, Iran's technological sophistication, its access to uranium and plutonium, and its experience launching satellites and missiles lend credence to the argument that it could theoretically build a nuclear weapon. But even after doing so, a weapon would require at a minimum one full year to complete—and American intelligence would almost certainly detect such efforts.

Nuclear latency does not violate Iran's international obligations, but it does arguably provide the Islamic Republic with a geostrategic equalizer in a region that America has dominated for decades. Numerous alternative explanations for opposing Iran's program have been offered: Iran's nuclear program will stunt the growth of nascent and future democracies in the region, fatally undermine the Nuclear Non-Proliferation Treaty, cause Iran's Arab neighbors to lean toward Tehran, or encourage nuclear proliferation throughout the Middle East.

Some of these concerns hold merit, others are more far-fetched. But all of them fall under the umbrella of a larger concern—arguably America's primary concern—regarding Iran's nuclear program: a nuclear-capable Iran will enable the emergence of a regional power that fundamentally rejects the notion of a Pax Americana for the Middle East.

And therein lies the rub: Iran will not enter into the regional security framework as it exists today, and the United States will not change the existing framework to accommodate Iranian preferences and goals. At face value, this seemingly zero-sum game puts Washington and Tehran on a collision course that can only end in war unless one side blinks.

The saving grace, which prevents this scenario from becoming a foregone conclusion, is that to date, diplomacy has not really been tried. There has been one forty-five minute bilateral meeting between the United States and Iran during Obama's first four years in office. This does not constitute a real diplomatic effort. Embarking upon a sustained diplomatic process on Iran's nuclear program will not solve the larger U.S.-Iran conflict. But it can serve as an important foundation from which dialogue can continue on other equally important issues.

## DRINKING THE CUP OF POISON

Overall, sanctions have succeeded in putting tremendous pressure on the Iranian economy. Rather than show greater flexibility, however, the Iranian government's response thus far has been responding in kind by increasing pressure on the West. Tehran has continued to expand its nuclear program, it has sought ways to circumvent sanctions rather than acquiesce to them, and it has doubled down on the foreign-threat mindset that empowers Iran's hardline security and intelligence communities—the very elements that benefit from a continuation of the crisis. All this indicates a significant gap between the stated goals of the sanctions policy—a change in the Iranian calculus in regard to its nuclear program—and what sanctions have actually achieved.

Some sanction advocates posit that sanctions will not necessarily yield results in a linear manner; Tehran, they explain, may be able to resist sanctions for an extended period of time, only to massively yield to the pressure after an inflection point has been reached. The view suggests that judging the track record of sanctions thus far is therefore inappropriate and misleading. In an arena where diplomatic efforts are judged harshly and expected to yield extensive results almost instantaneously, this argument also accepts a political reality in which timelines and deadlines for sanctions can hardly be guaranteed.

However, even if the notion of a non-linear process is accepted, signs of an inflection point must become evident at some stage, such as the emergence of a narrative within the elite that challenges the status quo policy and presses for a change. The existence of widespread discontent and anger against the Iranian regime should not be misconstrued as such an inflection point, that is, as pressure from society (or stakeholders) to shift Iran's nuclear policy per se.

Sanctions have thus far failed to produce an inflection point, nor are they likely to do so. The combination of suppressing open debates about the nuclear issue, the manner in which sanctions "vindicate" Ayatollah Khamenei's narrative of Western animosity aimed at "defeating Iran," and the absence of convincing and enticing incentives—such as meaningful sanctions relief—to change Iran's nuclear policy has prevented the emergence of a credible counter narrative within the Iranian elite. In the words of Roberto Toscano, a former Italian ambassador to Iran:

> [P]ragmatic voices within the regime . . . should be capable of convincingly stressing that both national interest and regime survival would be better pursued by abandoning not only [Iran's] provocative rhetoric but also its

ideological intransigence. The problem is that this is made more difficult by sanctions, a godsend for those who are trying to rally Iranians around the regime and against external pressure.

Moreover, stakeholders in the system such as the business community have focused on seeking economic concessions from the regime rather than lobbying for a shift in Iran's nuclear stance. The absence of meaningful sanctions relief on the negotiating table appears to have prevented the emergence of incentives for the business community to forcefully challenge the regime's nuclear strategy.

Successful cases in which enormous external pressure shifted the Islamic Republic's policy on a central national security issue—such as Ayatollah Ruhollah Khomeini's decision to "drink the cup of poison" and end the debilitating war with Iraq—included both a challenge to the dominant narrative and influential stakeholders pushing for a policy shift. In the case of the Iraq-Iran war, this was made possible because it was clear to the Iranians that accepting a UN-mediated truce would unquestionably end the war with Iraq *and* they had confidence that Saddam Hussein could deliver on his end of the bargain. Tehran does not perceive a similar situation today, as two key issues remain unclear to the regime: What sanctions would be lifted if Iran were to succumb to Western pressure, and perhaps more importantly, whether the West has the political ability to deliver on sanctions relief.

## AN EXISTENTIAL CONCERN

A pressure strategy that lacks the sophistication and flexibility to help unravel the dominant narrative in the sanctioned state and entice stakeholders to push for policy changes is unlikely to succeed and may be counter-productive. In the case of Iran, a continuation of the current approach will likely consolidate the anti-Western narrative and render a compromise more difficult.

The United States and the EU believe sanctions have put Iran on a one-way path toward economic collapse unless it yields on the nuclear issue. Accepting the P5 + 1 proposal is a rational move, as they see it, and rejecting it is either the result of miscalculation or ideological rigidity.

Iran perceives a different reality. Khamenei's behavior suggests he is aware of his regime's unpopularity. Since 2009, the regime has lost several constituencies, rendering the few who support the regime and believe it to be legitimate all the more politically crucial to regime survival. To these constituencies, the narrative of resistance against the West to uphold Iran's independence is essential. Any move by the regime that will be perceived by this constituency as a capitulation to Western demands, i.e., a violation of the regime's narrative, risks turning them against Khamenei. Mindful of Khamenei's already weak support base, the loss of these last constituencies could be existential and prove a greater threat to the regime's survival than even a military confrontation with the United States. While the regime does not hold out hope for actually winning a war against the U.S., it certainly believes it can *survive* a war—and even come out of it stronger at home. Thus, it is highly unlikely that the regime will succumb to the sanctions pressure at a time when its narrative remains unchallenged within the elite, key stakeholders are not visibly lobbying for policy shifts, no meaningful sanctions relief is put on the table by the P5 + 1, and capitulation poses an existential threat to the regime.

Any calibration of the sanctions policy should focus on promoting a discourse that can undo the consolidated narrative that Western governments are opposed to Iran's progress, *and* can offer a solid prospect—such as meaningful sanctions relief—and clear arguments to Iranian stakeholders who have the ability to change the debate inside Iran. These measures can dramatically change the prospects of shifting Iran's nuclear calculus.

## CRITICAL THINKING QUESTIONS

1. In terms of their importance, rank the factors driving U.S. sanctions policy toward Iran.
2. How would you expect the United States to respond if economic sanctions were put in place against it? How is this different from how Iran has responded?
3. On a scale of 1–10, how would you rate the success or effectiveness of U.S. sanctions? What needs to be done to raise the score?

# Emerging Issues

As the United States has experienced on more than one occasion, surprise is an inescapable feature of world politics. To its dismay, the United States was surprised by the Japanese attack on Pearl Harbor (1941). Decades later it was surprised that the Shah of Iran fell (1979), and after that it was surprised that its embassy was seized by Iranian protesters. News of the terrorist attacks of 9/11 in 2001 was met with disbelief and then horror. Most recently it was surprised by the attack on its diplomatic outpost at Benghazi (2012) and the sudden appearance of ISIS as a major force in international terrorism due to its involvement in the Syrian civil war, which began in 2011. Surprises, however, are not always unwelcome, as the unexpected fall of communism in Russia and the ending of the Cold War (1991) demonstrated. It should be noted as well that the United States is also capable of surprising the world, as was the case with the announcement of President Richard Nixon's trip to China (1972), which began the process of diplomatic recognition and normalizing U.S.-China relations.

Preventing surprise, or at least minimizing its consequences, requires that policy makers engage in three types of calculations in formulating foreign policy. First, they need to look to the future and prioritize the problems and situations they anticipate will confront them. In doing so they must weigh two considerations. The first is the seriousness of the potential situation: How great a threat does it represent to core national interests? The second is the likelihood that this situation will occur. When a situation is judged to be highly threatening and likely to occur, it is easily defined as a foreign policy problem worthy of considerable attention and the expenditure of significant resources. Those situations judged not to be of great consequence nor likely to occur are easily ignored. The great majority of foreign policy issues are found in between, requiring that difficult choices be made.

The second calculation is that policy makers must seek to learn from the past. The typical starting point for this is George Santayana's often quoted admonition that those who fail to learn from the past are condemned to repeat it. Left unsaid for the most part is, what part of the past is one to learn from? Was George W. Bush's failed Iraq policy the result of a poorly conceived line of action or one that could have succeeded had it been implemented properly? Both positions have been advanced by those studying U.S. post–Saddam Hussein foreign policy toward Iraq. A very different starting point for learning from the past has been suggested by contemporary terrorism experts who argue that if a policy succeeds today, it will fail tomorrow because the enemy will adapt. The implication here is clear: not only must policy makers avoid past failures but they also cannot become overly attached to past successes. Just because a military strategy defeated an enemy in less than two months, such as the United States did against Saddam Hussein, it does not mean that strategy can be repeated successfully in the future.

Third, policy makers must look to the present in order to understand how leaders and citizens of other states view the global problems and situations they are concerned with. What U.S. officials see as an unwarranted aggressive set of actions may be seen by leaders in another country as a legitimate set of defensive moves. A policy the United States sees as designed to preserve international order and peace may be seen by another state as an effort by the United States to condemn it to the status of a second-rank state whose sovereignty is constantly infringed on by more powerful states.

The challenge of devising a foreign policy that could meet future challenges appeared to be high on Obama's initial foreign policy agenda. His early speeches called for "a new era of engagement" with the world. In particular, he called for an end to the "cycle of suspicion and discord" that had come to exist in relations between the Muslim world and the United States. In recognition of the growing importance of China to U.S. economic and security interests, a "pivot" to Asia was placed high on his priority list of new foreign policy initiatives.

It was not long, however, before this forward-looking agenda came to fall into the shadows of pressing current problems, such as the emergence of pro-democracy movements throughout the Middle East and North Africa, the desire to end the U.S. military presence in Afghanistan and Iraq, and the crises in Ukraine and Syria. The redirection of attention from future issues to current ones is not unique to the Obama administration. Few presidents have been able to avoid it for long periods of time. This points to yet another dimension of the challenge of avoiding surprise. Making foreign policy is not simply an intellectual challenge of connecting dots or imagining new worlds. It is also a political challenge in which a consensus must be created among often competing institutional interests and societal interests and values.

Our first reading in this final part is an excerpt from the "Global Trends 2030" report produced by the National Intelligence Council. It presents a series of possible scenarios they have constructed to help policy makers and citizens think about the future. In the second reading, "More Small Wars," Max Boot presents ten important lessons that policy makers need to take away from Afghanistan and Iraq if the United States is to successfully fight future small wars. In 2015 the Millennium Development Goals established by the United Nations in 2000 will expire. The problem of economic development, however, will continue. In "Delivering Development after 2015," Molly Elgin-Cossart discusses the process, politics, and policies of financing sustainable development in the future.

Climate change issues also promise to be an ongoing problem that U.S. foreign policy will need to incorporate into its planning for the future. The next reading is an excerpt from the World Resource Institute working paper "A Critical Decade for Climate Policy." In it, Taryn Fransen and Casey Cronin present an overview of different types of climate policies and discuss how we might go about establishing a climate monitoring system so we can judge if we are achieving our objectives. Without such a system, surprise is virtually inevitable. Yet another emerging foreign policy problem area centers on the use of drones as a counterterrorism tool. In "Is the U.S. Drone War Effective?" Michael J. Boyle notes that while many see drones as a key tool to defeat terrorism while holding American casualties to a minimum, it has also stirred up new levels of hostility toward the United States, especially in South Asia. The end result could be heightened regional instability.

## BIG PICTURE QUESTIONS

1. Identify five possible foreign policy problems the United States will face in the next decade. For each, evaluate the likelihood they will happen and the degree of threat they present to the U.S. national interest.
2. What is the best way for policy makers to understand how leaders and citizens of other states view U.S. foreign policy and define foreign policy problems?
3. What are the three most important lessons one should learn from past foreign policy failures? What are the three most important lessons one should learn from past foreign policy successes?

## SUGGESTED READINGS

Eric Farnsworth, "Reinvent the Summit of the Americas," *Current History* 112 (February 2013), 75–76.

Clare Lockhart, "Fixing US Foreign Assistance," *World Affairs* 176 (January 2014), 84–93

Gerami Nima, "Attracting a Crowd: What Societal Verification Means to Arms Control: The U.S. Response," *Bulletin of the Atomic Scientists* 69 (May 2013), 14–18.

P. W. Singer and Alan Friedman, *Cybersecurity and Cyber War* (New York: Oxford University Press, 2014).

Ramesh Thakur, *The Global Governance Architecture of Nuclear Security* (Muscatine, IA: Stanley Foundation, March 2013).

# 24

# Global Trends 2030

## ALTERNATIVE WORLDS

The world of 2030 will be radically transformed from our world today. By 2030, no country—whether the United States, China, or any other large country—will be a hegemonic power. The empowerment of individuals and diffusion of power among states and from states to informal networks will have a dramatic impact, largely reversing the historic rise of the West since 1750, restoring Asia's weight in the global economy, and ushering in a new era of "democratization" at the international and domestic level. In addition to individual empowerment and the diffusion of state power, we believe that two other *megatrends* will shape our world out to 2030: demographic patterns, especially rapid aging; and growing resource demands which, in the cases of food and water, might lead to scarcities. These trends, which are virtually certain, exist today, but during the next 15–20 years they will gain much greater momentum. Underpinning the megatrends are *tectonic shifts*— critical changes to key features of our global environment that will affect how the world "works" [see table 24.1].

Extrapolations of the megatrends would alone point to a changed world by 2030—but the world could be transformed in radically different ways. We believe that six key *game-changers*—questions regarding the global economy, governance, conflict, regional instability, technology, and the role of the United States—will largely determine what kind of transformed world we will inhabit in 2030. Several potential *Black Swans*—discrete events—would cause large-scale disruption [see table 24.2]. All but two of these—the possibility of a democratic China or a reformed Iran—would have negative repercussions.

Based upon what we know about the megatrends and the possible interactions between the megatrends and the game-changers, we have delineated four archetypal futures that represent distinct pathways for the world out to 2030. None of these *alternative worlds* is inevitable. In reality, the future probably will consist of elements from all the scenarios.

Excerpted from the Executive Summary of "Global Trends 2030: Alternative Worlds," National Intelligence Council, December 2012, iii–xiv.

## TABLE 24.1

### Tectonic Shifts Between Now and 2030

| | |
|---|---|
| **Growth of the Global Middle Class** | Middle classes most everywhere in the developing world are poised to expand substantially in terms of both absolute numbers and the percentage of the population that can claim middle-class status during the next 15-20 years. |
| **Wider Access to Lethal and Disruptive Technologies** | A wider spectrum of instruments of war—especially precision-strike capabilities, cyber instruments, and bioterror weaponry—will become accessible. Individuals and small groups will have the capability to perpetrate large-scale violence and disruption—a capability formerly the monopoly of states. |
| **Definitive Shift of Economic Power to the East and South** | The US, European, and Japanese share of global income is projected to fall from 56 percent today to well under half by 2030. In 2008, China overtook the US as the world's largest saver; by 2020, emerging markets' share of financial assets is projected to almost double. |
| **Unprecedented and Widespread Aging** | Whereas in 2012 only Japan and Germany have matured beyond a median age of 45 years, most European countries, South Korea, and Taiwan will have entered the post-mature age category by 2030. Migration will become more globalized as both rich and developing countries suffer from workforce shortages. |
| **Urbanization** | Today's roughly 50-percent urban population will climb to nearly 60 percent, or 4.9 billion people, in 2030. Africa will gradually replace Asia as the region with the highest urbanization growth rate. Urban centers are estimated to generate 80 percent of economic growth; the potential exists to apply modern technologies and infrastructure, promoting better use of scarce resources. |
| **Food and Water Pressures** | Demand for food is expected to rise at least 35 percent by 2030 while demand for water is expected to rise by 40 percent. Nearly half of the world's population will live in areas experiencing severe water stress. Fragile states in Africa and the Middle East are most at risk of experiencing food and water shortages, but China and India are also vulnerable. |
| **US Energy Independence** | With shale gas, the US will have sufficient natural gas to meet domestic needs and generate potential global exports for decades to come. Increased oil production from difficult-to-access oil deposits would result in a substantial reduction in the US net trade balance and faster economic expansion. Global spare capacity may exceed over 8 million barrels, at which point OPEC would lose price control and crude oil prices would collapse, causing a major negative impact on oil-export economies. |

# MEGATRENDS AND RELATED TECTONIC SHIFTS

## Megatrend 1: Individual Empowerment

Individual empowerment will accelerate substantially during the next 15–20 years owing to poverty reduction and a huge growth of the global middle class, greater educational attainment, and better health care. The growth of the global middle class constitutes a tectonic shift: for the first time, a majority of the world's population will not be impoverished, and the middle classes will be the most important social and economic sector in the vast majority of countries around the world. Individual empowerment is the most important megatrend because it is both a cause and effect of most other trends—including the expanding global economy, rapid growth of the developing countries, and widespread exploitation of new communications and manufacturing technologies. On the one hand, we see the potential for greater individual initiative as

## TABLE 24.2

## Potential Black Swans That Would Cause the Greatest Disruptive Impact

| | |
|---|---|
| Severe Pandemic | No one can predict which pathogen will be the next to start spreading to humans, or when or where such a development will occur. An easily transmissible novel respiratory pathogen that kills or incapacitates more than one percent of its victims is among the most disruptive events possible. Such an outbreak could result in millions of people suffering and dying in every corner of the world in less than six months. |
| Much More Rapid Climate Change | Dramatic and unforeseen changes already are occurring at a faster rate than expected. Most scientists are not confident of being able to predict such events. Rapid changes in precipitation patterns—such as monsoons in India and the rest of Asia—could sharply disrupt that region's ability to feed its population. |
| Euro/EU Collapse | An unruly Greek exit from the euro zone could cause eight times the collateral damage as the Lehman Brothers bankruptcy, provoking a broader crisis regarding the EU's future. |
| A Democratic or Collapsed China | China is slated to pass the threshold of US$15,000 per capita purchasing power parity (PPP) in the next five years or so—a level that is often a trigger for democratization. Chinese "soft" power could be dramatically boosted, setting off a wave of democratic movements. Alternatively, many experts believe a democratic China could also become more nationalistic. An economically collapsed China would trigger political unrest and shock the global economy. |
| A Reformed Iran | A more liberal regime could come under growing public pressure to end the international sanctions and negotiate an end to Iran's isolation. An Iran that dropped its nuclear weapons aspirations and became focused on economic modernization would bolster the chances for a more stable Middle East. |
| Nuclear War or WMD/Cyber Attack | Nuclear powers such as Russia and Pakistan and potential aspirants such as Iran and North Korea see nuclear weapons as compensation for other political and security weaknesses, heightening the risk of their use. The chance of nonstate actors conducting a cyber attack—or using WMD—also is increasing. |
| Solar Geomagnetic Storms | Solar geomagnetic storms could knock out satellites, the electric grid, and many sensitive electronic devices. The recurrence intervals of crippling solar geomagnetic storms, which are less than a century, now pose a substantial threat because of the world's dependence on electricity. |
| US Disengagement | A collapse or sudden retreat of US power probably would result in an extended period of global anarchy; no leading power would be likely to replace the United States as guarantor of the international order. |

key to solving the mounting global challenges over the next 15–20 years. On the other hand, in a tectonic shift, individuals and small groups will have greater access to lethal and disruptive technologies (particularly precision-strike capabilities, cyber instruments, and bioterror weaponry), enabling them to perpetrate large-scale violence—a capability formerly the monopoly of states.

## Megatrend 2: Diffusion of Power

The diffusion of power among countries will have a dramatic impact by 2030. Asia will have surpassed North America and Europe combined in terms of global power, based upon GDP, population size, military spending, and technological investment. China alone will probably have the largest economy, surpassing that of the United States a few years before 2030. In a tectonic shift, the health of the global economy increasingly will be linked to how well the developing world does—more so than the traditional West. In addition to China, India, and Brazil, regional players such as Colombia, Indonesia, Nigeria, South Africa, and Turkey will become especially important to the global economy. Meanwhile, the economies of Europe, Japan, and Russia are likely to continue their slow relative declines.

The shift in national power may be overshadowed by an even more fundamental shift in the *nature* of power. Enabled by communications technologies, power will shift toward multifaceted and amorphous networks that will form to influence state and global actions. Those countries with some of the strongest fundamentals—GDP, population size, etc.—will not be able to punch their weight unless they also learn to operate in networks and coalitions in a multipolar world.

## Megatrend 3: Demographic Patterns

We believe that in the world of 2030—a world in which a growing global population will have reached somewhere close to 8.3 billion people (up from 7.1 billion in 2012)—four demographic trends will fundamentally shape, although not necessarily determine, most countries' economic and political conditions and relations among countries. These trends are: aging—a tectonic shift for both for the West and increasingly most developing countries; a still-significant but shrinking number of youthful societies and states; migration, which will increasingly be a cross-border issue; and growing urbanization—another tectonic shift, which will spur economic growth but could put new strains on food and water resources. Aging countries will face an uphill battle in maintaining their living standards. Demand for both skilled and unskilled labor will spur global migration. Owing to rapid urbanization in the developing world, the volume of urban construction for housing, office space, and transport services over the next 40 years could roughly equal the entire volume of such construction to date in world history.

## Megatrend 4: Growing Food, Water, and Energy Nexus

Demand for food, water, and energy will grow by approximately 35, 40, and 50 percent respectively owing to an increase in the global population and the consumption patterns of an expanding middle class. Climate change will worsen the outlook for the availability of these critical resources. Climate change analysis suggests that the severity of existing weather patterns will intensify, with wet areas getting wetter and dry and arid areas becoming more so. Much of the decline in precipitation will occur in the Middle East and northern Africa as well as western Central Asia, southern Europe, southern Africa, and the U.S. Southwest.

We are not necessarily headed into a world of scarcities, but policymakers and their private sector partners will need to be proactive to avoid such a future. Many countries probably won't have the wherewithal to avoid food and water shortages without massive help from outside. Tackling problems pertaining to one commodity won't be possible without affecting supply and demand for the others. Agriculture is highly dependent on accessibility to adequate sources of water as well as on energy-rich fertilizers. Hydropower is a significant source of energy for some regions while new sources of energy—such as biofuels—threaten to exacerbate the potential for food shortages. There is as much scope for negative tradeoffs as there is the potential for positive synergies. Agricultural productivity in Africa, particularly, will require a sea change to avoid shortages. Unlike Asia and South America, which have achieved significant improvements in agricultural production per capita, Africa has only recently returned to 1970s levels.

In a likely tectonic shift, the United States could become energy-independent. The United States has regained its position as the world's largest natural gas producer and expanded the life of its reserves from 30 to 100 years due to hydraulic fracturing technology. Additional crude oil production through the use of "fracking" drilling technologies on difficult-to-reach oil deposits could result in a big reduction in the U.S. net trade balance and improved overall economic growth. Debates over environmental concerns about fracturing, notably pollution of water sources, could derail such developments, however.

# GAME-CHANGERS

## Game-Changer 1: The Crisis-Prone Global Economy

The international economy almost certainly will continue to be characterized by various regional and national economies moving at significantly different speeds—a pattern reinforced by the 2008 global financial crisis. The contrasting speeds across different regional economies are exacerbating global imbalances and straining governments and the international system. The key question is whether the divergences and increased volatility will result in a global breakdown and collapse or whether the development of multiple growth centers will lead to resiliency. The absence of a clear hegemonic economic power could add to the volatility. Some experts have compared the relative decline in the economic weight of the United States to the late 19th century when economic dominance by one player—Britain—receded into multi-polarity.

A return to pre-2008 growth rates and previous patterns of rapid globalization looks increasingly unlikely, at least for the next decade. Across G-7 countries, total nonfinancial debt has doubled since 1980 to 300 percent of GDP, accumulating over a generation. Historical studies indicate that recessions involving financial crises tend to be deeper and require recoveries that take twice as long. Major Western economies—with some exceptions such as the United States, Australia, and South Korea—have only just begun deleveraging (reducing their debts); previous episodes have taken close to a decade.

Another major global economic crisis cannot be ruled out. The McKinsey Global Institute estimates that the potential impact of an unruly Greek exit from the euro zone could cause eight times the collateral damage as the Lehman Brothers bankruptcy. Regardless of which solution is eventually chosen, progress will be needed on several fronts to restore euro zone stability. Doing so will take several years at a minimum, with many experts talking about a whole decade before stability returns.

Earlier economic crises, such as the 1930s Great Depression, also hit when the age structures of many Western populations were relatively youthful, providing a demographic bonus during the postwar economic boom. However, such a bonus will not exist in any prospective recovery for Western countries. To compensate for drops in labor-force growth, hoped-for economic gains will have to come from growth in productivity. The United States is in a better position because its workforce is projected to increase during the next decade, but the United States will still need to increase labor productivity to offset its slowly aging workforce. A critical question is whether technology can sufficiently boost economic productivity to prevent a long-term slowdown.

As we have noted, the world's economic prospects will increasingly depend on the fortunes of the East and South. The developing world already provides more than 50 percent of global economic growth and 40 percent of global investment. Its contribution to global investment growth is more than 70 percent. China's contribution is now one and a half times the size of the U.S. contribution. In the World Bank's baseline modeling of future economic multipolarity, China—despite a likely slowing of its economic growth—will contribute about one-third of global growth by 2025, far more than any other economy. Emerging market demand for infrastructure, housing, consumer goods, and new plants and equipment will raise global investment to levels not seen in four decades. Global savings may not match this rise, resulting in upward pressure on long-term interest rates.

Despite their growing economic clout, developing countries will face their own challenges, especially in their efforts to continue the momentum behind their rapid economic growth. China has averaged 10 percent real growth during the past three decades; by 2020 its economy will probably be expanding by only 5 percent, according to several private-sector forecasts. The slower growth will mean downward pressure on per capita income growth. China faces the prospect of being trapped in middle-income status, with its per capita income not continuing to increase to the level of the world's advanced economies. India faces many of the same problems and traps accompanying rapid growth as China: large inequities between rural and urban sectors and within society; increasing constraints on resources such as water; and a need for greater investment in science and technology to continue to move its economy up the value chain.

## Game-Changer 2: The Governance Gap

During the next 15–20 years, as power becomes even more diffuse than today, a growing number of diverse state and nonstate actors, as well as subnational actors, such as cities, will play important governance roles. The increasing number of players needed to solve major transnational challenges—and their discordant values—will complicate decision making. The lack of consensus between and among established and emerging powers suggests that multilateral governance to 2030 will be limited at best. The chronic deficit probably will reinforce the trend toward fragmentation. However, various developments —positive or negative—could push the world in different directions. Advances cannot be ruled out despite growing multipolarity, increased regionalism, and possible economic slowdowns. Prospects for achieving progress on global issues will vary across issues.

The governance gap will continue to be most pronounced at the domestic level and driven by rapid political and social changes. The advances during the past couple decades in health, education, and income—which we expect to continue, if not accelerate in some cases—will drive new governance structures. Transitions to democracy are much more stable and long-lasting when youth bulges begin to decline and incomes are higher. Currently about 50 countries are in the awkward stage between autocracy and democracy, with the greatest number concentrated in Sub-Saharan Africa, Southeast and Central Asia, and the Middle East and North Africa. Both social science theory and recent history—the Color Revolutions and the Arab Spring—support the idea that with maturing age structures and rising incomes, political liberalization and democracy will advance. However, many countries will still be zigzagging their way through the complicated democratization process during the next 15–20 years. Countries moving from autocracy to democracy have a proven track record of instability.

Other countries will continue to suffer from a democratic deficit: in these cases a country's developmental level is more advanced than its level of governance. Gulf countries and China account for a large number in this category. China, for example, is slated to pass the threshold of U.S. $15,000 per capita purchasing power parity (PPP) in the next five years, which is often a trigger for democratization. Chinese democratization could constitute an immense "wave," increasing pressure for change on other authoritarian states.

The widespread use of new communications technologies will become a double-edged sword for governance. On the one hand, social networking will enable citizens to coalesce and challenge governments, as we have already seen in the Middle East. On the other hand, such technologies will provide governments—both authoritarian and democratic—an unprecedented ability to monitor their citizens. It is unclear how the balance will be struck between greater IT-enabled individuals and networks and traditional political structures. In our interactions, technologists and political scientists have offered divergent views. Both sides agree, however, that the characteristics of IT use— multiple and simultaneous action, near instantaneous responses, mass organization across geographic boundaries, and technological dependence—increase the potential for more frequent discontinuous change in the international system.

The current, largely Western dominance of global structures such as the UN Security Council, World Bank, and IMF probably will have been transformed by 2030 to be more in line with the changing hierarchy of new economic players. Many second-tier emerging powers will be making their mark—at least as emerging regional leaders. Just as the larger G-20—rather than G-7/8—was energized to deal with the 2008 financial crisis, we expect that other institutions will be updated—probably also in response to crises.

## Game-Changer 3: Potential for Increased Conflict

Historical trends during the past two decades show fewer major armed conflicts and, where conflicts remain, fewer civilian and military casualties than in previous decades. Maturing age structures in many developing countries point to continuing declines in intrastate conflict. We believe the disincentives will remain strong against great power conflict: too much would be at stake. Nevertheless, we need to be cautious about the prospects for further declines in the number and intensity of intrastate conflicts, and interstate conflict remains a possibility.

Intrastate conflicts have gradually increased in countries with a mature overall population that contain a politically dissonant, youthful ethnic minority. Strife involving ethnic Kurds in Turkey, Shia in Lebanon, and Pattani Muslims in southern Thailand are examples of such situations. Looking forward, the potential for conflict to occur in Sub-Saharan Africa is likely to remain high even after some of the region's countries graduate into a more intermediate age structure because of the probable large number of ethnic and tribal minorities that will remain more youthful than the overall population. Insufficient natural resources—such as water and arable land—in many of the same countries that will have disproportionate levels of young men increase the risks of intrastate conflict breaking out, particularly in Sub-Saharan Africa and South and East Asian countries, including China and India. A number of these countries—Afghanistan, Bangladesh, Pakistan, and Somalia—also have faltering governance institutions.

Though by no means inevitable, the risks of interstate conflict are increasing owing to changes in the international system. The underpinnings of the post–Cold War equilibrium are beginning to shift. During the next 15–20 years, the United States will be grappling with the degree to which it can continue to play the role of systemic guardian and guarantor of the global order. A declining U.S. unwillingness and/or slipping capacity to serve as a global security provider would be a key factor contributing to instability, particularly in Asia and the Middle East. A more fragmented international system in which existing forms of cooperation are no longer seen as advantageous to many of the key global players would also increase the potential for competition and even great power conflict. However, if such a conflict occurs, it almost certainly will not be on the level of a world war with all major powers engaged.

Three different baskets of risks could conspire to increase the chances of an outbreak of interstate conflict: changing calculations of key players—

particularly China, India, and Russia; increasing contention over resource issues; and a wider spectrum of more accessible instruments of war. With the potential for increased proliferation and growing concerns about nuclear security, risks are growing that future wars in South Asia and the Middle East would risk inclusion of a nuclear deterrent.

The current Islamist phase of terrorism might end by 2030, but terrorism is unlikely to die completely. Many states might continue to use terrorist groups out of a strong sense of insecurity, although the costs to a regime of directly supporting terrorists looks set to become even greater as international cooperation increases. With more widespread access to lethal and disruptive technologies, individuals who are experts in such niche areas as cyber systems might sell their services to the highest bidder, including terrorists who would focus less on causing mass casualties and more on creating widespread economic and financial disruptions.

## Game-Changer 4: Wider Scope of Regional Instability

Regional dynamics in several different theaters during the next couple decades will have the potential to spill over and create global insecurity. The **Middle East** and **South Asia** are the two regions most likely to trigger broader instability. In the Middle East, the youth bulge—a driving force of the recent Arab Spring—will give way to a gradually aging population. With new technologies beginning to provide the world with other sources of oil and gas, the region's economy will need to become increasingly diversified. But the Middle East's trajectory will depend on its political landscape. On the one hand, if the Islamic Republic maintains power in Iran and is able to develop nuclear weapons, the Middle East will face a highly unstable future. On the other hand, the emergence of moderate, democratic governments or a breakthrough agreement to resolve the Israeli-Palestinian conflict could have enormously positive consequences.

South Asia faces a series of internal and external shocks during the next 15–20 years. Low growth, rising food prices, and energy shortages will pose stiff challenges to governance in Pakistan and Afghanistan. Afghanistan's and Pakistan's youth bulges are large—similar in size to those found in many African countries. When these youth bulges are combined with a slow-growing economy, they portend increased instability. India is in a better position, benefiting from higher growth, but it will still be challenged to find jobs for its large youth population. Inequality, lack of infrastructure, and education deficiencies are key weaknesses in India. The neighborhood has always had a profound influence on internal developments, increasing the sense of insecurity and bolstering military outlays. Conflict could erupt and spread under numerous scenarios. Conflicting strategic goals, widespread distrust, and the hedging strategies by all the parties will make it difficult for them to develop a strong regional security framework.

An increasingly multipolar **Asia** lacking a well-anchored regional security framework able to arbitrate and mitigate rising tensions would constitute one of the largest global threats. Fear of Chinese power, the likelihood of growing Chinese nationalism, and possible questions about the United States remaining involved in the region will increase insecurities. An unstable Asia would cause large-scale damage to the global economy.

Changing dynamics in other regions would also jeopardize global security. **Europe** has been a critical security provider, ensuring, for example, Central Europe's integration into the "West" after the end of the Cold War. A more inward-focused and less capable Europe would provide a smaller stabilizing force for crises in neighboring regions. On the other hand, a Europe which overcomes its current intertwined political and economic crises could see its global role enhanced. Such a Europe could help to integrate its rapidly developing neighbors in the Middle East, Sub-Saharan Africa, and Central Asia into the global economy and broader international system. A modernizing Russia could integrate itself into a wider international community; at the same time, a Russia which fails to build a more diversified economy and more liberal domestic order could increasingly pose a regional and global threat.

Progress toward greater regional cohesion and integration in **Latin America** and **Sub-Saharan Africa** would promise increased stability in those regions and a reduced threat to global security. Countries in Sub-Saharan Africa, Central America, and the Caribbean will remain vulnerable, nevertheless, to state failure through 2030, providing safe havens for both global criminal and terrorist networks and local insurgents.

## Game-Changer 5: The Impact of New Technologies

Four technology arenas will shape global economic, social, and military developments as well as the world community's actions pertaining to the environment by 2030. **Information technology** is entering the big data era. Process power and data storage are becoming almost free; networks and the cloud will provide global access and pervasive services; social media and cybersecurity will be large new markets. This growth and diffusion will present significant challenges for governments and societies, which must find ways to capture the benefits of new IT technologies while dealing with the new threats that those technologies present. Fear of the growth of an Orwellian surveillance state may lead citizens particularly in the developed world to pressure their governments to restrict or dismantle big data systems.

Information technology–based solutions to maximize citizens' economic productivity and quality of life while minimizing resource consumption and environmental degradation will be critical to ensuring the viability of megacities. Some of the world's future megacities will essentially be built from scratch, enabling a blank-slate approach to infrastructure design and implementation that could allow for the most effective possible deployment of new urban technologies—or create urban nightmares, if such new technologies are not deployed effectively.

**New manufacturing and automation technologies** such as additive manufacturing (3D printing) and robotics have the potential to change work patterns in both the developing and developed worlds. In developed countries these technologies will improve productivity, address labor constraints, and diminish the need for outsourcing, especially if reducing the length of supply chains brings clear benefits. Nevertheless, such technologies could still have a similar effect as outsourcing: they could make more low- and semi-skilled manufacturing workers in developed economies redundant, exacerbating domestic inequalities. For developing economies, particularly Asian ones, the new technologies will stimulate new manufacturing capabilities and further increase the competitiveness of Asian manufacturers and suppliers.

Breakthroughs, especially for technologies pertaining to the **security of vital resources**—will be necessary to meet the food, water, and energy needs of the world's population. Key technologies likely to be at the forefront of maintaining such resources in the next 15–20 years will include genetically modified crops, precision agriculture, water irrigation techniques, solar energy, advanced bio-based fuels, and enhanced oil and natural gas extraction via fracturing. Given the vulnerabilities of developing economies to key resource supplies and prices and the early impacts of climate change, key developing countries may realize substantial rewards in commercializing many next-generation resource technologies first. Aside from being cost competitive, any expansion or adoption of both existing and next-generation resource technologies over the next 20 years will largely depend on social acceptance and the direction and resolution of any ensuing political issues.

Last but not least, new health technologies will continue to extend the average age of populations around the world, by ameliorating debilitating physical and mental conditions and improving overall well-being. The greatest gains in healthy longevity are likely to occur in those countries with developing economies as the size of their middle class populations swells. The health-care systems in these countries may be poor today, but by 2030 they will make substantial progress in the longevity potential of their populations; by 2030 many leading centers of innovation in disease management will be in the developing world.

## Game-Changer 6: The Role of the United States

How the United States' international role evolves during the next 15–20 years—a big uncertainty—and whether the United States will be able to work with new partners to reinvent the international system will be among the most important variables in the future shape of the global order. Although the United States' (and the West's) relative decline vis-à-vis the rising states is inevitable, its future role in the international system is much harder to project: the degree to which the United States continues to dominate the international system could vary widely.

The United States most likely will remain "first among equals" among the other great powers in 2030 because of its preeminence across a range of power dimensions and legacies of its leadership role. More important than just its economic weight, the United States' dominant role in international politics has derived from its preponderance across the board in both hard and soft power.

Nevertheless, with the rapid rise of other countries, the "unipolar moment" is over and Pax Americana—the era of American ascendancy in international politics that began in 1945—is fast winding down.

The context in which the U.S. global power will operate will change dramatically. Most of Washington's historic Western partners have also suffered relative economic declines. The post–World War II era was characterized by the G-7 countries leading both economically and politically. U.S. projection of power was dependent on and amplified by its strong alliances. During the next 15–20 years, power will become more multifaceted—reflecting the diversity of issues—and more contextual—certain actors and power instruments will be germane to particular issues.

The United States' technological assets—including its leadership in piloting social networking and rapid communications—give it an advantage, but the Internet also will continue to boost the power of nonstate actors. In most cases, U.S. power will need to be enhanced through relevant outside networks, friends, and affiliates that can coalesce on any particular issue. Leadership will be a function of position, enmeshment, diplomatic skill, and constructive demeanor.

The U.S. position in the world also will be determined by how successful it is in helping to manage international crises—typically the role of great powers and, since 1945, the international community's expectation of the United States. Should Asia replicate Europe's 19th- and early-20th-century past, the United States will be called upon to be a balancer, ensuring regional stability. In contrast, the fall of the dollar as the global reserve currency and substitution by another or a basket of currencies would be one of the sharpest indications of a loss of U.S. global economic position, strongly undermining Washington's political influence too.

The replacement of the United States by another global power and erection of a new international order seems the least likely outcome in this time period. No other power would be likely to achieve the same panoply of power in this time frame under any plausible scenario. The emerging powers are eager to take their place at the top table of key multilateral institutions such as UN, IMF, and World Bank, but they do not espouse any competing vision. Although ambivalent and even resentful of the U.S.-led international order, they have benefited from it and are more interested in continuing their economic development and political consolidation than contesting U.S. leadership. In addition, the emerging powers are not a bloc; thus they do not have any unitary alternative vision. Their perspectives—even China's—are more keyed to shaping regional structures. A collapse or sudden retreat of U.S. power would most likely result in an extended period of global anarchy.

## ALTERNATIVE WORLDS

The present recalls past transition points—such as 1815, 1919, 1945, and 1989—when the path forward was not clear-cut and the world faced the possibility of different global futures. We have more than enough information to suggest that however rapid change has been over the past couple decades, the rate of change will accelerate in the future. Accordingly, we have created four scenarios that represent distinct pathways for the world out to 2030: *Stalled Engines, Fusion, Gini Out-of-the-Bottle, and Nonstate World*. As in previous volumes, we have fictionalized the scenario narratives to encourage all of us to think more creatively about the future. We have intentionally built in discontinuities, which will have a huge impact in inflecting otherwise straight linear projections of known trends. We hope that a better understanding of the dynamics, potential inflection points, and possible surprises will better equip decision makers to avoid the traps and enhance possible opportunities for positive developments.

## Stalled Engines

*Stalled Engines*—a scenario in which the risk of interstate conflict rises owing to a new "great game" in Asia—was chosen as one of the book-ends, illustrating the most plausible "worst case." Arguably, darker scenarios are imaginable, including a complete breakdown and reversal of globalization due potentially to a large-scale conflict on the order of a World War I or World War II, but such outcomes do not seem probable. Major powers might be drawn into conflict, but we do not see any such tensions or bilateral conflict igniting a full-scale conflagration. More likely, peripheral powers would step in to try to stop a conflict. Indeed, as we have stressed, major powers are conscious of the likely economic and political damage to engaging in any major conflict. Moreover, unlike in the interwar period, completely undoing economic interdependence or globalization would seem to be harder in this more advanced technological age with ubiquitous connections.

*Stalled Engines* is nevertheless a bleak future. Drivers behind such an outcome would be a United States and Europe that turn inward, no longer interested in sustaining their global leadership. Under this scenario, the euro zone unravels quickly, causing Europe to be mired in recession. The U.S. energy revolution fails to materialize, dimming prospects for an economic recovery. In the modeling which McKinsey Company did for us for this scenario, global economic growth falters and all players do relatively poorly.

## Fusion

*Fusion* is the other book-end, describing what we see as the most plausible "best case." This is a world in which the specter of a spreading conflict in South Asia triggers efforts by the United States, Europe, and China to intervene and impose a ceasefire. China, the United States, and Europe find other issues to collaborate on, leading to a major positive change in their bilateral relations, and more broadly leading to worldwide cooperation to deal with global challenges. This scenario relies on political leadership, with each side overruling its more cautious domestic constituencies to forge a partnership. Over time, trust is also built up as China begins a process of political reform, bolstered by the increasing role it is playing in the international system. With the growing collaboration among the major powers, global multilateral institutions are reformed and made more inclusive.

In this scenario, all boats rise substantially. Emerging economies continue to grow faster, but GDP growth in advanced economies also picks up. The global economy nearly doubles in real terms by 2030 to $132 trillion in today's dollars. The American Dream returns with per capita incomes rising $10,000 in ten years. Chinese per capita income also expands rapidly, ensuring that China avoids the middle-income trap. Technological innovation—rooted in expanded exchanges and joint international efforts—is critical to the world staying ahead of the rising financial and resource constraints that would accompany a rapid boost in prosperity.

## Gini Out-of-the-Bottle*

This is a world of extremes. Within many countries, inequalities dominate—leading to increasing political and social tensions. Between countries, there are clear-cut winners and losers. For example, countries in the euro zone core which are globally competitive do well, while others on the periphery are forced to leave the EU. The EU single market barely functions. The United States remains the preeminent power as it gains energy independence. Without completely disengaging, the United States no longer tries to play "global policeman" on every security threat. Many of the energy producers suffer from declining energy prices, failing to diversify their economies in time, and are threatened by internal conflicts. Cities in China's coastal zone continue to thrive, but inequalities increase and split the Party. Social discontent spikes as middle-class expectations are not met except for the very "well-connected." The central government in Beijing, which has a difficult time governing, falls back on stirring nationalistic fervor.

In this scenario, economic performance in emerging and advanced economies leads to non-stellar global growth, far below that in our *Fusion* scenario, but not as bad as in *Stalled Engines*. The lack of societal cohesion domestically is mirrored at the international level. Major powers are at odds; the potential for conflicts rises. More countries fail, fueled in part by the dearth of international cooperation on assistance and development. In sum, the world is reasonably wealthy, but it is less secure as the dark side of globalization poses an increasing challenge in domestic and international politics.

## Nonstate World

In this world, nonstate actors—nongovernmental organizations (NGOs), multinational businesses, academic institutions, and wealthy individuals—as well

---

*The "Gini" in this scenario title refers to the *Gini Coefficient*, which is a recognized statistical measurement of inequality of income.

as subnational units (megacities, for example), flourish and take the lead in confronting global challenges. An increasing global public opinion consensus among elites and many of the growing middle classes on major global challenges—poverty, the environment, anti-corruption, rule-of-law, and peace—form the base of their support. The nation-state does not disappear, but countries increasingly organize and orchestrate "hybrid" coalitions of state and nonstate actors which shift depending on the issue.

Authoritarian regimes find it hardest to operate in this world, preoccupied with asserting political primacy at home and respect in an increasingly "fully democratized" world. Even democratic countries, which are wedded to the notion of sovereignty and independence, find it difficult to operate successfully in this complex and diverse world. Smaller, more agile countries in which elites are also more integrated are apt to do better than larger countries that lack social or political cohesion. Formal governance institutions that do not adapt to the more diverse and widespread distribution of power are also less likely to be successful. Multinational businesses, IT communications firms, international scientists, NGOs, and others that are used to cooperating across borders and as part of networks thrive in this hyper-globalized world where expertise, influence, and agility count for more than "weight" or "position."

This is nevertheless a "patchwork" and very uneven world. Some global problems get solved because networks manage to coalesce, and some cooperation occurs across state and nonstate divides. In other cases, nonstate actors might try to deal with a challenge, but they are stymied because of opposition from major powers. Security threats pose an increasing challenge: access to lethal and disruptive technologies expands, enabling individuals and small groups to perpetuate violence and disruption on a large scale. Economically, global growth does slightly better than in the *Gini Out-of-the-Bottle* scenario because more cooperation occurs on major global challenges in this world. The world is also more stable and socially cohesive.

---

# CRITICAL THINKING QUESTIONS

1. Do you agree with the NIC's assessment of best and worst case scenarios?
2. Which should be of greater concern to the United States: underlying trends or game-changers?
3. This document is produced every four years. What needs to be changed in thinking about the next Global Trends report?

# 25

# More Small Wars

## COUNTERINSURGENCY IS HERE TO STAY

Max Boot

Although the wars in Afghanistan and Iraq are far from the costliest the United States has ever fought in terms of either blood or treasure, they have exacted a much greater toll than the relatively bloodless wars Americans had gotten used to fighting in the 1990s. As of this writing, 2,344 U.S. troops have been killed in Afghanistan and 4,486 in Iraq, and tens of thousands more have been injured. The financial costs reach into the trillions of dollars.

Yet despite this investment, the returns look meager. Sunni extremists from the Islamic State of Iraq and al-Sham (ISIS), also known as the Islamic State, and Shiite extremists beholden to Iran have divided the non-Kurdish parts of Iraq between them. Meanwhile, the Taliban and the Haqqani network remain on the offensive in Afghanistan. Given how poorly things have turned out, it would be tempting to conclude that the United States should simply swear off such irregular conflicts for good.

If only a nation as powerful and vulnerable as the United States had the option of defining exactly which types of wars it wages. Reality, alas, seldom cooperates. Over the centuries, U.S. presidents of all political persuasions have found it necessary to send troops to fight adversaries ranging from the Barbary pirates to Filipino *insurrectos* to Haitian *cacos* to Vietnamese communists to Somali warlords to Serbian death squads to Taliban guerrillas to al Qaeda terrorists. Unlike traditional armies, these enemies seldom met U.S. forces in the open, which meant that they could not be defeated quickly. To beat such shadowy foes, American troops had to undertake the time-intensive, difficult work of what's now known as counterinsurgency, counterterrorism, and nation building.

There is little reason to think the future will prove any different, since conflict within states continues to break out far more frequently than conflict

Max Boot is Jeane J. Kirkpatrick Senior Fellow for National Security Studies at the Council on Foreign Relations and the author of *Invisible Armies: An Epic History of Guerrilla Warfare from Ancient Times to the Present*. Reprinted by permission of *Foreign Affairs* 93, no. 6 (November/December 2014). Copyright © 2014 by the Council on Foreign Relations, Inc., www.ForeignAffairs.com.

among states. Although the world has not seen a purely conventional war since the Russian invasion of Georgia in 2008, more than 30 countries—including Colombia, Iraq, Israel, Mexico, Nigeria, Pakistan, Somalia, and Ukraine, to name a few—now find themselves fighting foes that rely on guerrilla or terrorist tactics. One such conflict, the civil war in Syria, has killed over 170,000 people since 2011. Given how many of these conflicts involve U.S. allies or interests, it is wishful thinking to imagine that Washington can stay aloof. Indeed, President Barack Obama himself, who campaigned against the war in Iraq, has been compelled to fight again there because of the threat from ISIS.

Even if the United States does not send substantial numbers of ground troops to another war anytime soon, it will surely remain involved in helping its allies fight conflicts similar to those in Afghanistan and Iraq, and as has become clear in recent months, it will stay involved in Afghanistan and Iraq, too. Since Washington doesn't have the luxury of simply avoiding insurgencies, then, the best strategy would be to fight them better. Drawn from more than a decade of war, here are ten lessons for how to do so, which U.S. policymakers, soldiers, diplomats, and spies should keep in mind as they try to deal with the chaotic conflicts to come.

## THE BEST-LAID PLANS

The first lesson may sound like a no-brainer, but it has been routinely ignored: plan for what comes after the overthrow of a regime. In Afghanistan and Iraq, the George W. Bush administration failed to adequately prepare for what the military calls "Phase N," the period after immediate victory—an oversight that allowed law and order to break down in both countries and insurgencies to metastasize. Yet Obama, despite his criticism of Bush's conduct of the Iraq war, repeated the same mistake in Libya. In 2011, U.S. and NATO forces helped rebels topple Muammar al-Qaddafi but then did very little to help the nascent Libyan government establish control of its own territory. As a result, Libya remains riven by militias, which have plunged the country into chaos. Just this past July—almost two years after U.S. Ambassador Christopher Stevens was killed in Benghazi—the State Department had to evacuate its entire embassy staff from Tripoli after fighting there reached the airport.

This is not a problem confined to Bush or Obama. The United States has a long tradition of bungling the conclusions to wars, focusing on narrow military objectives while ignoring the political end state that troops are supposed to be fighting for. This inattention made possible the persecution of freed slaves and their white champions in the South after the American Civil War, the eruption of the Philippine insurrection after the Spanish-American War, the rise of the Nazis in Germany and the Communists in Russia after World War I, the invasions of South Korea and South Vietnam after World War II, and the impetus for the Iraq war after the Gulf War. Too often, U.S. officials have assumed that all the United States has to do is get rid of the bad guys and the postwar peace will take care of itself. But it simply isn't so. Generating order out of chaos is one of the hardest tasks any country can attempt, and it requires considerable preparation of the kind that the U.S. military undertook for the occupation of Germany and Japan after 1945—but seldom did before and has seldom done since.

# THINK AGAIN

An equally important lesson is to challenge rosy assumptions during the course of a conflict. Following the overthrow of Saddam Hussein, the Bush administration opted for the smallest possible footprint in Iraq. The faster U.S. forces pulled out and the more elections Iraqis held, they reasoned, the more likely Iraqis would be to take responsibility for their own problems. This strategy was plausible—and wrong. By the end of 2005, at the latest, Bush; his secretary of defense, Donald Rumsfeld; and the commander of coalition forces in Iraq, General George Casey, should have known that their strategy was failing. Yet Bush did not reevaluate it until the end of 2006, at the 11th hour, when defeat was imminent. Rumsfeld and Casey never seemed to reevaluate it at all.

The same pathology afflicted U.S. division, brigade, and battalion commanders, who always seemed convinced that they were making progress in their areas of operations. On regular visits to Iraq from 2003 on, I never heard someone giving a brief say the situation was getting worse; commanders invariably painted a picture of challenges that were being overcome. (The usual subtext: "The previous unit in this area really screwed things up, but we've got it headed in the right direction.") It's not as if alternative assessments were hard to come by: all you had to do was pick up the *New York Times* or the *Washington Post* to find out that Iraq was degenerating into civil war. Many lower-level soldiers even admitted as much privately. But those higher up in the chain of command dismissed bad news as mere data points that failed to capture the hidden progress Iraq was supposedly making.

The Bush administration's political commitment to the Iraq war was partly to blame, since it blinded decision makers to evidence that their initiatives were failing. Likewise, generals developed an emotional attachment to the strategies they implemented. The Pentagon's can-do culture also got in the way. The U.S. military's greatest virtues—its commitment to following orders, its unwillingness to accept excuses for failure, its insistence on achieving objectives no matter the obstacles—are also its greatest vulnerabilities. They can make it hard for junior soldiers to tell their superiors uncomfortable truths (or even to think such dangerous thoughts).

The success of the "surge" in Iraq started with the willingness of General David Petraeus, who was named commander of coalition forces in Iraq in early 2007, to acknowledge that the war was in danger of being lost. With an additional 30,000 troops, he put in place a new, and ultimately more successful, strategy that focused on protecting the population. To get an accurate picture of events on the ground, Petraeus bypassed the chain of command and sought information directly from junior soldiers and civilian experts, including report-ers and think tankers. The military needs to institutionalize a similar culture of second-guessing (or "red teaming") and regularly seek outside information in order to escape the tyranny of yes men in the chain of command.

## STRATEGIC STAFFING

The United States also needs to cultivate better strategic thinkers in both the military and the civilian spheres. The country's best and brightest made mis-takes in Afghanistan and Iraq that were just as monumental as the ones famously made by their predecessors in Vietnam. A decade of war exposed the flaws of experienced, highly credentialed civilians, such as Vice President Dick Cheney, Rumsfeld, Paul Bremer (the head of the Coalition Provisional Author-ity in Iraq), and Richard Holbrooke (the special envoy to Afghanistan and Pakistan); of equally experienced and equally credentialed military officers, such as Casey, Tommy Franks, Ricardo Sanchez, John Abizaid, and David McKiernan; and of a few officers turned senior civilians, such as Karl Eiken-berry (the U.S. ambassador to Afghanistan).

Petraeus and Ryan Crocker, the U.S. ambassador to Iraq who led the civil-ian side of the surge in 2007–2008, represent two of the very few senior offi-cials to emerge from the wars with their reputations improved. That's because they exhibited a rare quality in the U.S. military: strategic acumen. Not even General Stanley McChrystal, who achieved legendary status for his success in running the Joint Special Operations Command, was able to make the transi-tion to a theater-level commander in Afghanistan; he was forced to resign in 2010 after his staff made impolitic comments to a *Rolling Stone* reporter.

It's no coincidence that Petraeus and Crocker also had unusual back-grounds. Unlike most generals, Petraeus did not attend a war college for mid-career studies; he got a Ph.D. in international relations from Princeton instead. Crocker, too, did graduate studies at Princeton. He also spent time as a truck driver, a construction worker, a bartender, a cabby, and a waiter, and he once hitchhiked from Amsterdam to Calcutta. "It nearly killed me but gave me a view of the region that no diplomat will ever get," he told me. Obviously, the Pentagon cannot mandate that all its future leaders spend time driving taxis, attend Ivy League schools, or travel across Eurasia. But it should encourage up-and-comers to pursue diverse experiences rather than follow a well-trodden path. And it should abandon its practice of promoting officers on the basis of their operational excellence alone and also consider their strategic intelligence.

## TRAINING DAY

Another lesson the Pentagon should take to heart is the importance of training for more than just short conventional operations. The U.S. government ran into trouble in Afghanistan and Iraq in large part because it simply was not set up to do nation building and counterinsurgency. When it became clear after

Saddam's downfall in April 2003 that Iraq wouldn't automatically govern itself, the job was given first to the Office of Reconstruction and Humanitarian Assistance and then to the Coalition Provisional Authority—both ludicrously ill prepared for the monumental challenges they faced. Whereas military units train for years to take down regimes like Saddam's, their civilian counterparts had at most a few weeks to prepare for the much more difficult task of governing a foreign land.

The situation wasn't much better in Afghanistan. Although a provisional government formed within just weeks after the Taliban's downfall, it enjoyed tenuous authority. President Hamid Karzai was in practice little more than the mayor of Kabul, yet the Bush administration and the U.S. military did not consider it their job to extend his authority. The result was a power vacuum, which was filled by corrupt warlords and a resurgent Taliban. In both Afghanistan and Iraq, the U.S. military's narrow focus on hunting down insurgents, rather than denying them a raison d'etre, engendered more support for them because it resulted in the imprisonment or death of so many innocent individuals.

Through trial and error, the U.S. military learned to wage counterinsurgency and build functional states rather than simply conduct firepowerintensive operations. Yet there is a real danger it could lose that expertise as it lays off veterans due to budget cuts and returns to its real passion: preparing for conventional wars that never quite arrive. It is not comforting to learn, for example, that in October, the army shuttered the Army Irregular Warfare Center at Fort Leavenworth, Kansas, which was set up in 2006 to reintroduce counterinsurgency into military thinking. Counterinsurgency needs to remain part of the military curriculum, and the Pentagon needs to issue a manual and inaugurate a school dedicated to governance. (A new institute devoted to the subject is just now being developed at the U.S. Army John F. Kennedy Special Warfare Center and School, at Fort Bragg, North Carolina; a full-fledged school should have opened long ago.)

The civilian side is in even worse shape. For all the talk of a "civilian surge" in Afghanistan and Iraq, the State Department and other government agencies could never provide enough skilled personnel in such areas as governance and economic development to complement the military's efforts; soldiers wound up filling many of the jobs. The problem is that no agency within the U.S. government views nation building as its assignment. The closest any comes is the U.S. Agency for International Development, but it has a nebulous mission and scant resources of its own. It is high time to revamp USAID, making it into an organization focused not on development for its own sake but on state building in countries of strategic concern, from Mali to Pakistan. As part of this shift, USAID should hire some of the soldiers the U.S. Army and the Marine Corps are laying off who have considerable expertise in nation building.

## SPEAKING IN TONGUES

Preparing for nation building also requires the U.S. government to boost its cultural and linguistic skills. The biggest vulnerability for U.S. forces in

Afghanistan and Iraq was their lack of local knowledge, a problem made clear by an experience I had in an area southwest of Baghdad in August 2003. I was traveling with a group of marines when an improvised explosive device blew up near our convoy. While the marines searched for the culprit, an Iraqi man approached us and tried to tell us something, but he spoke no English and we spoke no Arabic. The military partially rectified this problem by hiring many interpreters and so-called cultural advisers, who could communicate with the people of Afghanistan and Iraq.

But those countries represent only two battlefields of many in the broader struggle against Islamist extremism. Today, the U.S. government is as deficient in cultural and linguistic knowledge about Iran, Libya, Mali, Nigeria, Pakistan, and Syria as it once was about Afghanistan and Iraq. The United States simply doesn't have many soldiers, diplomats, or intelligence officers who are fluent in such languages as Arabic, Farsi, Pashto, and Urdu, to say nothing of the local dialects spoken throughout much of Africa and South Asia. And it's not just a question of knowing foreign languages; even more important in many ways is a country's power structures, customs, and mindsets.

The U.S. Army's decision in 2012 to create regionally aligned brigades, each one focused on a particular part of the world, counts as a small step in the right direction, but it's doubtful that most troops will have much time or energy to devote to cultural and language studies, given the countless other tasks they must perform. To make matters worse, the army's policy of nonstop rotations means that soldiers rarely stay in one unit or one region long enough to acquire true expertise.

The military does already have a corps of foreign area officers, who have regional expertise, but they rarely secure important command assignments. The Pentagon needs to mainstream these officers by giving them more credit for their expertise in the promotion and assignment process, and it should permit some of them to stay in hot spots for years, even decades, giving them a chance to gain knowledge and influence. Some of these volunteers should be foreign-born; the Pentagon needs to expand its Military Accessions Vital to the National Interest, or MAVNI, program, which allows immigrants who don't have green cards but do have needed skills to enlist. This initiative has brought in highly qualified soldiers, including Sergeant Saral Shrestha, a Nepalese immigrant whom the army named Soldier of the Year in 2012. But with just 1,500 slots a year (many of which are reserved for technical positions), MAVNI is far too small. The Pentagon should also create an organization dedicated to advising foreign counterparts—arguably the most important mission in the years ahead, but one that today often gets relegated to the lowest-rated officers who have been pulled out of regular combat formations.

## THE RIFLEMAN ON THE CORNER

When facing future counterinsurgencies, the U.S. military also needs to learn that it cannot rely too much on high-tech firepower and special operations forces. Afghanistan and Iraq laid bare the shortcomings of precision bombing, drone strikes, and commando raids. In Iraq, all these capabilities proved important, but none was sufficient to turn the tide; the situation didn't begin to improve until the U.S. military adopted a population-centric strategy in 2007. The same was true in Afghanistan, where it did not implement a counterinsurgency strategy until 2010. Before then, special operations raids had no lasting impact; new insurgents quickly replaced those captured or killed. Only after U.S. and Afghan forces entered the provinces of Helmand and Kandahar in massive numbers could they secure districts the Taliban had long controlled.

When it comes to enforcing regime change, there is still no replacement for a rifleman on a street corner. Drone strikes and raids can eliminate terrorist leaders, but they cannot uproot entire terrorist organizations. That requires controlling enough terrain to prevent insurgent organizations from regenerating themselves in the way that al Qaeda, Hamas, Hezbollah, ISIS, and the Pakistani Taliban, among others, have after the loss of their leaders.

Yet the U.S. government is once again cutting ground forces and becoming overly reliant on drone strikes and special operations forces. In essence, policymakers are repeating the mistake Rumsfeld made before 9/11, when he openly contemplated cutting two divisions from the army—only now, they are slashing even more combat power. Congress needs to reverse the destructive decline in the number of active-duty soldiers, which, if the most drastic budget cuts take effect, could fall from a peak of 570,000 in 2011 to as few as 420,000 over the next decade.

In the past decade, even 570,000 troops proved insufficient for coping with two limited conflicts against relatively primitive foes who lacked the high-tech weapons that future adversaries will likely wield. Were the number to drop to 420,000, the army would have trouble fighting even one ground war, given that less than one-third of all troops can be sent to battle at any given time (most of the others are either recovering from deployment or preparing for it). Fighting two wars at a time—once the gold standard of U.S. military strategy—would be utterly impossible. Those who think the United States will never fight another ground war should remember that many people thought the same after World War I—and then after World War II, the Korean War, the Vietnam War, and the Gulf War.

## BASING INSTINCT

The next lesson may seem to get into the weeds but in fact has high-level ramifications: don't let logistics drive strategy. The U.S. military created a massive logistical footprint in Afghanistan and Iraq, erecting a series of heavily fortified Little Americas that offered troops everything from ice cream to large-screen TVs. These compounds proved staggeringly expensive to resupply. In the summer of 2006, when both conflicts were going strong, U.S. Central Command had more than 3,000 trucks delivering supplies and another 2,400 delivering fuel to its bases, and these convoys had to be protected by either troops or contractors. The military thus became what soldiers sometimes called a "self-licking ice cream cone"—an organization that fought to sustain itself rather than to achieve a mission.

It is doubtful that senior commanders ever gave much thought to these logistical requirements; they more or less operated on autopilot. Each base commander would bring in a few more amenities to make life better for the troops, a commendable impulse. But in the process, commanders not only created supply-line vulnerabilities but also cut off troops from the populace, neglecting an essential part of any successful counterinsurgency campaign. In the future, the Pentagon should resist the temptation to build up huge bases unless doing so accomplishes the objectives of the war.

## MANAGING MERCENARIES

Another specific yet vital lesson is that the U.S. government needs to exercise greater authority over contractors on the battlefield. After its post–Cold War downsizing, the military lacked enough troops to control both Afghanistan and Iraq. So the Pentagon relied heavily on contractors for everything from doing laundry at bases to protecting convoys. Although most were not armed, a significant minority were (16 percent of those in Afghanistan at the end of 2013), and they generated numerous complaints about their alleged abuses. Driving armored black SUVs, contractors frequently careened through towns in Afghanistan and Iraq, forcing civilian cars· off the road and sometimes shooting at vehicles that got too close. The most notorious offender was Blackwater, whose employees killed 17 people in Baghdad's Nisour Square in 2007.

Although security contractors usually got the job done, sometimes heroically, the way their job was defined was itself a problem. The U.S. government hired them to move goods or people from Point A to Point B, no matter the consequences. Unlike troops, who were told to win hearts and minds, contractors had virtual carte blanche to achieve their narrow objectives. They were effectively exempt from prosecution under the Uniform Code of Military Justice and even from lesser forms of discipline.

The inevitable result of setting loose all these armed, aggressive men was a series of abuses that harmed U.S. relations with the locals. Both Karzai and Iraqi Prime Minister Nouri al-Maliki grew exercised about the contractors' behavior over time and threatened to kick them out. Congress reacted in 2004 by amending U.S. law to allow the prosecution of U.S. contractors by U.S. courts. So far, however, only 12 people have been charged under these statutes, including six Blackwater guards implicated in the Nisour Square shooting. One pled guilty, another had the charges against him dropped, and the remaining four went on trial in federal court in Washington, D.C., in the summer of 2014—a scandalous six years after their indictment.

Continued downsizing will mean that the military won't be able to stop relying on contractors in future conflicts. But it can control them better. One possible model is the way that U.S. commanders exercise authority over foreign troops. Just as the troops from contributing nations plug into a U.S.-led command structure, contractors could, too. In the future, the U.S. government should write its contracts differently. Security firms working for any branch of the U.S. government, including the State Department and USAID, and operating on a battlefield where the U.S. military is present should fall under the operational control of a senior U.S. military officer who has the power to revoke their contracts and prosecute their employees in case of misdeeds.

## PLAYING NICE TOGETHER

Another lesson involves what the military calls "interoperability," the ability of various components to work together smoothly. One of the U.S. government's biggest successes in Afghanistan and Iraq was the improvements it made in getting U.S. forces to cooperate with foreign forces and getting different types of U.S. forces to cooperate with one another.

In particular, special operations and regular forces learned to work hand in hand after years of mutual resentment. During the Gulf War, General Norman Schwarzkopf looked at special operations forces with so much suspicion that he tried to keep them off the battlefield altogether. In the early years of Afghanistan and Iraq, many conventional commanders also complained about special operations forces entering their areas without permission and undertaking operations (such as a raid on an influential sheik) without considering how such actions might destroy carefully nurtured relationships.

Those problems never entirely went away, but by 2007, special operations forces (in particular, the elite members of the Joint Special Operations Command) came to occupy a central place in U.S. strategy in Afghanistan and Iraq, and their dealings with regular troops became far more harmonious. Relations between U.S. forces and allied ones also improved, even if Australia, Canada, and the United Kingdom continued to complain about Washington's proclivity to deny them the most sensitive intelligence—yet another area where there is room for improvement.

Some U.S. military commanders developed close relationships with their civilian advisers, but just as often, the relationships were antagonistic and dysfunctional. In the future, the conventional military and its civilian, foreign, and special operations counterparts must train together, which should help smooth their relations in the field.

## THE LONG HAUL

Finally, Washington must recognize that counterinsurgency and nation building take time. In Iraq, the United States had all but won by 2011, when U.S. troops had to leave because Obama failed to negotiate a new status-of-forces agreement, in part because he never made it a priority. Now, ISIS has gained control of a chunk of Syria and Iraq larger than the United Kingdom and declared a caliphate, and violence in Iraq has shot back to its 2008 level. A similar disaster could occur in Afghanistan if the United States pulls out completely in 2016, as Obama has pledged. In any given conflict, Washington needs to make a long-term commitment, as in Kosovo, where U.S. troops have been deployed since 1999. Otherwise, it shouldn't bother to get involved in the first place.

Skeptics argue that a fickle American public will never support long-term deployments of U.S. soldiers, and so serious counterinsurgency campaigns are a nonstarter. In fact, Americans have shown impressive patience with the wars in Afghanistan and Iraq, which explains why the United States has remained involved in those conflicts far longer than anyone initially imagined possible. The public may not be enthusiastic about these campaigns, but neither has the country seen protests of the scale it did during the Vietnam War.

The only time when either of the two recent wars became a major political issue was in 2006 and 2007, when U.S. fatalities in Iraq reached over 100 a month and the war looked lost. The one thing that the U.S. public won't tolerate is making sacrifices for a losing cause. But after the success of the surge, public opposition waned. Had Obama struck a status-of-forces agreement with Iraq in 2011, he would have faced no serious political obstacle to keeping thousands of troops there. Likewise, no political obstacle prevents him from keeping thousands of troops in Afghanistan past 2014, or even past 2016.

Some of these recommendations call for little more than new policies; others entail major changes in the institutional culture of the military and the broader U.S. government. None will be easy to implement; there will be fierce opposition on Capitol Hill to boosting defense spending or creating a nation-building agency, for example, and fierce opposition in the Pentagon to revising the military's personnel system or emphasizing culture and language as much as traditional war-fighting skills. And even if policymakers take all these lessons to heart, they can hardly guarantee success in undertakings as grueling and complicated as counterinsurgency and nation building. But refusing to heed these lessons practically guarantees that the United States' future wars will, at best, succeed at a much higher cost than necessary—and, at worse, fail outright.

## CRITICAL THINKING QUESTIONS

1. Will there be more small wars in the future? Why or why not?
2. Which of the ten lessons is the most important lesson to remember?
3. Which of the ten lessons is the least persuasive?

# 26

# Delivering Development after 2015

Molly Elgin-Cossart

World leaders are set to meet in September 2015 to agree on a set of goals to replace the Millennium Development Goals, which will expire in 2015. People from all over the world have been engaged in opining, discussing, debating, and even voting on what those new goals should be.

While significant attention is being paid to the vision of the post-2015 agenda, less attention has focused on the details of how to achieve this vision by 2030, the assumed deadline for the next set of goals.

Fortunately, the conversation is now turning from the "what" to the "how" with the recent announcement of the Third International Conference on Financing for Development, or FFD, conference to take place in July 2015 in Addis Ababa, just ahead of the September 2015 U.N. summit to adopt the post-2015 framework.

The Addis conference will focus on channeling the resources and tools necessary to achieve the new set of development goals. The proposed goals submitted to the U.N. General Assembly cover a broad range of issues, from economic growth to social issues to global public goods. The post-2015 agenda will be much more ambitious than the MDGs. To have any chance of realizing this vision, a just-as-ambitious plan for financing and implementation is needed.

## DEFINITIONS

Advanced market commitment, or AMC: A legally binding agreement for an amount of funds to subsidize the purchase, at a given price, of an as-yet-unavailable vaccine against a specific disease that causes high morbidity and mortality in developing countries. AMCs incentivize pharmaceutical companies to develop innovative vaccines.

Molly Elgin-Cossart is a senior fellow with the National Security and International Policy team at the Center for American Progress. This brief includes substantial contributions from Annie Malknecht, Pete Ogden, and Varad Pande. This piece was originally published by the Center for American Progress in August 2014. Reprinted with permission from the Center for American Progress.

**Bilateral export credits:** Export credits are government financial supports that facilitate the sale of national goods abroad through loans, risk guarantees, and insurance.

**Concessional flows:** Loans extended on terms that are more generous than market loans. The concessionality is achieved either through interest rates below those available on the market, grace periods, or a combination of these. Concessional loans typically have long grace periods.

**Foreign direct investment, or FDI:** The category of international investment that reflects the objective of a resident entity in one economy to obtain a lasting interest in an enterprise resident in another economy.

**Official development assistance, or ODA:** Government aid designed to promote the economic development and welfare of developing countries, but does not include loans and credits for military purposes. Aid may be transferred bilaterally, from government to government, or through multilateral institutions such as the World Bank or United Nations.

**Other official flows, or OOF:** Transactions by the official sector with countries on the list of aid recipients that do not meet the conditions for eligibility as ODA, either because they are not primarily aimed at development, or because they have a grant element of less than 25 percent.

The MDGs' financing and implementation policies were not agreed upon until the 2002 Monterrey Consensus of the International Conference on Financing for Development—two years after the Millennium Declaration, which set out commitments for poverty eradication, development, and the environment, was signed. Holding the financing conversation earlier in the process is a welcome development, one proposed by the High Level Panel on Post-2015—on which CAP founder and former Chair John Podesta served—which called for a conference "in the first half of 2015 to address in practical terms how to finance the post-2015 agenda."

The timing does, however, raise the stakes: The FFD conference will be the first of four major multilateral meetings in 2015, followed by the September Heads of State and Government Summit to agree to the next development agenda; the December U.N. Framework Convention on Climate Change, or UNFCCC, Conference of Parties meeting in Paris to agree to a climate treaty; and the December ministerial-level meeting of the World Trade Organization. Though these are separate processes, they are substantively interlinked. With FFD occurring first in this sequence, there will be significant pressure for a successful agreement to lay the foundation for agreements in the other major multilateral venues.

In addition to the timing, the content of the discussion will be more challenging than that at Monterrey. Monterrey embodied an implicit bargain between donors and developing countries, though middle-income countries' interests received relatively less attention. It solidified support for more official development assistance, or ODA, from donor countries—reversing a decade of decline in aid flows—in return for developing countries committing to social reforms in key goal areas, such as poverty, health, and education. A 2008 follow-up conference in Doha, Qatar, reiterated this commitment, even in the midst of the financial crisis.

Such a bargain will not work this time around. Seismic economic shifts have overturned the development landscape: Some of the world's largest economies are home to the largest numbers of people living in extreme poverty, while traditional donor countries are struggling with slow growth and sluggish economies. And the next development agenda is likely to be universal, meaning that the goals will be relevant for all countries, not just low-income countries. The political deal that needs to be struck in Addis is more difficult than previous financing agreements, with many competing demands and a swiftly changing economic context.

This issue brief provides an outline of the process, politics, and policies of financing sustainable development.

## THE ROAD TO ADDIS

The government of Ethiopia, as the host country, will play a pivotal role in shaping the Addis conference and its outcome, though the precise nature of that role—and Ethiopia's role in the process leading up to the conference—remain unclear. In many ways, Ethiopia is ideally suited to host a conference on financing inclusive and sustainable development, with enormous gross domestic product, or GDP, growth; one of Africa's largest social protection programs; and a Climate-Resilient Green Economy Strategy to achieve carbon-neutral middle-income country status by 2025.

The Intergovernmental Committee of Experts on Sustainable Development Financing has issued its report, which establishes the empirical foundation for the conference's outcome document and outlines policy options that could be developed into the financing deal that will underpin the post-2015 agenda. Nongovernmental organizations and other groups, such as the World Economic Forum, have issued reports on financing and the post-2015 agenda that will also provide useful background.

The outcome document for the Addis conference will be negotiated in advance, with U.N. diplomats discussing and drafting throughout the winter of 2014 and early spring of 2015 and producing a first draft in February 2015 that will serve as the reference point for negotiations at the conference itself.

Consultations—60 of which have been proposed—will generate additional input on the conference outcome document, with meetings beginning this fall and continuing through January 2015. The Norwegian and Guyanese U.N. ambassadors will facilitate the process and preparations for the conference and aim to balance the interests of developed and developing countries.

The conference itself will be attended by heads of state and ministers of finance, foreign affairs, development, and trade, who will negotiate any changes to the outcome document and then adopt it as the major reference point for international development cooperation going forward.

Conference participation is open to all U.N. member states, specialized agencies, and observers in the U.N. General Assembly. Following the models for openness and participation used in previous international conferences, civil society groups, business actors, and organizations are also invited to attend and to facilitate their own multistakeholder events in both New York and Addis around the summit. The involvement of nongovernmental actors can bolster the ambition of the final outcome and provide a platform to launch of external initiatives that complement and strengthen the intergovernmental agreement.

Although the greater part of the FFD negotiations will take place in New York leading up to the Addis conference, a wider audience—especially national governments—need to be meaningfully engaged for the conference to be a success. Expect to see discussions about post-2015 financing at both the fall and spring annual meetings of the World Bank and the International Monetary Fund, or IMF; the World Economic Forum meeting in Davos next January; side meetings at the G-20 meeting in Brisbane; and at the G-7 meeting in June 2015. The BRICS countries—Brazil, Russia, India, China, and South Africa—already referenced the process in the Fortaleza Declaration, which announced the New Development Bank and could play an important role in development financing needs. There will also be a high-level Organisation for Economic Co-operation and Development, or OECD, development finance meeting in December 2014 that will focus on ODA.

## TIMELINE FOR THE FINANCING FOR DEVELOPMENT PROCESS

- **September 16, 2014:** Opening of the 69th session of the U.N. General Assembly.
- **October 10–12, 2014:** Annual World Bank and International Monetary Fund meetings, Washington, D.C.
- **November 15–16, 2014:** G-20 Leaders Summit, Brisbane, Australia.
- **November 30, 2014:** U.N. secretary-general's synthesis report on the post-2015 development agenda presented to the U.N. General Assembly.
- **December 15–16, 2014:** Organisation for Economic Co-operation and Development DAC High-Level Meeting, Paris, France.
- **January 21–24, 2015:** World Economic Forum, Davos, Switzerland.
- **April 17–19, 2015:** 2015 spring meetings of the World Bank and International Monetary Fund, Washington, D.C.
- **June 4–5, 2015:** G-7 Annual Heads of State and Government Meeting, Schloss Elmau, Germany.
- **July 13–16, 2015:** Financing for development meeting, Addis Ababa, Ethiopia.
- **September 15–28, 2015:** 70th session of the U.N. General Assembly, New York, New York.
- **November 30–December 11, 2015:** 21st Conference of the Parties to the U.N. Framework Convention on Climate Change, Paris, France.
- **December 2015:** 10th World Trade Organization Ministerial Conference.

# KEY ISSUES FOR NEGOTIATORS TO ADDRESS

Although the global economy's recovery from the 2008 crisis has been slow, the outlook for global development is not quite as dire as it may seem. Developing countries continue to grow much faster than developed countries; non-ODA sources of financing, such as foreign direct investment, or FDI, continue to grow; and as a result of implementing the MDGs for the past 15 years, there is more knowledge about how to use development resources wisely.

While the Addis conference is referred to as the "financing for development" conference, money is only part of the story. There are many potential sources of development financing and investment, but the strategies, institutions, and policies that help to increase, improve, and channel funds, align incentives, and drive action toward goals that improve the lives of people and protect the natural environment are equally important.

The Monterrey Consensus provides a good start for the FFD financing discussion. It includes fairly comprehensive coverage of the range of financial flows for development, including domestic financial resources, international public financing, and international trade, and addresses systemic issues. It will need to be updated, however, to reflect the needs of the post-2015 agenda—especially the greater focus on global public goods and jointly tackling economic, social, and environmental challenges.

## Improving Domestic Resource Mobilization

Mobilizing domestic resources is the main mechanism for achieving goals at the national level. The good news is that developing countries are growing, and this GDP growth has the potential to generate increased funds for health, education, and other core components of development. But too often, developing countries lack the capacity and systems to collect taxes, reduce tax evasion, and account properly for financing allocations. If growth is to lead to improvements in quality of life, responsible and effective institutions and policies will be required, both domestically and internationally.

Improving domestic resource mobilization has several components that could be discussed in Addis, with actions to be taken by both developed and developing countries. Developed countries can help to get their own houses in order, improving transparency, reducing illicit flows and tax evasion, and ensuring that more revenue stays where it is generated. According to Global Financial Integrity, an estimated $946.7 billion left developing countries in illicit financial outflows during 2011, often ending up in banks in developed countries or tax havens. Initiatives such as the Extractive Industries Transparency Initiative, or EITI, and the Dodd-Frank bill are promising attempts to improve transparency and decrease abuse of transfer pricing and other tax-avoidance tactics, but the effectiveness of such initiatives and legislation is still being tested.

Developing countries have work to do, too. Improving the capacity of domestic tax systems can help stem illicit flows and tax avoidance, and development assistance could play a role in shoring up these capacities. Developing countries collect significantly less in taxes as a percentage of GDP than developed countries do and, as a result, tend to be dependent on a narrow tax base, which has economic and political consequences. While high-income countries collect an average of about 35 percent of their GDP in taxes, half of the countries in sub-Saharan Africa collect less than 17 percent. Ensuring that government spending is focused on concrete benefits for citizens is a final challenge, and such a drive for accountability must be domestically driven. A broader tax base and more targeted subsidies can help achieve this objective and should be part of the policy packages discussed for FFD.

## Improving Development Assistance and Cooperation

Though domestic resource mobilization is the most powerful financing tool for development, traditional development assistance is the most discussed. Monterrey notably called for developed countries to dedicate 0.7 percent of their gross national income, or GNI, toward official development assistance, a call that is likely to be repeated in Addis. Fulfilling this target is a major concern for developing countries, which point out that only six countries have met this target. Although many others call attention to the dwindling role of ODA, especially in rapidly growing developing countries, it would be a mistake to neglect this central component of financing. Especially for low-income and vulnerable countries and those trapped in cycles of violence, it is difficult or impossible to attract other forms of financing. Yet economic growth and the access to good jobs are key to escaping cycles of poverty, violence, and poor governance and overcoming vulnerability to shocks such as natural disasters and the effects of climate change.

The FFD conference is likely to feature discussions of how to better use aid to accomplish development aims. One emerging solution with the potential to play a larger role in the future is the International Aid Transparency Initiative, or IATI. More than 260 organizations have published data to the IATI standard, including governments, multilaterals, nongovernmental organizations, foundations, and private-sector companies, but it remains to be seen how widely this system is adopted and utilized.

Improving the availability, quality, and transparency of information about where foreign assistance money is spent and its impact is a major issue and has hit some political stumbling blocks. The most complete source of information on development assistance is the OECD Development Assistance Committee, or DAC, which tracks not only ODA, but also other official flows using data from the IMF and nations' central banks.

Many question whether the DAC systems will work in the new development landscape. DAC is considered to be a rich country club. Its 29 members are all classified as upper income and are required to meet criteria about their development cooperation strategies, institutions, and policies. Yet, increasingly, development cooperation transcends the traditional divide between developed and developing countries. Many middle-income countries, such as China and Brazil, now both give and receive aid, engaging in cooperation with other developing countries in what is called south-south cooperation. Seventeen non-DAC members report aid transactions to DAC on a voluntary basis but most emerging market economies do not, and it appears unlikely that they will. They consider the DAC to be too Western-driven and want to maintain independence over their development assistance and when and how it is monitored.

The lack of a complete and coherent system to track and monitor, however, makes it difficult to assess how much money is being spent on development and whether it is improving people's lives. Some non-DAC donors are beginning to discuss developing their own system for development cooperation, and this is a good starting point, but much work remains to be done. Creating a clearer picture of the many sources of support available for development, including flows between developing countries, is a necessary part of achieving the ambitious aims of the post-2015 development agenda.

## Unlocking Climate Finance

Perhaps the most difficult question in Addis will be the relationship between climate and development financing. While there is no official number of how much public and private climate finance is currently flowing around the world, the Climate Policy Initiative estimates that public and private climate investments amount to approximately $360 billion per year. The share of public financing provided by developed countries has grown over the past years to between $10 billion and $20 billion annually.

While there is a shared understanding that the current scale of climate finance is insufficient to meet the challenge of climate change and must be increased, developing countries worry that climate financing will compete with development financing or that donors will simply repackage ODA as climate financing. They argue that the two should be kept completely separate to ensure that any climate finance is in fact additional.

In an agenda that integrates economic, social, and environmental issues, however, it is hard to separate climate and poverty challenges on the ground, especially since climate change affects the poor most immediately and severely. Especially in areas such as agriculture and nutrition, water, and energy, climate is inherently linked to development.

It is hard to see how this political impasse can be unlocked, but better and smarter financing will be needed to both tackle poverty and the catastrophic effects of climate change.

## NEW OPPORTUNITIES AND CHALLENGES

Building on Monterrey, the discussion of resources will need to go beyond business as usual to include not only the more efficient and effective use of current financing flows, but also ways to catalyze additional resources and enable creative problem solving to meet the needs of a more ambitious development agenda.

## Private Financing

Private financing flows—FDI, equity, and others—were discussed in Monterrey, but have become a much larger part of financing that flows into developing countries in the years since then. Net FDI flows to developing countries reached $471.6 billion in 2011, while ODA and other official flows totaled only $227 billion. In 2012, private flows to developing countries totaled $222.5 billion, while its official development flows amounted to just $150 billion, and many other OECD DAC countries have greater amounts of private flows than official aid flows.

Private flows are potentially more plentiful and more sustainable than concessional grants, but they do not necessarily reap development benefits. The effectiveness of FDI in financing development objectives depends upon how the flows are catalyzed, leveraged, and channeled. More work needs to be done in this area. Public funding is still necessary—the two are complementary in fulfilling development needs. Private finance flows to areas of expected return, and public finance can fill the gap in areas where risk is too high, the returns are hard to monetize—in public goods, for example—or there are asymmetries of information.

Public financing can also serve as an investment or catalyst, attracting private finance for greater development gains. The Global Environment Facility, or GEF, which funds environmental projects such as building agricultural sustainability and developing renewable groundwater resources in arid lands, has provided $12.5 billion in grants since 1991, attracting an additional $58 billion in project co-financing from the private sector. For every $1 of public financing invested, GEF attracted $5 in additional private financing. Imagine if all development assistance were used to catalyze additional financing on the same scale—hundreds of billions of additional dollars could be made available for vital needs such as nutrition, education, basic shelter, and health care.

While the economics are appealing, the politics of private finance are tricky. Many developing countries are suspicious of private-sector involvement, contending that private financing does not replace the need for public financing. On the other hand, many Western countries encourage the inclusion of private-sector flows but are hesitant to include specific recommendations for businesses, in particular reporting on the social and environmental effects of their activities. As a result, the discussion on private-sector financing is likely to be contentious but is worth pursuing anyway. The reality is that private finance will be part of achieving the post-2015 goals, and ensuring that it is channeled and invested wisely and responsibly is an important topic for FFD. Negotiators should not be afraid to have an open conversation with each other and with the business and finance communities about these topics.

## The Role of Middle-Income Countries

One emerging topic in development financing is the role of middle-income countries, or MICs. Nations with per-capita gross national incomes of more than $1,045 but less than $12,746 are classified as "middle income" by the World Bank, a category that encompasses a wide variety of countries and capabilities, from the BRICS to key regional players such as Turkey and Mexico to populous-but-fragile countries such as Pakistan. Many of the world's wealthiest and most powerful countries have large numbers of people living in extreme poverty. For example, India, a booming economy and information technology hub, is also home to more than one-third of the world's extreme poor.

MICs confront a dual challenge: tackling poverty while also growing their economies inclusively and sustainably. With growing middle classes and rapid urbanization, they need to finance extensive investment in power, water, and other development needs. MICs still need to build most of their infrastructure. For example, India still needs to build 70 percent of the infrastructure it will need by 2030, according to global consultancy McKinsey & Company. MICs have the opportunity to leapfrog to low-carbon, sustainable infrastructure. Investment of this kind requires large amounts of upfront financing, and neither ODA nor domestic resources are sufficient to meet this need.

Nonconcessional loans, bilateral export credits, FDI, commercial debt, technical cooperation, and specific regulations and actions to spur market development hold greater promise in tackling MICs' challenges. A growing focus on infrastructure from the G-20 and the New Development Bank started by the BRICS are initial steps in the right direction. The mechanisms to support MICs' development are weak, and this nascent conversation deserves much more attention in the post-2015 era, especially given its profound implications for global issues such as resource scarcity and climate change.

## Innovative Financing

There is much buzz about innovative financing, an ill-defined term that stretches from advanced market commitments to fund medicines to taxing airline tickets with proceeds directed at development. The current discussion on innovative financing is vague and sometimes controversial and will need to be more closely tied to specific recommendations or specific sectors to gain more traction. Successful models can help to breakthrough such negotiation deadlocks. For example, the Pneumococcal Advanced Market Commitment—with funding from the Canadian, Italian, Norwegian, Russian, and U.K. governments and the Bill and Melinda Gates Foundation—has facilitated the rollout of newly developed pneumococcal vaccines, which are generally available only in wealthier countries, to children in low-income countries. Such tools have the potential to help bring together partners and direct funding toward the achievement of post-2015 goals in areas from health to conserving environmental resources.

# A POLITICAL DEAL?

Although an agreement that takes all of the various sources of development finance into account is crucial, the make-or-break decisions for the post-2015 agenda will come down to highly political topics such as global governance, international trade, technology transfer and intellectual property, migration, and debt relief. Especially for many middle-income countries, these broader issues are more relevant than development financing, which has limited impact for their economies. Additionally, these political issues have a broad consensus among the MICs, compared topics such as south-south cooperation, aid transparency, and their own needs.

If the post-2015 agenda is to live up to its hype as a transformative agenda that moves beyond tackling absolute poverty to put the world on track toward more-inclusive and more-sustainable globalization, these issues are central. At the same time, negotiators will be wary of wading into the waters of other multilateral negotiations, such as those on trade and intellectual property. It remains to be seen how much of a financing deal can be forged at FFD, especially with climate and trade talks yet to come. A good financing deal that offers something to all sides can help build trust, resolve some aspects of these controversial issues, and create space for deals in other areas.

The contours of a political deal are clear—greater influence in the global system for developing countries in return for increased responsibilities. But the details are still muddy. Such a deal is a tall order for a multilateral system that is struggling to make progress on trade, climate, and other areas of international cooperation. And if there is no agreement on development, it is hard to see how progress is possible in other areas. With such high expectations, will the leaders who turn up in Addis rise to the occasion?

---

## CRITICAL THINKING QUESTIONS

1. Which of the major changes that have occurred in the development field make it unlikely past bargains can be recreated?
2. Is it more important to find ways of mobilizing local, private, or international resources to meet future development goals?
3. Outline a political deal that would allow the millennium development goal effort to continue and move forward.

# 27

# A Critical Decade for Climate Policy

## TOOLS AND INITIATIVES TO TRACK OUR PROGRESS

Taryn Fransen with Casey Cronin

We are in the midst of a critical decade for climate policy. Global GHG [Greenhouse Gas] emissions must peak by 2017 to retain even a 50 percent chance of limiting the average global temperature increase to 2C, yet they continue to climb—according to the International Energy Agency's 2012 World Energy Outlook, carbon dioxide emissions from fossil fuel combustion reached a record high in 2011. A dramatic change in course seems unlikely in the absence of immediate and effective policy intervention by the governments of the world's largest economies.

In this context, it becomes imperative to track closely the development, adoption, implementation, and effect of the specific policies and measures that countries undertake to advance their transition to a low-carbon economy. At the domestic level, timely access to this information can help policymakers and other stakeholders identify barriers, facilitate course correction, and understand how policy interventions are affecting GHG emissions and other issues of national concern. Internationally, it can enhance trust among countries regarding the extent of national action, determine the extent to which needed reductions are likely to occur as a result of existing approaches, improve targeting of international assistance and climate finance to address key barriers, and help countries learn from one another's experience. Taken together, these functions can help maximize the extent to which countries deliver on their international GHG reduction pledges as well as on their domestic policy commitments.

Taryn Fransen is a senior associate with the World Resources Institute, where she serves as project director for the Open Climate Network, an independent, international partnership that tracks and reports on climate change policy. Casey Cronin is the associate director of global research at the ClimateWorks Foundation. This is excerpted from a piece originally published by the World Resources Institute in March 2013. Reprinted with permission from the World Resources Institute.

Independent observers and civil society organizations play a legitimate and fundamental role in environmental governance, and this is particularly true in the case of tracking climate change policy. These actors not only supplement government perspectives on policy potential and effectiveness, but they also fill in gaps in accurate and timely reporting of climate policy information that has emerged slowly and inconsistently through official channels.

This paper examines efforts that have emerged in recent years to address the need for climate policy tracking, with a special emphasis on independent tracking efforts, and with a view toward identifying remaining information gaps and opportunities to fill them. As a basis for the discussion, it introduces definitions and concepts related to climate policy tracking and presents the background and context for current climate policy tracking initiatives, including efforts within and outside of the UNFCCC [United Nations Framework Convention on Climate Change]. It then describes international climate policy tracking efforts, as well as illustrative country-specific and sector-specific approaches, and analyzes these efforts with regard to a range of variables. Finally, it identifies priorities for future climate policy tracking efforts.
. . .

## BACKGROUND AND CONTEXT

### Defining "Climate Policy Tracking"

In this paper, climate policies refer to actions that can be taken or mandated by a government to accelerate the application and use of measures that curb GHG emissions. Examples of climate policies include carbon taxes, fossil fuel taxes, cap-and-trade programs, renewable energy incentives, energy efficiency standards, and land use policies. Additional examples and explanations are provided in table 27.1.

**Climate policy tracking** refers to the ongoing observation—or monitoring—of metrics related to climate policy development, adoption, implementation, and effect. It also comprises climate policy evaluation, when conducted on a periodic basis in the interest of tracking policy effectiveness over time. We propose these terms—tracking, monitoring, and evaluation—with the understanding that they are used differently by different communities of practice.

Climate policy metrics may be designed to address any stage in the policy lifecycle. They may capture:

- Financial, technical, sociopolitical, or human resource inputs
- Distinct actions associated with stages of developing, adopting, or implementing the policy
- Effects or results of the policy, including changes in GHG emissions, related sector- or policy-specific interim outcomes, or other costs or benefits

## TABLE 27.1

## Types of Climate Policies

| POLICY TYPE | DESCRIPTION | EXAMPLES |
|---|---|---|
| Regulations and standards | These specify abatement technologies (technology standards) or minimum requirements for pollution output (performance standards). They may also set obligations or mandates for specific sectors (e.g., 20% of electricity supply must be from renewable sources). | Vehicle fuel economy standards (Canada, China, European Union, Japan, South Korea, United States) Power plant performance standards (United States) |
| Taxes and charges | A levy imposed on each unit of activity by an emissions source (e.g., fuel tax, carbon tax, traffic congestion charge, import or export tax). | Carbon pricing mechanism (Australia) Coal tax (India) Carbon dioxide tax (Norway) |
| Tradable permits | A program that establishes a limit on aggregate emissions by specified sources, requires each source to hold permits equal to its actual emissions, and allows permits to be traded among sources. Tradable permits can also be issued for attributes other than emissions (see India example, right). | Emissions Trading Scheme (European Union) Perform Achieve Trade Scheme (India) |
| Voluntary agreements | An agreement between a government authority and one or more private parties beyond compliance to regulated obligations (e.g., with the aim of improving environmental performance). Not all VAs are truly voluntary; some include rewards and/or penalties associated with participating in the agreement or achieving the commitments. | Energy Efficiency Benchmarking Covenant (Netherlands) Kaidanren Voluntary Action Plan on the Environment (Japan) |
| Subsidies and incentives | Direct and indirect benefits and payments, tax reductions, rebates, price supports or the equivalent thereof, from a government to an entity for implementing a practice or performing a specified action. | Renewable energy feed-in tariffs (China, Germany, India, Japan, Thailand, United Kingdom) Production Tax Credit (United States) |
| Information instruments | Required public disclosure of information (e.g., environmentally related information), generally by industry to consumers. These include labeling programs, rating, and certification systems, as well as information campaigns aimed at changing behavior. | Green Light Programme (European Union) Bureau of Energy Efficiency Star Label (India) ENERGY STAR (United States) |
| Research and development (R&D) | Activities that involve direct government funding and investment aimed at generating innovative approaches to the physical and social infrastructure (e.g., to reduce emissions). Examples of these are funding and incentives for technological advances. | High Tech Strategy 2020 (Germany) Sun Shot Initiative (United States) |
| Public procurement policies | Policies requiring that specific attributes (e.g., environmental attributes) be considered as part of public procurement processes. | Sustainable Public Procurement in Urban Administrations (China) Green Procurement Law (Japan) |
| Infrastructure programs | Provision of sustainable infrastructure (e.g., high speed rail). | Integrated Transport Network (Curitiba, Brazil) Janmarg (Ahmedabad, India) |
| Financing and investment | Grants or loans (e.g., to support development strategies or policies). | The American Recovery and Reinvestment Act of 2009 (United States) |
| Strategies framed in terms of desired outcomes | Government or private sector strategies (e.g., increasing renewable energy generation or reducing deforestation by 20% by 2020). | Action Plan to Prevent and Control Deforestation in the Amazon (Brazil) Jawaharlal Nehru National Solar Mission (India) |

*Source:* Adapted from GHG Protocol (2012).

■ Underlying circumstances and external drivers that influence policy development, adoption, implementation, and effectiveness

In contrast to **monitoring**, which involves collecting data over time, climate policy **evaluation** makes use of data to answer specific questions about policy implementation, effects, or other related issues. Outcome or impact evaluations seek to identify the effect of a particular policy program, intervention, or investment. Evaluations may assess policy effectiveness vis-à-vis environmental impact, cost, or other qualities. Evaluations can be qualitative or quantitative in nature. They can take place on an ex-ante or ex-post basis, and can occur as one-off efforts or on a periodic basis throughout the lifecycle of a particular policy effort.

. . .

## Objectives of Climate Policy Tracking

Both within and outside of the UNFCCC, climate policy tracking has facilitative functions, which promote policy effectiveness, as well as accountability functions, which provide assurance that policy commitments are being met. Information generated by tracking climate policies can facilitate effectiveness in a number of ways. First, it can provide policymakers and other stakeholders with timely information on policy implementation processes and their effects, allowing them to correct course when implementation or an external driver does not proceed as intended or to meet targets in more effective ways during the implementation process. Second, it may be able to facilitate the flow of funds to support the policy—for example through international climate finance mechanisms, which have monitoring requirements. Third, climate policy tracking—in particular, evaluation—can identify success factors and barriers and inform the design and adoption of more effective policies based on lessons learned, including by creating greater certainty around effective and ineffective methods of policy implementation and identifying best practices. To the extent that policy tracking documents positive policy outcomes, this may also serve to build political capital in support of climate policy.

In addition to facilitating effectiveness, climate policy tracking can also promote accountability of public institutions for implementing appropriate, ambitious, and effective policies, and for delivering on GHG-related and other policy commitments. Tracking promotes accountability by providing the necessary information to determine whether governments are on track to meet GHG targets and other policy goals, and whether policies are sufficiently ambitious. By improving transparency of the climate policy implementation process, tracking can also facilitate stakeholder participation. This, in turn, can contribute to adoption of appropriate policy measures to which stakeholders can hold their governments accountable.

Ensuring that these objectives are met requires monitoring individual policies throughout their lifecycle—from development to adoption to implementation and effect. It also requires understanding how a portfolio of policies, taken together, relates to what countries have pledged to deliver, what is technically possible to deliver, and what is required to limit temperature increase. Finally, it requires evaluation to understand and replicate the factors that contribute to policy effectiveness.

Figure 27.1 illustrates what a climate policy tracking landscape that meets these needs might encompass. For example:

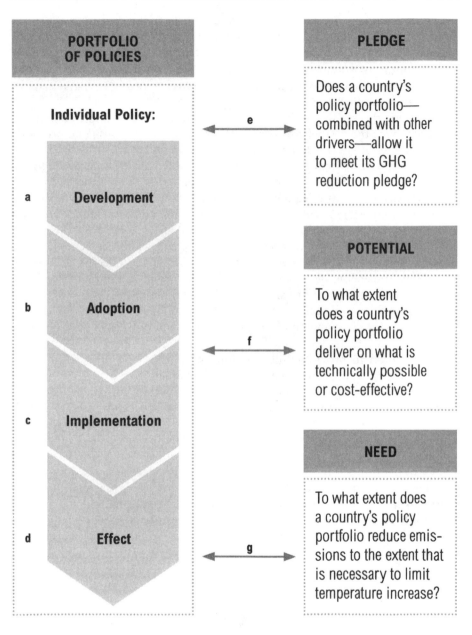

**FIGURE 27.1**
Climate Policy Tracking Landscape

- Tracking policy development (*a* in figure 27.1) facilitates stakeholder participation and can help build and maintain political momentum for future progress.
- Adoption (*b*) provides a discrete point to begin to quantify likely and full potential policy outcomes as well as to evaluate a policy's relative risk, certainty, and/or strength.
- Tracking the extent to which an adopted policy is being implemented (*c*) and having the desired effect (*d*) facilitates course correction and promotes accountability at the domestic policy level.
- Measuring the extent to which a country's policy portfolio is likely to deliver on its pledge (*e*) promotes accountability at the international level.
- Comparing a country's policy portfolio to what is technically possible or cost-effective (*f*) provides a measure of ambition and can identify areas for further policies or actions.
- Quantifying the extent to which policies or pledges, if implemented, would limit atmospheric GHG concentrations (*g*) promotes collective accountability and encourages course correction toward global mitigation goals.
- Monitoring the effect of particular policies (*c*) may be necessary for developing countries to secure international climate finance, and it can also contribute to learning and future effectiveness of policies in development.

In addition to providing information across this landscape, an effective climate policy information system will also be characterized by a range of other attributes. For example, information should be accurate, consistent, and comprehensive in its coverage (i.e., of geographies, sectors, and gases). Analysis should be methodologically transparent, elucidate barriers and success factors, and generate conclusions relevant to users. Information and analysis should be publicly available, user-friendly, and released in a timely manner to support policy decision-making. Strong communications strategies should leverage credible messengers and target audience interests to help ensure that the information will be used. In the context of climate policy tracking, there is a particular need to ensure that analysis and communications strategies are designed to inform domestic policy debates, in addition to the international negotiations and venues.

. . .

## RESULTS AND DISCUSSION

This section presents and discusses results from the mapping exercise—including the landscape mapping, technical aspects, and strategic aspects.

### LANDSCAPE MAPPING

This section describes the point in the policy lifecycle—development, adoption, and/or implementation—at which various initiatives track (or, in some cases, "count" abatement resulting from) climate policies. The adoption of new policies provides a discrete moment at which they can be considered. While policy development and implementation are equally critical to policies' ultimate effect, these stages in the lifecycle are addressed by fewer initiatives.

### Policy Development

The ClimateWorks Foundation uses its Campaign Expected Path tool to identify the activities and circumstances necessary to lead to a policy under development gaining momentum and being successfully adopted. The Open Climate Network tracks major policies under development according to expert surveys and published literature.

### Policy Adoption

Several initiatives track or evaluate policies at the point of their adoption. For example, the GLOBE *Climate Legislation Study* has provided an annual summary of newly adopted climate-related legislation in over 30 countries for the past three years. The Climate Action Tracker (v1.5) quantifies the effect of the "top three" adopted policies—collectively—on projected national GHG emissions across a range of countries, and in v2.0 examines adopted policies against a menu of best practice policy options. The ClimateWorks Foundation's Gigatonne Scorecard quantifies the expected and full effect of key adopted policies. The Open Climate Network also tracks adopted policies and describes—as far as feasible—their state of implementation and expected effects.

### Policy Implementation

In many situations, a significant gap can emerge among policy adoption, implementation, and ultimate effect, due to gaps in implementation (for example, lack of compliance and enforcement) or changes in external drivers (for example, macroeconomic trends or fuel prices that differ from what had been expected). ClimateWorks' Campaign Expected Path tool also provides a framework for identifying paths and obstacles to implementation, as does the Open Climate Network Policy Implementation Toolkit.

. . .

# CONCLUSIONS AND RECOMMENDATIONS

## Conclusions

Countries are pursuing a wide variety of policies to mitigate GHG emissions, and a range of tools are needed to monitor and evaluate them as they move through development, past adoption, and into implementation. The field of climate policy tracking will continue to evolve as it experiments with different approaches to meet these needs. Based on a review of the major efforts that have developed over the past several years, as well as many spirited discussions with our peers and colleagues, we offer the following observations regarding the current climate policy tracking landscape.

**The climate policy tracking community has developed a diverse portfolio of methodologies and frameworks to address a range of policy tracking needs.** The portfolio includes both qualitative and quantitative approaches for monitoring and evaluating climate policy through various life-cycle phases (i.e., development, adoption, and implementation) and in comparison to several possible reference points (i.e., pledges, potential, and atmospheric need). A notable exception is tracking co-benefits of climate policies, where we have found less work to date. The methodologies and frameworks are at varying stages of maturity and acceptance, and further evolution and refinement should be expected (and encouraged), but they provide a foundation on which to base further efforts.

**Nevertheless, information about climate policies remains patchy.** Several organizations and initiatives—including the Climate Action Tracker, GLOBE, and the IEA—monitor climate policies as they are adopted by countries. As a result, information on policy adoption has improved significantly over the past two to three years. Nonetheless, significant gaps remain regarding information on policy development and implementation. Certain geographies (both national and subnational) are less well covered, and challenges remain regarding quantitative information on GHG impact and projected national GHG emissions. Our assessment identified the following gaps:

- Limited information is available on policies under development (i.e., policies under consideration that have not yet been adopted), including on robustness of their design and likelihood of adoption and implementation.
- Once climate policies have been adopted, implementation is not necessarily well monitored. This can be particularly important in developing countries, where capacity and institutional barriers can prevent adopted policies from delivering on their potential.
- Geographical coverage is uneven. Countries like Russia and South Korea, for example, are poorly represented by international tracking efforts despite their status as major emitters. However, even countries that are addressed by all of the international initiatives are subject to the limitations described above. Information on subnational policies, as well, is lacking for a range of countries.
- Estimates of the GHG effect of policy interventions are limited. Where available, the methodologies used to derive them are often neither consistent nor transparent.
- Projections of national GHG emissions under different climate policy scenarios vary widely by country. The Climate Action Tracker and the IEA provide a critical resource in this regard, but are limited in the policies and assumptions they can consider compared to country-specific efforts, which are inconsistent.

Many climate policy tracking efforts target the needs of an international audience, though some good examples exist at the country level. Our landscape assessment found that most major climate policy tracking efforts—particularly independent ones—target international audiences, venues, and influence opportunities. While this is valuable, robust and independent policy monitoring is essential at the national level as well to more effectively target and influence domestic policy debates. This function can be provided by independent authorities established by the government, as in the examples of Australia and the United Kingdom, as well as by NGOs. In either case, it is made possible by human resource capacity—that is, a "deep bench" of technical experts, by access to data and information, and by institutional arrangements that promote independent research, commentary, and policy recommendations.

Technical abatement potential serves as a useful goalpost but lacks political and policy context. Theoretical estimates of what could and should be possible, given currently available technology and assumptions around future economic indicators and growth trajectories, are vital for setting goals and targets. Even the most sophisticated modeling of technical abatement potential, however, will not address many other relevant characteristics such as institutional effectiveness, political economy, and competing national and business priorities. Governments and private industry can apply more sophisticated context to these types of analyses, but often have an inherent incentive to underestimate what is theoretically possible. Events that defy prediction can also lead to broader, transformative change that previously would have seemed impossible.

## Recommendations

The landscape described above will change as the climate policy tracking community gains experience—and further review of country-level and sector-specific tracking efforts may also shed new light on these conclusions. At present, we recommend that practitioners, funders, and governments consider the following actions to strengthen policy tracking in the near term.

Deepen tracking of policy implementation and of policies under development. As noted above, monitoring of policy development and implementation remains relatively weak in comparison to monitoring of policy adoption. As a result, opportunities to strengthen policy design and implementation can be obscured, and estimates of policy impact or projections of progress toward future climate mitigation goals can rest on incorrect assumptions. Efforts to enhance this information can draw on several resources:

- The Open Climate Network's policy landscape assessment series identifies policies under development for a number of key countries. These could be prioritized for further monitoring and evaluation in a coordinated manner.

- The Climate Action Tracker identifies the "top three" new climate policies for a range of countries in terms of potential GHG impact, while the IEA compiles many emerging and existing policies into their "New Policies" and "Current Policies" scenarios. These lists of policies could be reviewed by national experts to select priority policies for tracking development and implementation.
- The ClimateWorks Campaign Expected Path framework, the Open Climate Network Policy Implementation Toolkit, the GHG Protocol Policy Accounting Standard, and the UK Committee on Climate Change all provide tools that can be adopted or adapted to enhance monitoring of policies in these stages.

**Strengthen climate policy tracking at the country level, while maintaining internationally focused efforts.** Efforts to strengthen country-level tracking efforts can benefit from engagement by a range of actors, and should recognize and build on the diversity of policy environments, governance structures, and capacities at the country level. Important roles and functions may include:

- In-country practitioners: Identify key policy decision points, information needs, and data and information resources; develop and implement tracking frameworks
- International practitioners: Share methodologies and lessons learned; incorporate country-level information into international tracking efforts as appropriate
- Governments: Make data, information, and assumptions transparent and publicly available; consider possible benefits of establishing an independent policy tracking authority

**Enhance coordination and collaboration among climate policy tracking practitioners.** Many synergies between climate policy tracking initiatives have yet to be fully exploited. For example, information collected by initiatives that monitor climate policy adoption can feed into the monitoring of implementation and effect. Aggregated information on implementation and effect can inform future scenarios on which GHG projections are based. When policy evaluations uncover critical factors in policy effectiveness, these factors can then be incorporated into monitoring efforts and define key performance metrics. Dialogues such as the Practitioners' Workshop on Climate Policy Tracking, as well as stakeholder collaborations like the GHG Protocol, the LEDS Global Partnership, the Mitigation Action Plans and Scenarios Programme, the Measurement and Performance Tracking Project, and the Open Climate Network can provide constructive fora for collaboration. These groups might consider further efforts at:

- Co-developing, testing, reviewing, and standardizing technical approaches for quantifying outcomes and effects (e.g., through the GHG Protocol pilot testing period)

- Improving links and synergies between "stages" of policy tracking—from early groundwork to policy development, adoption, implementation, and effect
- Enhancing international understanding of countries' reported figures and projections
- Considering communications in a national context to inform policy debates and reviews
- Coordinating timing and publishing of future reports or evaluations with policy windows
- Learning from additional efforts to supplement this analysis with new areas of expertise

## CRITICAL THINKING QUESTIONS

1. What are the five most important climate policies presented in this reading?
2. Which of the three stages of the climate policy lifecycle (development, adoption, and implementation) is most important?
3. Can the climate policy tracking system presented here be adapted to other global problem areas? Provide an example with your answer.

# 28

# Is the U.S. Drone War Effective?

Michael J. Boyle

Among the most distinctive features of U.S. President Barack Obama's counterterrorism strategy has been his reliance on unmanned aerial vehicles—more commonly known as drones—to target terrorist operatives around the globe. The use of drones has rapidly expanded beyond the battlefields where U.S. troops have openly engaged in conflict, such as Afghanistan and Iraq, to a range of undeclared combat zones, including Pakistan, Yemen, and Somalia. According to an official estimate, the U.S. military launched 1,160 drone strikes in Afghanistan alone between 2009 and 2012.

In many respects, it is not surprising that the Obama administration would resort to drone strikes as a way of keeping pressure on Al Qaeda and the Taliban as the U.S. military prepares to withdraw from Afghanistan. What is more unusual is the extent to which the administration has employed drones to target militants in countries where the United States is not formally at war. According to an estimate by the New America Foundation (which has conducted one of the most comprehensive studies), the Obama administration launched 321 drone strikes in Pakistan and 83 in Yemen between 2009 and 2013. There have also been scattered strikes in countries such as Libya, Somalia, and Mali. Under Obama's leadership, the American drone war has grown far beyond its original limits under President George W. Bush, and now stretches across wide swaths of South Asia, the Middle East, and North Africa.

The use of drones has proven widely controversial for a number of moral and legal reasons. Some critics argue that drones are increasingly becoming a substitute for real military combat—a cheap and seductive way to fight dirty little wars without raising taxes or imposing sacrifices on the American people. Others object that drone warfare does not conform to traditional notions of heroic warfare, in which combatants face an equal risk of death. Still others have argued that the illusion of a bloodless war produced by drones raises a moral hazard that could lead the United States to more frequently engage in wars abroad on the assumption that it can do so without cost.

* Michael J. Boyle is an assistant professor of political science at La Salle University and the author of *Violence after War: Explaining Instability in Post-Conflict States*. Reprinted with permission from *Current History* magazine (April 2014). Copyright © 2015 Current History, Inc.

The legal criticisms mainly question the right of the United States to engage in drone strikes in countries against which it has made no formal declaration of war, as well as the extent to which the original Authorization for Use of Military Force passed by Congress after the terrorist attacks of September 11, 2001, has been stretched beyond its original intent to cover drone strikes against groups unrelated to, or only loosely affiliated with, Al Qaeda. A number of civil libertarians have also expressed concern about the dangers of a president wielding the power to kill people abroad (even U.S. citizens, in some cases) without a judicial finding of guilt or appropriate Congressional scrutiny. These legal and moral issues have deepened the sense of unease in Washington over the use of drones and raised additional questions about the wisdom of deploying them so frequently in South Asia.

## DEFINING EFFECTIVENESS

For many, however, the most immediate question is whether or not drones are effective in targeting terrorist operatives and producing tangible security gains for the United States. On this point, the administration has been emphatic that drones are indeed highly effective and have become, in the words of former Secretary of Defense Leon Panetta, the "only game in town" when it comes to destroying Al Qaeda. The security gains from drones, according to the administration, are indisputable. Panetta asserted in 2011 that drones have so radically improved American counterterrorism efforts that their use has put the United States within reach of "strategically defeating Al Qaeda." If drones have been so effective in bringing Al Qaeda to its knees, some advocates argue that the case for using them is self-evident and that many of the legal and moral objections therefore become secondary.

Yet the questions surrounding the effectiveness of drones are more complicated than the Obama administration's account suggests. At the most basic level, what it means for a drone strike to be effective is rarely defined. Are drone strikes considered effective if they yield only tactical gains, such as the elimination of "bad guys" from the battlefield? What are the possible long-term strategic costs of drones? How should they be measured against these tactical victories? The Obama administration's public arguments about the effectiveness of drones have tended to conflate tactical and strategic gains, implying without evidence that they are the same.

The administration's drone policy has not directly addressed some key measurement issues. How, for example, would the United States know if it had achieved a tangible security gain from a drone strike? How can it measure the effect of drone strikes on the organizational capacities of the militant groups it targets? As a number of critics have noted, the effectiveness of drones is highly dependent on the extent to which they do not indirectly generate or recruit more militants than they eliminate. If the United States is merely trading existing militants for new ones in the future, as critics allege, the argument that drones are effective due to their immediate impact on Al Qaeda needs to be reexamined.

More generally; this debate over effectiveness also needs to consider both on-the-ground blowback and the political consequences of drone strikes. The administration has argued that blowback will be minimal because its drone attacks are highly precise and cause relatively few civilian casualties. Yet this argument confuses effectiveness with precision. Even if drones are precise, their strategic utility can be undermined if they provoke a call for revenge from the social, tribal, and family networks of their victims. Similarly, the political costs of drones must be weighed against their utility in killing militant leaders. Particularly in Afghanistan and Pakistan, drones have stirred up new levels of hostility against the United States and endangered the stability and cooperation of the local governments, with potential long-term consequences for the stability of the South Asian region.

## TACTIC OR STRATEGY?

According to the Obama administration, drone strikes have been highly effective in terms of decapitating the top Al Qaeda leadership and placing the organization under intense pressure. There is some evidence to suggest that this claim is true. Papers discovered in Osama bin Laden's house in Abbottabad after his death showed that he encouraged his colleagues to flee Pakistan's northwestern region of Waziristan in order to avoid drones. He also recommended a range of operational security measures, such as traveling by road infrequently, carefully monitoring movements so as not to attract attention, and moving on overcast days to evade the gaze of drones.

By one estimate, more than 50 senior Al Qaeda and Taliban leaders have been killed by drone strikes. Bin Laden himself recognized that drones have hollowed out the top leadership of Al Qaeda and left the leadership ranks populated with younger, less experienced operatives. In the eyes of the Obama administration, drones have degraded the capacity of the organization and made it harder for its leaders to plan for the future. As Obama remarked in his speech at the National Defense University in May 2013, "Today, the core of Al Qaeda in Afghanistan and Pakistan is on the path to defeat. Their remaining operatives spend more time thinking about their own safety than plotting against us. They did not direct the attacks in Benghazi or Boston. They've not carried out a successful attack on our homeland since 9/11."

While the administration is correct that drones have degraded Al Qaeda's ability to operate in Afghanistan and Pakistan by removing its top operational leadership, it is not clear that this fact alone proves the effectiveness of drone strikes. The administration's standard of effectiveness is a tactical one, generally concentrating on whether drones eliminate the "bad guys." Yet the strategic question regarding drones—that is, do they cause sufficient harm to Al Qaeda to produce durable security gains for the United States—extends beyond a tally of leaders removed from the battlefield.

Even if Al Qaeda is under organizational pressure due to drones, this may have unintended consequences. As Micah Zenko of the Council on Foreign Relations has pointed out, drones tend to force operatives to leave one theater for another, diffusing rather than destroying the threat. For example, pressure on Al Qaeda in the "AfPak" theater has forced its operatives to move to Yemen, Somalia, and parts of the Levant—especially Syria. For a number of reasons, including the pressure placed on it by drones, Al Qaeda has become less a hierarchical terrorist organization than a franchise brand that local groups can adopt for their own purposes and exploit for funding, training, and other resources. Instead of pushing Al Qaeda to the edge of strategic collapse, drones may have accelerated its fragmentation into a series of local affiliates, most of which are weaker than Al Qaeda's central organization was at its height before 9/11.

Here the effectiveness argument is murkier than it initially appears: Drones have degraded the central organization of Al Qaeda, but they have also turned one enemy into a series of loosely connected smaller foes. It is not yet clear whether this fragmentation will render Al Qaeda strategically weaker than it was beforehand, or whether in fact this dynamic will give Al Qaeda a second life as a franchise outside its original theater in South Asia.

Moreover, the United States has not limited its drone strikes to the Al Qaeda leadership alone. The Obama administration has expanded the number of targeted groups to a range of Islamist networks affiliated, often in different ways, with Al Qaeda. The New America Foundation found that the majority of drone strikes targeted not Al Qaeda, but rather the Taliban, the Haqqani network, and various smaller Islamist groups, some of which are allied as factions under the umbrella of the Tehrik-e-Taliban in Pakistan (TTP). In some cases, the identity of a drone strike's target remains unknown; in others, the United States is occasionally unsure which militant group a known target belongs to. Some of the Islamist factions targeted by drone strikes are so small that U.S. officials have found it difficult to distinguish between them in the general atmosphere of militancy brewing in Pakistan.

The same scattering dynamic is also present with the use of drones against these local groups in Pakistan. In this case, many factions of the ITP have fled from the Federally-Administered Tribal Areas (FATA) and relocated to cities like Karachi, where they are increasingly targeting Pakistani civilians with terrorist attacks. While their capacities have been degraded in the FATA, the effect of drones on their organization as a whole is less clear.

## WEAK LINKS

The Obama administration has expanded its targeting to local groups in Pakistan, Yemen, and elsewhere under the argument that they are linked or affiliated with Al Qaeda or the Taliban. Yet the problem here concerns the slippery concept of linkage: In this complex environment, many local groups will be in some way "linked" to Al Qaeda or the Taliban, yet those connections can mean anything from direct combat support to parallel independent operations against U.S. forces (as with the Haqqani network in Afghanistan), or a range of lesser, even incidental, relationships. Much of the reporting on drone strikes merely accepts the word of U.S. or local officials that a militant was "linked" to Al Qaeda, without questioning the precise nature of that connection.

One potential danger of this catchall approach is that the United States may wind up creating more enemies by targeting groups only indirectly affiliated with Al Qaeda. Some evidence of this dynamic already exists: The Times Square bomber Faisal Shahzad was allegedly trained and deployed by a faction of the TTP to attack New York City in 2010 in revenge for U.S. drone strikes. This event is particularly significant because the TTP's principal enemy is the Pakistani government; it only tried to attack the United States after its leadership was targeted by an American drone strike. It is possible that smaller Islamist groups, such as Jaish-e-Mohammed or Lashkar-e-Taiba, could take similar action in response to the pressure that they have experienced under drone strikes.

While the Obama administration tends to speak about drones as a tool against Al Qaeda alone, the reality is that drone strikes are targeting organizations with varying links to Al Qaeda and the Taliban, as well as other Islamist groups whose main quarrel is with the governments of their own countries. Given the blowback risk, analyzing the effectiveness of these drone strikes is more complex than the administration's argument implies. The United States has racked up a series of tactical victories by removing high-ranking Al Qaeda and Taliban operatives from the battlefield, but it still remains unclear whether Al Qaeda is close to collapse or simply more dispersed and amorphous. Most of these strikes amount to tactical hits against Al Qaeda, the Taliban. and a growing array of other Islamist networks. Yet the larger strategic question is whether those drone strikes will push all of these groups toward defeat and contribute to long-term stability in the AfPak theater. There is no evidence at present that the Taliban, for example, is close to defeat in Afghanistan or Pakistan. While drone strikes have certainly weakened Al Qaeda's leadership, local hostility to the strikes has also given the organization a powerful propaganda tool. Drones have now replaced Guantanamo Bay as the preferred recruiting theme for militants.

The danger of the Obama administration's approach revolves around the conceptual questions of what "linkage" means and what that implies for U.S. policy. The administration has remained vague on what it means to say that a group is "linked" to Al Qaeda and therefore a justified target for a drone strike. Due to the slipperiness of this concept, and the temptation to use drones preventively, the United States may be overemploying them and creating a series of smaller, less capable local enemies in Afghanistan and Pakistan. If so, the drone campaign is facilitating a process by which the United States replaces a single transnational terrorist network with an array of locally embedded new foes. The debate over the strategic effectiveness of drones must weigh the creation of these local enemies against the elimination of "bad guys" in the short term.

# COUNTING CASUALTIES

In part, the question of the strategic utility of drones ties into a controversial debate over the number of civilian casualties caused by drone strikes. Much of the existing debate conflates precision with effectiveness, implying that if drones are precise, they must be effective. Yet even the evidence for the precision of drones is less clear than the Obama administration's public arguments suggest. The exact number of people killed by drone strikes is unknown. In Afghanistan, the casualty tolls are difficult to ascertain, since drone strikes occur most often amidst combat operations. Distinguishing who was killed from a drone strike, as opposed to other means, is often impossible.

Estimates of casualties from the covert drone campaigns in Pakistan and Yemen are more readily available. The New America Foundation estimates that between 2,080 and 3,428 people have been killed by drones in Pakistan (2004–2013) and another 717 to 927 in Yemen (2002–2013). But casualties from drone strikes are notoriously difficult to measure and verify. Most of the strikes are conducted in distant—sometimes ungoverned—territories of Pakistan and Yemen, where few have the ability to interview survivors or even count the dead. Moreover, it is well known that the Taliban and other local Islamist groups inflate casualty counts for propaganda purposes.

Many newspaper accounts of drone strikes toss around words like "militants" and "civilians" casually, often without evidence. The underlying difficulties of reporting strikes in these countries have been compounded by the U.S. decision to adopt a classification scheme that counts any male between the ages of 18 and 70 killed in a drone strike as a "militant" unless posthumous evidence is presented to clear his name. For this reason, almost all of the data on casualties from drone strikes needs to be treated with a healthy degree of skepticism.

Advocates of drones compare their relative precision favorably with other methods of warfare, and note that drones cause fewer civilian casualties than air strikes or ground assaults. The Obama administration has adopted a similar line of argument, stating that its stringent guidelines for selecting targets ensure that relatively few, if any, civilians are killed in drone strikes. In 2011, Obama's then-chief counterterrorism adviser, John Brennan, claimed that there had been no civilian casualties from U.S. drone strikes for nearly a year due to their precision. Obama publicly argued in 2012 that the drone program is "a targeted, focused effort at people who are on the list of active terrorists." The administration has emphasized that strikes have a "surgical" character and are conducted with a "laser-like focus." In his May 2013 speech at the National Defense University, the president acknowledged the reality of civilian casualties from drone strikes but insisted that "before any strike is taken, there must be near certainty that no civilians will be killed or injured—the highest standard we can set."

Is this correct? Estimates provided by the New America Foundation suggest that the percentage of civilian deaths varies, depending on whether the high or low casualty number from a given range is used. In Pakistan, for example, the data suggest that between 12.4 percent and 8.9 percent of the casualties were civilians. In Yemen, the estimate runs between 10.9 and 9.0 percent. The Bureau of Investigative Journalism (TBIJ), an independent London-based organization, has produced alternative estimates that put the figures of civilians killed by drone strikes somewhat higher. In Pakistan, for example, the highest range of the TBIJ estimate suggests that 26 percent of those killed by drone strikes were civilians. Similarly, the TBIJ data suggest that as much as 13 percent of the victims of drone strikes in Yemen were civilians.

By either estimate, the hyperbolic arguments of some critics—that drones are a wholly indiscriminate weapon of war, killing more civilians than terrorists—can be rejected. Moreover, both data sets suggest that the precision of drones is increasing over time, and the rates of civilian casualties from drone strikes have dropped significantly under the Obama administration.

## RISKING REVENGE

Yet the fact that drones are not as indiscriminate as other weapons of war should not be confused with the argument that they are so precise as to avoid consequences from their use. To confuse precision with effectiveness, as much of the debate over drones does, is to sidestep some pressing questions about who is killed and what blowback their deaths may bring.

While drone strikes do not indiscriminately harm civilians, they are increasingly targeting non-Al Qaeda groups, such as the Taliban and other local Islamist networks operating in countries like Pakistan and Yemen. These local groups are dominated by recruits who are often not full-time fighters, but rather fight in their own villages or regions on a part-time basis. Unlike Al Qaeda operatives, many of whom are from Arab countries and have few local connections, local Taliban or other Islamist fighters have families and dense webs of social networks in the regions in which they are targeted. The risk that the families and friends of such fighters killed in drone strikes will be motivated to seek revenge is likely to be higher than it is with Al Qaeda targets.

Akbar Ahmed of American University has argued that drone strikes in the Pashtun regions of Afghanistan and Pakistan may activate latent codes of revenge that obligate tribesmen to fight the Americans, either directly or by joining militant networks opposed by them, in response to the death of their relatives. As one Pakistani man who lost relatives in a drone strike remarked to researchers from Stanford and New York Universities: "We won't forget our blood, for two hundred, two thousand, five thousand years—we will take our revenge for these drone attacks."

This risk of blowback is even greater because the Obama administration has expanded the targeting of drones to lower-ranking operatives of these organizations. An estimate by the New America Foundation suggests that only 2 percent of the casualties from drone strikes are "high-value targets" or key commanders of Islamist groups.

Lower-ranking fighters are particularly likely to be enmeshed in a variety of family, religious, and cultural networks in their local communities. This makes them more likely to have family and friends who will seek to avenge their deaths by joining militant organizations than the foreigners who typically fill the ranks of Al Qaeda. Expanding the drone war to local Islamist networks and targeting lower-ranked operatives of these organizations magnifies the risks of revenge-fueled blowback against the United States or its local allies.

The implicit assumption that drones are effective because they are precise permeates much of the debate over these weapons. Yet there are reasons to believe that a relatively precise weapon—perhaps even one that could be called "humane" compared with many other alternatives—may produce local blowback that undermines its effectiveness in the long run. The decision to target non–Al Qaeda groups and lower-ranked operatives from these organizations has doubtlessly produced an unknown number of new militants, while taking others off the battlefield.

At present, it is impossible to know the net effects of drones. The causality between drone strikes and militant recruiting is particularly complex: Strikes might be increasing in areas of high militancy because the threat is increasing, or these organizations might be growing in strength because the tempo of drone strikes has provoked outrage among the local population. But there is no reason to assume that even a relatively precise weapon like drones could be used without risking blowback in the long run.

## PAKISTANI BACKLASH

A thorough analysis of the effectiveness of drones should also consider the larger political ramifications. If drones end up creating high levels of political opposition to the United States, or to a local government whose cooperation is crucial to Washington, this effect may offset the tactical gains achieved by removing enemies from the battlefield.

A growing number of critics from inside the Obama administration have come forward to voice this concern. In 2011, former Director of National Intelligence Dennis Blair wrote that drone attacks did decimate the leadership of Al Qaeda, but they also "increased hatred of America" and harmed "our ability to work with Pakistan [in] eliminating Taliban sanctuaries, encouraging Indian-Pakistani dialogue, and making Pakistan's nuclear arsenal more secure." Similarly, General James Cartwright, former vice chairman of the Joint Chiefs of Staff, in 2013 said regarding the drone policy in Pakistan, "We're seeing that blowback. If you're trying to kill your way to a solution, no matter how precise you are, you're going to upset people even if they're not targeted."

Public backlash over drones can make it harder for local governments to say "yes" to the United States, thus raising the costs of strategic cooperation. In Pakistan, for example, drone strikes have become a flashpoint of debate and placed the government under intense pressure to appear as if it is not standing idly by while the United States strikes its territory. Of course, the reality has always been more complex: The Pakistani government has traditionally consented to at least some of the strikes, and privately applauded when they took out its own enemies.

Throughout 2010–2012, political pressure began to build in Pakistan as the drone strikes increased in tempo. In 2012, Pakistan's parliament denounced the strikes and demanded that they be halted. while some nationalist politicians began to talk about shooting down American drones in the country's airspace. In many respects, this was a cynical double game: Pakistani military officials secretly approved drone strikes and allowed some to launch from their air bases while the political class grandstanded against the United States for domestic consumption.

By early 2013, this situation had become untenable due to mounting public anger. After he came to power in June 2013 elections, Pakistan's new prime minister, Nawaz Sharif, declared that "the policy of protesting against drone strikes for public consumption, while working behind the scenes to make them happen," would not continue. Throughout the past year, Sharif has consistently called on Washington to reduce the number of drone strikes in order to mollify public opinion. In February 2014, it was revealed that the United States had agreed to curtail drone strikes while the Pakistani government sought a peace agreement with the TTP.

Although the controversy has died down recently, the salience of the issue in Pakistani public life illustrates some of the strategic costs associated with the drone campaign. As some critics have noted, only a minority of Pakistani civilians is even aware that the U.S. drone program exists, due to illiteracy and low access to radio and television. Yet those who are informed about it are fiercely opposed to unilateral drone strikes on Pakistani territory. According to a 2012 survey by the Pew Global Attitudes Project, 97 percent of informed Pakistani respondents viewed the drone program as "bad" or "very bad." Another Pew poll in 2012 revealed that 74 percent of Pakistanis considered the United States an enemy, up from 59 percent in 2010.

This anti-American atmosphere has placed the Pakistani government under intense domestic pressure from nationalist forces to stand up to Washington. Among the most prominent of these critics is Imran Khan, a former cricket star turned politician, who publicly named the CIA's Islamabad station chief in November 2013 in order to embarrass the United States and capitalize on the widespread discontent about the drone campaign. Even though drones have successfully taken out insurgents fighting Pakistan's government, and weakened or scattered elements of the TTP, this has come at the cost of deep political polarization and increasing hostility toward America.

## AFGHAN GRANDSTANDING

In Afghanistan, a different set of political consequences has arisen. President Hamid Karzai has used civilian casualties from drone strikes to manufacture new crises with the United States and strengthen his bargaining position.

During contentious negotiations over a bilateral security agreement, Karzai has capitalized on accidental deaths from drone strikes to grandstand and burnish his credentials with parts of the population hostile to the American mission. While Karzai's position on drones is cynical and opportunistic (he has said relatively little about civilian casualties caused by the Taliban) it has nevertheless deepened the crisis over the unfinished agreement and led Obama to threaten to withdraw all U.S. troops.

Moreover, there is some limited evidence that drones might serve as a recruiting tool for the Afghan Taliban. The Taliban leadership recently criticized the use of drone strikes, calling them an attempt to mask America's defeat in the country, and commenting that "the affected local populations, traumatized by such attacks, begin to view the Americans as a discriminate and immoral force that is willing to sacrifice the lives of the locals in order to attack a small number of their enemies."

Politically, the casualties associated with drone strikes in Afghanistan, while minimal in comparison with Pakistan, have nevertheless played into the hands of both Karzai and the Taliban, and undermined long-term U.S. priorities in the country.

# LONG-TERM DANGERS

Most of the Obama administration's arguments for the effectiveness of drones have been short-term and tactical, concentrating on how drone strikes remove key enemies from the battlefield, and why they may be the best of a selection of bad options in difficult terrain. Yet, with some exceptions, members of the administration have avoided discussing the possible long-term costs of the drone program.

The debate is a difficult one, in large part because many of the details of the drone program remain shrouded in secrecy, and many of its costs will not be known for years to come. But even today there is considerable evidence to suggest that drone strikes, no matter how precise, have negative consequences sufficient to offset the administration's strongest arguments in their favor.

The dangers—that drone strikes may inadvertently produce new, locally embedded enemies, or that their use will generate political crises that damage relationships with key American partners—all suggest that Washington may pay a price for overreliance on drones as opposed to other counterterrorism tools. In South Asia, this overreliance has exacerbated anti-American sentiment and produced a backlash effect that may undermine the legitimacy of the governments of both Pakistan and Afghanistan.

This does not mean that the United States should never use drones for fear of their potential long-term repercussions. But it does suggest that Washington is best advised to exercise considerable caution, and selectivity in choosing targets, when authorizing drone strikes in the future. It also means that the Obama administration should be more circumspect in claiming that tactical victories from drones can be achieved today without the risk of potentially painful costs tomorrow.

———

## CRITICAL THINKING QUESTIONS

1. Which standard is most important in measuring the use of drones: legal, moral, strategic, or tactical?
2. How does one weigh short-term benefits versus long-term risks?
3. Are there conflict situations in which drones should not be used?